THE NEW HOME PLANS BOOK

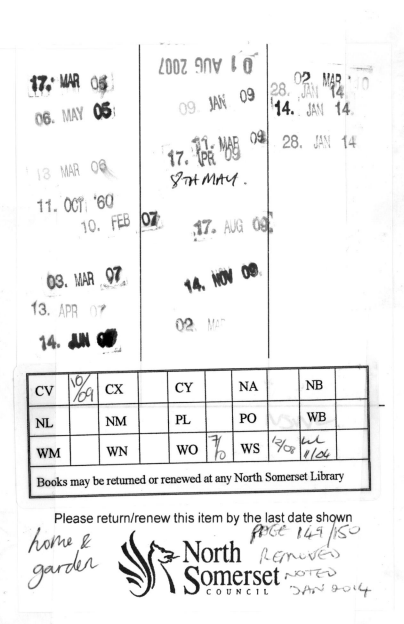

THE NEW HOME PLANS BOOK

DAVID SNELL AND
MURRAY ARMOR

EBURY PRESS
LONDON

First published in Great Britain in 2003

1 3 5 7 9 10 8 6 4 2

First published in the United Kingdom in 2003 by Ebury Press
Random House
20 Vauxhall Bridge Road
London SW1V 2SA

Random House Australia (Pty) Limited
20 Alfred Street, Milsons Point, Sydney
New South Wales 2061, Australia

Random House New Zealand Limited
18 Poland Road, Glenfield
Auckland 10, New Zealand

Random House South Africa (Pyt) Limited
Endulini, 5a Jubilee Road, Parktown 2193, South Africa

The Random House Group Limited Reg. No. 954009

www.randomhouse.co.uk

A CIP catalogue record for this book is available from the British Library

Designed by Jerry Goldie Graphic Design

ISBN 0 09 189447 6

Papers used by Ebury Press are natural, recyclable products made from wood grown in sustainable forests.

This book contains only general advice, and neither the author nor the publishers will accept responsibility of any sort for the consequence of the application of this advice to specific situations, in particular, planning and other legislation is described in outline only, and professional help should always be obtained when dealing with these matters. No company has paid for any of their material to be used in this book and the authors take no responsibility for the accuracy of any of the plans reproduced.

Printed in China by Midas

CONTENTS

INTRODUCTION

This is the second book of self build plans that I have compiled and, like the first, it continues to draw on a wide spectrum of package deal companies, architects and designers working within this industry. Most of the plans are new. A very few are repeated, not least because I wish the two books to stand alone and if plans from a certain company have a particular and continuing relevance to a category, then I do not want new readers to be deprived.

In the introductory pages to the previous book I waxed lyrical about the influences that self builders have had on design and the general acceptance of new innovations in home building. I commentated on changes in design requirements that I had seen over the years and speculated on changes that I saw coming. I am pleased to report that many of those forecasts and some I had not foreseen are now represented in the new plans within this book.

Out goes the idea of a hatchway between kitchens and dining rooms. Out, in many cases, has gone the over-large utility room to be replaced with a smaller back scullery, porch or mudroom with the freed-up space being utilised to increase the kitchen/breakfast room areas. There has been recognition that the activities that take place in the kitchen and utility rooms are not always related. Kitchens are for cooking whereas utility rooms are often concerned with the laundry. Therefore why do they have to be adjoining and, even more radically, why can't the laundry room and linen cupboards go upstairs?

Many cooks will also be pleased to note the return of the larder. Also, within the cooking/eating and utility areas, changes in the regulations, brought about by the requirement for disabled access have meant that space need no longer be wasted in providing a lobby between kitchens and the downstairs toilet. Staying on the subject of eating, the dining room is often the most expensively furnished and least used room in the house. With appliances becoming ever quieter and extraction systems becoming ever more efficient, the idea of the kitchen/dining room, often doubling up as the family room or general living area has become more popular. Dining or 'great halls' combine the space previously 'wasted' in circulation with the eating area. And, with vaulted ceilings becoming ever more acceptable, galleries have come into their own as sitting or sewing areas.

Above all, what I do see is the idea of accommodation flexibility. The naming of rooms on a plan is, after all, just a paper exercise. What that room is used for can change and if, for example, a room can begin life as a dining room and then move on to become a playroom and, finally, a downstairs bedroom, then that is no more than the proper evolution of the family home.

This book is meant to give you ideas for the design of your new home. If there is a plan that suits you in every sense then the best thing to do might be to contact the practice or company responsible. More likely, I suspect, is that elements of various designs take your fancy and in that case it is perhaps best if you approach those whose ideals most closely match your own, for a bespoke design.

Important copyright notice
Copyright of any plans or drawings resides with the originators until or unless they agree otherwise. Even if you commission a bespoke design and you pay the bill in full, that does not mean that the copyright will pass to you, unless you have made specific arrangements for it to do so.

All of the plans within this book remain the copyright of the contributing companies and practices and they may not be used, copied or reproduced in any form or for any purpose without the express consent of those copyright holders.

No contributor has paid to have their plans included within this book.

ABOUT THE PLANS

If and when you contact the companies and practices featured within this book, you may find that their measurements, and particularly their overall areas, do not tally with those given in this book. I have re-measured and re-calculated all of the drawings in an attempt to show like for like. Some companies working within the industry, for operational reasons, give their overall sizes as either being over frame or overall brickwork. I have reduced these measurements to the net internal dimensions. The areas given are, therefore, calculated on the basis of the dimensions inside the external walls for each floor of the home.

Where garages are illustrated on the plans, they are included in the overall dimensions and areas, but their individual area is also given. Also included are ancillary rooms such as sunrooms, workrooms, storage rooms and conservatories, where they form a deliberate part of the accommodation. Rooms, including conservatories in some obvious cases, that are quite specifically meant to be future additions or options are, however, left out of the calculations.

Some of the contributors, as a matter of course in their literature, deduct the garage from the overall area, maintaining that the garage should not be costed at the same rate as the house. I can see some logic in that but not a lot. If the garage is integral or attached then it will share the same foundations and the same walling and roofing materials as the rest of the building. The garage door may well cost more than an equivalent sized window, the trades of electrician and plumber will be represented and, in all probability, so will the plasterer. If the garage is detached there may indeed be some saving but in many cases, with a pitched roof and sharing the same materials as the house, it is really just a small bungalow building and, as such, is likely to cost almost as much per square metre to build. Above all, I object to the danger of the garage being left out of the calculation altogether. These areas do not come for free and, especially in the initial budgeting stages, it is, in my opinion, best to include them in the overall costings at the same rate as for the rest of the house.

Some of the companies might not like what I have done because, in some cases, the effect is that the living accommodation provided is less than they advertised and therefore, when they talk about costs in relation to size, their figures might not add up. I make no apology for this. I believe that when considering design and costs you need a 'level playing field' if you are to compare one design against another and get a true picture of what you can afford to build.

A three bedroom family home centred around a great hall and gallery – see page 269

Planning to build your own home

This book is concerned with the design of your new home and the choices that lead up to your final plans.

Many will skip these first pages and go straight to the plans. But how can you think about design, except in the broadest sense, if you have not yet found your plot? How can you consider even what size your new home is going to be if you have not set your budget and decided just how much is left for the building costs? These things and many others are discussed in detail in the sister book by the same authors *'Building Your Own Home'* and it behoves the serious would-be self builder to read that book thoroughly before getting too far down the line.

'Building Your Own Home', which has been a best seller for all of its 17 editions, is not a technical manual; it is a book that goes through the whole business of self building. It offers advice on how to find and evaluate the plot, the legal aspects and pitfalls of buying land, choosing who will design your new home and understanding the basics of valuation. It is concerned with self build finance and all aspects of insurance and warranties. It discusses in detail the ins and outs of planning and building regulations and goes on to advise on how to find and manage subcontract labour or building contractors. It has chapters on the many choices that the self builder will face as well as advice on the sourcing and buying materials.

DESIGN CONSIDERATIONS

Studying the plans within this book is meant to excite you and lead to you drawing plans of your own and making lists of your design likes and dislikes. I hope that you will begin to think about things like tabled verges, great halls, roof pitches and playrooms. I hope that from these pages you will be able to decide exactly what your new home should include and that when you come to commission your architect or designer, you are able to give them precise details that will enable them to draw up exactly what you want.

You may therefore think it strange when I introduce a brake on your enthusiasm.

Many people are tempted to think in terms of a detailed design, even going to the extent of commissioning an architect or designer, before they have even found the plot. They then go looking for a site upon which they can fit their chosen design. This is wrong. It is putting the cart before the horse. Always find the plot first and then design the house to fit the plot. Designs are infinitely variable. Plots are hard to come by and if you go around discounting sites because your chosen design won't fit on them, you'll never get beyond first base with your self build project.

The plot is the most important factor in the self build. Without a plot there will be no self build. With a plot, the local vernacular, the planners requirements and the dictates of the site such as the levels, its size and its carrying capacity in terms of just what sort of house or bungalow it is economically viable to build there, all become paramount.

That doesn't mean that you shouldn't think, perhaps in quite detailed format, about what you want and what you're hoping to achieve. What it does mean is that you should make 'wish lists', take photographs of what you like and don't like, draw rough plans and decide on size and style, but that is as far as it should go until you've found the plot.

Well that's the end of the lecture – now down to the serious business of thinking about the design of your new home and the questions that you should ask yourselves: -

What are you hoping to achieve?

Examine your motives for self building before you commission the design. Is this the culmination of a long standing desire to create something permanent that you can be proud of and which will be there long after you've gone? Or is this merely a step on the ladder to your eventual dream home? Are you doing this in order to have a home that fits your family's lifestyle and individual needs or are you more interested in the possible gains in value that are to be made? Is it all about more accommodation, particularly more bedrooms, or is it about quality? Is kerb appeal and instant attraction more important than having a home that grows upon you or opens up in unexpected ways when you walk through it? If the answers to these questions prove that the proposed new home is just going to be a temporary phase in your lives, then the motto of 'least in most out' must apply and every design specification and all material choices must be weighed against cost versus general acceptability. If the answers mean that this home is something special to you then, although cost effectiveness may still be a prime consideration, personal preferences must also play their part.

What part are the planners going to play in the design of your new home?

Travel around the area where your site is located and look out for new buildings or those that have been built in the past few years. Discount many of the larger sites and concentrate on the single dwellings. Compare these with the older properties. Do they share the same design characteristics? They may not. They may sympathise with them but not emulate them in any way. Modern architecture has often, and quite rightly, grown into and evolved certain styles that seem to have no reference from the past. Unfortunately there are also many parts of the realm where modern architecture is simply just a pastiche of what has gone before.

Be that as it may, study these new buildings and make a note of what you like and dislike. Keep a camera handy and photograph distinctive features. Take notes and cut out plans from magazines that serve to illustrate a point or feature.

What you see built before you is a demonstration of what has been accepted by the planners in your area. In all probability what is demonstrated within these buildings is encapsulated in word and diagrammatic form in the Local Plan/Framework or planning policy document produced by the local authority and available for inspection at their offices. This document is a rolling policy that is replaced every five years and is therefore under constant review. That does not, however, mean that its impermanence in any way detracts from the fact that, as far as the planning authorities are concerned, this established and ratified policy governs all of their decisions.

I am not for one moment suggesting that you think at this stage of going to Appeal – an appeal, as you will read in Building Your Own Home is always the last resort. But to demonstrate the importance of the Local Plan, the advice from the

A four bedroom, heavy timbered home with an impressive porch – see page 191

Inspectorate is that appeals for applications that run counter to adopted and ratified planning policy, have a fairly slim chance of success.

So study the local plan. Consult with the planners about your specific site. Learn about local architectural vernacular. This does not mean that you have to slavishly follow some design dictate. It does mean that if you are going to achieve what you want, you may have to learn to compromise and you may have to develop skills of communication and learn to use the planners' own arguments and policies to your advantage.

One other aspect of design that the local authority will influence is the requirement, this time under the Building Regulations rather than planning, for disabled access. All new dwellings must have disabled access and, within the entrance floor, provision needs to be made for wheelchair access to a toilet. These regulations may well be cranked up in the future with talk of space having to be allocated or identified for possible provision of a lift. At the moment the requirement is for the access to at least one entrance door to have a ramp no longer than ten metres for gradients of 1:15 or five metres for gradients up to 1:10. If the site has a steeper slope then a stepped approach is allowed so long as the steps have a width of no less than 900mm, the rise for each step is between 75mm and 150mm and the rise between each landing is no more than 1.8 metres. If there are more than three risers, there has to be a continuous handrail on one side with a gripable profile. The entrance door, which can be a secondary door on the main entrance floor should have a clear opening of at least 775mm. It should also have a level threshold or cill although if one is unavoidable, this should be no more than 150mm.

Internal doorway and passageway widths are also prescribed by the following table: -

Doorway clear opening width	Corridor/passageway width
750mm or wider	900mm when approach to the door is head on
750mm	1200mm when approach to the door is not head on
775mm	1050mm when approach to the door is not head on
800mm	900mm when approach to the door is not head on

There has to be a toilet on the ground or entrance storey. Whilst it is recognised that it may not always be practicable for a wheelchair to be fully accommodated within the compartment, access must, however, be as easy as possible. This is often satisfied by having the door opening outwards with the washbasin positioned so as not to impede access.

Although not impinging on the design of your new home, power sockets must be a minimum of 450mm from the floor and light switches must be a maximum of 1200mm from the floor.

What impact does the site have on your new home?

Quite apart from the fact that the location of your site will determine the Planning Authority and the dictates you have to comply with, the site itself is obviously the governing factor in any design. The shape of the building will be ruled by the shape of the land. If it is a narrow or a sloping plot there will be special design considerations. That does not mean that you necessarily have to be restricted in what you can build but it may well mean that ingenuity in design, as demonstrated within these pages, will have to come to the fore. In fact many of the more innovative design solutions and some of the most exciting designs have evolved in order to overcome a particular site 'problem'.

Trees can affect design. In bad ground they may well dictate additional foundation costs, therefore reducing the size of the building through the constriction on your budget. In other situations their retention may affect the design either by restricting the area available to build on or by requiring different window configurations to avoid shading or retain views.

Access is also important and satisfaction of Highways requirements can often impact on the space that is left for the house. On sloping ground, in particular, large tracts may be needed to provide driveways at the required minimum gradients, together with parking and turning. Pay particular attention to any requirement for visibility splays. These may seem innocuous but if they require rights over other land, and these are not readily available, it can mean that a site cannot be developed. These and other related matters are discussed in great detail in Building Your Own Home where you will find a comprehensive site details checklist.

Have you properly considered the budget?

Have you worked out your finances and established just how much you can afford to spend on your new home? Are you aware that differing methods of building and the level of your own involvement with the build process will impact on the costs and therefore the proposed size of your new home? At the time of writing average building costs seem to be as follows: -

When built by a medium sized NHBC registered builder	£570 - £850 per sq. m.
When built to weathertight shell stage only by a small NHBC registered builder with subcontractors used for the second fix trades	£500 - £770 per sq. m.
When built on a direct labour basis using subcontractors for each trade	£490 - £720 per sq. m.
When built on a direct labour basis using subcontractors but with the self builder doing a reasonable amount of DIY	£450 - £680 per sq. m.

The observant will see that there are huge variations within these figures. In parts of Eire and Northern Ireland many self builders will achieve much lower figures than these whereas, in London, some of the Home Counties and in the Channel Islands, the final figures could be much higher.

The point is that you have to start somewhere. These figures are going to keep on changing and the important thing is for you to make yourselves aware of the current costs in order to set your budget and decide, in broad terms, the size of your proposed new home. A detailed analysis of build costs throughout the British Isles is published monthly in Homebuilding & Renovating magazine. Divide your building budget by the appropriate figure to set the guideline size but then be aware that this is an interim costing and that, before proceeding too far with the design, you should arrange for a more detailed cost analysis.

Are you going to go right up to, or even slightly beyond the limit of your finances, and trust to inflation to sort out any shortfall or are you going to play it safe? Have you considered whether a contingency sum would be appropriate? Have you put the budget at the top of the requirements list that you will eventually be presenting to your architects/designers?

Are limited finances affecting what you're trying to achieve?

If the plot is more expensive than you had hoped for and has seriously eroded your ability to build just what you had wanted, could you look at things another way? Is it possible that you could think in terms of a design that could be built in stages or one that could evolve as finances permit? Would it be possible to scale down your requirements? Could you cheapen the specification in some way in order to gain more space on the understanding that at some time in the future you could strip some things out and put better ones in place? Bearing in mind what I have said above, could you think in terms of changing the method of building and having more on site involvement yourself?

Could/should you think about a more economical shape? The more complicated the design, the more expensive it will be to build. If cost is the problem, stick wherever possible, to standard or rectangular configurations. This doesn't mean that you have to build a box. Unattractive designs can sometimes prove to be a false economy if the consequence of simplicity is a reduced market value. But simplicity does not have to equate with boring. Many of the classic design styles of previous ages have at their root, simple shapes and symmetry.

It is the 'fussy' designs, such as those with multiple roof planes and abutments, valleys and hips that cost the most to build. Whilst it may be essential to occupy the roof, consider the fact that a roof light can often be cheaper than dormers. Cut and pitch roofs are also expensive and time consuming. A trussed roof can be 'slung' in a few days whereas a roof made on site from sawn lumber might take weeks. If you've decided that your new home has to be a complex shape then even some trussed roofs may have sections such as hip and valley trees that have to be made up on site. But this, together with the use of girder trusses, is still cheaper than having the whole roof constructed on site.

It may also be cheaper to consider attic trusses if you want rooms in the roof, rather than having a cut and pitch roof. They may necessitate a crane having to be on site but they are often cheaper and quicker. If your budget is tight and you may need more space one day, urgently consider substituting the ordinary trusses for attic trusses at a fairly minimal extra cost that will give you the scope and opportunity for future expansion when finances permit.

How long are you likely to live there?

Whatever you think now, the chances are that within five years you will be moving on, perhaps to another self build. If you've decided that you're only going to build it and live in it for the minimum time to escape a Capital Gains Tax liability then you need to keep a constant eye on the resale value versus the building costs.

A home might not be for life but it should be capable of evolving and adapting to changing needs. If you're going to be in the same house whilst you raise your children will you need to think ahead for their accommodation requirements and the maintenance of your own sanity? What about visitors? Do you have family or friends who will often want to visit and if so, do you have to design around the ability to put them up with relative comfort? If you opt for all of this extra accommodation, what use will it have when the family has left home? If you're planning to live in the home through to old age should you make adjustments to the design to accommodate ground floor living/sleeping or the possibility of physical disability in later life? Could part of the building provide either a granny annex or accommodation for a carer?

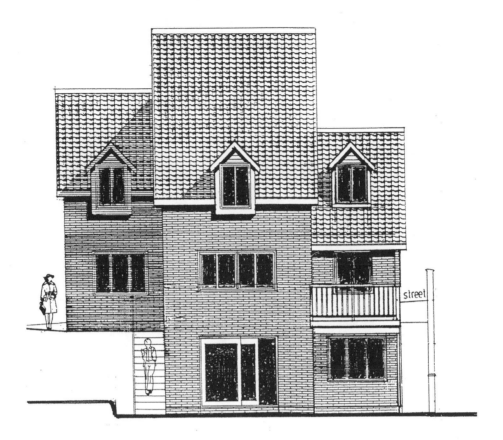

Externally, what do you want it to look like?

As discussed above, the planners are going to have a lot to do with what your home looks like from the outside, how big it is and what materials will be used. In fact they probably get the blame for many 'ordinary' houses when the real culprits are the self builders who, having rubbished the designs of most developers, then create pale imitations of the same thing.

That's not always wrong of course. Modern design reflects the best of a modern lifestyle and its evolution is an ongoing factor as I have already discussed. It is also a fact that if and when you come to sell you'll be doing so to a non self building buyer. They won't have the same ideals as you. They won't know anything about many of the design considerations and technical innovations that you as a self builder take for granted. If your home is too far out of the norm, you might find that you've cut down on the marketability of your home and that, within your price range, you're tying to reach a very small proportion of the buyers.

Are you ready to push the boat out in design terms? Do you want something that is truly individual? If so are you ready for the negotiation and hassle that being different will entail? Will your site lend itself to new innovations and design ideas or is this the wrong place or period of your life to buck the trend or conduct experiments of that sort?

If you do decide to do something different, try to take the planners with you rather than see it as entering into some sort of duel. Planning officers spend day after day considering houses and bungalows that, to say the least, do not tax the

Awkward sloping sites call for imaginative solutions – see page 340

An imaginative five bedroom design with a Scottish flavour –see page 278

imagination. If you can 'invite' them into your scheme as partners in achieving something different, something that nevertheless conforms to their broad policy ideals and yet something that represents a leap forward in design terms, then their working lives will be made more interesting for a time and you may have some success.

Internally could you go for freedom of expression?

The planners are not usually concerned with the inside of a house. Nevertheless, the internal arrangements of most homes are remarkably predictable with a recognised progression of associated rooms. Do you feel the need to stick to conventional design formats? Does each area of your new home have to justify its existence by reference to a particular function or could you contemplate the idea of architectural space for its own sake? Could you envisage a layout or mixture of rooms that defies the accepted wisdom, yet fits in with your own lifestyle, or would that seriously affect any re-sale values? Do you care? Do you want a strict division of living and sleeping arrangements or are you aware of the fact that the names on each of the rooms does not mean that they will forever be used for that purpose? Do you want to create areas of your new home that are private from or even capable of being divided from other areas?

Are running costs important?

Have you examined the reasons behind your choices? Are you aware of the need to save money in the short as well as the longer term? Are you conscious of the fact that in later life your finances might be limited and that being saddled with high fuel costs might make it impossible to stay in your home? Are your motives purely personal or are you trying to save the planet? Are you cognisant of the fact that many of the energy saving devices and technologies have very high capital costs and that you might never recover those costs by strict reference to your subsequent outlays? Have you considered which relatively cheap ideas could lower your running costs and pay for themselves within a reasonable timescale?

At the moment active solar power, the use of solar and photovoltaic panels, does not have a reasonable payback time. Passive solar gain is, however, virtually free. The orientation of your new home is an important factor. A south facing home, plus or minus 45 degrees with most of the habitable room windows to this southern side and with shelter from the wind without shading, will be much more energy efficient. If a conservatory or atrium is introduced then this too can provide heat to the house and, even when not doing so, its existence means that the walls it is up against cease to be outside walls.

Compact shapes that minimise the external wall area, also have the effect of reducing heat loss and maximising energy efficiency.

Could the hall be given greater prominence?

The dining or great hall is a feature in many of the designs within this book. In previous years it was considered essential that the entrance area was kept distinct from the rest of the house and a large part of each floor was devoted to circulation and access with no other function. That belief seems to be falling away and many designers and their clients seem to have realised that this is an enormous waste of space. Now we have the dining halls, some with vaulted ceilings that provide grand entrances yet still serve a useful family function. We have the galleried seating areas to top landings, often overlooking the great hall or the lounge, utilising the landing and, through high level windows or roof lights, flooding light into the very centre of the home.

We also see the growth of the idea that there does not have to be just one entrance area. Many of us recognise that, for normal family purposes, the entrance lobby at the back or utility side of the house, is the one that we prefer. The one at the 'front door' is either largely unused or only occasionally opened to special or important guests. Therefore why does the toilet, if there is only going to be one, have to be near the front door? Would it not be more useful closer to the lobby/utility area?

What sort of living accommodation do you want?

Do you dare think in terms of open plan or is your requirement for open plan living part of the reasoning behind you wanting to self build in the first place? If you stick to convention, will any large lounge be used by the whole family? If there's a snug, will it ever get used? Will that usage continue or will the need for the children to have separate space where they can watch and listen to their own choice of TV and music become apparent in years to come? Do you need family rooms, music rooms, television rooms or even a cinema room? If you work from home or if you run a business from home do you need an office or even a suite of offices and, if so, is it necessary for them to have either a separate entrance or separate toilet facilities? Could you think in terms of the various living rooms being interconnected or even capable of being opened up to each other? Is it necessary for the living areas to have direct access to the garden?

Many pictures of lounges have as their centrepiece, a fireplace. Do you want this? If so have you considered the style and whether your favourite is the right choice for the general style of your house or the period it is emulating? A fireplace can dominate a room or it can complement it. A chimney is an expensive feature. If the fireplace is to be used as a focal point and there is no requirement for a fire in it then might it not be a better idea to leave out the chimney. It will save money and might save quite a bit of space on the floors above.

Granny annexes have their own section within this book. Planners are sometimes afraid of granny annexes, believing that they might be subdivided and let or sold off, thus turning what was supposed to be one household into two. The argument for a granny annex might be lost if too much attention is paid to it having a separate access or if, with granny supposedly infirm, the accommodation is all upstairs.

Examine why you need a separate or distinct access. Could the annex have a shared access with the rear lobby or utility area of the main house? Could it officially have no access other than from the main house, yet enjoy one by means of French doors into the lounge section? Does it have to have its own cooking facilities or will 'granny' be eating with you? And of course, an annex might not always be needed for a granny. Sometimes an annex is needed for other purposes – a disabled person, a member of staff or as guest or holiday accommodation.

Will the selection of certain external materials impact on your design?

The choice of external materials is dictated, in many cases, by the requirements of the local authority. Do you understand that if you are building in materials such as natural stone this may well affect the design of your new home, as the walls will be thicker and you will lose usable area? Certain traditional bricks, tiles and stone are no longer available and alternatives can be very expensive. Could you use the argument that modern buildings can empathise with traditional architecture whilst making their own statement in terms of design and the choice of materials? Are you aware that some roof coverings have to be laid at either a minimum or maximum pitch and that this can affect not only the design, but also the availability of loft space?

The principal difference that the self builder will notice in respect of external materials, is the cost and the impact this has on the size of the building. Building in natural stone with either plain clay tiles, natural slates or, even more expensively, natural stone slates is going to be the most expensive option. But in certain areas it's no use bleating about it. The planners are going to insist on it, it probably appears as a condition on the planning consent and their inclusion must be assumed at the very beginning rather than trusting to a vain hope that things might change.

Obviously the cheapest external materials are going to be rendered walling under concrete interlocking roof tiles. Be careful, some of the companies working within the industry are prone to quoting final build costs for their designs based on these cheaper materials. The fact that their use would be incongruous with their super designs does not seem to faze them. When things turn out more expensive they are able to point out that their package deal price has not altered and that it's the dastardly planners who are messing up your budget plans rather than them!

Windows are part and parcel of the external materials and both the planners and the building inspector may well have quite a bit to say about their style and the materials they are made of.

The most common, and the simplest, form of window is the casement window where an external frame supports opening lights that hinge on one side like a door. The window may be divided in several sections or have more than one opening light together with fixed lights and the simple hinges may be replaced with swivot hinges

A compact four bedroom home. An excellent design for a narrow site – see page 343

that swing the casement clear of the frame but essentially the mechanism and the look is the same. Sash windows open by sliding vertically with the window usually being divided horizontally into two parts with the top and bottom sections able to slide past each other independently. Traditional sash windows, known as 'box sashes' have a pulley and weight system hidden within the boxing of the side frame. Modern equivalents have a system of spiral spring assisted balances fixed directly to the sides or stiles. Pivot windows are similar to casement windows except that they have a double action pivoting arrangement that allows the window to be swung open in the vertical plane and to reverse fully so that both sides can be cleaned from the inside.

All of these types of window, and variations on their theme, can be divided by glazing bars into smaller areas of glass. Windows that are divided into a series of smaller areas are often called 'All bar' or 'Georgian'. Those with a single horizontal glazing bar across each light are often called 'Cottage' window and there are many other styles designed to emulate the windows of various ages including the Edwardian and Victorian eras. Leaded lights are usually achieved by introducing lead strips to either side of the external leaf of glass in a double glazed unit and, in some cases, but particularly with u-PVC windows, glazing bars to achieve an all bar or cottage look are introduced in the same way.

Windows can be made of softwood, hardwood, u-PVC, aluminium or metal. Softwood windows no longer rot as they used to as they are now pressure treated to last up to 30 years. Hardwood windows are expensive and to my mind are out of place because they are usually made from non-indigenous timber and may well contribute to the decimation of the rain forests. u-PVC or plastic windows are becoming increasingly popular. Planners, however, abhor them in certain sensitive

A very large and adaptable family home design – see page 253

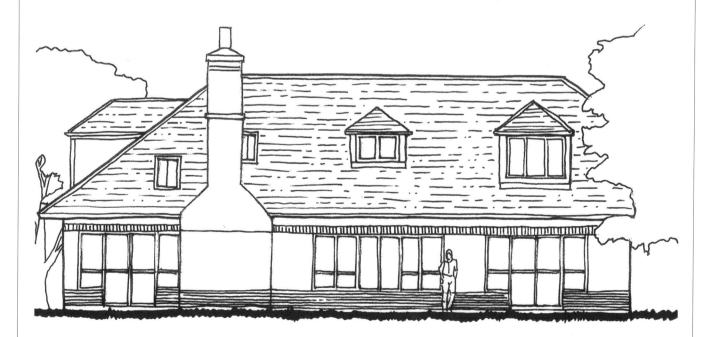

areas and may insist on painted softwood. Raw aluminium has lost much of its popularity but powder coated aluminium looks much better. Metal framed windows achieve a certain style due to the thinness of the frame and casement but they have problems satisfying the new thermal regulations.

Just like windows, doors come in various styles and can be made in all of the various materials. Planners don't seem to get quite as excited about which doors go on a house but there is no doubt that they are an important feature and can help determine the character of a building. Garage doors are of particular importance. Firstly, in many sites, if care is not given to the design, the garage door can become the dominant architectural feature of the house. It is possible to mitigate this. Where the garage door sits and the context of the building around it are important. Recessing the door, introducing roof overhangs and generally designing to take away the dominance of this feature is demonstrated by many of the contributors within this book. In particular, dividing a larger garage door into smaller ones and, wherever possible, facing garage doors across the plot rather than forwards, tends to look best.

Patio doors are an unashamedly modern arrangement. They should never display the glazing bars or leaded lights that the rest of the house's windows might have and should be left as clear glass. French doors do have basis in history. They can share the glazing bars and subdivisions of the other windows without compromising their architectural integrity.

Could/should you think in terms of incorporating a basement?

Does the slope on your site dictate a split level or partial basement design as the cost effective design solution? If there is a planning restriction on the overall size of the building, will the planners agree the basement as an extra or will they count it as part of the allowable area? Would it be extra living accommodation,

An impressive design which would be stunning in the right setting – see page 273

play/rumpus space or utility room? Can you provide windows at a higher level or consider light wells? If it's going to be windowless, have you considered ventilation adequate to its proposed usage? Are the soil conditions or water-table right for the building of basements in your area? Will you think in terms of a fully tanked basement or might you opt for one of the sump and pump systems? Are you aware that the space will cost at least as much per square metre as for the rest of the house and possibly more?

Could /should you plan to occupy the attic?

I have discussed the idea of using attic trusses above. Attic space is cheap space but its use or eventual use has to be planned for. If your roof is built with ordinary trusses then it is usually impossible to convert it into living space without virtually re-roofing the property. If there is ever a likelihood that you will want to occupy the attic then the roof must be built as either a purlin and spar roof or with attic trusses. What will you use your attic for? Will it be additional bedrooms or bathrooms? Will it be office space and if so can you get heavy office machinery and equipment up there? Will it be used as a play area? If so what are the implications for bedrooms immediately below? How will you gain access? Are you content for an occasional use to have access via a pull down staircase or loft ladder? If you want a permanent second staircase, is there room for its departure and arrival and is there sufficient headroom? Will the addition of a further habitable floor mean that fire regulations make you use fire doors to all doors leading from the landings and that escape facilities are provided?

A gracious five/six bedroom house providing spacious accommodation – see page 255

Cooking and eating

Do you really need a separate dining room? As I have said many times, the dining-room is the least used yet most expensively furnished room in the house. Most people when asked why they want a separate room say that they wouldn't want cooking smells going all around the house and they couldn't have guests eating in the same area as the food preparation. Is this clear thinking? Modern extraction systems mean that cooking smells can very quickly be disposed of. Who do you have to dinner? Do you really have strangers to dinner or are they normally family or friends? Do you really entertain thoughts of having your boss for dinner or is it more likely that in those circumstances you'd eat out? In any event, think about parties and dinner parties that you do have. Isn't it true that these days many guests gravitate to the kitchen and that when people come to dinner they normally end up chatting to you in the kitchen as you prepare the food – an exercise that often adds to the conviviality of the evening? What about a kitchen dining-room or an archway between the two areas? At least then the cook wouldn't have to be excluded from the dinner party.

Kitchens are one of the biggest selling points. Is yours the right kitchen for your home? Have you chosen from the brochure or for fashion's sake without thinking how it will look in your home without showroom lighting? Would a breakfast area be useful and much used space? What about the kitchen, breakfast area and family room being joined together as one area where the majority of family activity takes place?

A four bedroom house with a traditional look offers ample space for a narrow site – see page 346

Do you want an Aga/Rayburn? Many people swear by them but do they really fit in with a modern home. They are hugely expensive. They are frightfully heavy. They are relatively inefficient and they pump out heat into a room that, in a modern thermally efficient home, can be an embarrassment in the summer months. Above all, they can never be an afterthought. They have to be planned for. The flue needs thinking about and, given the weight, the substructure will also need attention.

Utility rooms and storage

I have already mentioned the utility room. When they first came into existence they began to rival the kitchen in size and in the level of fittings. What is the purpose of your utility room? Is its use allied to that of the kitchen and if not, does it have to connect to it? If it's really a laundry room, why cart clothes downstairs, wash them, and cart them back up again? Couldn't you have a laundry room upstairs instead? If it's a mudroom, somewhere for dirty dogs and wellies, could it just become a lobby and perhaps benefit from a toilet and/or shower room? What about the idea of it being a true wetroom with the floor draining to a gully? Dishwashers and washing machines used to make a noise like Concorde taking off. Now they can hardly be heard. If, therefore, space is at a premium, could the utility room be scrapped altogether in favour of, say a bigger kitchen or a breakfast area? If you're having underfloor central heating have you thought of where the necessary cupboards will go? Is there to be space for a central vacuum? Will the linen or airing cupboards be accessible to the communal areas or must they be in one of the bathrooms or bedrooms? Have you already got wardrobes or will you want built in and fitted ones?

And don't forget, as most big house developers do, about storage for brooms, mops, vacuum cleaners and floor polishers.

A distinctive design offering ample space for a family – see page 260

A large home with a self-contained annex and bedroom – see page 266

What about the number of bedrooms?

You might only want two or three bedrooms. But adding that extra room to the design takes you into a completely different price bracket. A house with three large bedrooms compared with an identically sized house with four smaller ones might have considerably less value. Yet its build costs might be substantially the same. If you're absolutely convinced that you only want the smaller number of bedrooms then why not plan them so that they can easily be subdivided? The dressing room or nursery room, directly adjoining the master suite can always, if it has a separate door, be walled off and turned into that extra bedroom. Be aware though that many prospective purchasers might not be able to fully comprehend such a change and that you might be better advised to carry out the alterations yourself in the event of you selling up. What about bedroom sizes? It's your house so are you going to insist that the master suite takes the lion's share of the space? Will you want dressing rooms? Do you want the remaining bedrooms to be more or less equal in size or could one or more of them be smaller and given over to occasional or some other use?

Bathrooms, toilets and washing facilities

Do you need a downstairs toilet by the front door or would it be more useful in the utility area, accessible from the garden? Might you not need both? An en-suite is de rigueur in most larger family homes. Do you want it to be a shower room or a full bathroom? Are you aware that having an en-suite to at least one of the bedrooms might take your new home into a different price league but that if its provision means that the bedrooms are made too small, any advantage on that side may be lost? With the communal bathroom do you want the toilet to be separate or have you thought of a completely separate toilet in any case? What about en-suite

An exotic three storey design centred round a courtyard – see page 264

accommodation for other bedrooms, or for at least one that you can call a guest suite? Could the idea of one bathroom being directly accessible to and serving two bedrooms fit in with your family arrangements? Have you thought through the family routines, especially in the mornings? Would doubling up the number of hand basins help? Could you put hand basins in some bedrooms?

The method of construction & technological innovations

In most conventional designs the method of construction is secondary to the design. Certain specific construction forms do, however, facilitate or in some cases dictate the design. Are you sure that the construction method you favour will be able to provide you with what you want in design terms? Are you aware that to add in a fireplace to some of the Scandinavian sealed home systems might negate much of their energy saving concept? Do you realise that some of the post and beam systems can provide clear open space that would otherwise be unattainable? Have you thought that open spaces and high or vaulted ceilings will require specific heating solutions if you are to maintain the same level of comfort as in other areas? Have you thought of running costs? Have you considered what the full height glass wall will be like in summer as well as winter?

The garage

Considered almost essential by the market, yet very rarely used for the housing of motor cars. Do you want one at all and if so, will you ever use it and what for? Could you think in terms of building more house or could you think in terms of incorporating the garage space within the home on the understanding that if it ever comes to re-sale, it can be put back to its original purpose? Could you have a carport instead? Should the garage be attached, integral or detached? Planners feel that detached garages reflect the rural character whilst attached and integral garages are an urban solution to the problem of what to do with the motor car. If the garage is detached or attached to the side of your new home, could it be left until later so as to concentrate available monies on the actual home?

If there is an historical background to the garage it is found in the coach house. Why build horrid little rectangles? Why not build something that harks back to the coach or cart house roots, possibly open at the front and with associated accommodation similar to some of those illustrated in this book? Why not vary the shape? Why not include living, office or play accommodation within the roof area?

Contents and furniture

Have you made a list of your favourite furniture? Most modern furniture is designed to fit through door openings as narrow as 760mm or else be capable of disassembly; but antique furniture certainly is not. How much space will that grand piano take up? Is the dining area large enough to accommodate your dining table fully extended and is there room enough around it for chairs and circulation? Are the ceilings going to be high enough for antique wardrobes, dressers or clocks? If your snooker table is going in the loft, can you get it up there and if so, will the floor take the weight? Is there enough space to use it? A snooker or table tennis table needs at least two metres all around.

Can you incorporate the garden into the home?

I have said many times that the garden should be an extension of the living space within the home rather than a separate entity. A home never stands in isolation. The most wonderful design can look horrible in drab surroundings. The least attractive design can look better in a well thought out and planted setting. Many of the illustrations of houses rely upon some softening of the more stark architectural features with plants or shrubs and, in some cases, climbing plants.

Do you want the garden to be separate entity or should it fit into the natural progression between rooms? If so should access to it be from the sunroom or conservatory? Will you want the main living rooms to have direct access to the garden? Are you worried about children and dogs bringing in dirt?

THE CONTRIBUTORY COMPANIES AND PRACTICES

As I have said above, none of the companies or practices represented within this book have paid to have their designs featured and all have submitted plans at my invitation. Some of the companies are package deal companies working within the self build industry. Many of these are timber frame companies but others work with traditional masonry construction. All of them are concerned to supply their drawings as part and parcel of a recognised package deal of materials or a kit supply. Their drawings are prepared in order to sell their products and they are very unlikely to want to sell or allow their plans to be used without the rest of their service.

The architectural practices may have a slightly different perspective on things in that they may, in certain circumstances, be persuaded to sell or licence the use of their drawings, particularly if you are out of their area. In any of these cases you cannot assume that these drawings are for sale. The copyright always belongs to the originator and you cannot use these drawings without their consent or agreement.

However, as I have said above, I suspect that for many if not most of you, the plans within this book will be used to give you ideas for your own individual self build design. In that case what you are after is a bespoke design and many if not all of the contributors to this book are happy to provide that service. I suggest therefore that what you do is contact the company that you feel most closely represents or encapsulates your design ideals and that you talk to them about what they can do for you.

Associated Self Build Architects (ASBA)

For many years architects, and particularly the crustier ones, virtually excluded themselves from the self build market, refusing to listen to what their prospective clients wanted and instead, trying to dictate what they should have. Then, in 1992, ASBA came into being to show just how much architects had to offer and to promote, through a like-minded membership, the principle of architects working for and with their clients in order to achieve what the self builder wanted rather than that which the architect thought they should have. Their rules for membership mean that only the smaller practices can join and they must be members of the RIBA or RIAS. They must also carry the appropriate professional indemnity insurance. ASBA architects must also agree to provide an initial consultation, free of charge, and most importantly, their members must possess the appropriate design skills and a general commitment to one-off houses. They are also required to have an unpretentious attitude to the work and their clients. As architects, their members can provide a range of services ranging from initial design right though to full build supervision.

The architect or architectural practice is shown beside the ASBA copyright notice on each drawing. You might like to quote this when contacting them.

Telephone 0800 387310

e-mail: asba@asba-architects.org

The Border Design Centre

This exciting design practice with its unashamedly Scottish houses and bungalows has links with major timber frame manufacturers who are members of the UK Timber Frame Association (UKTFA), effectively forming the design and planning arm of their service. Their designs, although fitted into a brochure, are always bespoke designs, drawn to suit their client's needs and the dictates of the site. They handle the planning and building regulations applications and prepare a full specification to enable you to obtain competitive quotations for the construction. Although there is an initial charge for the design service, this is recoverable from their associated timber frame manufacturers.

Telephone/fax 01578 740218

e-mail: borderdesign@constructionplus.net

T.J.Crump OAKWRIGHTS Ltd

The enthusiasm with which the proprietors and staff of this company espouse their products has to be seen to be believed. This is middle ages technology brought into the modern world with a massive skeleton of heavy oak timbers forming the frame. This frame is erected in their yard and each piece of timber is given a carpenter's mark before being dispatched to site and erected permanently. In its single skin form the infill panels are fitted with a sophisticated system of water bars, trims and weather seals before being rendered on the outside with the oak framing visible both internally and externally. In their clad systems they use Structurally Insulated Panels as the external leaf. They have a full range of designs and will undertake bespoke designs, taking care of all of the planning and building regulations and effectively providing a 'turnkey' service.

Telephone 01432 353353

Fax 01432 357733

e-mail: enquiries@oakwrights.co.uk

Custom Homes Ltd.

This company has been running in one form or another for over 30 years and they have a lot of experience in dealing with one-off self builders. Their service is usually based upon a design study, produced as a result of site meetings. This will include the initial drawings which are then followed up by a quotation for their timber frame supply and erect service plus an estimate of probable completion costs. They provide an energy efficient timber frame package covering everything including the planning and building regulations applications through to the supply and erection of the frame. Some of their clients prefer to self manage their projects whilst others prefer to take advantage of their in-house project management service.

Telephone 01293 822898
Fax 01787 377622
e-mail: admin@customhomes.co.uk

Designer Homes

The company specialises in providing plans for use in either timber frame or brick and block construction. If you are building in timber frame they will hope to be involved in providing and erecting the timber frame. If you are building in brick and block they will supply the plans only. You then make your own applications for planning and building regulations. Whilst they have a comprehensive range of designs, they can undertake alterations. They have regional managers and can arrange for a project management service.

Telephone/fax 01450 870127

Design & Materials Ltd.

This company was first established in 1971 and they are well known in the self build industry for their championing of the brick and block forms of construction. Most of their designs are bespoke and their head of design, Beverley Pemberton has become one of the best known and respected designers in the country. Their service commences, following an initial site meeting, with the preparation of a design study including initial drawings and a quotation for their materials supply service, together with an assessment of completion costs. If this is acceptable they handle all of the planning and building regulations applications and use the intervening period to help source labour or builders so that a start can be made on site as soon as practicable.

Telephone 01909 730333
Fax 01909 730201
E-mail: designandmaterials@lineone.net

Potton Ltd

This company is regarded by many as being synonymous with self building and has been, for a long time, the market leader in many respects. They are best known for their 'Heritage' range of houses built on the 'aisle frame' principle. This is a unique form of construction that employs massive timber uprights supporting a skeleton frame that takes all of the major loadings, therefore the walling panels are free to take up different configurations. Other designs within their ranges use a conventional open panel system of building. Their services include the initial design, the planning and building regulations applications and the supply and erection of the timber frame including second fix. They have a comprehensive list of builders and subcontractors and a host of bolt on extras such as supplier discounts and financial advice and packages. They hold regular seminars at their Wyboston Lakes Business and Leisure Park and have a show village of fully furnished houses.

Telephone 01480 401401
Fax 01480 401444
e-mail: sales@potton.co.uk

The Self Build House Company Ltd.

This company is a branch of the well known Scandia-Hus Ltd. The company was formed when they realised that there was a completely separate market for those who did not want so much hand holding and merely wanted to purchase a really well made timber frame from a British based company. They do have a design service and although they will undertake to deal with the planning and building regulations and will offer help in finding builders etc., these are optional extras. The quality is governed by the ideals championed by Scandia-Hus but the specification and service are tailored for the cost conscious.

Telephone 01342 312513
Fax 01342 312613
e-mail: sales@sbhc.co.uk

Scandia-Hus Ltd

For many this company, which has been in the same ownership and management for nearly thirty years, is the epitome of package deal and timber frame companies. They make no pretence or claim of cheapness. They delight in being thought of as the 'Rolls Royce' way of building. Their designs and their specification borrow the very best from Scandinavian ideals and technology and marry these to the requirements of the British climate and planning controls. The service is described by them as a 'hand holding' service covering every aspect of self building from initial design, through planning and building control right through to the supply, erection and completion of the timber frame house or bungalow on a full 'turnkey' basis to include most if not all of the second fix items to Scandinavian standards.

Telephone 01342 327977

Fax 01342 315139

e-mail: sales@scandia-hus.co.uk

Scottish Architects Network (ScAN)

This is essentially the Scottish equivalent of ASBA. It has the same ideals and very much the same rules as that association of architects with which it is closely linked. Some of the contributing architectural practices within this book who are members of both associations have chosen to have some of their designs listed under ScAN with others, drawn for clients south of the border, listed under ASBA.

The architect or architectural practice is shown beside the ScAN copyright notice on each drawing. You might like to quote this when contacting them.

Telephone 0800 731 3405

Fax 0141 331 2751

e-mail: architectu@aol.com

The Swedish House Company Ltd.

The kits provided by this long established company are based on the Scandinavian 'closed panel' system and manufactured in Sweden from timber grown in their own forests. This provides quality control from the planting right though to the completion of the new home. The kits are delivered to site in storey high sections up to nine metres long, all fully insulated and with the vapour barrier fitted. The company then fits out and finishes them to an extremely high standard to include things like triple glazing and heat recovery and mechanical ventilation as standard. They have standard designs or can produce bespoke designs and they handle all of the planning and building regulations applications. They will assist in finding builders or labour or else provide a 'turnkey' service.

Telephone 08707 700760

Fax 08707 700759

e-mail: sales@swedishhouses.com

THE PLANS

BUNGALOWS UNDER 140 SQ.M.

Although there is still an affection for the simple rectangular bungalows and there are places within the Realm where their long established presence has made them the architectural norm, in many other areas they have fallen out of favour. Planners and the general public, led by the example of self builders, have come to realise that the ranch style bungalow has no real historical foundation other than as an import from the Raj.

They have also realised, as is demonstrated within these pages, that single storey dwellings do not have to be boring and that they can borrow from the true architectural vernacular of the various regions and provide exciting and innovative homes.

One word of warning about small bungalows. Whilst the smaller size is sometimes dictated by budget restraints rather than choice, these smaller sizes lose out in economy of scale. This means that although the cost of the building may well be low in overall terms, in pounds per square metre it is often appreciably higher than for larger dwellings. This is brought about by the fact that many of the features, fittings and requirements such as the driveway, the service connections, the sanitaryware, the kitchen units and the boilers do not cost that much, if anything, less than for the larger dwellings. And yet they have a smaller area to amortise over.

Contributors in this section:
Associated Self Build Architects
The Border Design Centre
T.J.Crump OAKWRIGHTS Ltd.
Custom Homes Ltd.
Design & Materials Ltd.
Designer Homes
Potton Ltd.
The Self Build House Company Ltd.
Scottish Architects Network
Scandia-Hus Ltd.
The Swedish House Company Ltd.

LAURA LODGE

The copyright belongs to Custom Homes Ltd.

46.6 sq. m.

Overall dimensions 9.9 x 7.9m

In a world where everything has to be big, it is refreshing to see a bungalow that is unashamed to call itself small. It may just have one bedroom, a lounge and a kitchen plus a bathroom but nothing is cramped and this lovely home would suit a couple or a single person down to the ground. It is illustrated with a ramped access, something that is in any case required under the latest Building Regulations for all new homes.

FRONT ELEVATION

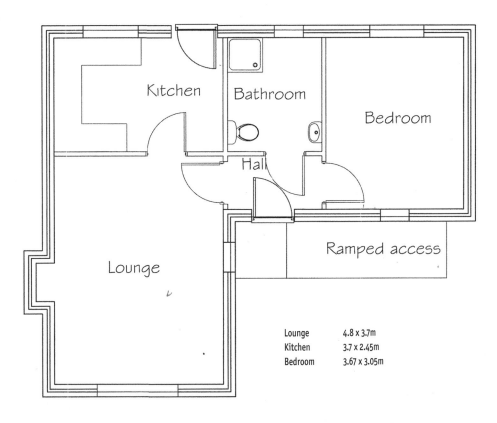

Lounge	4.8 x 3.7m
Kitchen	3.7 x 2.45m
Bedroom	3.67 x 3.05m

GROUND FLOOR

RODBRIDGE

The copyright belongs to Custom Homes Ltd.

74.4 sq. m.

Overall dimensions 10.9 x 10.5m

It may be a small bungalow covering a total area of less than the entrance halls of some of the larger houses but this is by no means cramped. All of the rooms are of a good size and this bungalow would be suitable for a single person or a retired couple, especially if they had disabilities of some sort as the layout is uncluttered and eminently suitable for wheelchair access to all rooms.

FRONT ELEVATION

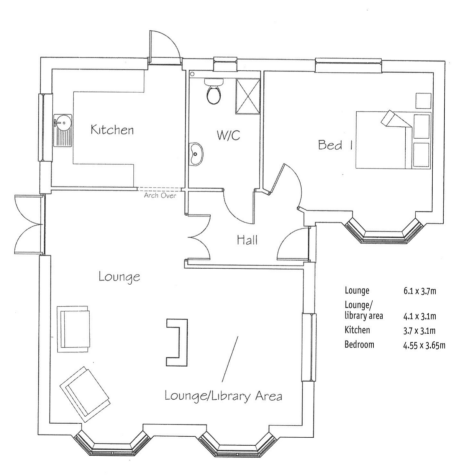

Kitchen

W/C

Bed 1

Arch Over

Hall

Lounge

Lounge	6.1 x 3.7m
Lounge/library area	4.1 x 3.1m
Kitchen	3.7 x 3.1m
Bedroom	4.55 x 3.65m

Lounge/Library Area

GROUND FLOOR

ROUNDTHWAITE

The copyright belongs to an ASBA architectural practice – S. Buttler

79 sq. m.

Overall dimensions 14.0 x 10.1m

FRONT ELEVATION

The kitchen and living room are grouped around an entrance located on the sheltered side of the home, looking directly out over the views. The sleeping accommodation is located off the living room via a separate lobby. This lobby and the entrance hall could be linked with a simple re-arrangement of the bathroom. The attic is also large enough for future occupation.

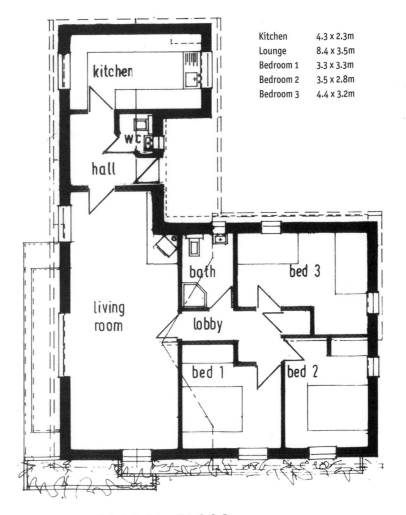

Kitchen	4.3 x 2.3m
Lounge	8.4 x 3.5m
Bedroom 1	3.3 x 3.3m
Bedroom 2	3.5 x 2.8m
Bedroom 3	4.4 x 3.2m

GROUND FLOOR

LINSELL

The copyright belongs to The Swedish House Company Ltd.

83 sq. m.

Overall dimensions 10.95 x 10.05m

Proof positive that very small bungalows don't have to look boring. By introducing the split in the walling whilst keeping both offset sections beneath the same roofline, interest is given without excessive increase in cost or complexity in building. The roof runovers allow for the porch to be sheltered and give a covered patio area accessible from the sitting room.

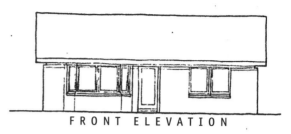

FRONT ELEVATION

SIDE ELEVATION

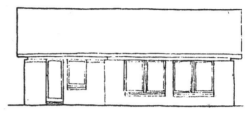

REAR ELEVATION

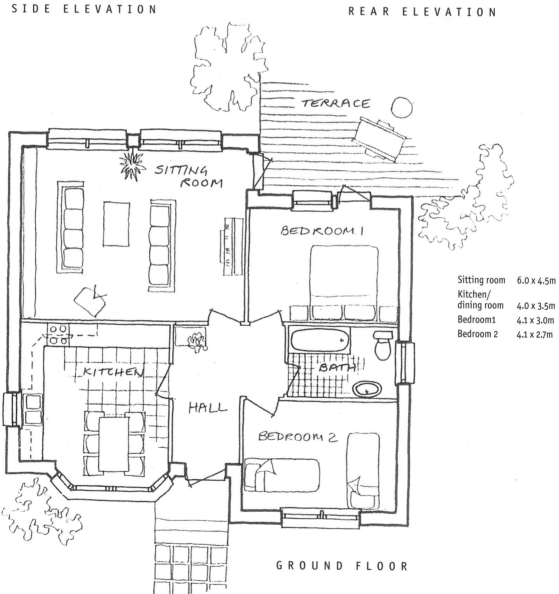

Sitting room	6.0 x 4.5m
Kitchen/dining room	4.0 x 3.5m
Bedroom1	4.1 x 3.0m
Bedroom 2	4.1 x 2.7m

GROUND FLOOR

THE ATHENA

The copyright belongs to Scandia-Hus Limited

88 sq. m.

Overall dimensions 10.51 x 10.51m

There is a distinct Greek influence to this home, dispelling the notion that bungalows have to look boring. The open fire in the lounge is shared by the entrance hall giving a warm welcome and the open plan of the living area gives a feeling of spaciousness normally felt in a much larger property.

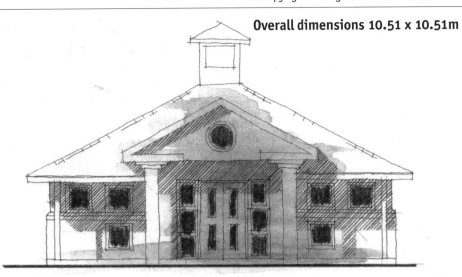

REAR ELEVATION

FRONT ELEVATION

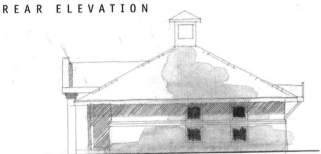

SIDE ELEVATION

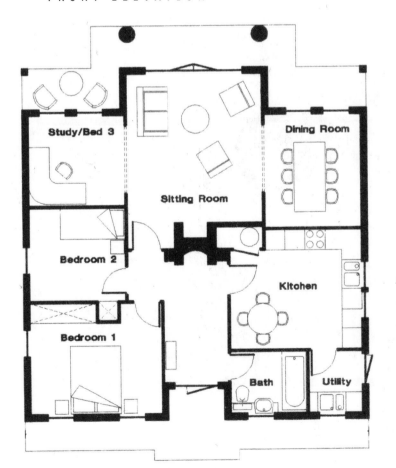

GROUND FLOOR

Kitchen	3.9 x 3.4m
Dining room	3.2 x 2.8m
Sitting room	5.0 x 4.0m
Study/ Bedroom 3	2.8 x 2.6m
Master bedroom	3.9 x 3.2m
Bedroom 2	2.8 x 2.7m

THE ONSALA

The copyright belongs to Scandia-Hus Limited

95 sq. m.

Overall dimensions 14.71 x 7.51m

FRONT ELEVATION

The classic rectangular bungalow is an economic form of construction that with careful external treatment can be made to blend in to most situations. All of the living areas are to one end of the building. The sleeping accommodation could be isolated by a simple door in the corridor.

SIDE ELEVATION

Kitchen	3.1 x 2.4m
Dining area	2.4 x 2.4m
Sitting room	5.6 x 4.4m
Master bedroom	3.8 x 2.8m + wardrobe
Bedroom 2	3.8 x 2.8m + wardrobe
Bedroom 3	2.8 x 2.5m

GROUND FLOOR

ROBIN

The copyright belongs to Designer Homes

107 sq. m.

Overall dimensions 13.80 x 9.60m

F R O N T   E L E V A T I O N

This pretty little cottage style bungalow provides three good sized bedrooms one of which is en-suite. The addition of the porch at the front prevents it looking like a railway carriage and gives it interest as well as providing space for the separate cloakroom, something that small bungalows often lack. If space permitted, the utility room could be put in a side extension to maximise the space in the kitchen/breakfast room.

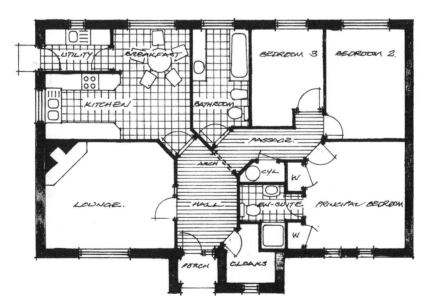

G R O U N D   F L O O R

Lounge	4.65 x 3.75m
Kitchen/ breakfast room	5.25 x 3.85m max
Utility	2.30 x 1.50m
Principal bedroom	3.75 x 3.65m + wardrobes & en-suite
Bedroom 2	3.85 x 2.90m
Bedroom 3	3.40 x 2.60m

THE EKUDDEN

The copyright belongs to Scandia-Hus Limited

109 sq. m.

Overall dimensions 14.71 x 9.91m

The simple expedient of off-setting each section of this bungalow home means that the entrance area can be covered by a deep porch and the sitting room enjoys a covered verandah. Once again the good design of this bungalow shows in the division of living and sleeping accommodation.

Kitchen area	3.2 x 2.9m
Dining area	3.2 x 2.9m
Sitting room	5.8 x 4.5m
Master bedroom	4.0 x 3.5m + wardrobe
Bedroom 2	4.2 x 2.8m
Bedroom 3	3.5 x 2.2m

FRONT ELEVATION

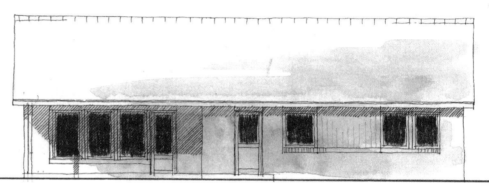

REAR ELEVATION

GROUND FLOOR

THE BOSCOBEL

The copyright belongs to Scandia-Hus Limited

110 sq. m.

Overall dimensions 15.91 x 9.71m

Although the main footprint of this bungalow is a basic rectangle, it is broken up on the front and on the back by means of a gable projection that turns this home into something special. This theme is continued by the projecting bay windows. The living area is illustrated as open plan if prefered, it would be easy to sub divide.

FRONT ELEVATION

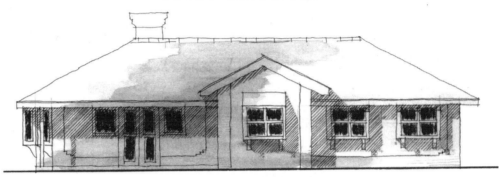

REAR ELEVATION

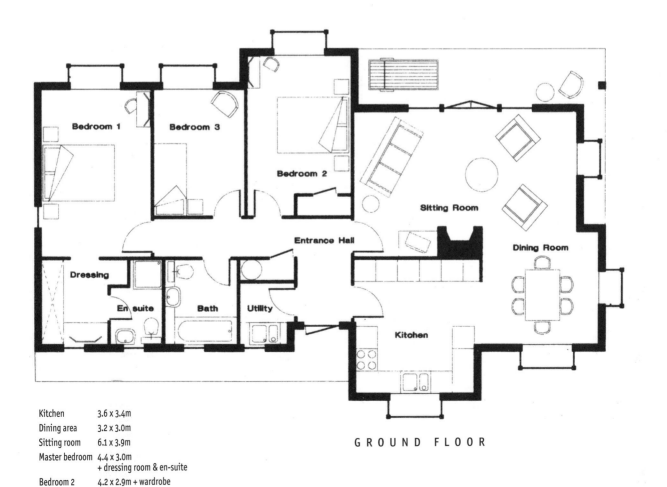

GROUND FLOOR

Kitchen	3.6 x 3.4m
Dining area	3.2 x 3.0m
Sitting room	6.1 x 3.9m
Master bedroom	4.4 x 3.0m
	+ dressing room & en-suite
Bedroom 2	4.2 x 2.9m + wardrobe
Bedroom 3	3.4 x 2.4m

WEEPING WILLOW

The copyright belongs to Designer Homes

117 sq. m.
including a garage of 16 sq. m.

Overall dimensions 13.70 x 12.25m

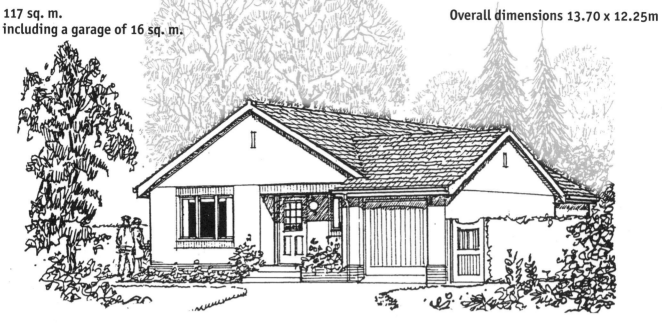

FRONT ELEVATION

This attractive bungalow demonstrates how the clever use of roof planes with the roofline over the garage coming down over the door, and the recessing of the porch and bedroom three window, actually decreases the visual impact of the garage door. The large lounge and dining area at the rear is left open plan but the kitchen remains enclosed.

Lounge	5.03 x 4.50m
Dining area	2.90 x 2.06m
Kitchen/ breakfast room	3.81 x 3.73m max
Utility	1.80 x 1.80m
Bedroom 1	3.88 x 3.43m + en-suite & wardrobe
Bedroom 2	3.43 x 3.20m + wardrobe
Bedroom 3	2.97 x 2.59m + wardrobe
Garage	5.30 x 3.00m

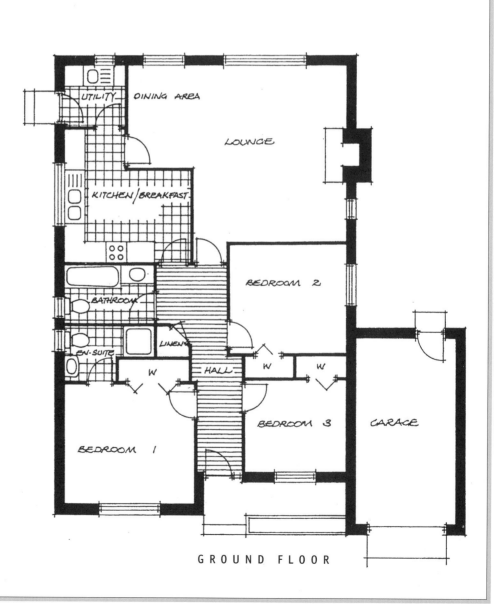

GROUND FLOOR

ASHMORE-P

The copyright belongs to Potton Ltd.

121 sq. m. including a garage of 16 sq. m.

Overall dimensions 15.3 x 11m

In recent years there has been a trend away from the traditional 'ranch style' bungalow to more complex shapes. Nevertheless there is still a place for the rectangular bungalow but, this time, it is cheered up by a forward projection and by hipping one end of the roof.

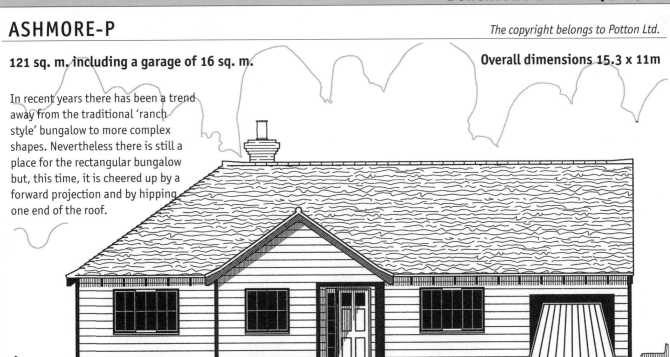

FRONT ELEVATION

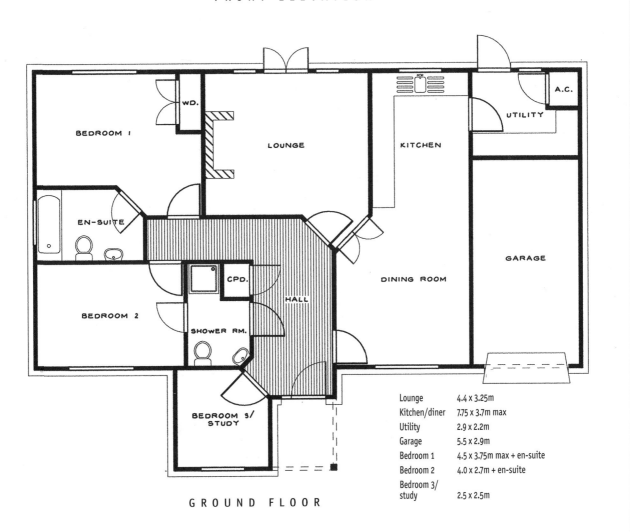

Lounge	4.4 x 3.25m
Kitchen/diner	7.75 x 3.7m max
Utility	2.9 x 2.2m
Garage	5.5 x 2.9m
Bedroom 1	4.5 x 3.75m max + en-suite
Bedroom 2	4.0 x 2.7m + en-suite
Bedroom 3/ study	2.5 x 2.5m

GROUND FLOOR

CAIRNDOW

The copyright belongs to a ScAN architectural practice – Design Practice

122 sq. m.

Overall dimensions 14.3 x 9.0m

F R O N T   E L E V A T I O N

The style of the windows and the lobby to both the front and the back doors give the clue to the fact that this bungalow was originally designed for a Scottish site. Many would lose the hall in favour of a larger lounge area while maintaining the division between living and sleeping accommodation.

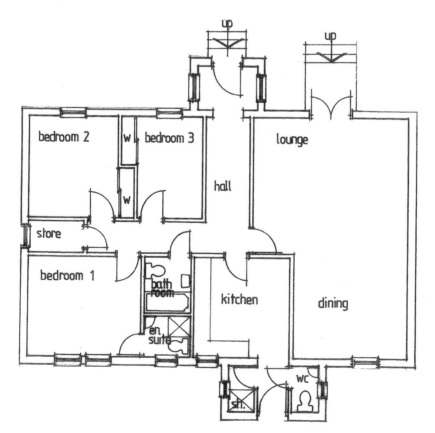

Lounge area	5.5 x 4.75m
Dining area	4.1 x 3.7m
Kitchen	3.5 x 3.5m
Bedroom 1	4.1 x 3.5m + en-suite
Bedroom 2	3.5 x 3.2m + wardrobe
Bedroom 3	3.5 x 2.4m + wardrobe

G R O U N D   F L O O R

WILLOW

The copyright belongs to Designer Homes

124 sq. m.
including a garage of 23 sq. m.

Overall dimensions 13.50 x 13.00m

The position of the garage at the side and the 'T' shape of its roof with the main bungalow lifts this gable-end design out of the ordinary. The rear lobby, providing access to the utility room has the knock on effect of creating workroom space within the garage. Storage cupboards to the utility and hall areas are also a useful addition.

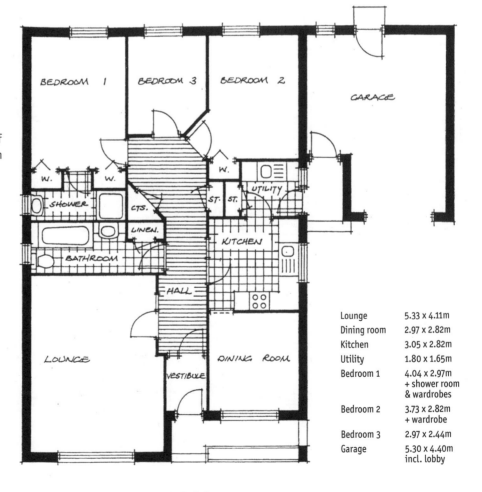

Lounge	5.33 x 4.11m
Dining room	2.97 x 2.82m
Kitchen	3.05 x 2.82m
Utility	1.80 x 1.65m
Bedroom 1	4.04 x 2.97m + shower room & wardrobes
Bedroom 2	3.73 x 2.82m + wardrobe
Bedroom 3	2.97 x 2.44m
Garage	5.30 x 4.40m incl. lobby

GROUND FLOOR

ENVIKEN

The copyright belongs to The Swedish House Company Ltd.

127 sq. m.

Overall dimensions 16.56 x 9.45m

The simple rectangular bungalow still has its place and when it provides this level of accommodation under one simple roof, it is easy to see why. Some might feel that the 'loss of space' given over to the roof runover and covered terrace was not worthwhile, whilst others might agree that it adds considerable interest.

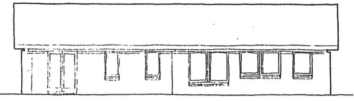

REAR ELEVATION

SIDE ELEVATION

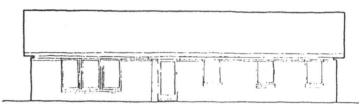

FRONT ELEVATION

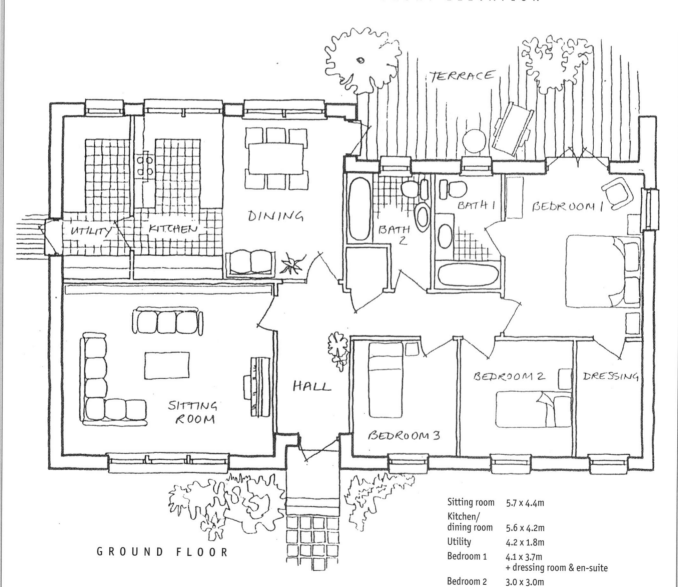

GROUND FLOOR

Sitting room	5.7 x 4.4m
Kitchen/dining room	5.6 x 4.2m
Utility	4.2 x 1.8m
Bedroom 1	4.1 x 3.7m + dressing room & en-suite
Bedroom 2	3.0 x 3.0m
Bedroom 3	3.0 x 2.8m

HEYWOOD 00-054

128 sq. m.

Overall dimensions 17.2 x 9.9m

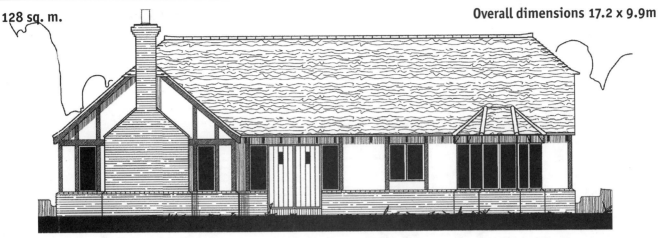

FRONT ELEVATION

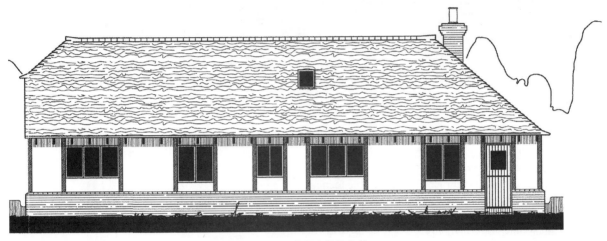

REAR ELEVATION

The long rectangular shape of this bungalow could have meant that it would look boring from the outside. The designers, however, have avoided this by adding in differing wall treatments and features and by introducing other roof planes. The large hallway, opening onto the lounge makes it a useful room rather than just wasted space.

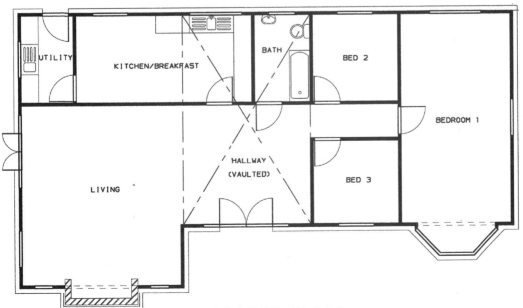

GROUND FLOOR

Lounge	5.9 x 5.4m
Kitchen/ breakfast	5.9 x 2.9m
Utility	2.9 x 1.8m
Dining hall	4.3 x 3.9m
Bedroom 1	6.8 x 3.8m
Bedroom 2	2.9 x 2.9m
Bedroom 3	2.9 x 2.9m

MALLARD

The copyright belongs to Designer Homes

128 sq. m.
including a garage of 21 sq. m.

Overall dimensions 16.20 x 15.70m

FRONT ELEVATION

Without the garage this bungalow could be fitted onto quite a narrow plot but with it, it takes on a much more impressive role. The forward projection has its roof supported on pillars to form the porch and provide the runover roof to the bay in the lounge. The sleeping accommodation is all on one side of the hall and passageway, giving it privacy and if more was required, the archways could be substituted for doors.

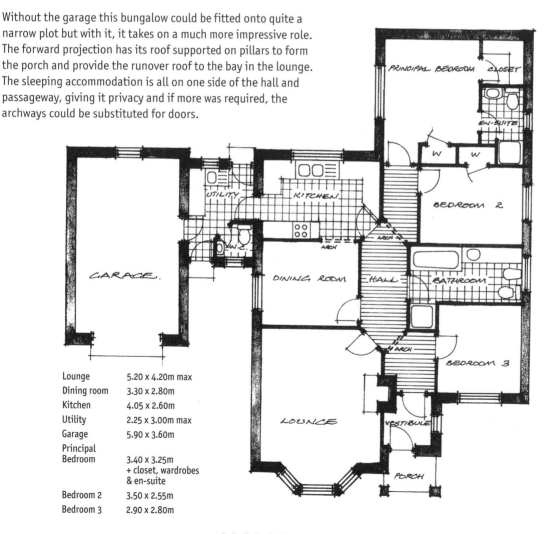

Lounge	5.20 x 4.20m max
Dining room	3.30 x 2.80m
Kitchen	4.05 x 2.60m
Utility	2.25 x 3.00m max
Garage	5.90 x 3.60m
Principal Bedroom	3.40 x 3.25m + closet, wardrobes & en-suite
Bedroom 2	3.50 x 2.55m
Bedroom 3	2.90 x 2.80m

GROUND FLOOR

THE BJORKHAM

The copyright belongs to Scandia-Hus Limited

133 sq. m.

Overall dimensions 15.01 x 14.71m

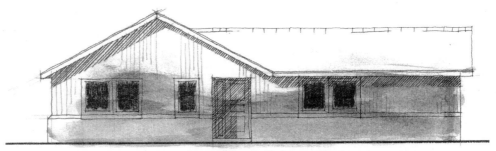

FRONT ELEVATION

REAR ELEVATION

This is the classic 'L' shaped bungalow and this simple design expedient, of putting the lounge into the extension, means that four bedrooms are easily achieved. The bedrooms are all on one side of the bungalow and the open plan living areas would open onto a sheltered patio.

Kitchen	3.1 x 3.0m
Dining area	4.1 x 3.7m
Sitting room	7.1 x 4.8m
Master bedroom	3.9 x 3.8m + en-suite
Bedroom 2	3.8 x 3.0m + wardrobe
Bedroom 3	3.0 x 2.5m
Bedroom 4	3.0 x 2.5m

GROUND FLOOR

SANDPIPER

The copyright belongs to Designer Homes

**133 sq. m.
including a garage of 16 sq. m.**

Overall dimensions 15.10 x 14.80m

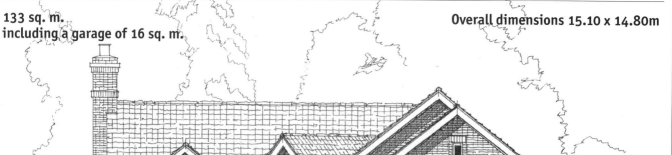

F R O N T   E L E V A T I O N

Having the porch across the angle of the two sections of this bungalow gives it an interesting façade. In many ways this home could fit onto a quite a narrow site. The bedrooms are all on the back and there is some mixing of living and sleeping accommodation meaning that this design lends itself to intimate family life or quiet retirement.

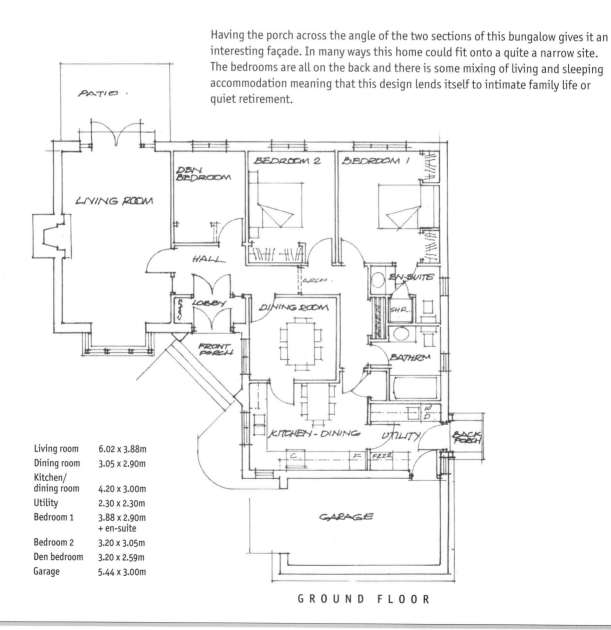

Living room	6.02 x 3.88m
Dining room	3.05 x 2.90m
Kitchen/ dining room	4.20 x 3.00m
Utility	2.30 x 2.30m
Bedroom 1	3.88 x 2.90m + en-suite
Bedroom 2	3.20 x 3.05m
Den bedroom	3.20 x 2.59m
Garage	5.44 x 3.00m

G R O U N D   F L O O R

M104

133 sq. m.

Overall dimensions 18.75 x 11.67m

F R O N T   E L E V A T I O N

A traditional bungalow that is given a new twist by the fact that the dining hall could easily have a staircase added, running from front to back and arriving at a top floor, just above the airing cupboard. This would mean that a further two bedrooms could be provided together with an additional upstairs bathroom. If more space was required in the kitchen, the utility room could move out and take up the space occupied by the shower room.

S I D E   E L E V A T I O N

Lounge	5.26 x 3.70m
Kitchen	5.25 x 3.80m including utility
Conservatory	3.70 x 3.70m
Dining hall	4.28 x 3.70m
Master bedroom	5.16 x 3.96m
Bedroom 2	4.56 x 3.70m
Bedroom 3	3.36 x 3.20m

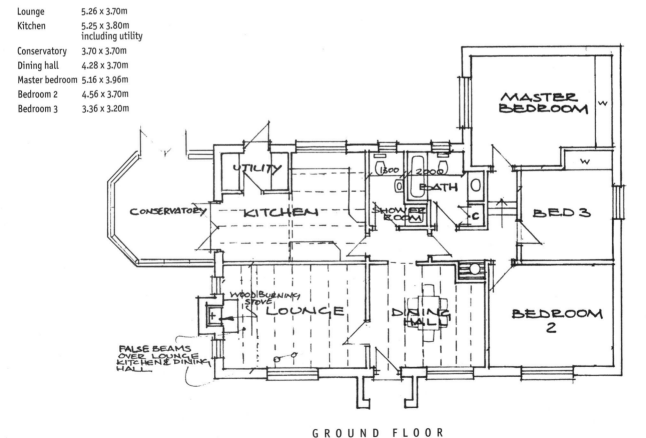

G R O U N D   F L O O R

BRIAR COTTAGE

The copyright belongs to Designer Homes

133 sq. m. including a garage of 15 sq. m.

Overall dimensions 14.50 x 14.50m

FRONT ELEVATION

SIDE ELEVATION

This cottage style bungalow looks pretty small from the front elevation but by putting the lounge and dining room, together with the master bedroom's en-suite, in the rear projection there is a lot more scope. This kind of design trick can be used quite effectively where it is necessary to lessen the visual impact to the street scene. Having the garage just that bit shorter than the main house also creates a break in the roofline and elevation, to the same effect.

Living room	5.40 x 3.90m
Dining room	3.60 x 3.00m
Kitchen	4.60 x 3.90m
Utility	3.00 x 1.50m
Garage	5.10 x 3.00m
Bedroom 1	4.00 x 3.00m + en-suite
Bedroom 2	4.00 x 3.00m
Bedroom 3	4.00 x 3.00m

living room

en-suite

dining room

bedroom 1

linen

utility

w

st

kitchen

w

hall

bathroom

coats

w

bedroom 2

garage

bedroom 3

porch

GROUND FLOOR

THE ACACIA

The copyright belongs to Scandia-Hus Limited

135 sq. m.

Overall dimensions 17.7 x 11.11m

FRONT ELEVATION

SIDE ELEVATION

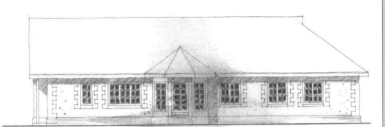

REAR ELEVATION

There is the distinct flavour of a rural school or chapel conversion behind this design. The lounge and entrance hall are illustrated as being on a lower level with steps up to the rest of the home and the layout neatly divides the comfortable living areas from the bedrooms.

GROUND FLOOR

Kitchen/ breakfast area	6.1 x 4.0m
Dining room	4.1 x 3.5m
Sitting room	7.1 x 4.9m
Master bedroom	3.8 x 3.4m + dressing area & en-suite
Bedroom 2	2.9 x 2.8m
Bedroom 3	2.7 x 2.2m

GLENKINCHIE

The copyright belongs to The Border Design Centre

**136 sq. m.
including a garage of 17 sq. m.**

Overall dimensions 14.9 x 13.7m

FRONT ELEVATION

Although a small bungalow, this design includes a tower as the hallmark feature of this contributor. It was originally designed for a farm manager on a Borders farm. There is a large farmhouse kitchen that could double up as the main living area, whilst the living room itself remains aloof as a 'best' room.

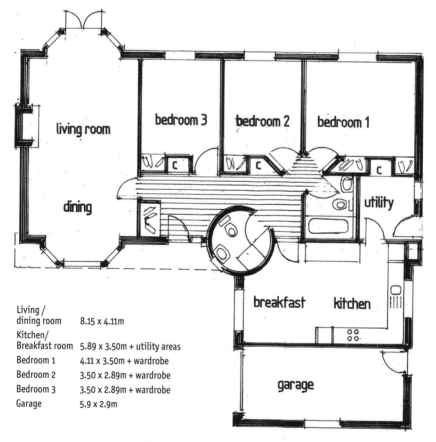

Living / dining room	8.15 x 4.11m
Kitchen/ Breakfast room	5.89 x 3.50m + utility areas
Bedroom 1	4.11 x 3.50m + wardrobe
Bedroom 2	3.50 x 2.89m + wardrobe
Bedroom 3	3.50 x 2.89m + wardrobe
Garage	5.9 x 2.9m

GROUND FLOOR

GOLDEN PHEASANT

The copyright belongs to Designer Homes

137 sq. m.

Overall dimensions 15.86 x 12.20m

FRONT ELEVATION

For its size this is a very special bungalow. All three bedrooms are self contained and could be shut off from the main living areas. They all have fitted wardrobes and the master bedroom has en-suite facilities. The kitchen/family room extends into the garden room and therefore into the garden area and/or the view. Having the lounge separated from all of the other accommodation means that it can be left for 'best'.

GROUND FLOOR

Lounge	5.03 x 4.15m + bay	Principal bedroom	3.58 x 3.30m + wardrobes & en-suite
Kitchen/ family room	6.25 x 3.50m		
Garden room	3.63 x 2.36m	Bedroom 2	3.58 x 3.12m + wardrobe
Utility	2.97 x 1.90m		
		Bedroom 3	2.97 x 2.82m + wardrobe

LAPWING

The copyright belongs to Designer Homes

139 sq. m.
including a garage of 16 sq. m.

Overall dimensions 15.60 x 14.50m

FRONT ELEVATION

Putting the entrance at the junction of the two parts of an 'L' shaped bungalow means that there is more scope with the interior arrangements. It does away with the need for long passageways and allows the creation of a central hall from which most rooms can flow. In this design that principle is extended by having the octagonal hallway with glazed screens giving and receiving borrowed light.

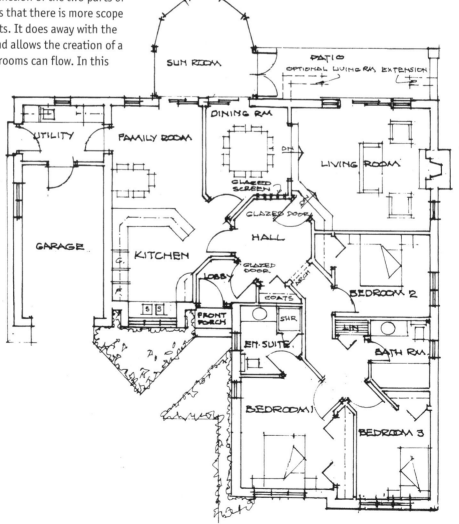

Living room	5.11 x 4.27m
Dining room	3.05 x 3.00m
Family room	3.61 x 3.50m
Kitchen	3.91 x 3.00m
Utility	3.00 x 1.98m
Garage	5.41 x 3.00m
Bedroom 1	3.88 x 3.30m
Bedroom 2	3.50 x 3.00m
Bedroom 3	3.00 x 2.69m

GROUND FLOOR

WAGTAIL

The copyright belongs to Designer Homes

140 sq. m.

Overall dimensions 17.20 x 14.30m

FRONT ELEVATION

Very little space is taken up with circulation in this design as the entrance hall gives access to most rooms. The lounge is shown with steps down into it from the main level but if this is not required, the removal of this feature would not compromise the design. The room beside the kitchen and behind the lounge could either be self contained as a study or it could be opened up to either or both of those rooms if a more open planned arrangement was preferred.

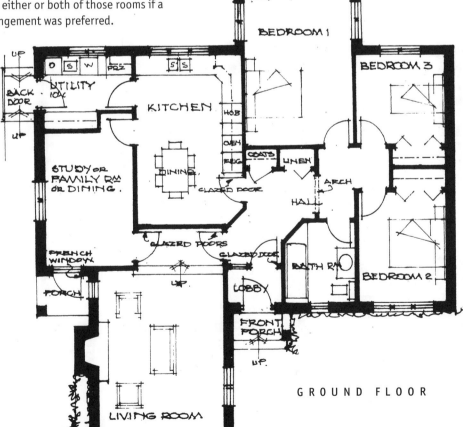

GROUND FLOOR

Living room	5.33 x 4.21m
Study/Family/ dining room	4.34 x 3.05m
Kitchen	5.49 x 3.61m
Utility	3.05 x 2.39m
Bedroom 1	4.52 x 3.66m + wardrobe & en-suite
Bedroom 2	3.61 x 3.05m + wardrobe
Bedroom 3	3.05 x 2.90m + wardrobe

SNOWFINCH

The copyright belongs to Designer Homes

140 sq. m.   **Overall dimensions 15.60 x 12.70m**

FRONT ELEVATION

It is so important to take care with the external features on a bungalow if it is not to look boring, and that is exactly what this designer has done. Attention has been paid to the roof lines. The bay windows have runover and lean-to roofs. Brick detail is indicated and that all important soft landscaping is illustrated to take off any hard lines. Inside there is ample four bedroom accommodation within an economical format.

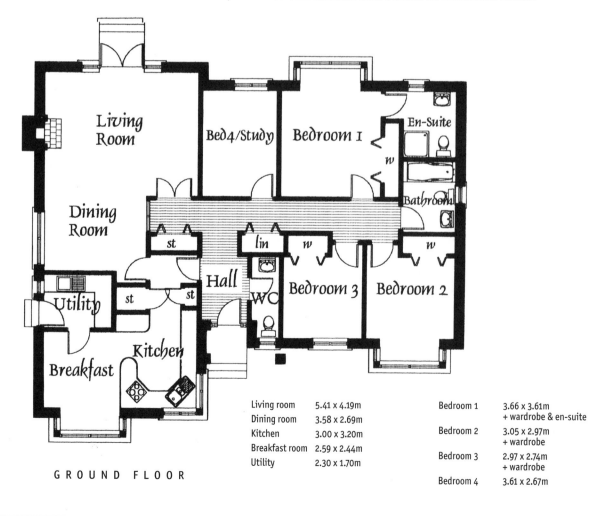

GROUND FLOOR

Living room	5.41 x 4.19m		Bedroom 1	3.66 x 3.61m + wardrobe & en-suite
Dining room	3.58 x 2.69m		Bedroom 2	3.05 x 2.97m + wardrobe
Kitchen	3.00 x 3.20m			
Breakfast room	2.59 x 2.44m		Bedroom 3	2.97 x 2.74m + wardrobe
Utility	2.30 x 1.70m			
			Bedroom 4	3.61 x 2.67m

BUNGALOWS OVER 140 SQ.M.

The larger bungalows can really spread their wings in design terms and some very interesting and innovative designs can result. Although still classed as bungalows many of these larger dwellings lend themselves to occupation of the roof void and a few of them have illustrated that fact. The criteria I have employed to classify them within this category is whether or not the ground floor can stand alone in accommodation terms.

Particular care needs to be taken with the design of a bungalow if the sleeping and living accommodation are not to muddle into each other, as there is no natural division between these two elements. In some bungalows it is possible to divide the two sections by means of a door within the passageway.

Bungalows need a considerably larger plot than a house of equivalent size. In situations where the foundation costs are inflated or an expensive roof covering is required, they may cost slightly more to build than a house. Nevertheless, this is often outweighed by a corresponding increase in value as those who need a bungalow are often in the later stages of home ownership and that, coupled with the fact that less bungalows are built than houses means that supply and demand drives the prices up.

Contributors in this section:
Associated Self Build Architects
The Border Design Centre
T.J.Crump OAKWRIGHTS Ltd.
Custom Homes Ltd.
Design & Materials Ltd.
Designer Homes
Potton Ltd.
The Self Build House Company Ltd.
Scottish Architects Network
Scandia-Hus Ltd.
The Swedish House Company Ltd.

REDSTART

The copyright belongs to Designer Homes

142 sq. m.

Overall dimensions 16.20 x 10.50m

FRONT ELEVATION

The theme with the living accommodation in this family bungalow is 'open plan'. The dining room is open plan to the lounge, separated only by an archway. The kitchen is open to the family room, which would probably serve as the main eating and congregating area for the family. What needs to be shut off is the utility room and here, many people will be delighted to see a built-in larder.

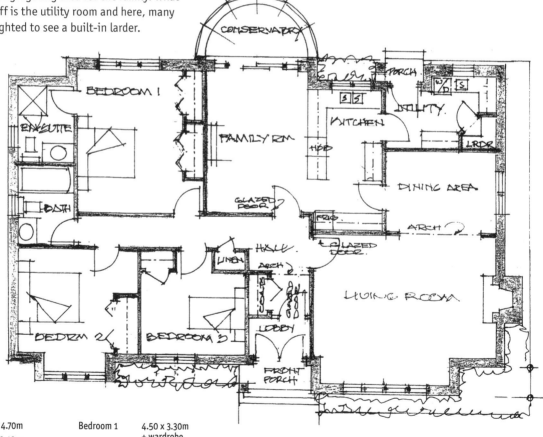

Living room	5.89 x 4.70m	Bedroom 1	4.50 x 3.30m + wardrobe & en-suite
Dining area	3.61 x 2.49m		
Kitchen	4.42 x 2.44m		
Utility	3.60 x 2.30m	Bedroom 2	3.61 x 3.30m
Family room	4.50 x 3.30m	Bedroom 3	3.40 x 2.59m

GROUND FLOOR

97-208

145 sq. m. plus optional 57 sq. m. upper part

Overall dimensions 15.31 x 14.78m

FRONT ELEVATION

This is a home with possibilities. On its own the ground floor accommodation provides either a two bedroom bungalow with four further reception rooms or areas. Change the denomination of the playroom and it becomes a three bedroom bungalow. Add in the upper part and you have more bedrooms or the possibility of home working or leisure facilities.

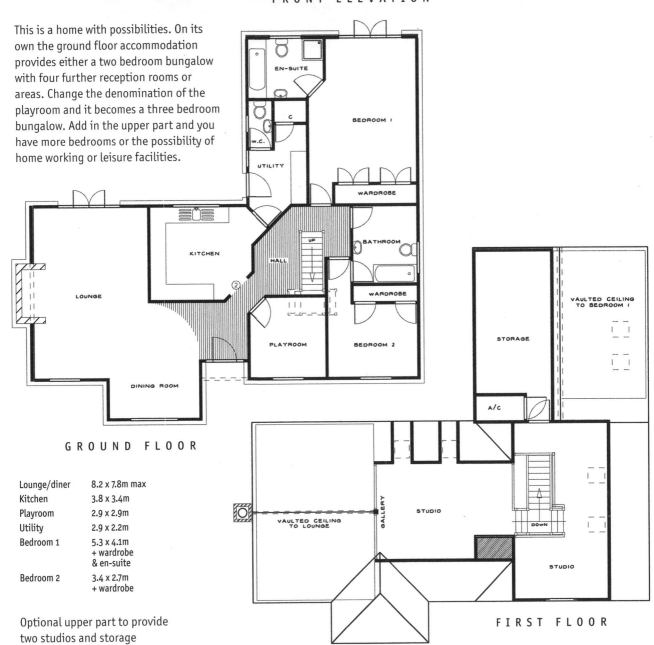

GROUND FLOOR

Lounge/diner	8.2 x 7.8m max
Kitchen	3.8 x 3.4m
Playroom	2.9 x 2.9m
Utility	2.9 x 2.2m
Bedroom 1	5.3 x 4.1m + wardrobe & en-suite
Bedroom 2	3.4 x 2.7m + wardrobe

Optional upper part to provide two studios and storage

FIRST FLOOR

MAPLETON-P

The copyright belongs to Potton Ltd.

143 sq. m. plus 30.4 sq. m. optional upper part

Overall dimensions 17.5 x 13.5m

FRONT ELEVATION

This is probably not a bungalow for a growing family. Nevertheless, its compact and ergonomically designed accommodation is eminently suitable for a single person or a couple who may want to entertain visitors from time to time. The option of further rooms in the roof would provide additional guest accommodation.

GROUND FLOOR

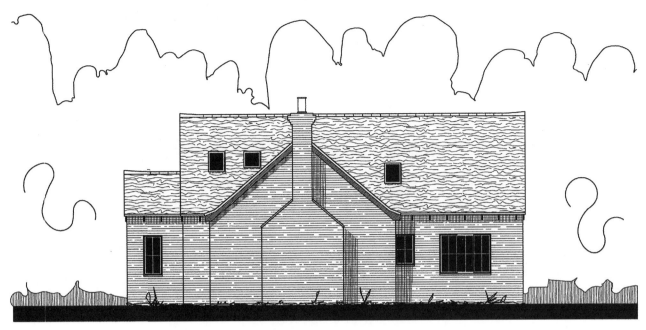

S I D E   E L E V A T I O N

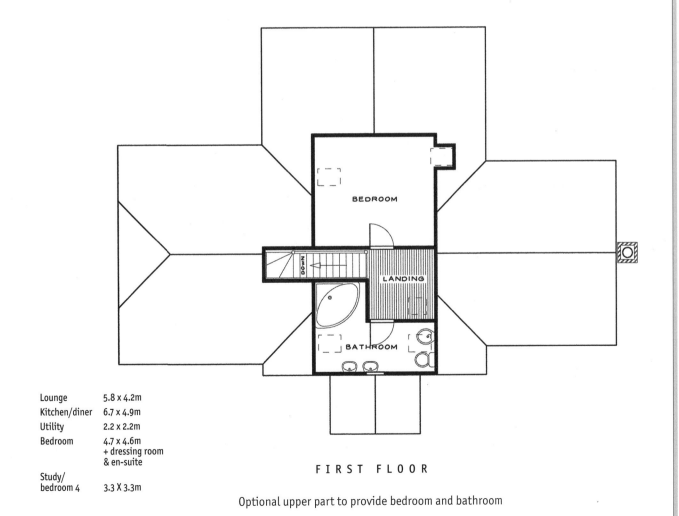

Lounge   5.8 x 4.2m
Kitchen/diner   6.7 x 4.9m
Utility   2.2 x 2.2m
Bedroom   4.7 x 4.6m
                + dressing room
                & en-suite
Study/
bedroom 4   3.3 X 3.3m

F I R S T   F L O O R

Optional upper part to provide bedroom and bathroom

KERRY

The copyright belongs to Designer Homes

146 sq. m.
including a garage of 19 sq. m.

Overall dimensions 15 x 13.80m

FRONT ELEVATION

At first sight this is an ordinary double fronted bungalow. A closer look, however, reveals the cut off corners to the two forward projections and the interesting effect this has on the two roof lines. The division between living and sleeping accommodation is largely brought about by confining each section to the front or rear with the kitchen tucking in behind the garage.

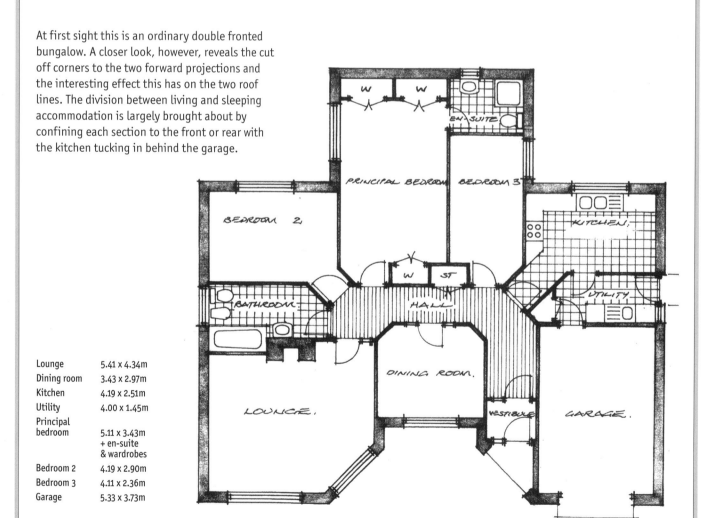

Lounge	5.41 x 4.34m
Dining room	3.43 x 2.97m
Kitchen	4.19 x 2.51m
Utility	4.00 x 1.45m
Principal bedroom	5.11 x 3.43m + en-suite & wardrobes
Bedroom 2	4.19 x 2.90m
Bedroom 3	4.11 x 2.36m
Garage	5.33 x 3.73m

GROUND FLOOR

SILJAN

The copyright belongs to The Swedish House Company Ltd.

147 sq. m.

Overall dimensions 17.53 x 9.43m

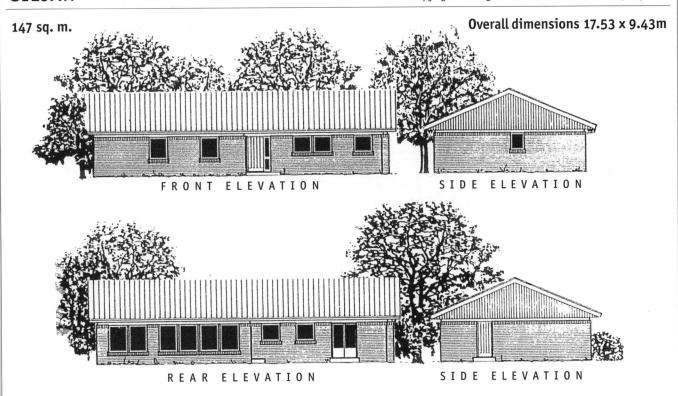

FRONT ELEVATION   SIDE ELEVATION

REAR ELEVATION   SIDE ELEVATION

Two important tricks have been used to make this bungalow more attractive. Firstly the accommodation has been split between living and sleeping so that one interferes as little as possible with the other. Secondly, by making the roof wider than the main accommodation, the two sections can be offset to each other, adding visual interest and creating wide covered areas to each main elevation.

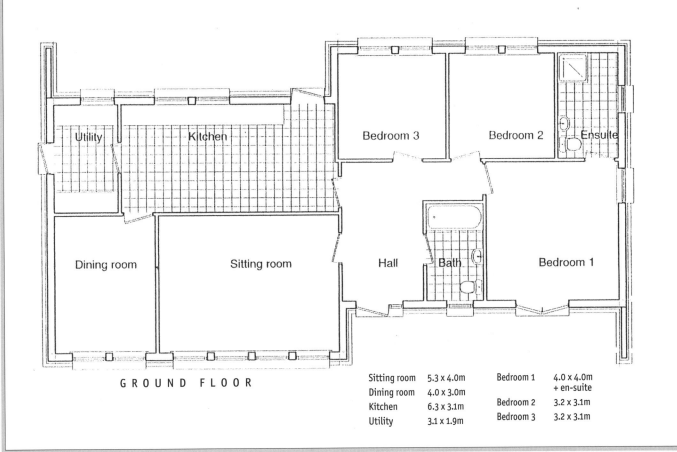

GROUND FLOOR

Sitting room	5.3 x 4.0m	Bedroom 1	4.0 x 4.0m + en-suite
Dining room	4.0 x 3.0m		
Kitchen	6.3 x 3.1m	Bedroom 2	3.2 x 3.1m
Utility	3.1 x 1.9m	Bedroom 3	3.2 x 3.1m

WOODCOCK

The copyright belongs to Designer Homes

149 sq. m.

Overall dimensions 17.66 x 13.76m

F R O N T   E L E V A T I O N

Separating the living and sleeping accommodation in a bungalow is essential and here, the designer has gone one step further and used separate parts of the building. A door in the hallway would give total privacy to the sleeping section with its four bedrooms including the principal bedroom, which is en-suite. The arrangements for the living accommodation flow nicely whilst remaining flexible.

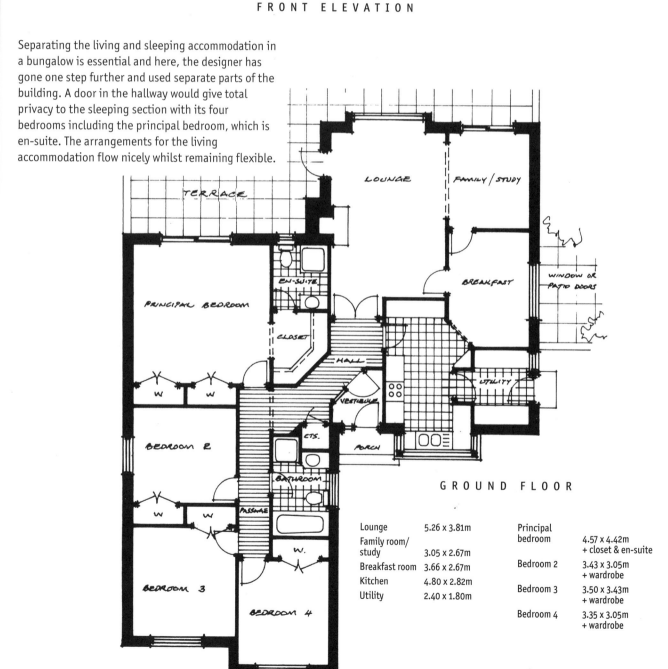

G R O U N D   F L O O R

Lounge	5.26 x 3.81m	Principal bedroom	4.57 x 4.42m + closet & en-suite
Family room/ study	3.05 x 2.67m	Bedroom 2	3.43 x 3.05m + wardrobe
Breakfast room	3.66 x 2.67m		
Kitchen	4.80 x 2.82m	Bedroom 3	3.50 x 3.43m + wardrobe
Utility	2.40 x 1.80m		
		Bedroom 4	3.35 x 3.05m + wardrobe

LEKSAND

The copyright belongs to The Swedish House Company Ltd.

149 sq. 2m.

Overall dimensions 15.5 x 12.75m.

The main hall in this 'L' shaped bungalow home opens up through a door into an inner hall from which the bedrooms are accessed. This divides and gives privacy to the sleeping accommodation. The large and combined sitting and dining room could, if required, be divided. As drawn, however, it provides open plan accommodation that can in part, take in the main hall.

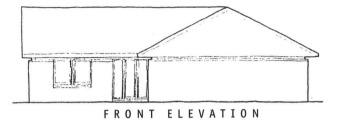

FRONT ELEVATION

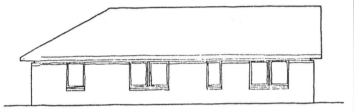

SIDE ELEVATION

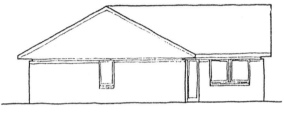

REAR ELEVATION

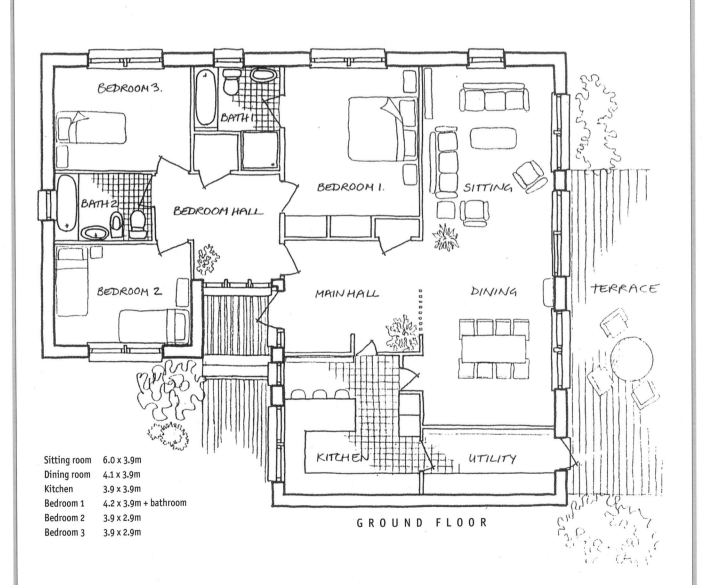

GROUND FLOOR

Sitting room	6.0 x 3.9m
Dining room	4.1 x 3.9m
Kitchen	3.9 x 3.9m
Bedroom 1	4.2 x 3.9m + bathroom
Bedroom 2	3.9 x 2.9m
Bedroom 3	3.9 x 2.9m

THE HARVARD

The copyright belongs to Scandia-Hus Limited

150 sq. m.

Overall dimensions 17.44 x 11.41m

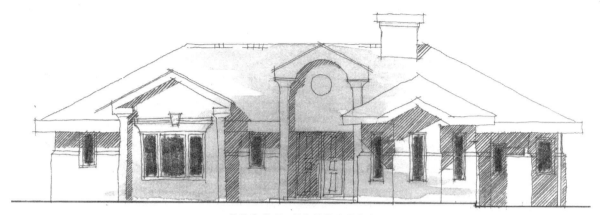

FRONT ELEVATION

Clever use of different levels within this bungalow allow for the creation of an individual ambience whilst maintaining the separate status of the sleeping sections. The imposing entrance tower gives character to the front elevation, reinforced by the hexagonal dining room projection.

GROUND FLOOR

Kitchen	4.2 x 3.2m
Dining room	3.8 x 3.2m
Sitting room	5.4 x 4.0m
Family room	5.8 x 3.9m
Master bedroom	4.0 x 3.7 m
	+ dressing area & en-suite
Bedroom 2	4.7 x 3.0m
Bedroom 3	3.3 x 2.8m

THE STOCKSUND

The copyright belongs to Scandia-Hus Limited

152 sq. m.

Overall dimensions 15.91 x 12.31m

F R O N T   E L E V A T I O N

This bungalow home offers character in abundance. The accommodation is on more than one level but if that presents a problem or the site dictates otherwise, it could be built on one level. Bay windows to most of the principal rooms project the interior into the garden and allow light to flood into the home.

S I D E   E L E V A T I O N

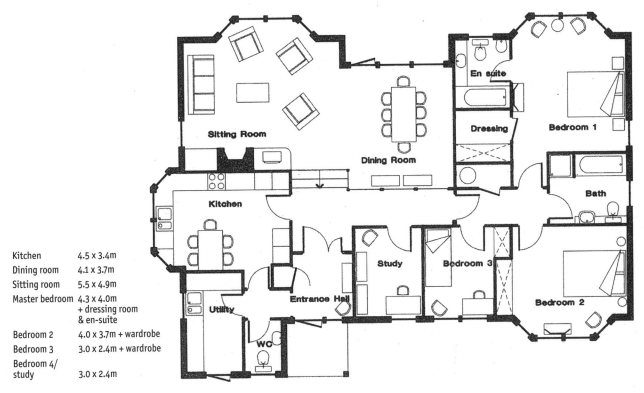

Kitchen	4.5 x 3.4m
Dining room	4.1 x 3.7m
Sitting room	5.5 x 4.9m
Master bedroom	4.3 x 4.0m + dressing room & en-suite
Bedroom 2	4.0 x 3.7m + wardrobe
Bedroom 3	3.0 x 2.4m + wardrobe
Bedroom 4/ study	3.0 x 2.4m

G R O U N D   F L O O R

MINARD

The copyright belongs to a ScAN architectural practice – Design Practice

153 sq. m.

Overall dimensions 16.2 x 14.5m

FRONT ELEVATION

The 'L' shaped bungalow is always popular, not least because the simple introduction of the extension means that so much more accommodation can be added without affecting the overall appearance. It also serves to help keep the sleeping and living accommodation in the separate wings.

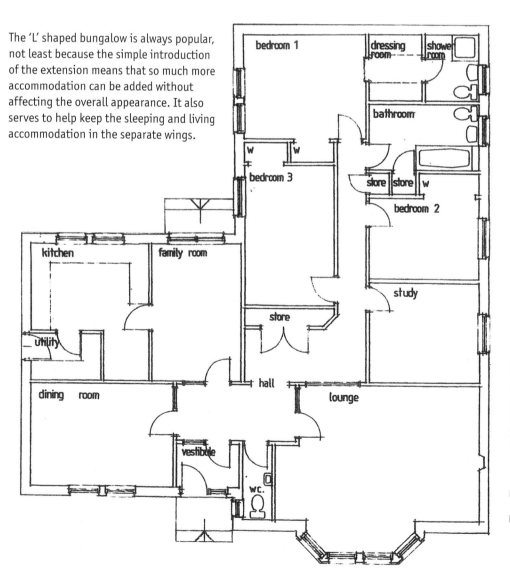

Lounge	6.2 x 4.0m + bay
Dining room	4.4 x 3.1m
Kitchen	3.6 x 2.6m
Utility	2.1 x 1.4m
Family room	4.1 x 2.8m
Study	3.3 x 3.0m
Bedroom 1	3.7 x 3.1m + wardrobe, dressing room & en-suite
Bedroom 2	3.3 x 3.15m + wardrobe
Bedroom 3	4.2 x 2.7m + wardrobe

GROUND FLOOR

GLENALMOND

The copyright belongs to The Border Design Centre

157 sq. m.

Overall dimensions 17.8 x 15.8m

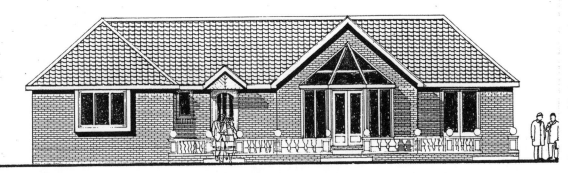

FRONT ELEVATION

The 'U' shape of this lovely bungalow home wraps around a sheltered courtyard overlooked by the kitchen and living room. The bedrooms, whilst not facing into the courtyard for reasons of privacy, nevertheless have easy access via the central hall and corridor.

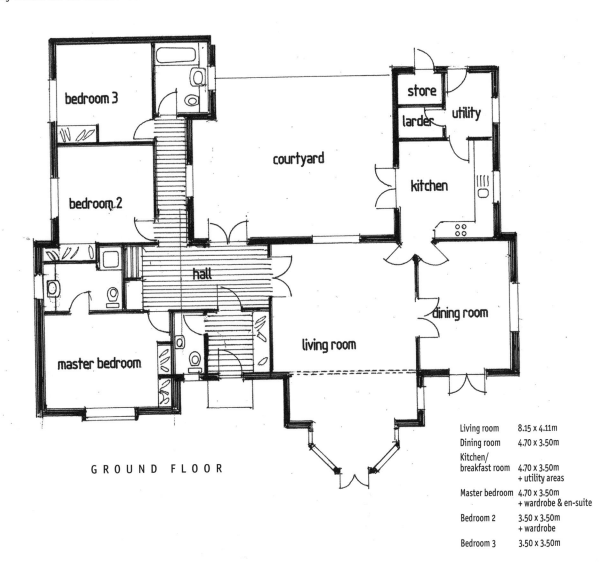

GROUND FLOOR

Living room	8.15 x 4.11m
Dining room	4.70 x 3.50m
Kitchen/ breakfast room	4.70 x 3.50m + utility areas
Master bedroom	4.70 x 3.50m + wardrobe & en-suite
Bedroom 2	3.50 x 3.50m + wardrobe
Bedroom 3	3.50 x 3.50m

HERON

The copyright belongs to Designer Homes

172 sq. m. including a garage of 33 sq. m.

Overall dimensions 22 x 18.50m

FRONT ELEVATION

Introducing a second floor tower room to a bungalow design gives it excitement, character and flexibility but still leaves it as a single storey dwelling. The three main ground floor bedrooms all open onto an inner hallway, which can be completely shut off from the rest of the living accommodation.

Living room	5.44 x 4.21m
Dining room	3.66 x 2.90m
Kitchen/ dining room	4.83 x 4.83m max
Utility	3.40 x 2.00m
Bedroom 1	4.76 x 4.17m + wardrobes & en-suite
Bedroom 2	3.96 x 3.43m + wardrobe
Bedroom 3	2.82 x 2.74m + wardrobe
Garage	6.04 x 5.44m
All purpose room	4.83 x 4.83m

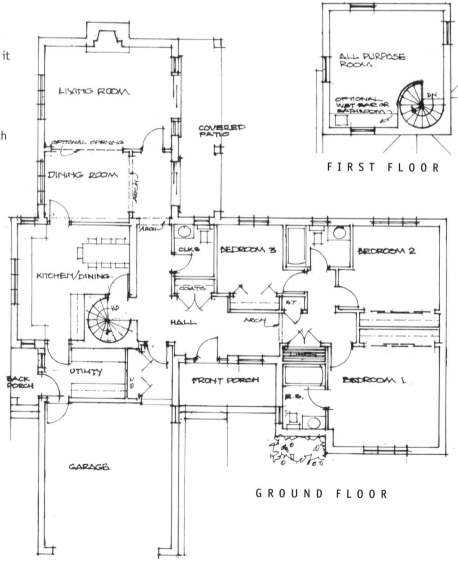

FIRST FLOOR

GROUND FLOOR

WREN

**173 sq. m.
including a garage of 26 sq. m.**

Overall dimensions 19 x 19m

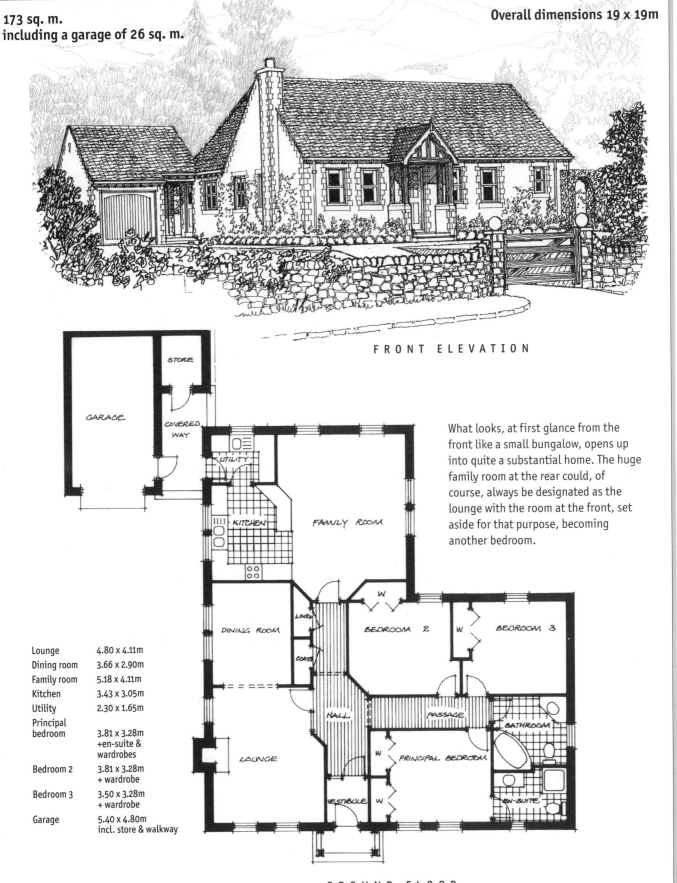

FRONT ELEVATION

What looks, at first glance from the front like a small bungalow, opens up into quite a substantial home. The huge family room at the rear could, of course, always be designated as the lounge with the room at the front, set aside for that purpose, becoming another bedroom.

Lounge	4.80 x 4.11m
Dining room	3.66 x 2.90m
Family room	5.18 x 4.11m
Kitchen	3.43 x 3.05m
Utility	2.30 x 1.65m
Principal bedroom	3.81 x 3.28m +en-suite & wardrobes
Bedroom 2	3.81 x 3.28m + wardrobe
Bedroom 3	3.50 x 3.28m + wardrobe
Garage	5.40 x 4.80m incl. store & walkway

GROUND FLOOR

HAWK

The copyright belongs to Designer Homes

**175 sq. m.
including a garage of 32 sq. m.**

Overall dimensions 17.51 x 17.36m

FRONT ELEVATION

This is the classic 'L' shaped bungalow given a new twist by the introduction of a reduced forward gable projection to add interest to the front elevation. The garage, in the other forward projection, linked to the main house by the utility room, has its doors facing across the plot. This reduces the visual impact of the garage doors.

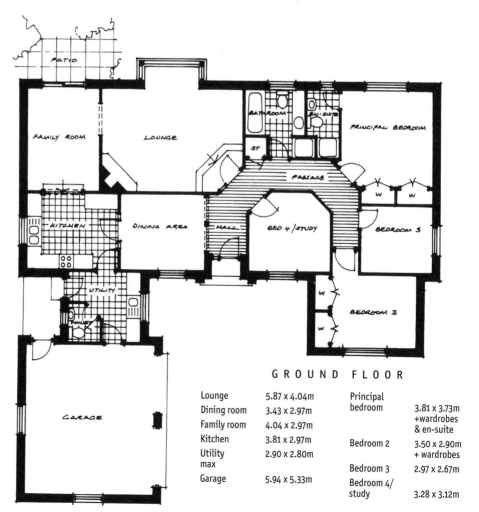

GROUND FLOOR

Lounge	5.87 x 4.04m	Principal bedroom	3.81 x 3.73m +wardrobes & en-suite
Dining room	3.43 x 2.97m		
Family room	4.04 x 2.97m		
Kitchen	3.81 x 2.97m	Bedroom 2	3.50 x 2.90m + wardrobes
Utility max	2.90 x 2.80m	Bedroom 3	2.97 x 2.67m
Garage	5.94 x 5.33m	Bedroom 4/ study	3.28 x 3.12m

HARRIER

The copyright belongs to Designer Homes

177 sq. m.
including a garage of 23 sq. m.

Overall dimensions 15.90 x 15.60m

F R O N T   E L E V A T I O N

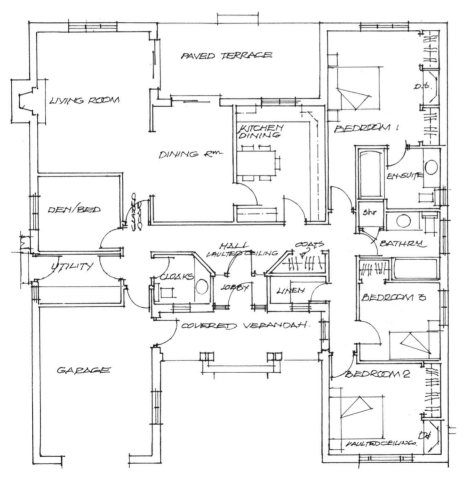

PAVED TERRACE

LIVING ROOM

KITCHEN DINING

DINING Rm.

BEDROOM 1

EN-SUITE

shr

DEN/BED

BATHRM

HALL VAULTED CEILING

COATS

UTILITY

CLOAKS

LOBBY

LINEN

BEDROOM 3

COVERED VERANDAH.

GARAGE

BEDROOM 2

VAULTED CEILING.

G R O U N D   F L O O R

The 'H' configuration for a bungalow means that you have a deep sheltered inset at the entrance and at the rear patio area. It also allows the sleeping accommodation to take up one wing of the building with the centre joining section and the other wing given over to the entrance area and the living accommodation.

Living room	5.13 x 4.21m
Dining room	4.17 x 3.00m
Den	3.05 x 2.74m
Kitchen/dining room	4.17 x 3.30m
Utility	3.05 x 1.83m
Garage	5.44 x 4.21m
Bedroom 1	4.21 x 4.17m + en-suite
Bedroom 2	4.21 x 3.30m
Bedroom 3	3.05 x 2.82m

THE GOTLAND

The copyright belongs to Scandia-Hus Limited

187 sq. m.

Overall dimensions 20.71 x 11.11m

FRONT ELEVATION

This spacious bungalow home is illustrated with a hipped roof, which tends to bring the eye down and reduce the visual impact, something that can be very helpful in a crowded street scene. Once again the living and sleeping accommodation are separated. The double backed chimney is an important feature for the family and sitting rooms.

SIDE ELEVATION

Kitchen	3.9 x 3.7m
Dining area	3.9 x 3.8m
Sitting room	7.1 x 5.7m
Family room	4.9 x 4.8m
Master bedroom	4.0 x 3.6m + en-suite
Bedroom 2	4.1 x 3.2m
Bedroom 3	3.8 x 2.9m
Bedroom 4	4.2 x 2.8m

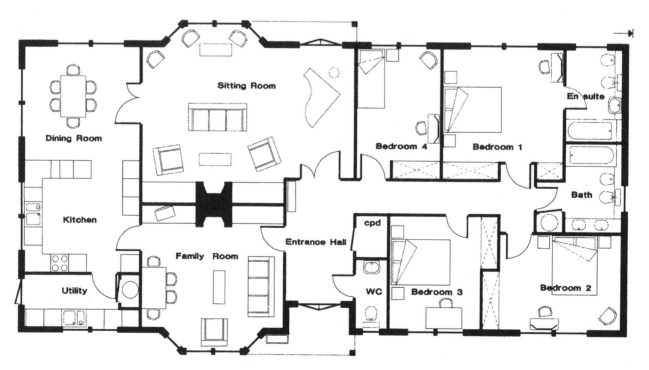

GROUND FLOOR

WOODLARK

The copyright belongs to Designer Homes

192 sq. m.
including a garage of 16 sq. m.

Overall dimensions 18.8 x 18m

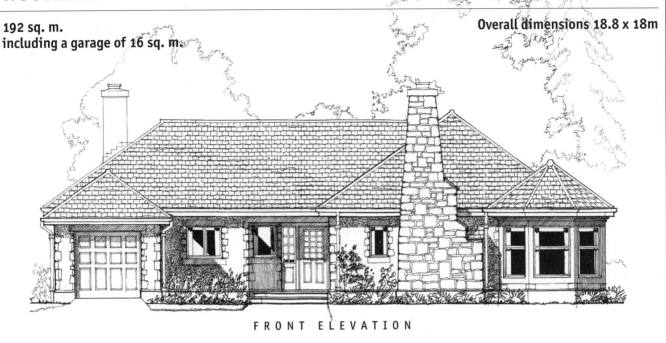

FRONT ELEVATION

The front elevation of this bungalow is enhanced by the addition of an octagonal tower providing extra accommodation and a window seat in the lounge. This theme is repeated internally with the octagonal shaped dining room. This allows the passageway to split two ways on either side leading to the two wings of the home.

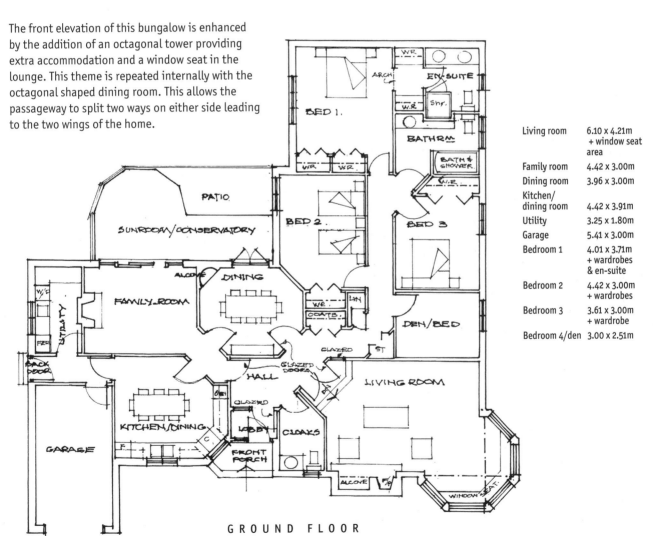

GROUND FLOOR

Living room	6.10 x 4.21m + window seat area
Family room	4.42 x 3.00m
Dining room	3.96 x 3.00m
Kitchen/dining room	4.42 x 3.91m
Utility	3.25 x 1.80m
Garage	5.41 x 3.00m
Bedroom 1	4.01 x 3.71m + wardrobes & en-suite
Bedroom 2	4.42 x 3.00m + wardrobes
Bedroom 3	3.61 x 3.00m + wardrobe
Bedroom 4/den	3.00 x 2.51m

CHAFFINCH

The copyright belongs to Designer Homes

203 sq. m.
including a garage of 37 sq. m.

Overall dimensions 19.50 x 15.60m

FRONT ELEVATION

A classic double fronted bungalow having a compact shape with the double garage as a forward projection. Within this garage there is space for a workbench and a door gives access to the main house via the utility area. The lounge is shown as being at a lower level with steps up to the dining area and steps within the entrance hall. This would be achieved by increasing the height of the room rather than dropping the ceiling level.

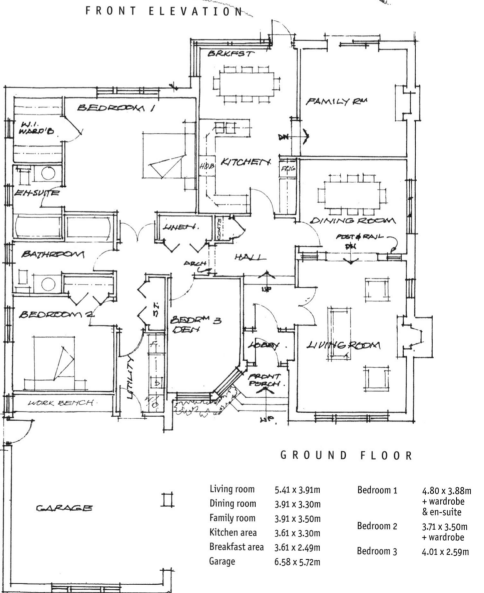

GROUND FLOOR

Living room	5.41 x 3.91m	Bedroom 1	4.80 x 3.88m	
Dining room	3.91 x 3.30m		+ wardrobe	
Family room	3.91 x 3.50m		& en-suite	
Kitchen area	3.61 x 3.30m	Bedroom 2	3.71 x 3.50m	
Breakfast area	3.61 x 2.49m		+ wardrobe	
Garage	6.58 x 5.72m	Bedroom 3	4.01 x 2.59m	

GLENELG

207 sq. m.
including a garage of 17 sq. m

Overall dimensions 25.5 x 17.8m

FRONT ELEVATION

What does one do when one has stunning panoramic views and one wants to let as many rooms as possible enjoy them? The answer could well be here with this double winged bungalow that presents each and every room to the rear whilst enclosing a central entrance area with an octagonal tower section to house the study.

FIRST FLOOR

Living room	6.50 x 6.50m
Kitchen/dining room	6.50 x 4.70m + utility areas
Master bedroom	4.11 x 3.50m + dressing room & en-suite
Bedroom 2	3.50 x 3.50m + wardrobe
Bedroom 3	4.11 x 3.50m
Garage	5.3 x 3.2m
Workshop	2.2 x 2.1m
Study	4.70 x 4.70m

GROUND FLOOR

THE UPPLAND

The copyright belongs to Scandia-Hus Limited

207 sq. m.

Overall dimensions 19.51 x 16.21m

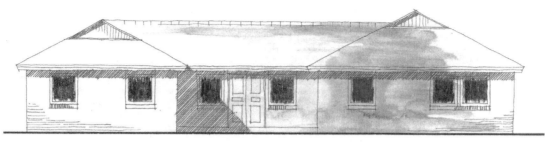

FRONT ELEVATION

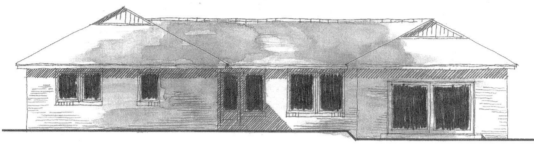

REAR ELEVATION

This is one of the largest of the single storey contributions from this company, offering a wealth of accommodation with up to five bedrooms and three bathrooms. The layout is an offset 'H' shape providing interest to the street scene with the opportunity of a sheltered patio area.

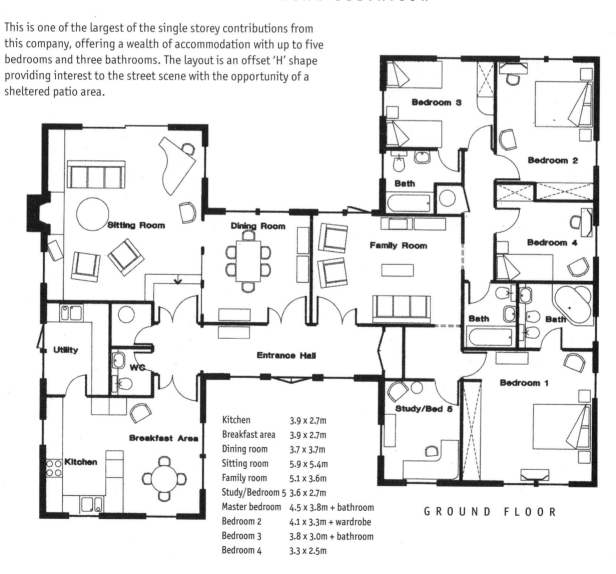

Kitchen	3.9 x 2.7m
Breakfast area	3.9 x 2.7m
Dining room	3.7 x 3.7m
Sitting room	5.9 x 5.4m
Family room	5.1 x 3.6m
Study/Bedroom 5	3.6 x 2.7m
Master bedroom	4.5 x 3.8m + bathroom
Bedroom 2	4.1 x 3.3m + wardrobe
Bedroom 3	3.8 x 3.0m + bathroom
Bedroom 4	3.3 x 2.5m

GROUND FLOOR

EAGLE

The copyright belongs to Designer Homes

214 sq. m.

Overall dimensions 20.60 x 19.70m

FRONT ELEVATION

Bay windows and gable projections abound in this interesting design, making it appear much more complex than it actually is. Inside, the dividing walls around the inner hall linking the principal reception areas are arranged in hexagonal and octagonal shapes and part shapes, creating interesting features. The section of the hall outside the minor bedrooms is utilised as a playroom.

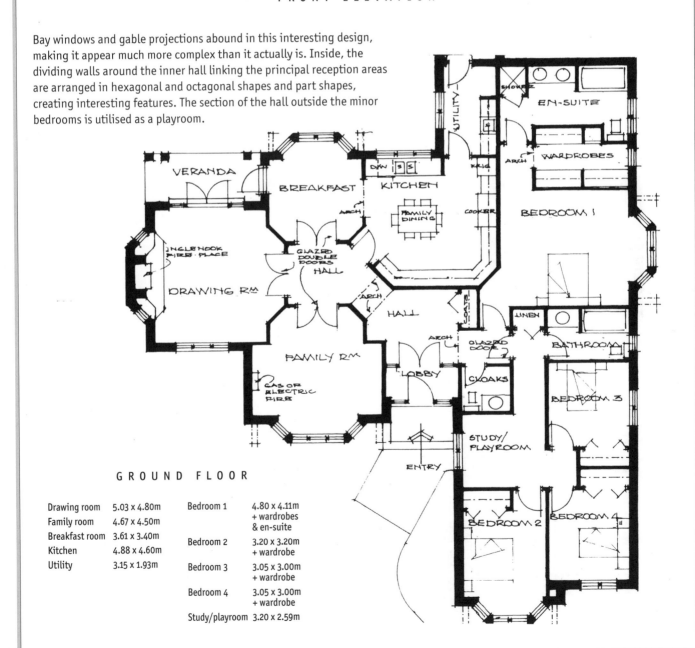

GROUND FLOOR

Drawing room	5.03 x 4.80m	Bedroom 1	4.80 x 4.11m + wardrobes & en-suite
Family room	4.67 x 4.50m		
Breakfast room	3.61 x 3.40m	Bedroom 2	3.20 x 3.20m + wardrobe
Kitchen	4.88 x 4.60m		
Utility	3.15 x 1.93m	Bedroom 3	3.05 x 3.00m + wardrobe
		Bedroom 4	3.05 x 3.00m + wardrobe
		Study/playroom	3.20 x 2.59m

IMPERIAL EAGLE

The copyright belongs to Designer Homes

218 sq. m.

Overall dimensions 17.47 x 14.80m

FRONT ELEVATION

At first sight this bungalow home looks as if it is one big square. Closer inspection reveals that it is a rectangular bungalow with two rear projections in a 'U' shape with the conservatory taking up part of the open space in between and a patio taking up the rest. This arrangement allows the whole of the accommodation to flow through with the patio serving as the link.

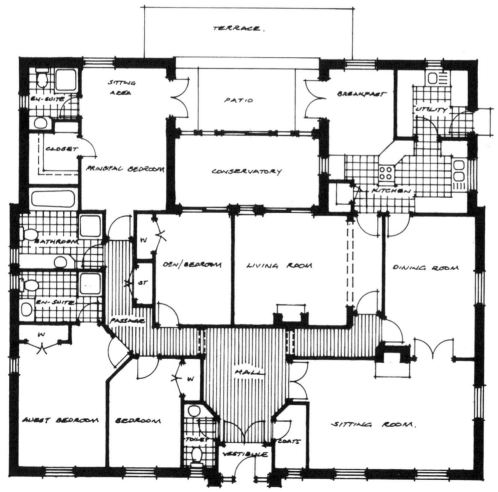

GROUND FLOOR

Sitting room	6.02 x 3.88m
Dining room	4.95 x 3.28m
Living room	5.49 x 3.88m
Kitchen	5.03 x 2.59m
Breakfast room	3.05 x 2.36m
Utility	2.55 x 2.30m
Conservatory	5.30 x 2.50m
Principal bedroom	5.03 x 3.20m + closet & en-suite
Guest bedroom	4.42 x 3.20m + en-suite
Bedroom	3.88 x 2.67m + wardrobe
Den/bedroom	3.88 x 2.90m + wardrobe

D170B

The copyright belongs to Design & Materials Ltd.

241 sq. m.
including a garage of 33 sq. m.

Overall dimensions 21.7m x 21.3m

FRONT ELEVATION

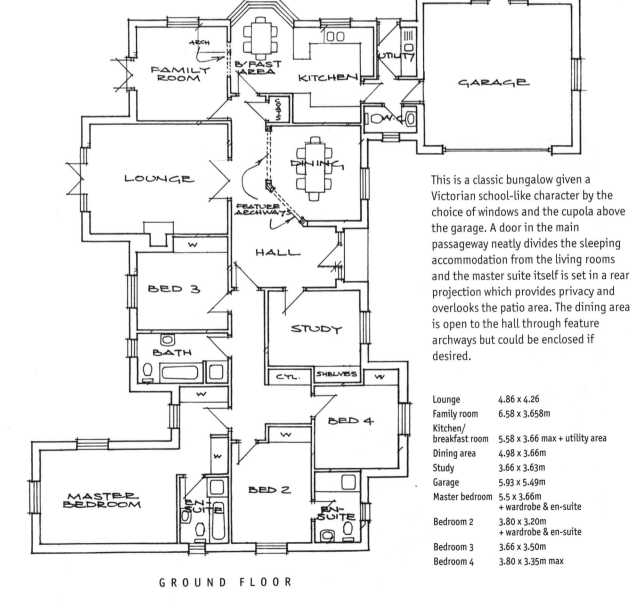

GROUND FLOOR

This is a classic bungalow given a Victorian school-like character by the choice of windows and the cupola above the garage. A door in the main passageway neatly divides the sleeping accommodation from the living rooms and the master suite itself is set in a rear projection which provides privacy and overlooks the patio area. The dining area is open to the hall through feature archways but could be enclosed if desired.

Lounge	4.86 x 4.26
Family room	6.58 x 3.658m
Kitchen/ breakfast room	5.58 x 3.66 max + utility area
Dining area	4.98 x 3.66m
Study	3.66 x 3.63m
Garage	5.93 x 5.49m
Master bedroom	5.5 x 3.66m + wardrobe & en-suite
Bedroom 2	3.80 x 3.20m + wardrobe & en-suite
Bedroom 3	3.66 x 3.50m
Bedroom 4	3.80 x 3.35m max

D271

The copyright belongs to Design & Materials Ltd.

266 sq. m.
including a garage of 31 sq. m.

Overall dimensions 23.37 x 17.00m

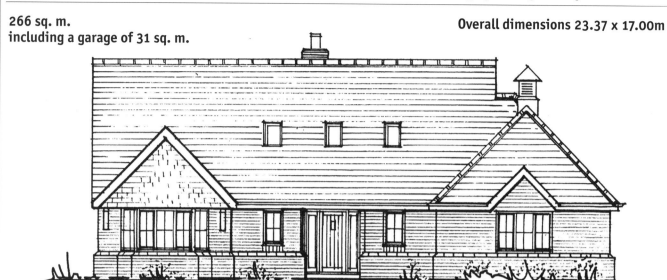

FRONT ELEVATION

There are several interesting features with this bungalow home. The sleeping accommodation to the ground floor is divided from the rest of the living accommodation by the wide hall and a door to an inner hall. An optional staircase can also lead to a room or rooms in the roof that could be used for guest accommodation. There are cupboards and wardrobes everywhere; something that is often sorely missed in bungalows.

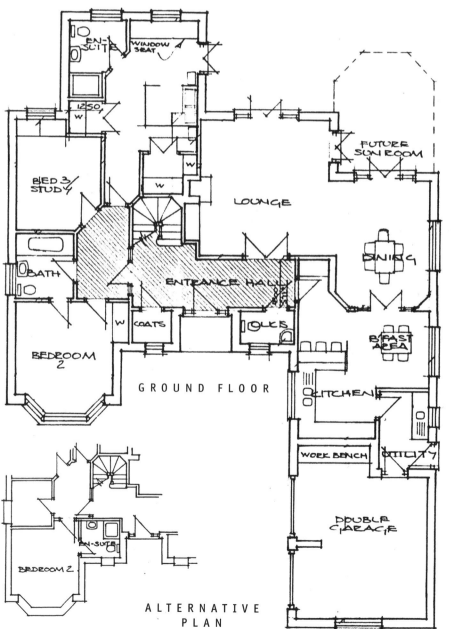

EN-SUITE
WINDOW SEAT
1250 W
BED 3/STUDY
FUTURE SUN ROOM
LOUNGE
W
W
DINING
BATH
ENTRANCE HALL
B'FAST AREA
W COATS
C'LKS
BEDROOM 2
GROUND FLOOR
KITCHEN
WORK BENCH
UTILITY
DOUBLE GARAGE

EN-SUITE
BEDROOM 2
ALTERNATIVE PLAN

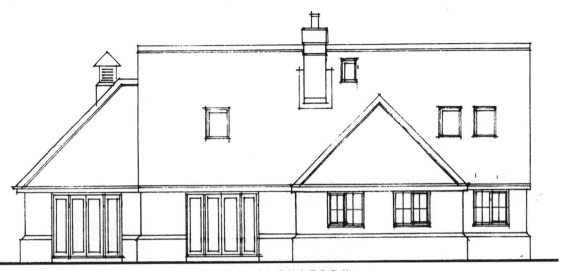

REAR ELEVATION

Lounge	5.18 x 5.12m
Dining area	4.90 x 3.66m
Kitchen/ breakfast room	5.20 x 4.88m max + utility area
Garage	6.63 x 5.20m max
Master bedroom	6.40 x 3.75m including walk-in wardrobes + en-suite
Bedroom 2	3.80 x 3.50m + wardrobe
Bedroom 3/ study	4.20 x 3.30m max
Upstairs bedroom	3.80 x 3.50m + en-suite

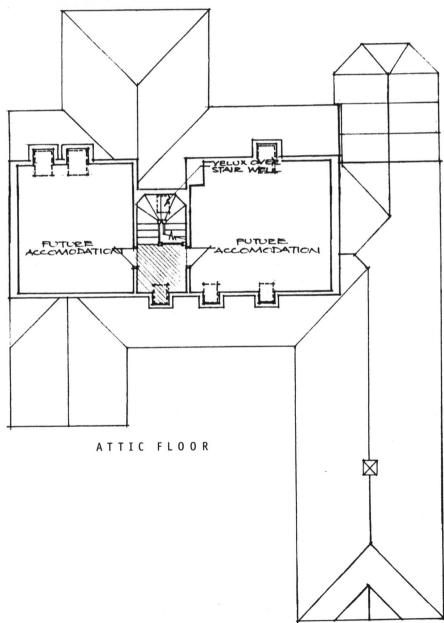

ATTIC FLOOR

ALDERNEY 01-007

The copyright belongs to Potton Ltd.

252 sq. m. plus optional 94 sq. m. upper part

Overall dimensions 21.9 x 14.5m

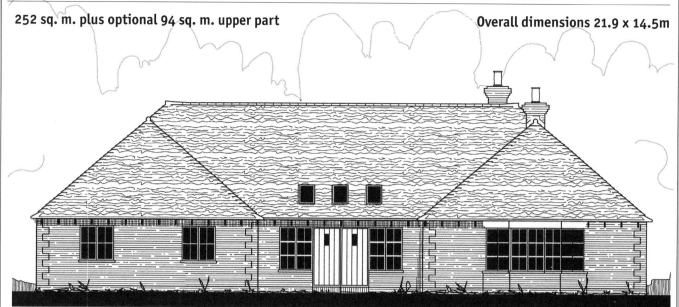

F R O N T   E L E V A T I O N

Entrances are always important and this courtyard entrance is very impressive. The large hallway with the vaulted ceiling gives access to and divides the sleeping accommodation from the living rooms. A further inner hall, behind double doors, gives added privacy to the bedrooms. The ground floor is perhaps sufficient in its own right but the addition of rooms in the roof increases the scope of the accommodation dramatically.

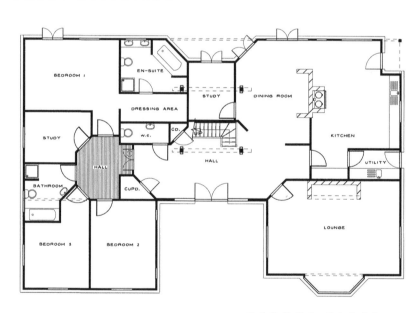

G R O U N D   F L O O R

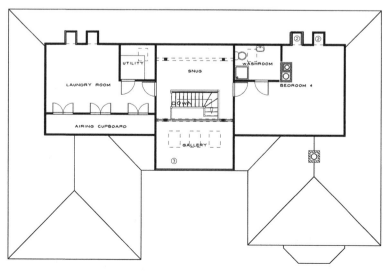

F I R S T   F L O O R

Lounge	7.5 x 5.1m
Kitchen	7.2 x 5.0m max
Dining room	5.7 x 4.2m
Study	3.15 x 2.6m
Additional study	3.8 x 2.8m
Bedroom 1	5.4 x 3.9m + dressing area & en-suite
Bedroom 2	4.9 x 3.7m
Bedroom 3	3.7 x 3.6m

Optional upper part to provide snug, further bedroom and bathroom and laundry/utility room

SALEN CONCEPT

The copyright belongs to The Swedish House Company Ltd.

297 sq. m.
including a garage of 46 sq. m.

Overall dimensions 22.8 x 15.0m.

F R O N T   E L E V A T I O N

R E A R   E L E V A T I O N

S I D E   E L E V A T I O N – E A S T

S I D E   E L E V A T I O N – W E S T

If the garage is not required then the space taken up by the lobby could become a fifth bedroom. The use of the word conservatory, to describe the room in this bungalow home, should not be confused with the normal interpretation of a glazed room sticking out from the main house, almost as an afterthought. Here, it refers to an integrated room with a vaulted ceiling, full height head gable windows and patio doors to both sides leading onto the patio.

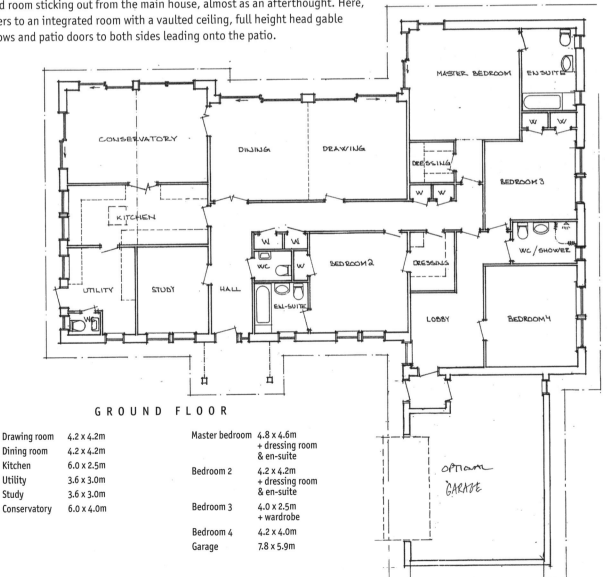

G R O U N D   F L O O R

Drawing room	4.2 x 4.2m	Master bedroom	4.8 x 4.6m + dressing room & en-suite	
Dining room	4.2 x 4.2m			
Kitchen	6.0 x 2.5m	Bedroom 2	4.2 x 4.2m + dressing room & en-suite	
Utility	3.6 x 3.0m			
Study	3.6 x 3.0m			
Conservatory	6.0 x 4.0m	Bedroom 3	4.0 x 2.5m + wardrobe	
		Bedroom 4	4.2 x 4.0m	
		Garage	7.8 x 5.9m	

HOUSES UP TO 140 SQ.M.

To bring these sizes into perspective it might help to realise that the average four bedroom house on an estate is around 110 sq. m. whilst the average size of a standard semi detached house, is usually just over 80 sq. m. Perhaps this will help you judge the scope of the accommodation in this and other categories. It might also leave you in admiration of just how much accommodation some of the cleverer designers are able to fit into a relatively small space. At the top end of this category it is often possible to fit in rooms such as a utility and en-suite shower rooms.

The decision that has to be made at an early stage in the design process is whether to go for fewer larger rooms or a greater number of smaller rooms. Estate agents value homes by their kerb appeal but more importantly, by the number of bedrooms. A four bedroom house is often going to be more valuable than a three bedroom property of the same size and styling. However, if what you want is two or three good bedrooms with an en-suite then that must be your choice. Downstairs the choice is often whether to have a separate lounge and dining room or whether to have a kitchen and utility or a larger kitchen/breakfast room.

Provision of a garage or parking space is important. Even if the plot is not in the 'narrow plot' category it is likely to be fairly restricted and the garage can often end up as the dominant architectural feature if you're not careful. Clever use, demonstrated within these pages, of tricks like recessing the garage doors or setting the garage such that the doors look across the plot can help to offset the problem.

Contributors in this section:
Associated Self Build Architects
The Border Design Centre
T.J.Crump OAKWRIGHTS Ltd.
Custom Homes Ltd.
Design & Materials Ltd.
Designer Homes
Potton Ltd.
The Self Build House Company Ltd.
Scottish Architects Network
Scandia-Hus Ltd.
The Swedish House Company Ltd.

THE CROFT

The copyright belongs to Scandia-Hus Limited

97 sq. m.

Overall dimensions 10.31 x 6.71m

FRONT ELEVATION

REAR ELEVATION

This traditional cottage would be equally at home in the Scottish Highlands or many English village streets. The farmhouse kitchen is situated at the centre of the ground floor accommodation. Both the dining and sitting rooms are illustrated with a fireplace, the chimneys of which give balance and character to the external appearance.

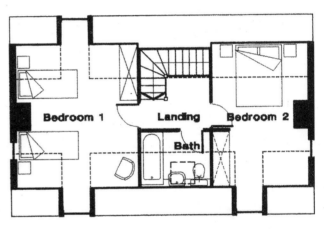

FIRST FLOOR

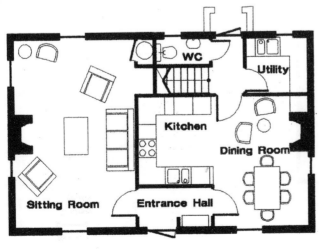

GROUND FLOOR

Kitchen	2.4 x 2.1m
Dining area	6.4 x 3.1m
Sitting room	6.1 x 4.0m
Master bedroom	6.4 x 4.0m
Bedroom 2	6.4 x 3.2m

HATLEY 98-094

The copyright belongs to Potton Ltd.

104 sq. m.

Overall dimensions 9.3 x 7.5m

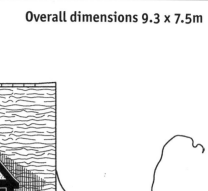

F R O N T   E L E V A T I O N

This three bedroom country cottage would blend into many rural situations. The large kitchen dining area would become a family living area whilst the self contained lounge with its inglenook fireplace would make a pleasant retreat.

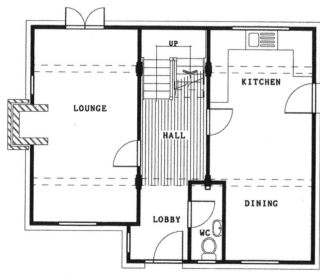

G R O U N D   F L O O R

F I R S T   F L O O R

Lounge	5.8 x 3.2m
Dining/kitchen	5.8 x 3.2m

Bedroom 1	4.35 x 3.5m
Bedroom 2	4.2 x 2.7m
Bedroom 3	3.2 x 3.0m

HERITAGE 01-322

The copyright belongs to Potton Ltd.

104 sq. m.

Overall dimensions 10.5 x 6.4m

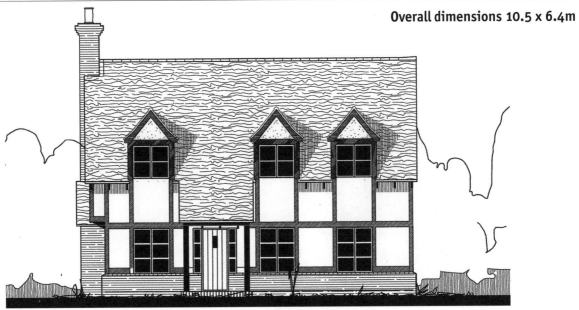

FRONT ELEVATION

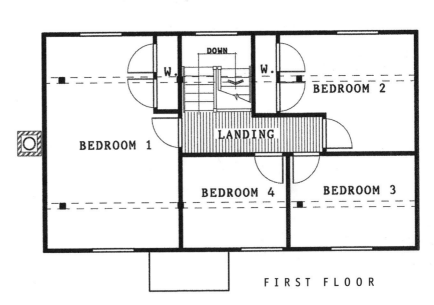

A distinctive little house of just over 100 sq.metres. The bathroom and toilet facilities are all on the ground floor and some might want to lose one bedroom upstairs to put the bathroom on the first floor and gain a dining room at the expense of the fourth bedroom.

FIRST FLOOR

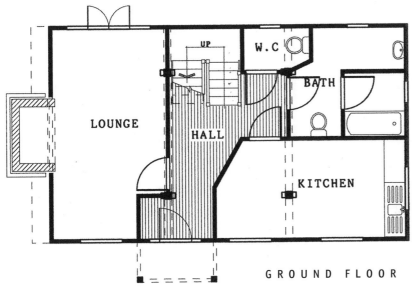

GROUND FLOOR

Lounge	5.75 x 3.2m
Kitchen	5.4 x 3.7m
Bedroom 1	5.8 x 3.7m + wardrobe
Bedroom 2	3.8 x 3.2m + wardrobe
Bedroom 3	3.6 x 2.5m
Bedroom 4	2.95 x 2.5m

THE GABLES

The copyright belongs to Scandia-Hus Limited

114 sq. m.

Overall dimensions 9.1 x 8.71m

FRONT ELEVATION

REAR ELEVATION

The exterior of this lovely home is illustrated in a Victorian style but the interior is also very true to the period. They may not have had en-suite facilities in that era but they would certainly have had the utility room, even if they did call it a scullery. A very versatile family home.

SIDE ELEVATION

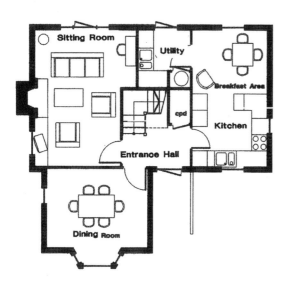

GROUND FLOOR

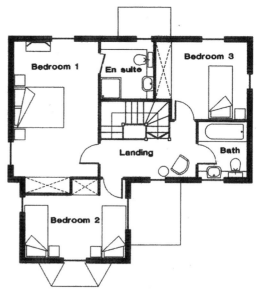

FIRST FLOOR

Kitchen	3.0 x 2.9m		Master bedroom	5.4 x 3.2m + en-suite
Breakfast area	2.9 x 2.1m			
Dining room	3.9 x 2.9m		Bedroom 2	3.9 x 2.9m
Sitting room	3.8 x 2.9m		Bedroom 3	3.5 x 2.9m

HATLEY 01-104

The copyright belongs to Potton Ltd.

114 sq. m.

Overall dimensions 9.8 x 7.5m

FRONT ELEVATION

This lovely cottage contains a wealth of accommodation within a relatively modest total area. As well as four bedrooms there is a separate study and dining room, whilst the kitchen has enough space for a useful breakfast area.

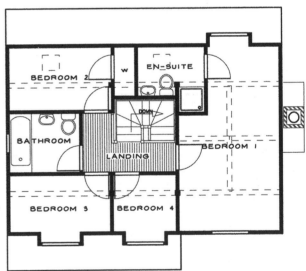

FIRST FLOOR

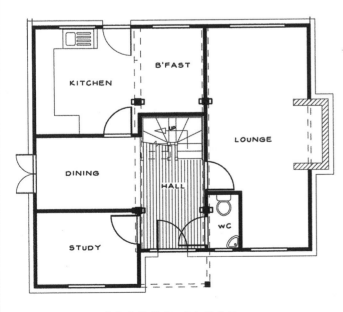

GROUND FLOOR

Lounge	6.85 x 3.2m		Bedroom 1	5.8 x 3.2m
Kitchen/breakfast	5.4 x 3.3m		Bedroom 2	3.25 x 2.0m
Dining room	3.35 x 2.25m		Bedroom 3	3.25 x 1.7m
Study	3.2 x 2.25m		Bedroom 4	2.15 x 1.7m

THE HIGHGROVE

The copyright belongs to Scandia-Hus Limited

116 sq. m.

Overall dimensions 9.91 x 8.0m

FRONT ELEVATION   REAR ELEVATION

The Georgian style called for symmetry, at least to the front elevations, although that was often taken away by later extensions. This house shews that symmetry and, with its relatively small footprint is perhaps suitable for the smaller site. It may not be a big house but it packs in a lot of spacious family accommodation.

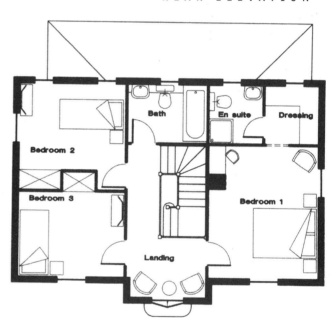

FIRST FLOOR

GROUND FLOOR

Kitchen/ breakfast area	4.2 x 2.6m
Dining room	3.3 x 3.0m
Sitting room	5.9 x 3.4m
Master bedroom	3.0 x 3.4m + dressing room & en-suite
Bedroom 2	3.5 x 3.2m
Bedroom 3	3.5 x 2.5m

PUMP HOUSE

The copyright belongs to T. J. Crump OAKRIGHTS Ltd.

117 sq. m.

Overall dimensions 10.66 x 9.77m

FRONT ELEVATION

SIDE ELEVATION

This compact home packs in a lot of accommodation for its size. The full height glazed wall to the sitting room would allow light to flood in and the open plan arrangement for the kitchen and dining room would increase the feeling of space.

FIRST FLOOR

GROUND FLOOR

Sitting room	5.00 x 3.81m
Dining room	4.97 x 3.98m
Kitchen	4.01 x 2.97m
Utility	2.97 x 1.87m
Bedroom 1	5.00 x 4.01m
Bedroom 2	3.98 x 2.84m
Bedroom 3	4.97 x 3.50m

THE AVINGTON

The copyright belongs to an ASBA architectural practice – Four Square Design Ltd.

120 sq. m.   **Overall dimensions 10 x 8.89m**

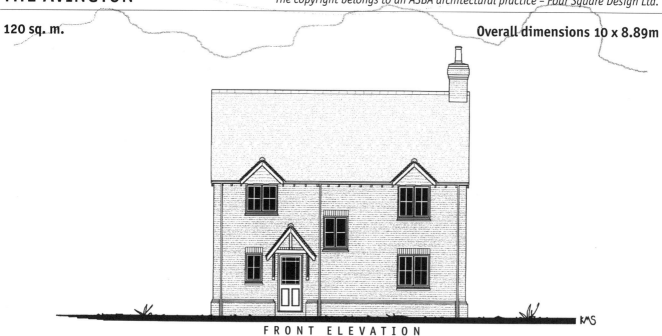

FRONT ELEVATION

This modest family home escapes from the traps that many smaller houses fall into – boring external design and lack of simple amenity space within the home. The external appearance avoids undue symmetry by off-setting the porch and by the inclusion of a mezzanine window. Inside, space is made for those essential cupboards and wardrobes and the master bedroom has full en-suite facilities.

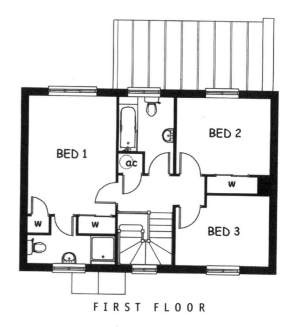

FIRST FLOOR

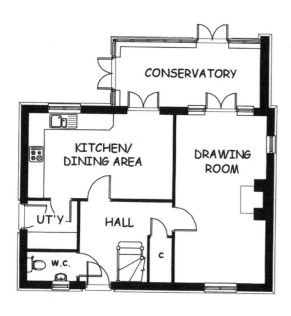

GROUND FLOOR

Drawing room	6.1 x 3.4m
Kitchen/dining area	5.4 x 3.1m
Utility	1.9 x 1.8m
Conservatory	5.4 x 2.3m
Bedroom 1	4.4 x 3.2m + wardrobes & en-suite
Bedroom 2	3.4 x 2.8m +wardrobe
Bedroom 3	3.4 x 2.6m

THE THATCH

The copyright belongs to Scandia-Hus Limited

122 sq. m.

Overall dimensions 12.01 x 7.51m

FRONT ELEVATION

REAR ELEVATION

This home derives its name and its inspiration from a traditional thatched cottage. The small windows and the cottage door add to the authenticity, as does the large inglenook fire to the sitting room. The dining and hall are combined so as to maximise the useable space and upstairs, three good sized bedrooms enjoy all the modern facilities.

FIRST FLOOR

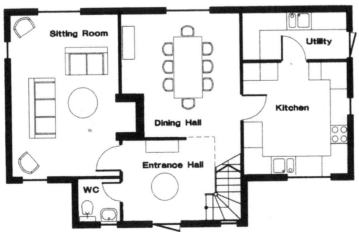

GROUND FLOOR

Kitchen	3.7 x 3.6m
Sitting room	5.4 x 3.7m
Dining hall	4.0 x 4.0m
Master bedroom	5.4 x 3.5m + en-suite
Bedroom 2	3.7 x 3.0m
Bedroom 3	3.7 x 2.3m

GAMLINGAY 97-205

The copyright belongs to Potton Ltd.

124 sq. m.

Overall dimensions 10.5 x 7.5m

F R O N T   E L E V A T I O N

Varied roof planes and eaves lines allow this small cottage to stand out in the crowd. The large open plan lounge and dining area could be divided if preferred and there is plenty of room for a generous study. Upstairs the main bedroom has en-suite facilities.

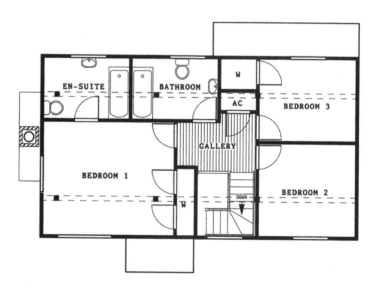

F I R S T   F L O O R

Lounge	4.82 x 3.33m
Diningroom	3.64 x 3.3m max
Kitchen	3.27 x 3.3m
Utility	2.22 x 1.6m
Study	3.3 x 1.8m
Bedroom 1	4.42 x 3.7m
Bedroom 2	3.27 x 3.0m
Bedroom 3	3.27 x 2.9m

G R O U N D   F L O O R

GAMLINGAY 95-068

The copyright belongs to Potton Ltd.

125 sq. m.

Overall dimensions 11.1 x 7.5m

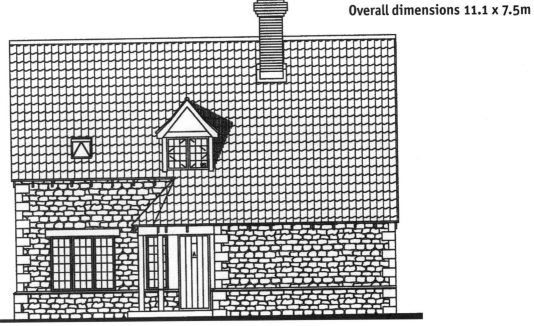

F R O N T   E L E V A T I O N

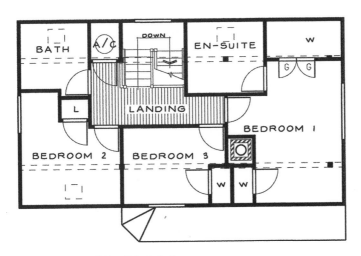

F I R S T   F L O O R

Illustrated in a stone finish, this cottage has a solidity about it. All of the rooms requiring drainage are at the rear and with a slight re-arrangement of the kitchen window this could suit a site with limited depth.

Lounge	6.9 x 3.7m
Dining room	4.2 x 3.1m
Kitchen	3.3 x 2.5m
Bedroom 1	4.5 x 2.85m
Bedroom 2	3.5 x 3.25m
Bedroom 3	3.3 x 2.9m

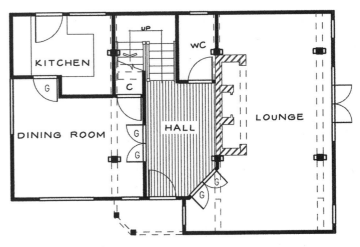

G R O U N D   F L O O R

WEYBRIDGE

The copyright belongs to Custom Homes Ltd.

129 sq. m.

Overall dimensions 21.9x 22m

FRONT ELEVATION

This is a lot of home for its size. It would also fit on quite a small plot. The rectangular shape is broken up at the front by lowering the eaves line and introducing two raised gables. This means that, from the side, the house has an asymmetric roof line and that those rooms on the first floor at the front will have sloping ceilings.

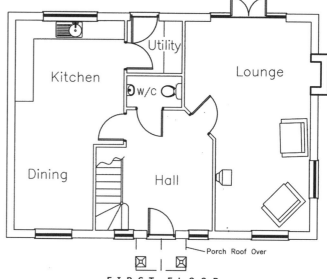

Porch Roof Over

FIRST FLOOR

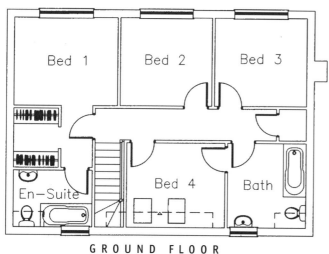

GROUND FLOOR

Lounge	6.7 x 4.1m max
Kitchen/diner	6.7 x 3.6m max
Utility	1.8 x 1.65m
Bedroom 1	3.4 x 2.8m + dressing room & en-suite
Bedroom 2	3.05 x 2.8m
Bedroom 3	3.05 x 2.8m
Bedroom 4	3.27 x 2.7m

THE BEAUFORT

The copyright belongs to an ASBA architectural practice – Julian Owen Associates

130 sq. m.

Overall dimensions 14.09 x 10.0m

FRONT ELEVATION

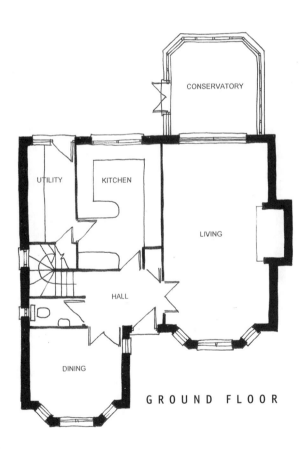

CONSERVATORY

UTILITY   KITCHEN

LIVING

HALL

DINING

GROUND FLOOR

Proof positive that small three bedroom houses don't have to look like little boxes. Although it hasn't been put into that category, this home could fit onto quite a narrow plot, especially if one of the dormer windows to the second bedrooms was sacrificed. Three bedrooms with en-suite facilities to the master bedroom, rather than four bedrooms, are becoming increasingly acceptable in market terms.

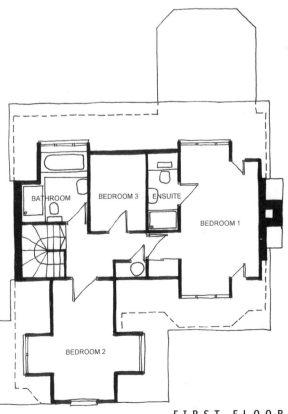

BATHROOM   BEDROOM 3   ENSUITE

BEDROOM 1

BEDROOM 2

FIRST FLOOR

Living room	7.0 x 4.0m		Bedroom 1	5.0 x 3.0m + en-suite
Conservatory	3.0 x 3.0m		Bedroom 2	4.0 x 4.0m
Dining room	3.2 x 3.0m		Bedroom 3	3.0 x 2.0m
Utility	3.5 x 1.75m			
Kitchen	4.4 x 3.1m			

EDENSIDE COTTAGE

The copyright belongs to a ScAN architectural practice - Buttler

131 sq. m.

Overall dimensions 12.4 x 8.6m

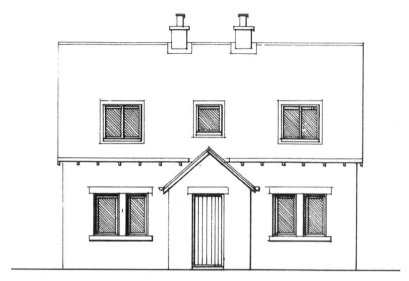

F R O N T   E L E V A T I O N

This design gives flexible living accommodation with an open plan arrangement that can be divided off by means of sliding screens. Upstairs there are two equally sized bedrooms whilst the ground floor study could also be a bedroom with access to its own en-suite arrangements and further access through the utility area, making it fairly self contained.

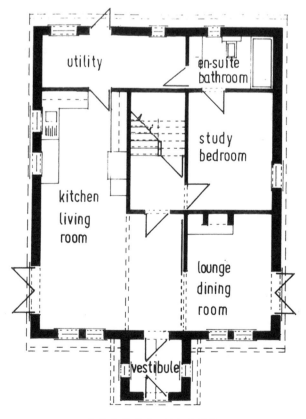

G R O U N D   F L O O R

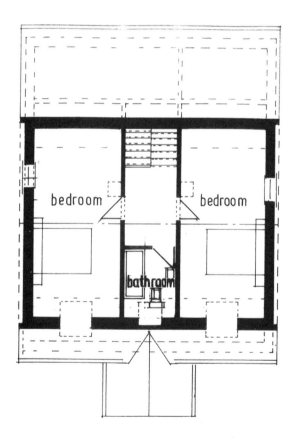

F I R S T   F L O O R

Kitchen/ living room	7.9 x 4.9m max		Bedroom 1	6.3 x 2.9m
Lounge/ dining room	3.9 x 2.9m		Bedroom 2	6.3 x 2.9m
Study/bedroom	3.9 x 2.9m			
Utility	4.9 x 1.7m			

PETTERIL COTTAGE

The copyright belongs to a ScAN architectural practice – S. Buttler

131 sq. m.
including a garage of 27 sq. m.

Overall dimensions 14.7 x 14.6m

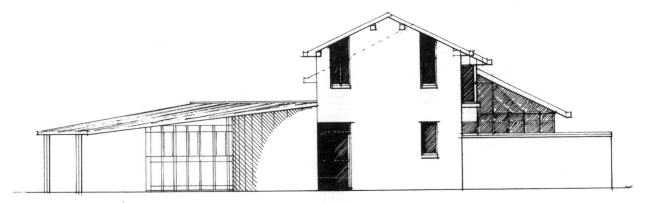

F R O N T   E L E V A T I O N

This stunning home was originally conceived for an awkward plot by a stream. The design has been cleverly manipulated to create three bedroom accommodation with garage parking and minimal gardens. It may be small, it may be an odd shape, but it is certainly an inspiring design that would be a pleasure to live in.

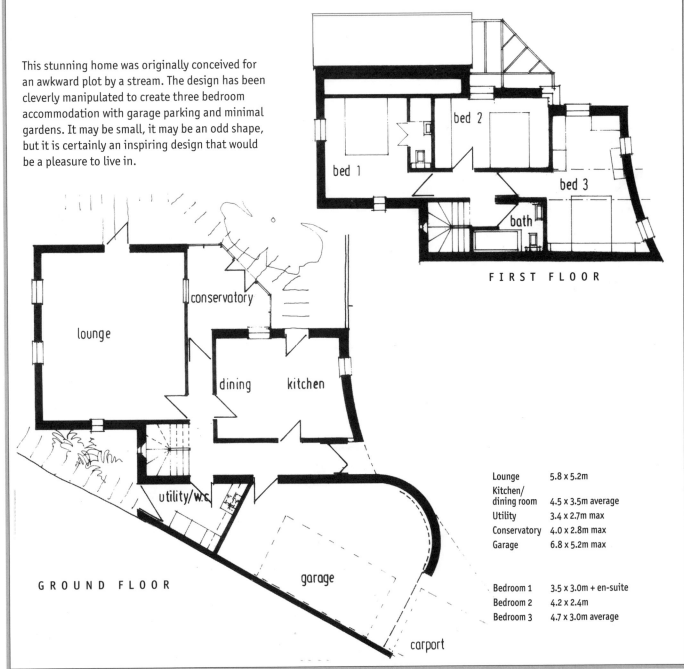

F I R S T   F L O O R

G R O U N D   F L O O R

Lounge	5.8 x 5.2m
Kitchen/ dining room	4.5 x 3.5m average
Utility	3.4 x 2.7m max
Conservatory	4.0 x 2.8m max
Garage	6.8 x 5.2m max
Bedroom 1	3.5 x 3.0m + en-suite
Bedroom 2	4.2 x 2.4m
Bedroom 3	4.7 x 3.0m average

D273

The copyright belongs to Design & Materials Ltd.

133 sq. m.

**Overall dimensions
12.30 x 8.40m**

FRONT ELEVATION

A simple crofting type cottage that, nevertheless, provides four good sized bedrooms plus the usual reception rooms. The low ridge height would mean that this might fit into a sensitive planning environment and the relatively narrow width would mean that it could fit onto quite a narrow plot. The trick with small simple and economical shapes is to keep them interesting and this one does that.

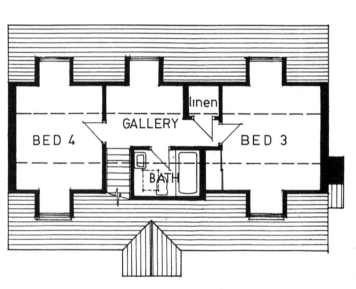

FIRST FLOOR

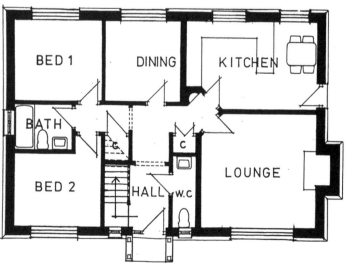

GROUND FLOOR

Lounge	4.42 x 4.27m
Kitchen	4.93 x 3.33m
Dining room	3.05 x 2.95m
Bedroom 1	3.35 x 3.05m
Bedroom 2	3.35 x 2.74m
Bedroom 3	4.42 x 4.19m
Bedroom 4	4.19 x 3.89m

THE HOLTWOOD

The copyright belongs to an ASBA architectural practice – Four Square Design Ltd.

135 sq. m.

Overall dimensions 9.44 x 9.25m

FRONT ELEVATION

With its tabled verges and its symmetrical design, this moderately sized family home would fit into many village street situations. The drawing room has double French doors leading onto the sheltered patio area, which would also be overlooked from the kitchen. Upstairs there are four good sized bedrooms one of which has en-suite facilities.

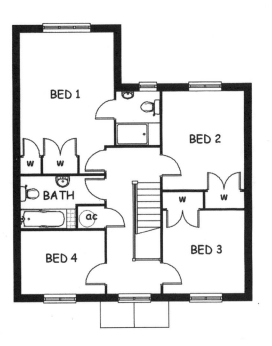

FIRST FLOOR

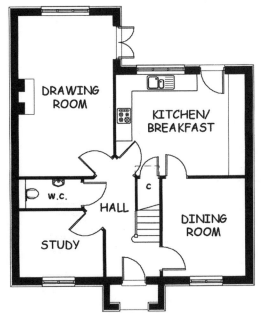

GROUND FLOOR

Kitchen	4.7 x 3.7m		Bedroom 1	4.4 x 3.5m + en-suite
Drawing room	5.8 x 3.5m		Bedroom 2	3.6 x 3.1m + wardrobe
Dining room	3.6 x 3.1m		Bedroom 3	3.1 x 3.0m + wardrobe
Study	3.1 x 2.4m		Bedroom 4	3.1 x 2.3m

DUCHRAY

The copyright belongs to a ScAN architectural practice – Design Practice

136 sq. m.

Overall dimensions 11.9 x 6.1m

FRONT ELEVATION

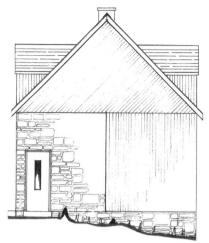

SIDE ELEVATION

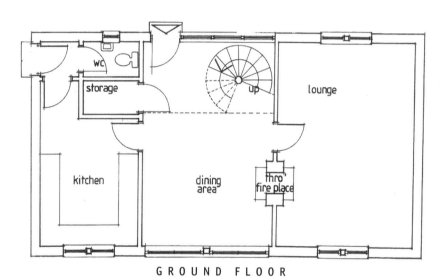

GROUND FLOOR

A lesson in how a simple rectangle can be made to look interesting. The central dining hall with its spiral staircase is obviously a feature of this house and equally striking is the exterior with the full height gable head windows. The lounge and the dining hall share a fireplace. The stone walling and the stone surrounds to the windows betray this design's Scottish origins.

Lounge	6.0 x 4.15m
Dining hall	6.0 x 4.0m
Kitchen	3.7 x 2.95m + lobby
Bedroom 1	6.0 x 4.15m
Bedroom 2	4.1 x 3.1m
Bedroom 3	4.1 x 2.75m

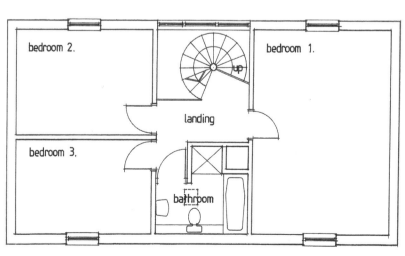

FIRST FLOOR

E119

The copyright belongs to Design & Materials Ltd.

138 sq. m.

Overall dimensions 11.13 x 8.32m

F R O N T   E L E V A T I O N

Homes where the major bedrooms are on the ground floor with just a couple of extra bedrooms and a bathroom on the top floor are eminently suitable for perhaps older couples who might wish to occupy their homes as a bungalow but who have to think in terms of being able to house the family when they visit. The window seats in the lounge and second bedroom add interest and the dining room could just as easily be a sunroom.

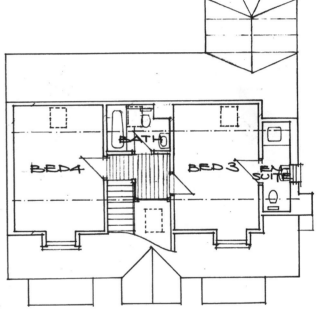

F I R S T   F L O O R

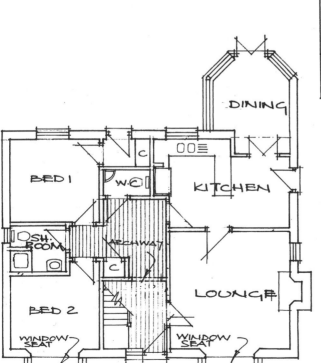

G R O U N D   F L O O R

Lounge	4.57 x 4.27m
Kitchen	4.57 x 3.35m
Dining room	3.60 x 2.90m
Bedroom 1	3.35 x 3.05m
Bedroom 2	3.35 x 2.74m
Bedroom 3	4.62 x 3.35m
Bedroom 4	4.62 x 3.35m

WILLESDEN

The copyright belongs to Designer Homes

138 sq. m.
including a garage of 16 sq. m.

Overall dimensions 13.40 x 11.30m

FRONT ELEVATION

This attractive family home manages to get four good sized bedrooms, one of them en-suite plus the usual reception rooms and a garage into a relatively small overall size. The garage is shewn linked to the house at the side. If the plot was narrower then the garage could easily be detached and brought to the front.

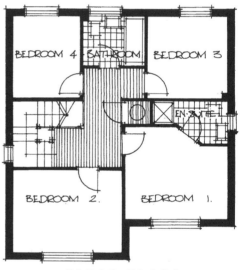

FIRST FLOOR

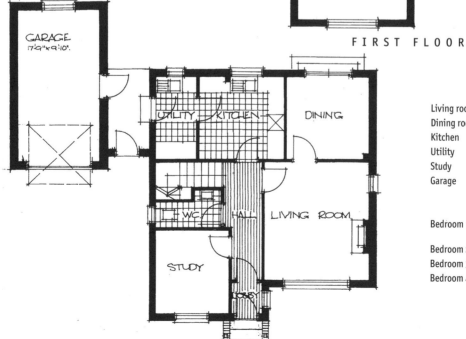

GROUND FLOOR

Living room	4.19 x 3.81m
Dining room	3.00 x 2.90m
Kitchen	3.10 x 2.90m
Utility	2.90 x 1.45m
Study	2.90 x 2.69m
Garage	5.41 x 3.00m
Bedroom 1	3.81 x 3.05m + en-suite
Bedroom 2	3.91 x 3.00m
Bedroom 3	3.00 x 2.90m
Bedroom 4	2.90 x 2.39m

TWEED

The copyright belongs to Designer Homes

140 sq. m.
including a garage of 19 sq. m.

Overall dimensions 18.72 x 9.55m

FRONT ELEVATION

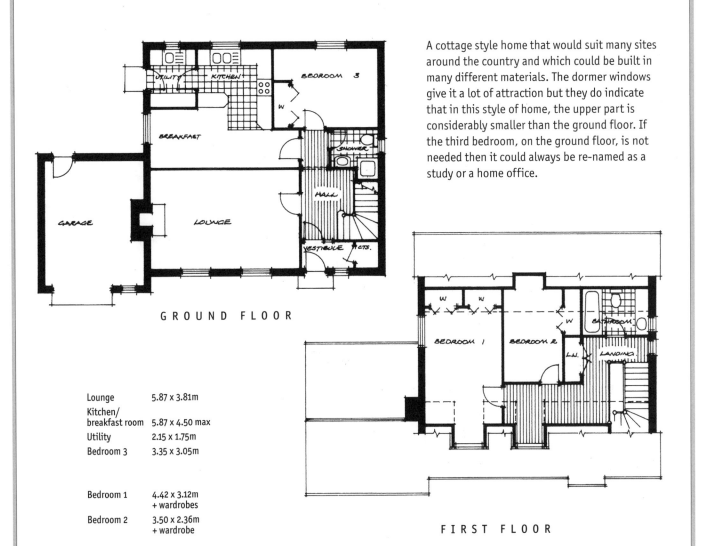

GROUND FLOOR

A cottage style home that would suit many sites around the country and which could be built in many different materials. The dormer windows give it a lot of attraction but they do indicate that in this style of home, the upper part is considerably smaller than the ground floor. If the third bedroom, on the ground floor, is not needed then it could always be re-named as a study or a home office.

FIRST FLOOR

Lounge	5.87 x 3.81m
Kitchen/ breakfast room	5.87 x 4.50 max
Utility	2.15 x 1.75m
Bedroom 3	3.35 x 3.05m
Bedroom 1	4.42 x 3.12m + wardrobes
Bedroom 2	3.50 x 2.36m + wardrobe

BLAIRHULLICHAN COTTAGE

The copyright belongs to a ScAN architectural practice – Walter Wood Associates

140 sq. m. **Overall dimensions 12.1 x 9.8m**

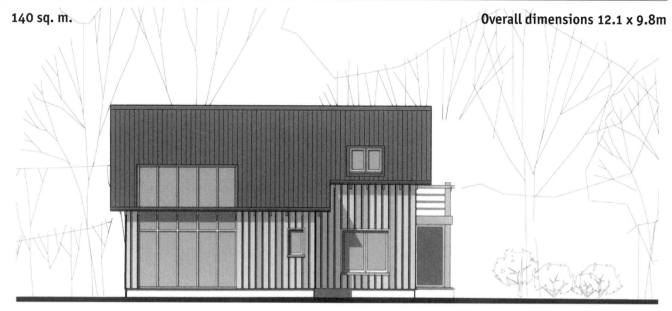

FRONT ELEVATION

An unashamedly modern home built and clad in contemporary materials. The lovely walk in bay to the lounge allows a balcony to the master bedroom. Sliding doors are shown where space is at a premium or in order to provide the ability to open up one room to another. A compact and economical design for modern day living.

FIRST FLOOR

GROUND FLOOR

Lounge	5.85 x 3.6m + bay
Kitchen/ dining room	5.15 x 4.5m
Sun room	4.5 x 2.0m
Utility	2.26 x 1.9m
Bedroom 1	4.6 x 3.6m + wardrobe, store & balcony
Bedroom 2	3.62 x 2.89m + wardrobe
Bedroom 3	3.62 x 2.89m + wardrobe

THE RECTORY

The copyright belongs to Scandia-Hus Limited

140 sq. m.

Overall dimensions 12.60 x 7.31m

FRONT ELEVATION

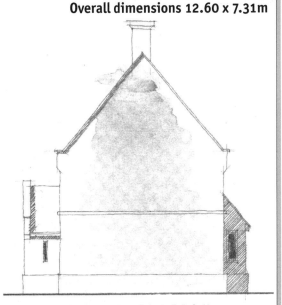

SIDE ELEVATION

The inspiration for this traditional two storey home comes from the Cotswolds where symmetry is frowned upon and buildings seem to go out of their way to avoid it. This would look good in any external material but it would look particularly fine in natural stone cladding with stone mullioned windows and a stone or slate roof.

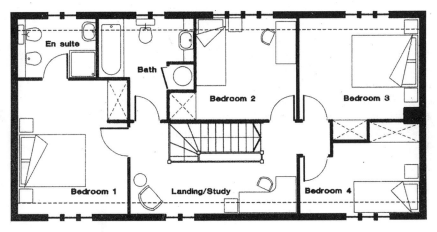

FIRST FLOOR

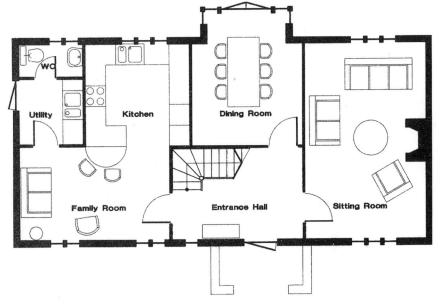

GROUND FLOOR

Kitchen	3.0 x 2.9m
Dining area	3.7 x 3.3m
Sitting room	5.7 x 3.5m
Family room	4.4 x 2.7m
Master bedroom	3.8 x 3.2m + en-suite
Bedroom 2	3.0 x 2.9m
Bedroom 3	3.6 x 2.9m + wardrobe
Bedroom 4	3.6 x 2.7m + wardrobe
Landing/study	5.0 x 2.7m

BIRGHAM

The copyright belongs to Designer Homes

140 sq. m.

Overall dimensions 9.80 x 9.35m

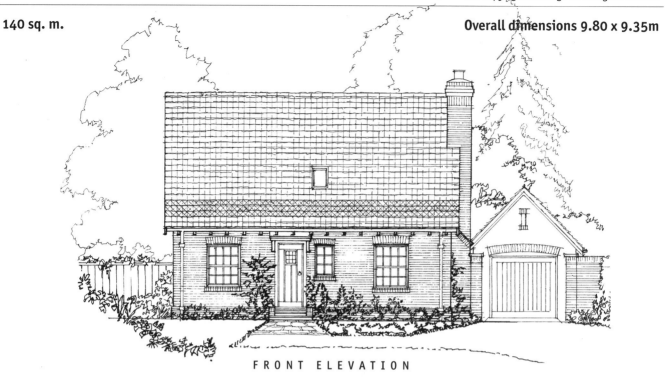

FRONT ELEVATION

A wolf in sheep's clothing. What looks like a bungalow from the road elevation is in fact a house. The windows for the bedrooms are on the gable ends whilst a small rear projection allows the bathroom and en-suite to have windows which would be obscure glazed. If more light was required the bedrooms could have extra roof lights, similar to the one that serves the staircase.

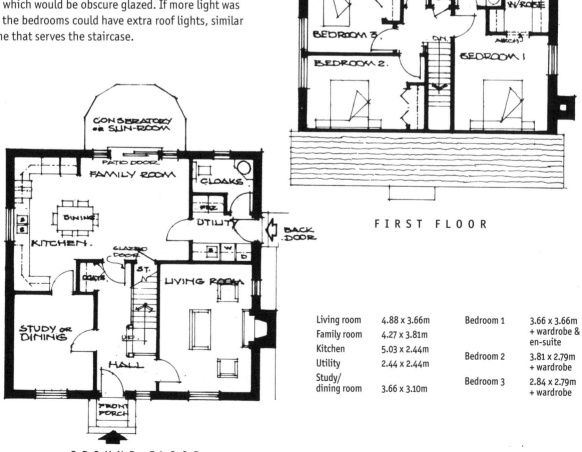

FIRST FLOOR

GROUND FLOOR

Living room	4.88 x 3.66m	Bedroom 1	3.66 x 3.66m + wardrobe & en-suite
Family room	4.27 x 3.81m		
Kitchen	5.03 x 2.44m	Bedroom 2	3.81 x 2.79m + wardrobe
Utility	2.44 x 2.44m		
Study/ dining room	3.66 x 3.10m	Bedroom 3	2.84 x 2.79m + wardrobe

HOUSES 141 TO 160 SQ.M.

Houses in this category are reaching twice the size of the average semi detached home on an estate and although not yet classed as big houses, many of the features and accommodation provided by much larger homes start to become possible. By the time you get up to this size the question of whether it is necessary to have a combined lounge and dining room has largely fallen away and the choice, if that's what you want, is yours. So too with the kitchen area where a utility may not mean having to give up on the idea of a breakfast area. Upstairs the en-suite can even be a proper bathroom rather than a restricted shower room.

The hallway and landing might still take up quite a bit of space. It's open for you to decide what you feel about the idea of doing away with them altogether by combining their space with the main living accommodation on the ground floor and leaving the landing as an extra sitting area to the upper floor.

Care may still have to be exercised with the garaging, parking and turning. Too big a garage could limit the ground floor accommodation whilst too small could limit the resale value as, certainly at the higher end of this category, a buyer might expect a double garage.

Contributors in this section:
Associated Self Build Architects
The Border Design Centre
T.J.Crump OAKWRIGHTS Ltd.
Custom Homes Ltd.
Design & Materials Ltd.
Designer Homes
Potton Ltd.
The Self Build House Company Ltd.
Scottish Architects Network
Scandia-Hus Ltd.
The Swedish House Company Ltd.

THE TRONNING

The copyright belongs to Scandia-Hus Limited

141 sq. m.

Overall dimensions 12.31 x 7.81m

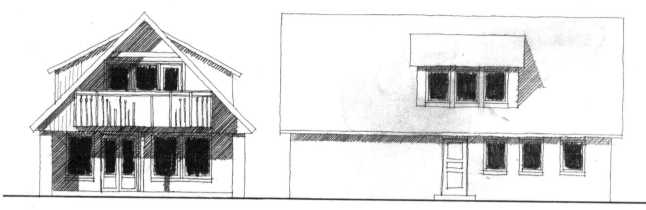

REAR ELEVATION

SIDE/ENTRANCE ELEVATION

This is perhaps the typical Scandinavian design that found so much favour when the concept was first introduced to this country. The balcony arrangement to the master bedroom provides a sheltered verandah to the sitting room and family room and creates a natural flow between inside and outside.

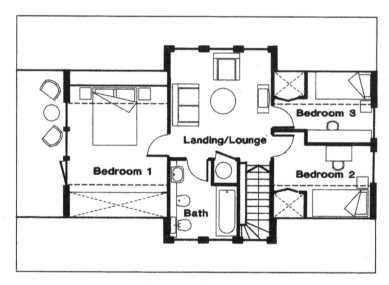

FIRST FLOOR

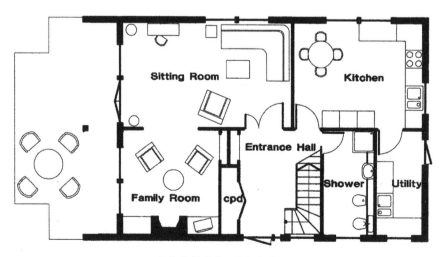

GROUND FLOOR

Kitchen	4.5 x 3.7m
Sitting room	5.9 x 3.7m
TV lounge	3.4 x 3.4m
Master bedroom	4.0 x 3.4m
Bedroom 2	3.4 x 2.4m
Bedroom 3	3.4 x 2.4m
Family room	3.6 x 3.5m

R113

143 sq. m.

Overall dimensions 11.1 x 10m

FRONT ELEVATION

In certain suburban streets there are rows and rows of bungalows like this one that have a lot of life left in them but, nonetheless, don't provide the accommodation and levels of comfort that modern homes provide. This one would fit neatly into such an environment. The third bedroom on the top floor is made more interesting with its en-suite arrangements and the gable windowed gallery. The walk in pantry would please many homeowners.

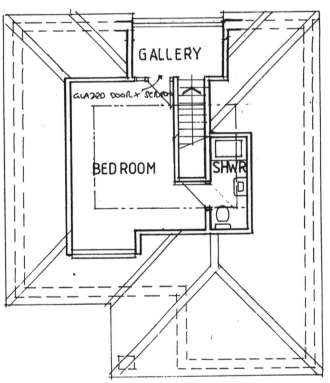

FIRST FLOOR

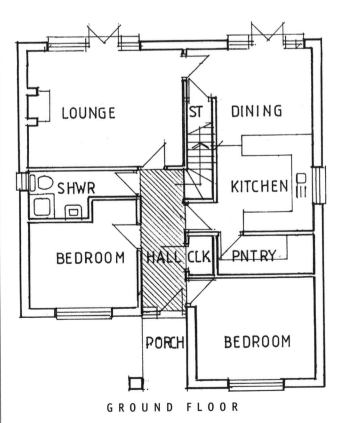

GROUND FLOOR

Lounge	5.10 x 3.76m
Dining area	4.20 x 2.85m max
Kitchen area	3.20 x 3.05m + walk in pantry
Bedroom 1	4.00 x 3.20m
Bedroom 2	3.55 x 2.75m
Bedroom 3	4.80 x 3.65m + gallery & shower room

FROGMORE

The copyright belongs to Custom Homes Ltd.

143 sq. m.
including a garage of 14.5 sq. m.

Overall dimensions 10.2 x 9.5m

A standard four bedroom family house that may well suit the younger family wishing to take the next step up the ladder from the starter home. It is illustrated here with hipped ends to the roof but in many areas these could be dispensed with to save costs.

FRONT ELEVATION

Lounge	4.6 x 4.6m
Dining room	4.28 x 3.34m
Kitchen	4.28 x 3.34m
Utility	2.64 x 2.18m
Garage	5.5 x 2.64m
Bedroom 1	4.21 x 3.04m + en-suite
Bedroom 2	3.64 x 3.1m
Bedroom 3	3.69 x 3.0m
Bedroom 4	2.65 x 2.62m

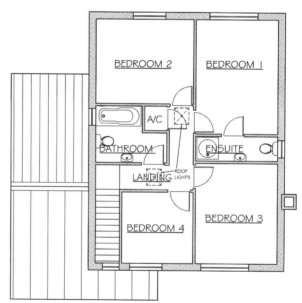

FIRST FLOOR

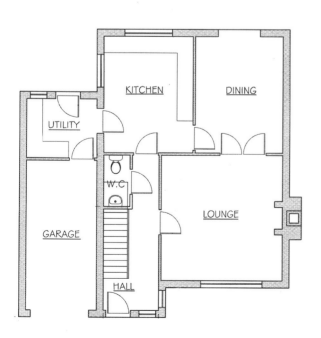

GROUND FLOOR

DIPLOMAT

145 sq. m.
including a garage of 17 sq. m.

Overall dimensions 11.25 x 10m

In many ways this design is probably the archetypal 'chalet bungalow' with its low eave lines and dormer windows. Despite the loss of space that this form of construction brings about on the upper floor, this home has everything that most families would want.

FRONT ELEVATION

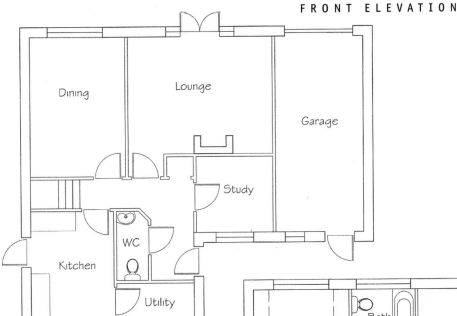

GROUND FLOOR

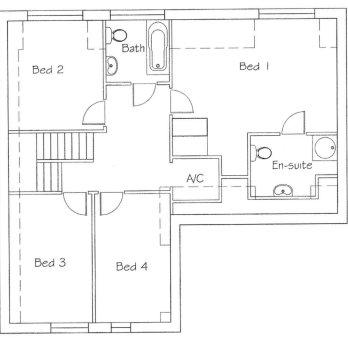

FIRST FLOOR

Lounge	4.6 x 3.6m
Dining room	4.3 x 3.1m
Kitchen	4.0 x 2.7m
Utility	2.4 x 1.75m
Study	2.4 x 2.4m
Garage	6.1 x 2.8m
Bedroom1	5.3 x 4.0m max including en-suite
Bedroom 2	3.4 x 2.7m
Bedroom 3	4.0 x 2.3m
Bedroom 4	4.0 x 2.1m

D270 - 1

The copyright belongs to Design & Materials Ltd.

**146 sq. m.
including a garage of 15 sq. m.**

Overall dimensions 13.87 x 8.22m

FRONT ELEVATION

SIDE ELEVATION

A lovely family home given a country feel through the choice of materials and the low ridgeline. The garage has access to the main house through the utility area. There is a large kitchen/breakfast room, together with a separate dining room and, in a country area these rooms would probably be the focus of the living area. The lounge, at the front, could then be kept for best.

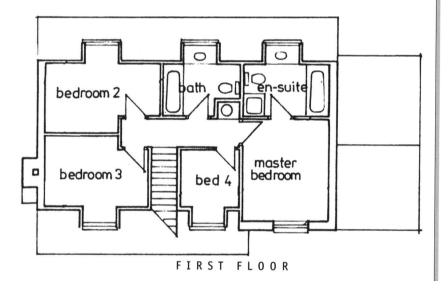

FIRST FLOOR

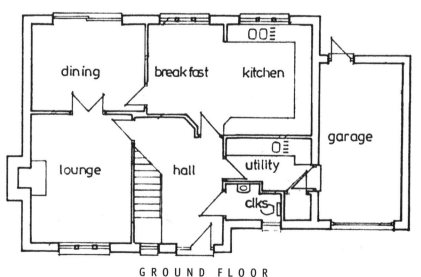

GROUND FLOOR

Lounge	4.47 x 3.66m
Dining room	4.12 x 3.05m
Kitchen/ breakfast room	5.79 x 3.81m + utility area
Garage	5.16 x 2.87m
Master bedroom	3.55 x 3.05m + en-suite
Bedroom 2	4.12 x 2.44m
Bedroom 3	3.66 x 2.44m
Bedroom 4	2.10 x 1.93m

THE OXLEY

The copyright belongs to The Self-Build House Company Ltd.

146 sq. m.

Overall dimensions 13.8 x 8.0m

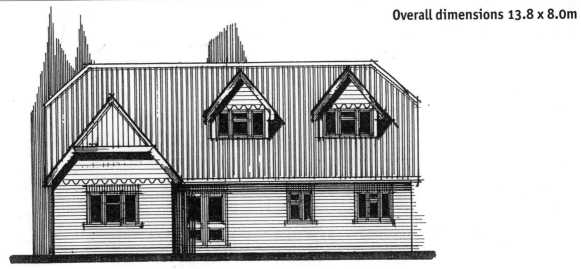

FRONT ELEVATION

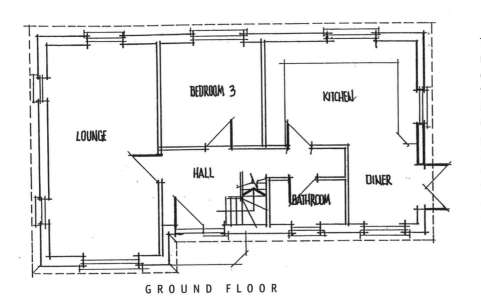

GROUND FLOOR

This pretty home has its two main bedrooms upstairs, complete with en-suite facilities, whilst the third bedroom or study is downstairs. The lounge is a generous size and whilst the kitchen/family room is shown combined with the dining area, for those who wanted a division, this would present no problems.

Kitchen/ family room	5.5 x 3.5m
Dining room	2.8 x 2.4m
Sitting room	7.3 x 4.0m
Bedroom 3	3.6 x 3.5m
Master bedroom	5.7 x 4.2m + bathroom
Bedroom 2	5.0 x 4.0m + bathroom

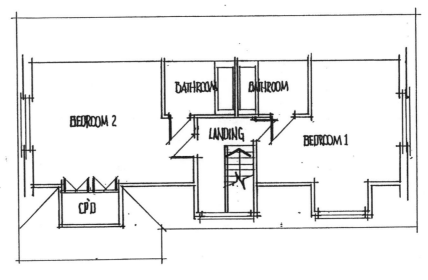

FIRST FLOOR

ELMDON 98-158

The copyright belongs to Potton Ltd.

146 sq. m.

Overall dimensions 11.9 x 11.43m

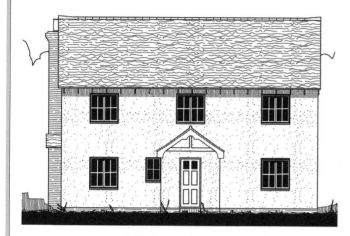

FRONT ELEVATION

REAR ELEVATION

This attractive and compact house packs in a lot of accommodation for its size. Many would think that one of the bathrooms should have been en-suite but some families might prefer it the way it is shown. The projection of the lounge into the sun room area is delightful with the inner part cosy around the inglenook and the outer part flooded with light.

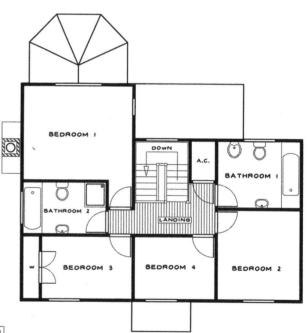

FIRST FLOOR

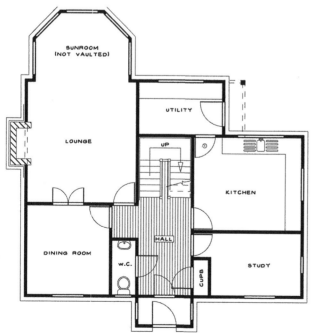

GROUND FLOOR

Lounge	6.9 x 4.1m	Bedroom 1	4.1 x 3.4m
Dining room	3.25 x 3.1m	Bedroom 2	3.25 x 3.1m
Kitchen	4.1 x 3.4m	Bedroom 3	3.4 x 2.3m
Study	3.4 2.25m		+ wardrobe
Utility	3.2 x 1.9m	Bedroom 4	3.0 x 2.3m

NEWBURY

The copyright belongs to Custom Homes Ltd.

**149 sq. m.
including a garage of 16 sq. m.**

Overall dimensions 12.35 x 9.8m

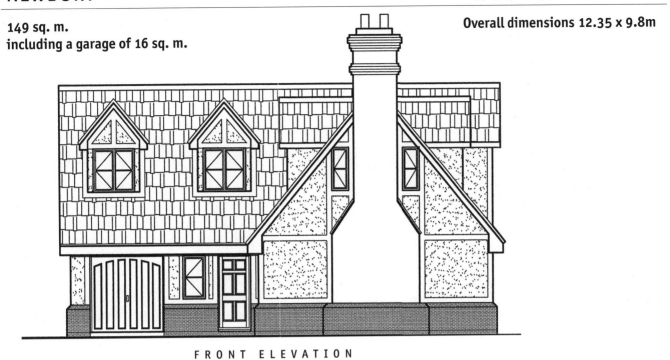

F R O N T   E L E V A T I O N

This is a compact family house. There is direct access to the house from the integral garage so that those who wanted extra space could easily convert this to another room, if there is adequate alternative parking.

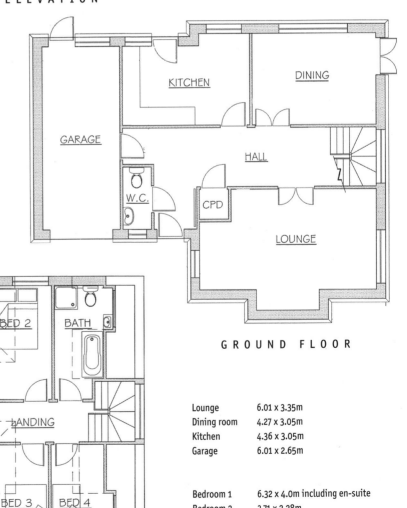

GARAGE

KITCHEN

DINING

HALL

CPD

W.C.

LOUNGE

G R O U N D   F L O O R

BED 2

BATH

MASTER BED

EN-SUITE

LANDING

BED 3

BED 4

F I R S T   F L O O R

Lounge	6.01 x 3.35m
Dining room	4.27 x 3.05m
Kitchen	4.36 x 3.05m
Garage	6.01 x 2.65m
Bedroom 1	6.32 x 4.0m including en-suite
Bedroom 2	3.71 x 2.28m
Bedroom 3	3.35 x 2.15m
Bedroom 4	3.35 x 1.76m

CAXTON D 95-067

The copyright belongs to Potton Ltd.

149 sq. m.

Overall dimensions 11.8 x 7.5m

FRONT ELEVATION

SIDE ELEVATION

This comfortable and solid four bedroom house would grace many a village street. The sitting room has space in plenty for a large and imposing inglenook fireplace and there is a passageway connecting this room with the dining room and kitchen so that the accommodation flows nicely.

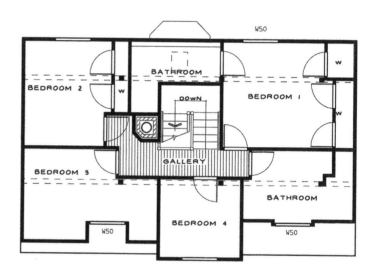

FIRST FLOOR

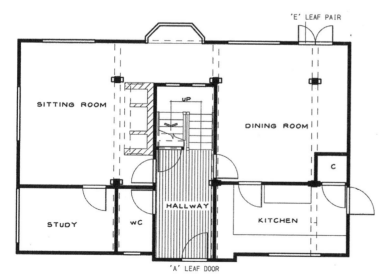

GROUND FLOOR

Sitting room	4.7 x 4.5m
Dining room	4.5 x 4.5m
Kitchen	4.5 x 2.2m
Study	3.25 x 2.1m
Bedroom 1	3.8 x 3.4m + wardrobe
Bedroom 2	3.4 x 3.0m + wardrobe
Bedroom 3	4.5 x 3.0m
Bedroom 4	2.7 x 2.6m

CAXTON 98-024

The copyright belongs to Potton Ltd.

149 sq. m.

Overall dimensions 11.8 x 10.4m

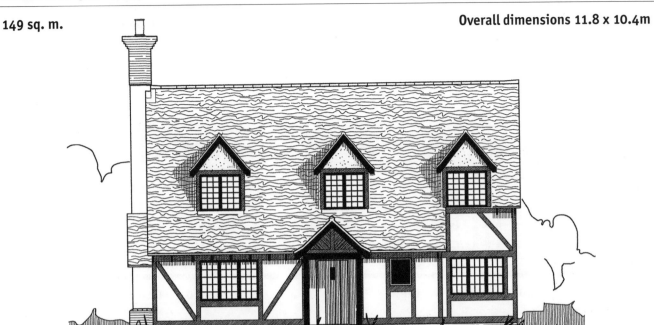

F R O N T   E L E V A T I O N

Although only modestly sized, this house has an imposing presence. The study could easily be designated as a fourth bedroom and the master bedroom has full en-suite facilities. Downstairs the large lounge is combined with a sun room for added interest.

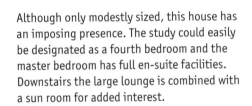

F I R S T   F L O O R

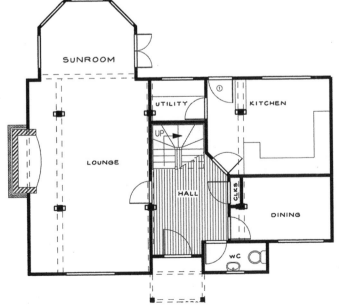

G R O U N D   F L O O R

Lounge	6.91 x 4.47m		Bedroom 1	5.81 x 3.38m + wardrobes & en-suite
Kitchen	4.56 x 3.47m			
Dining room	3.72 x 2.55m		Bedroom 2	3.26 x 2.67m
Utility	2.1 x 1.5m		Bedroom 3	3.05 x 2.7m
Sunroom	3.51 x 2.92m		Study	3.3 x 1.6m

3 BED BARN 02-909

The copyright belongs to Potton Ltd.

150 sq. m.

Overall dimensions 11.8 x 8.4m

FRONT ELEVATION

SIDE ELEVATION

Barn conversions aren't for everyone and it is notoriously difficult to gauge the costs involved. This house solves all that by closely emulating a barn conversion giving it a distinctly rural feel that might satisfy some delicate planning situations.

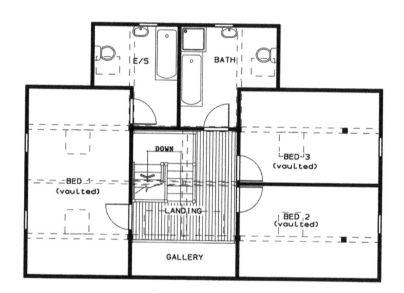

FIRST FLOOR

GROUND FLOOR

Lounge	5.7 x 4.4m
Dining/kitchen	5.7 x 3.2m
Utility	3.1 x 2.0m
Bedroom 1	5.7 x 3.2m + en-suite
Bedroom 2	4.4 x 2.8m
Bedroom 3	4.4 x 2.8m

GAMLND – P

The copyright belongs to Potton Ltd.

151 sq. m.

Overall dimensions 11 x 10.6m

F R O N T   E L E V A T I O N

This is one of the distinctive designs that brought this company to such prominence within the self build movement. The good sized lounge has an inglenook fireplace, the kitchen emulates a farmhouse kitchen and yet, the hall is large enough to give a first impression of space.

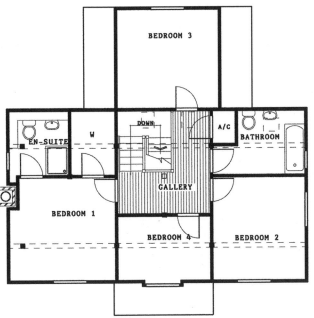

F I R S T   F L O O R

G R O U N D   F L O O R

Lounge	5.8 x 3.2m	Bedroom 1	3.7 x 3.5m + wardrobe & en-suite
Kitchen	4.3 x 3.4m		
Utility	3.4 x 1.4m		
Dining room	3.3 x 3.25m	Bedroom 2	3.5 x 3.25m
Study	3.25 x 2.3m	Bedroom 3	3.3 x 2.2m
		Bedroom 4	3.6 x 3.35m

D274

The copyright belongs to Design & Materials Ltd.

151 sq. m.
including a garage of 18 sq. m.

Overall dimensions 13.6x 10.8.m

FRONT ELEVATION

This isn't a very big house, yet it still manages to look quite grand. A deceptively complex shape actually breaks down into a simple 'T' section. The deep porch and the fully turned staircase leading up out of the entrance hall give it even more appeal and the conservatory areas to the lounge and the dining room effectively extend those rooms into the views for which this design was originally formulated.

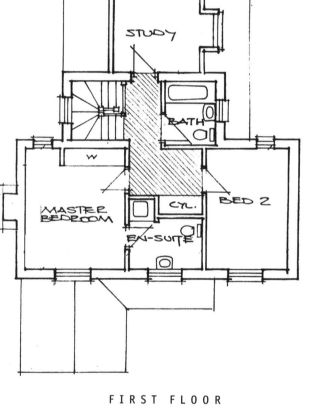

FIRST FLOOR

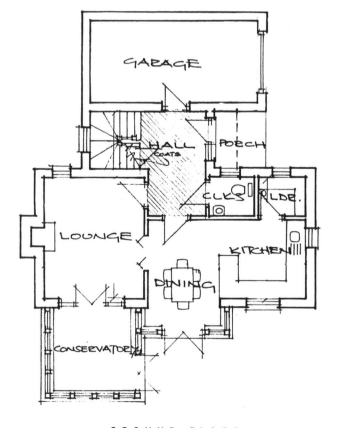

GROUND FLOOR

Lounge	4.28 x 3.66m	Master bedroom	4.27 x 3.66m + en-suite
Kitchen/ dining room	5.75 x 3.32m + larder	Bedroom 2	4.27 x 3.05m
		Study	3.19 x 2.98m
Garage	6.10 x 3.01m		

P304

152 sq. m.

Overall dimensions 14.25 x 12.95m

FRONT ELEVATION

Another home that could be sued as a bungalow with the upper part being used for visitor. The large dining hall, around which all of the major rooms are grouped, is the essential feature of this home. Note the cupboards in the hall and the larder off the kitchen. The lounge and the kitchen breakfast room also have vaulted ceilings with gable head windows.

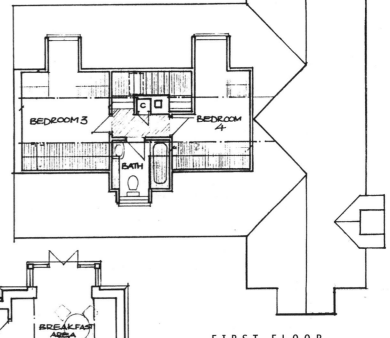

FIRST FLOOR

GROUND FLOOR

Dining hall	5.42 x 3.68m
Sitting room	4.57 x 3.96m
Kitchen/ breakfast room	5.87 x 3.96m + utility & larder
Master bedroom	3.35 x 3.05m + dressing room
Bedroom 2	3.35 x 2.74m
Bedroom 3	3.65 x 3.35m
Bedroom 4	3.65 x 3.05m max

131

CAXTG – P2

The copyright belongs to Potton Ltd.

153 sq. m. including a 16.5 sq. m. garage

Overall dimensions 13.9 x 8.5m

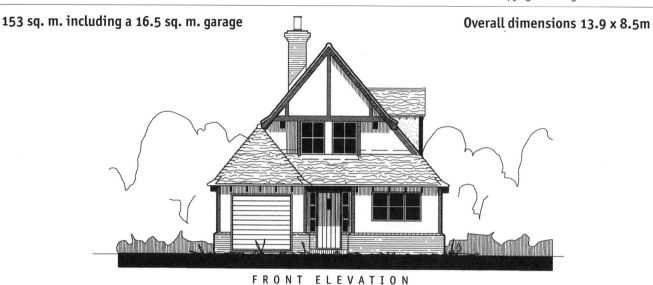

FRONT ELEVATION

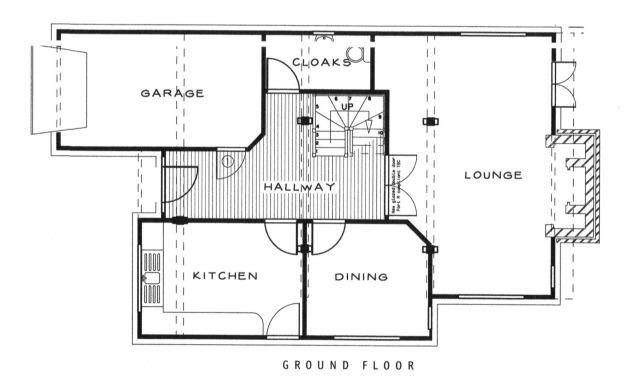

GROUND FLOOR

This a house for a deep but narrow site and, with the fourth bedroom either combined with one of the others or re-designated, it could fit on an even narrower one. Putting the pitched roof over the forward projecting garage is a masterstroke as it creates interest in what would other wise be a difficult elevation.

Lounge	6.9 x 4.4m
Diningroom	3.3 x 2.9m
Kitchen	4.4 x 3.3m
Garage	5.5 x 3.0m
Bedroom 1	3.7 x 3.65 m + en-suite
Bedroom 2	3.3 x 2.8m
Bedroom 3	3.3 x 2.8m
Bedroom 4	3.3 x 2.8m

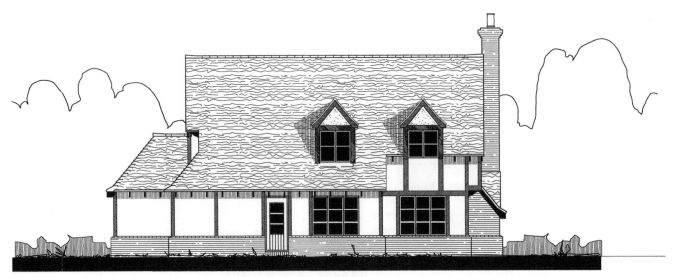

SIDE ELEVATION

REAR ELEVATION

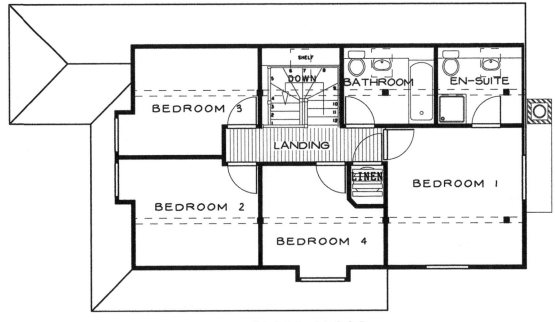

FIRST FLOOR

THE DOVECOTE

The copyright belongs to Scandia-Hus Limited

152 sq. m.

Overall dimensions 12.1 x 11.35m

FRONT ELEVATION

GROUND FLOOR

Kitchen	3.0 x 2.1m
Breakfast area	3.6 x 2.4m
Dining room	3.8 x 3.3m
Sitting room	6.0 x 3.9m
Study	3.9 x 2.8m
Master bedroom	3.9 x 3.2m
	+ wardrobe & en-suite
Bedroom 2	3.9 x 3.0m
Bedroom 3	3.7 x 2.6m
Landing lounge	4.4 x 2.0m

This beautiful home really looks as if it belongs in a fairy tale but most of its features and attractions are only too real. One of its inspirational features is the vaulted dining room, which opens right up to the apex on the top floor creating a feeling of space and light. The kitchen/breakfast room, in stark contrast to the cottagey feel of the rest of the house, features an entire wall of full height glazed panels.

FIRST FLOOR

OAKWELL-P

The copyright belongs to Potton Ltd.

153 sq. m.

Overall dimensions 14.8 x 9.6m

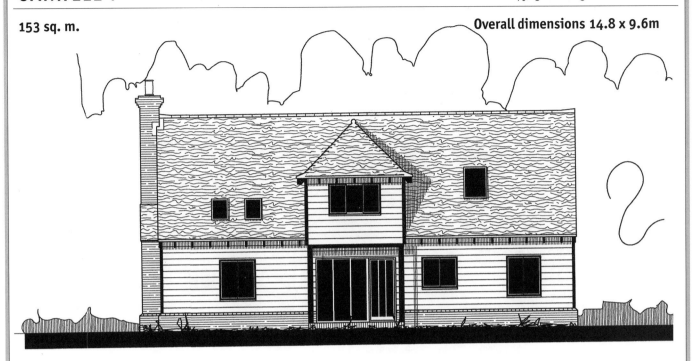

All elevations indicate that a rural barn was the starting point for the design of this home. No compromise is made to the internal arrangement with vaulted ceilings to the lounge and a generous use of the entire upper floor as the master suite.

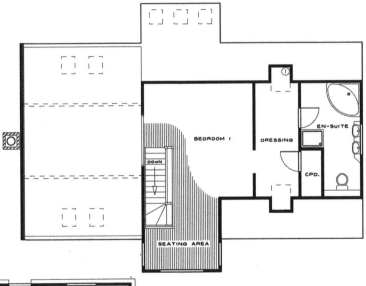

FIRST FLOOR

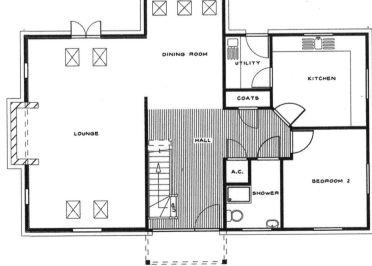

Lounge	7.4 x 4.7m
Diningroom	4.5 x 3.0m
Kitchen	3.8 x 3.5m
Utility	2.0 x 1.8m
Bedroom 2	3.75 x 3.4m
Bedroom 1	7.3 x 4.4m max + dressing and en-suite

GROUND FLOOR

CORNHILL

The copyright belongs to Designer Homes

154 sq. m.
including a garage of 16 sq. m.

Overall dimensions 14.15 x 10.60m

FRONT ELEVATION

Having a bedroom downstairs used to be looked upon as some sort of compromise. Increasingly, however, it is being thought of as giving flexibility to the home, especially in a time when the concept of 'homes for life' is discussed. A downstairs bedroom that is close to toilet and/or washing facilities can be very useful when an older or disabled person comes to stay.

FIRST FLOOR

GROUND FLOOR

Living room	4.80 x 3.91m	Bedroom 1	5.79 x 3.28m + wardrobes & en-suite
Family room	3.50 x 3.28m		
Kitchen	3.61 x 3.28m		
Utility	1.70 x 1.70m	Bedroom 2	3.61 x 2.39m + wardrobe
Dining room/ bedroom 4	3.28 x 3.28m	Bedroom 3	3.02 x 3.02m + wardrobe
Garage	5.25 x 2.60m		

STAMFORD

The copyright belongs to Designer Homes

155 sq. m.

Overall dimensions 14.85m x 12.90m

F R O N T   E L E V A T I O N

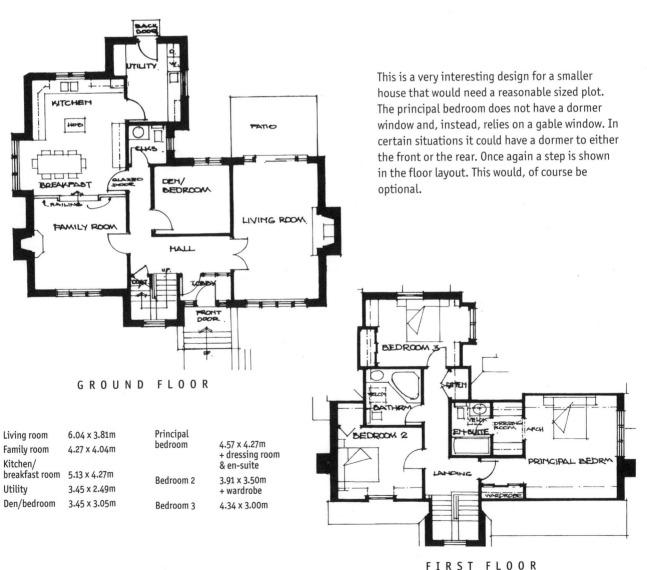

This is a very interesting design for a smaller house that would need a reasonable sized plot. The principal bedroom does not have a dormer window and, instead, relies on a gable window. In certain situations it could have a dormer to either the front or the rear. Once again a step is shown in the floor layout. This would, of course be optional.

G R O U N D   F L O O R

F I R S T   F L O O R

Living room	6.04 x 3.81m		Principal bedroom	4.57 x 4.27m + dressing room & en-suite
Family room	4.27 x 4.04m			
Kitchen/ breakfast room	5.13 x 4.27m		Bedroom 2	3.91 x 3.50m + wardrobe
Utility	3.45 x 2.49m			
Den/bedroom	3.45 x 3.05m		Bedroom 3	4.34 x 3.00m

137

SILVER BIRCH

The copyright belongs to Designer Homes

156 sq. m.
including a garage of 14 sq. m.

Overall dimensions 10.60 x 10.15m

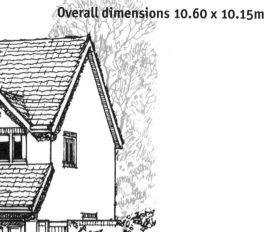

FRONT ELEVATION

This compact house is able to provide three reception rooms plus a kitchen and integral garage on the ground floor with four bedrooms upstairs, one of them with en-suite facilities. The design of the house, although normal height, manages to give the impression of a lower ridge by drawing the eye down with catslide and runnover roofs together with dormers and false dormers.

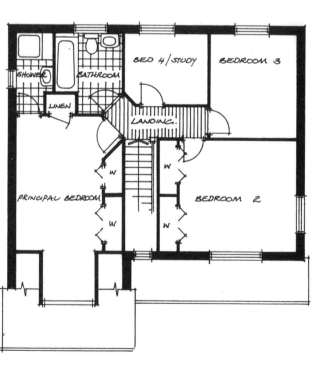

FIRST FLOOR

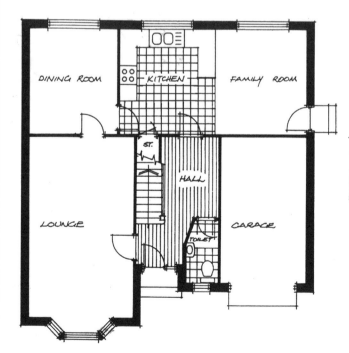

GROUND FLOOR

Lounge	5.94 x 3.58m	Principal bedroom	4.42 x 3.66m + wardrobes & en-suite
Dining room	3.50 x 2.97m		
Kitchen	3.50 x 3.28m		
Family room	3.50 x 3.20m	Bedroom 2	4.04 x 3.66m + wardrobes
Garage	4.80 x 2.95m		
		Bedroom 3	3.43 x 2.97m
		Bedroom 4/ study	2.82 x 2.36m

THE BEECHES

The copyright belongs to an ASBA architectural practice – Julian Owen Associates

159 sq. m.

Overall dimensions 15.0 x 11.5m

REAR ELEVATION

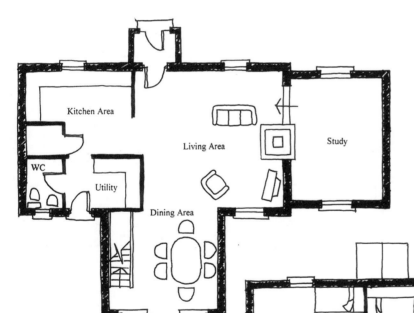

GROUND FLOOR

Once again this contributor has chosen to illustrate the rear elevation, this time to show off the full height glazed windows to the dining area which has vaulted ceilings. These are mirrored by the full length window serving both the living area and the master bedroom above.

FIRST FLOOR

Living area	5.5 x 5.5m
Dining area	4.0 x 3.5m
Kitchen area	4.2 x 2.0m
Study	4.5 x 3.4m
Utility	3.0 x 2.0m
Bedroom1	4.4 x 2.7m + en-suite
Bedroom 2	4.3 x 2.5m
Bedroom 3	4.5 x 2.5m

E120

The copyright belongs to Design & Materials Ltd.

159 sq. m.

Overall dimensions 13.27 x 9.03m

FRONT ELEVATION

This home present interesting shapes to the front elevation. The accommodation follows a standard pattern with the lounge separated from the rest of the living accommodation for use as a 'best' room. The rear entrance is through the stable door in the utility room. Upstairs, two of the bedrooms have en-suite facilities.

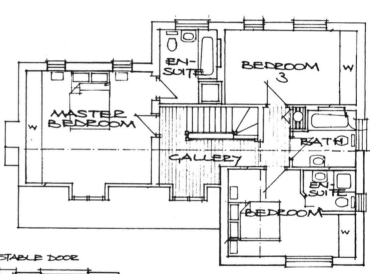

FIRST FLOOR

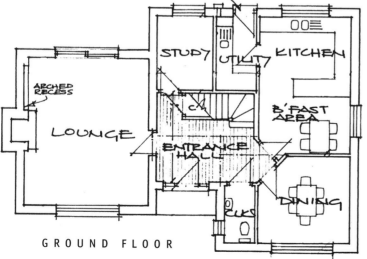

GROUND FLOOR

Lounge	5.49 x 4.88m
Kitchen/ breakfast room	5.13 x 3.50m
Dining room	3.50 x 3.20m
Utility	2.74 x 1.66m
Study	2.74 x 2.13m
Master bedroom	4.88 x 4.12m + en-suite
Bedroom 2	4.80 x 3.20m including en-suite
Bedroom 3	5.16 x 2.75m

D173

The copyright belongs to Design & Materials Ltd.

159 sq. m.

Overall dimensions 12.00 x 11.47m

FRONT ELEVATION

SIDE ELEVATION

This traditional house could fit into the Cotswolds, the North of England or indeed the South West but with a little tinkering could go almost anywhere. It is reminiscent of a cottage or farmhouse that has been extended, something that is known as additive development, which is a feature of many rural homes. The rooms are big. Some could be subdivided and a little re-arrangement could produce four bedrooms.

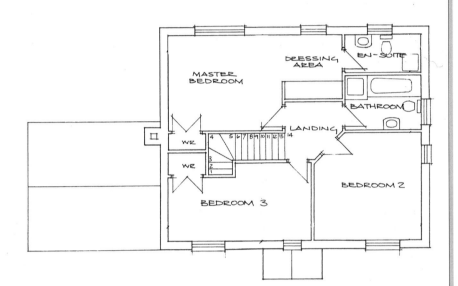

FIRST FLOOR

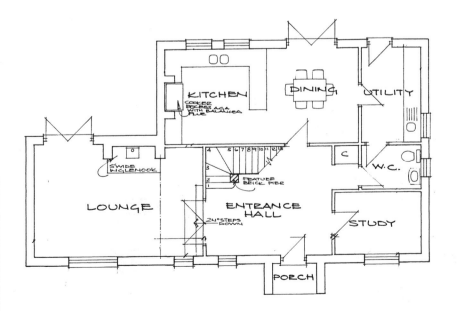

Lounge	6.10 x 3.96m
Kitchen/ding room	7.01 x 3.53m
Utility	3.35 x 2.13m
Study	3.05 x 2.13m
Master bedroom	6.40 x 3.35m max + en-suite
Bedroom 2	3.82 x 3.76m
Bedroom 3	5.32 x 2.76m

GROUND FLOOR

141

D194

The copyright belongs to Design & Materials Ltd.

159 sq. m.

Overall dimensions 12.0 x 11.47m

FRONT ELEVATION

REAR ELEVATION

This cottage presents a symmetrical and simple elevation to the street that is only challenged by having a chimney at one end only. As such it would fit into many village street scenes. The porch opens into an entrance lobby and then to a dining hall, a layout that would again have been a traditional feature and which is now coming back into favour. The rear elevation is much more complex with the mezzanine window and the roof extensions to the kitchen.

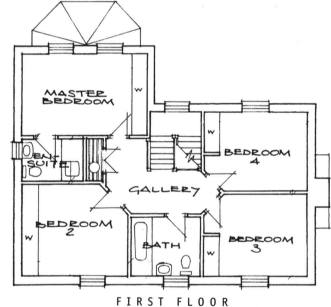

FIRST FLOOR

GROUND FLOOR

Lounge	6.10 x 3.96m
Dining hall	5.20 x 3.66m
Kitchen/ breakfast room	4.71 x 4.57m
Utility	3.05 x 1.60m
Study	3.05 x 2.13m
Master bedroom	4.71 x 2.90m + en-suite
Bedroom 2	3.96 x 3.50m
Bedroom 3	3.96 x 3.05m
Bedroom 4	3.96 x 2.95m

MARFIELD

The copyright belongs to Designer Homes

160 sq. m.

Overall dimensions 12.50 x 10.80m

F R O N T   E L E V A T I O N

An attractive family home providing three bedroom accommodation in a fairly standard layout. The external treatment shows how careful thought and attention to detail can transform what would otherwise have been an ordinary home into something special. Note the patterned roof tiling, the rendered gables with raised areas and the exposed rafter feet. Note also how the window style complements the design.

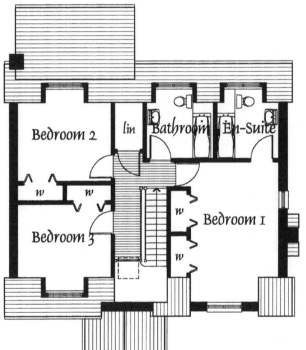

F I R S T   F L O O R

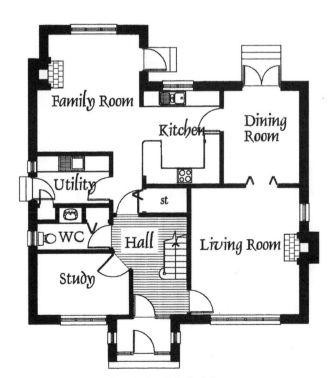

G R O U N D   F L O O R

Living room	5.03 x 4.14m		
Dining room	3.30 x 3.00m	Bedroom 1	5.33 x 3.43m + wardrobes & en-suite
Kitchen	3.30 x 2.84m		
Family room	4.42 x 3.96m	Bedroom 2	3.50 x 3.05m + wardrobe
Study	3.50 x 2.03m		
Utility	2.75 x 1.75m	Bedroom 3	3.50 x 2.74m + wardrobe

HERONGATE

The copyright belongs to Designer Homes

160 sq. m.

Overall dimensions 15.90 x 11.40m

FRONT ELEVATION

Having the principal bedroom suite downstairs means that this lovely home could be occupied as a bungalow with three further bedrooms upstairs for visiting family. When not in use the upper part radiators could be left on low. The open hall and dining area has an attractive feature staircase rising from it. The lounge is shown with the floor dropped and a higher ceiling.

GROUND FLOOR

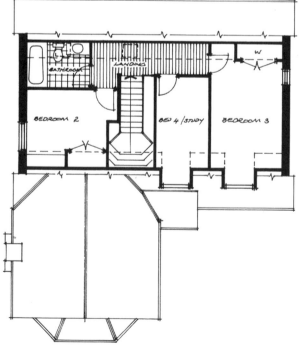

FIRST FLOOR

Lounge	5.03 x 4.34m	Bedroom 2	3.35 x 3.12m
Dining room	3.35 x 3.05m	Bedroom 3	4.34 x 3.05m
Kitchen	4.34 x 2.90m	Bedroom 4/ study	3.66 x 2.21m
Breakfast area	3.05 x 2.51m		
Garden room	3.12 x 2.29m		
Utility	4.34 x 1.52m		
Principal bedroom	3.66 x 3.58m + dressing area & en-suite		

HOUSES 161 TO 185 SQ.M.

O f all the size categories of houses, this is perhaps the one into which the majority of self build homes fall and for many, this is the size that personifies the ideal size for a family home. By now the study is really possible as part of the ground floor layout and the extension of the kitchen to include a breakfast eating area or an associated family/playroom is perfectly possible.

The bedrooms, if they are to remain at just four, start to be double rooms rather than single with fitted wardrobes as standard and en-suite facilities to at least the master suite.

With the house getting bigger the garage shrinks as a proportion of the whole and can therefore take its place as a part and parcel of the overall design format rather than being a complicating factor. It can be used to enhance the frontage in juxtaposition to the main house or it can be properly integrated within the main envelope.

Contributors in this section:
Associated Self Build Architects
The Border Design Centre
T.J.Crump OAKWRIGHTS Ltd.
Custom Homes Ltd.
Design & Materials Ltd.
Designer Homes
Potton Ltd.
The Self Build House Company Ltd.
Scottish Architects Network
Scandia-Hus Ltd.
The Swedish House Company Ltd.

THE LOVESTA

The copyright belongs to Scandia-Hus Limited

163 sq. m.

Overall dimensions 12.31 x 9.01m

FRONT ELEVATION

REAR ELEVATION

Once again the Swiss/Scandinavian ideal of a covered upper balcony providing a sheltered verandah to the main living rooms is employed to great effect. This is a home of flexibility, where a couple could live quite comfortably and economically or a growing or visiting family could easily be accommodated.

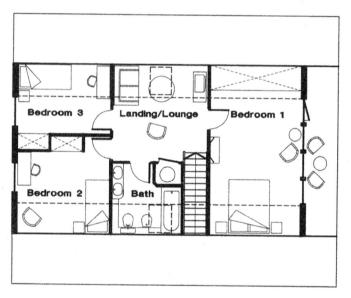

FIRST FLOOR

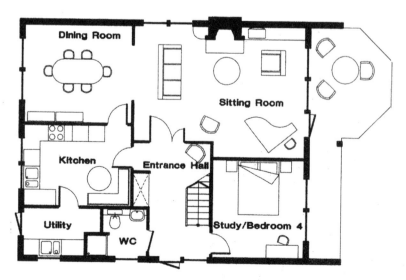

GROUND FLOOR

Kitchen	4.0 x 3.1m
Dining room	4.0 x 3.6m
Sitting room	6.4 x 3.7m
Study/bedroom 4	3.6 x 3.6m
Master bedroom	5.1 x 3.4m
Bedroom 2	3.4 x 3.4m
Bedroom 3	3.4 x 2.7m
Landing lounge	3.5 x 3.5m

MINTO

The copyright belongs to Designer Homes

**163 sq. m.
including a garage
of 18 sq. m.**

Overall dimensions 13.85 x 10.20m

FRONT ELEVATION

Cupboards are often forgotten, especially when
the design is restricted. The truth is, however,
that the smaller the design the greater the
need. This home abounds in them. A coat
cupboard in the hall. An understairs cupboard,
a larder and a storage cupboard in the utility.
Upstairs there is a large linen cupboard and
each of the bedrooms has fitted wardrobes.

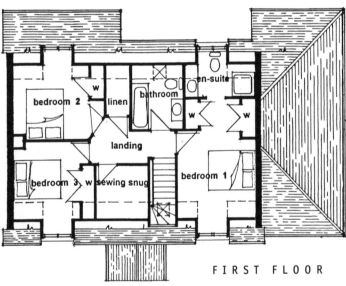

FIRST FLOOR

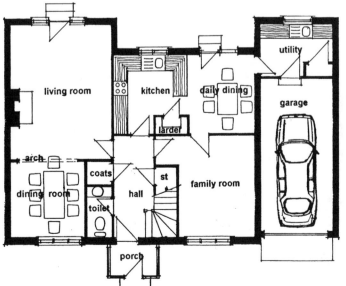

GROUND FLOOR

Living room 5.33 x 4.11m	Bedroom 1 3.43 x 3.12m + dressing/ wardrobe area & en-suite
Dining room 3.05 x 3.00m	
Kitchen 3.12 x 3.05m	
Daily dining room 3.12 x 2.75m	Bedroom 2 3.12 x 2.97m + wardrobe
Family room 4.04 x 3.12m	Bedroom 3 3.05 x 2.74m + wardrobe
Utility 3.00 x 2.10m	
Garage 6.10 x 3.00m	Sewing snug 2.10 x 2.10m

147

GULLANE

The copyright belongs to The Border Design Centre

165 sq. m.

Overall dimensions 14.9 x 10.7m

FRONT ELEVATION

This design was conceived for a tight walled garden site in a famous golfing village in East Lothian. In this design the stair is kept out of the main shell of the building and the corner bay window lends interest and allows a view through the entrance. Once again, a tower section is added to one corner of the building, creating a distinctive character and adding so much to the rooms it serves.

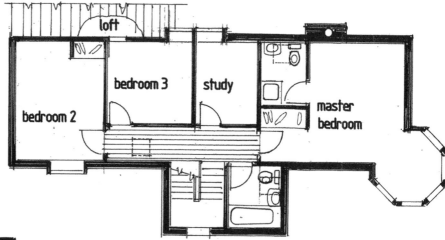

FIRST FLOOR

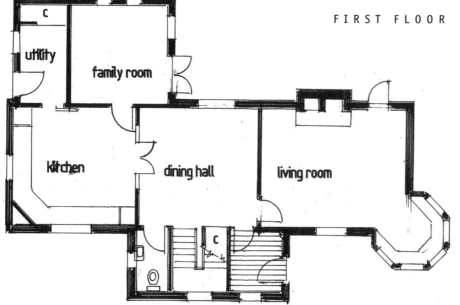

Living room	5.31 x 4.11m + tower section
Dining hall	4.39 x 4.11m
Kitchen	4.39 x 4.11m + utility area
Family room	3.50 x 3.50m
Study	2.31 x 2.29m
Master bedroom	4.11 x 3.50m + tower section & en-suite
Bedroom 2	4.11 x 3.20m
Bedroom 3	3.20 x 2.89m

GROUND FLOOR

FASKALLY

The copyright belongs to The Border Design Centre

165 sq. m.

Overall dimensions 16.1 x 10.7m

FRONT ELEVATION

Although not entered in the section, 'Homes for a sloping site', this design was originally conceived for a restricted steep site with beautiful views and it is used as an up-market bed and breakfast – hence the en-suites. In order to avoid costly underbuilding and a split level design, the house is built along the contours of the land with a narrow span. The dining hall is double height with a gallery.

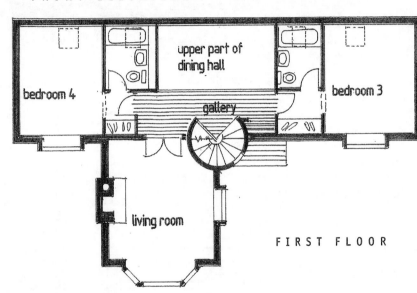

FIRST FLOOR

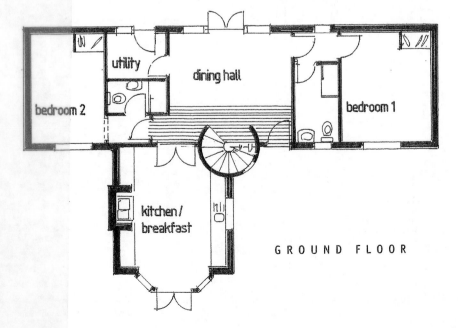

GROUND FLOOR

Dining hall	5.89 x 4.11m
Kitchen/ Breakfast room	5.21 x 4.11m + utility area
Bedroom 1	4.11 x 3.50m + en-suite
Bedroom 2	4.11 x 3.30m + en-suite

Living room	5.64 x 4.11m
Bedroom 3	3.11 x 3.50m + en-suite
Bedroom 4	4.11 x 2.89m + en-suite

E110

The copyright belongs to Design & Materials Ltd.

166 sq. m.

Overall dimensions 10.91 x 9.24m

FRONT ELEVATION

A home for tight rather than a narrow site, possibly where it has to contend with other properties or a limit on the ridge height. The eaves line is brought down to top floor window cill height, leaving the floor areas of the upstairs rooms unchanged but introducing skilling or sloping ceilings. The staircase and inner entrance hall are lit by a window set at mezzanine level and on the gallery above, the wall to the master bedroom is set at an angle.

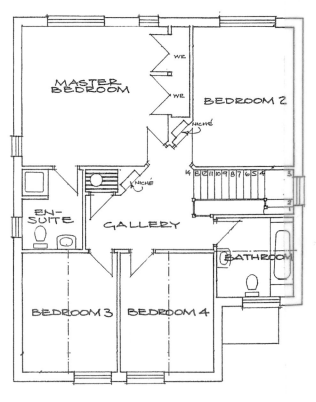

FIRST FLOOR

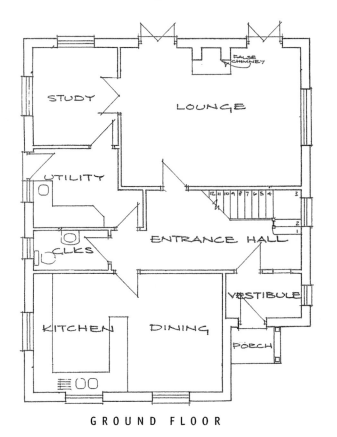

GROUND FLOOR

Lounge	5.80 x 4.27m		Master bedroom	4.64 x 4.27m + wardrobes & en-suite
Kitchen/dining room	6.10 x 3.66m			
Utility	2.74 x 2.44m			
Study	3.05 x 2.74m		Bedroom 2	4.27 x 3.20m
			Bedroom 3	3.66 x 3.00m
			Bedroom 4	3.66 x 3.00m

LIDDESDALE

The copyright belongs to The Border Design Centre

167 sq. m.
including a garage of 17 sq. m.

Overall dimensions 15.04 x 9.31m

FRONT ELEVATION

A farmer originally commissioned this design for a site that enjoyed views over rolling fields to the rear. It would be possible to change the denominations for one of the bedrooms and convert this into the master suite with the study providing the en-suite facilities. What is now called the master bedroom on the ground floor could then become the dining room.

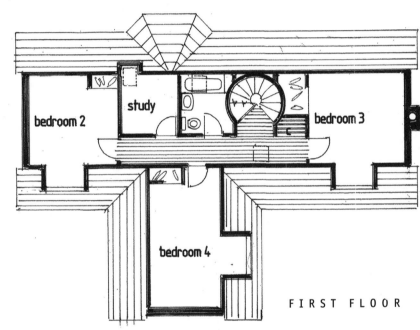

FIRST FLOOR

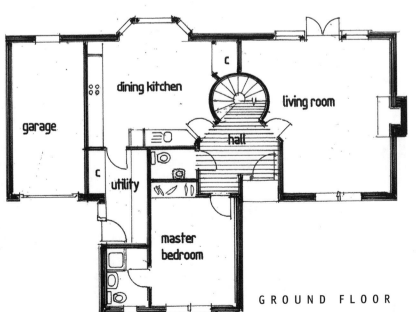

Living room	5.89 x 4.70m
Dining room/ kitchen	4.95 x 4.80m + utility area
Master bedroom	4.11 x 3.20m + wardrobe & en-suite
Garage	5.9 x 2.9m
Bedroom 2	3.50 x 3.50m
Bedroom 3	3.50 x 3.50m + wardrobe
Bedroom 4	4.11 x 2.79m
Study	2.20 x 2.20m

GROUND FLOOR

151

MERELANDS

The copyright belongs to T. J. Crump OAKRIGHTS Ltd.

170 sq. m.
including a garage of 17 sq. m.

Overall dimensions 14.75 x 12 m

FRONT ELEVATION

This is a truly open plan design on the ground floor, the principle of which is continued in the upper storey with open voids and the gallery overlooking the living areas. Simple tweaking could divide off some or all of the rooms and some might like a corridor between the ground floor toilet and utility, linking to the garage.

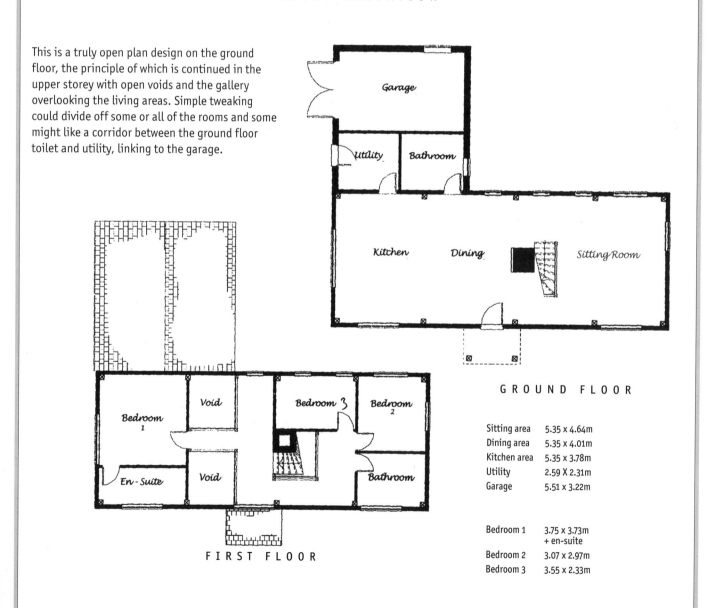

GROUND FLOOR

FIRST FLOOR

Sitting area	5.35 x 4.64m
Dining area	5.35 x 4.01m
Kitchen area	5.35 x 3.78m
Utility	2.59 X 2.31m
Garage	5.51 x 3.22m
Bedroom 1	3.75 x 3.73m + en-suite
Bedroom 2	3.07 x 2.97m
Bedroom 3	3.55 x 2.33m

ETTRICK

The copyright belongs to Designer Homes

172 sq. m.

Overall dimensions 14.30 x 13.10m

FRONT ELEVATION

The guest bedroom on the ground floor of this home would be eminently suitable for an older or disabled person as it is close by the downstairs shower room and close to all of the main reception rooms. The house is illustrated with a garage but this is not included in the plan or the dimensions above. The tabled verges and quoins would suit some areas but this home would look just as good in other materials.

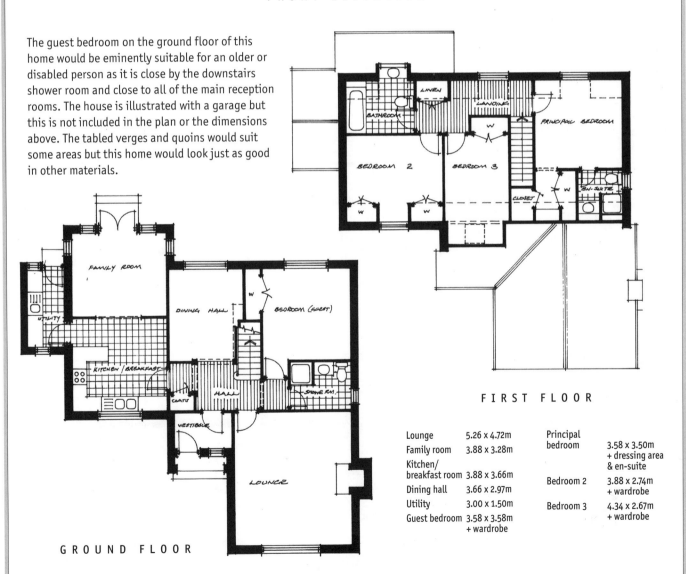

FIRST FLOOR

GROUND FLOOR

Lounge	5.26 x 4.72m		Principal bedroom	3.58 x 3.50m + dressing area & en-suite
Family room	3.88 x 3.28m			
Kitchen/ breakfast room	3.88 x 3.66m		Bedroom 2	3.88 x 2.74m + wardrobe
Dining hall	3.66 x 2.97m			
Utility	3.00 x 1.50m		Bedroom 3	4.34 x 2.67m + wardrobe
Guest bedroom	3.58 x 3.58m + wardrobe			

VENNACHER

The copyright belongs to The Border Design Centre

172 sq. m.

Overall dimensions 21.5 x 8.2m

FRONT ELEVATION

This home has conventional accommodation with all of the living rooms to the ground floor and all of the bedrooms and bathrooms to the upper part. But that's where the convention ends for, with twin towers, one at each end, the external appearance is changed dramatically and the four principal rooms are given a completely different twist.

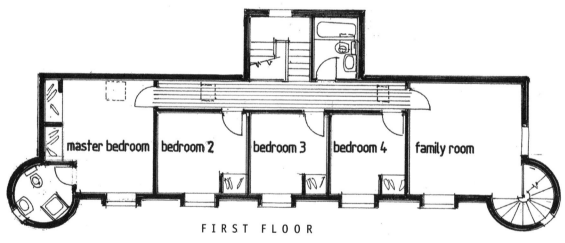

FIRST FLOOR

Living room	5.89 x 4.11m + tower study area	Family room	4.11 x 4.11m
Kitchen	4.11 x 3.50m + utility area	Master bedroom 4.11m x 3.20m + en-suite	
Dining room	4.11 x 4.11m	Bedroom 2	3.20 x 2.89m
		Bedroom 3	2.99 x 2.89m
		Bedroom 4	2.99 x 2.89m

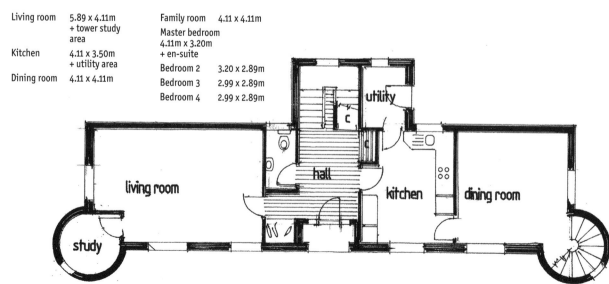

GROUND FLOOR

THE COURTFIELD

The copyright belongs to Scandia-Hus Limited

173 sq. m.

Overall dimensions 14.71 x 11.01m

FRONT ELEVATION

The dining room is illustrated as being at a higher level but is connected to the sitting room and the kitchen/breakfast areas by archways, providing an open yet individual feel to each room. Upstairs there are four good bedrooms with all of the usual facilities and use has been made of the large landing area to provide a further lounge.

FIRST FLOOR

GROUND FLOOR

Kitchen	3.2 x 2.1m
Dining room	3.8 x 3.7m
Sitting room	5.0 x 4.9m
Family/ breakfast room	4.9 x 3.9m
Study	3.2 x 2.8m
Master bedroom	4.7 x 3.5m + en-suite
Bedroom 2	3.8 x 3.7m
Bedroom 3	3.2 x 2.8m
Bedroom 4	3.1 x 2.4m
Landing lounge	4.1 x 3.5m

MAXTON

The copyright belongs to Designer Homes

173 sq. m. including a garage of 16 sq. m.

Overall dimensions 13.55 x 12.90m

FRONT ELEVATION

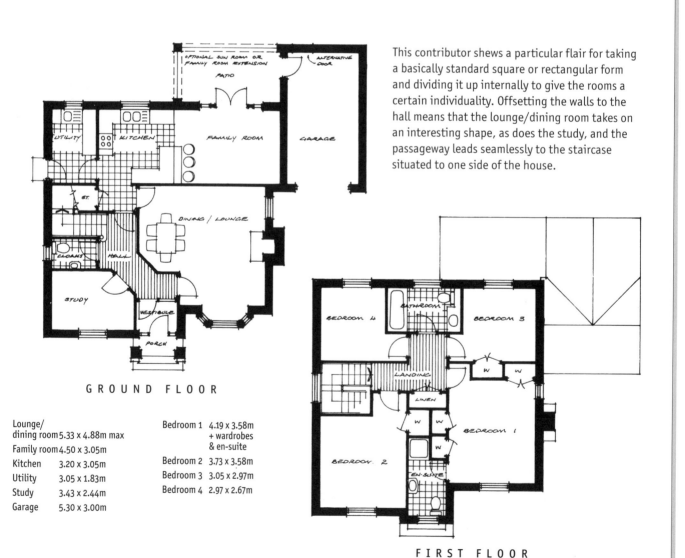

This contributor shews a particular flair for taking a basically standard square or rectangular form and dividing it up internally to give the rooms a certain individuality. Offsetting the walls to the hall means that the lounge/dining room takes on an interesting shape, as does the study, and the passageway leads seamlessly to the staircase situated to one side of the house.

GROUND FLOOR

FIRST FLOOR

Lounge/ dining room	5.33 x 4.88m max	
Family room	4.50 x 3.05m	
Kitchen	3.20 x 3.05m	
Utility	3.05 x 1.83m	
Study	3.43 x 2.44m	
Garage	5.30 x 3.00m	

Bedroom 1	4.19 x 3.58m + wardrobes & en-suite
Bedroom 2	3.73 x 3.58m
Bedroom 3	3.05 x 2.97m
Bedroom 4	2.97 x 2.67m

PRESTWICK

The copyright belongs to Designer Homes

173 sq. m.

Overall dimensions 11.90 x 11.90m

FRONT ELEVATION

The words 'family home' can mean so many things. This home illustrates just how a home can be designed around the needs of a modern family. The TV/study might be somewhere that the kids go to watch television. Alternatively there might be a television in the lounge and that's where the kids watch what they want to while the study becomes available for quieter pursuits. The family kitchen fulfils the needs of the busy family leaving the formal dining room for special occasions.

FIRST FLOOR

GROUND FLOOR

		Principal	
Lounge	5.20 x 4.10m	bedroom	4.60 x 3.20m
Dining room	3.45 x 2.95m		+ wardrobes
Kitchen/			& en-suite
family room	7.60 x 3.45m	Bedroom 2	4.05 x 3.50m
TV/Study	4.10 x 2.95m		+ wardrobes
Utility	1.90 x 1.70m	Bedroom 3	3.75 x 3.70m max
		Bedroom 4	3.60 x 2.65m

EDSBYN

The copyright belongs to The Swedish House Company Ltd.

176 sq. m.

Overall dimensions 12.75 x 8.55m.

This attractive three bedroom chalet bungalow could be built across the plot for maximum visual impact and kerb appeal. Alternatively, on a narrow site, the home could be positioned down the plot. The rooms are all of a generous size and the ethos behind Scandinavian design is reflected in the use of light and the integration of the outside with the decking.

FRONT ELEVATION

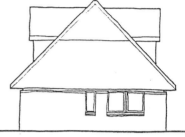

SIDE ELEVATION

REAR ELEVATION

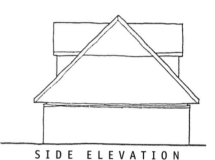

SIDE ELEVATION

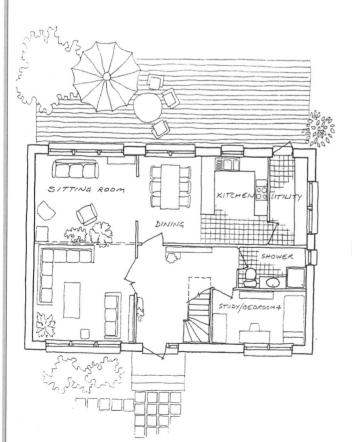

GROUND FLOOR

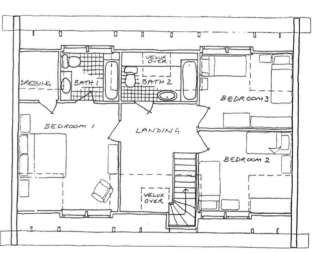

FIRST FLOOR

Sitting room	7.8 x 4.4m		Bedroom 1	4.4 x 4.4m
Dining room	3.6 x 2.7m			+ dressing room
Kitchen	3.6 x 3.0m			& bathroom
Utility	3.6 x 1.7m		Bedroom 2	4.1 x 3.4m
Study	4.1 x 2.2m		Bedroom 3	4.1 x 3.1m

THE DALSLAND

The copyright belongs to Scandia-Hus Limited

176 sq. m.

Overall dimensions 12.05 x 9.91

FRONT ELEVATION

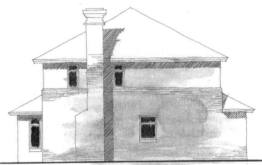

REAR ELEVATION

REAR ELEVATION

A traditional looking design for a modern four bedroom house that would easily blend into most street scenes. The entrance hall gives access to all of the major reception rooms. The lounge has a built-in extension adding interest to the rear elevation and projecting this room into the garden via the patio doors. Upstairs there are four good sized bedrooms and the master suite includes a dressing room and en-suite.

FIRST FLOOR

GROUND FLOOR

Kitchen	3.7 x 3.7m	Master bedroom	4.0 x 3.8m + dressing room & en-suite
Dining room	3.7 x 3.3m		
Sitting room	5.6 x 5.5m	Bedroom 2	4.8 x 3.3m + wardrobe
Study/ bedroom 5	3.8 x 2.7m	Bedroom 3	3.8 x 3.3m + wardrobe
		Bedroom 4	3.2 x 2.7m + wardrobe

159

TOSTOCK

The copyright belongs to Custom Homes Ltd.

176 sq. m.

Overall dimensions 13.4 x 10.65m

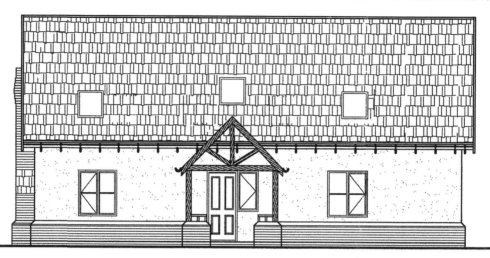

F R O N T   E L E V A T I O N

From the illustration of the front elevation you might think that I have put this home into the wrong category and that it should be amongst the bungalows. Well with a little re-arrangement and a change of designation on some of the rooms that is exactly what it could be. If the family room and study became bedrooms and the utility room became the bathroom then the ground floor becomes a self-contaned single storey home.

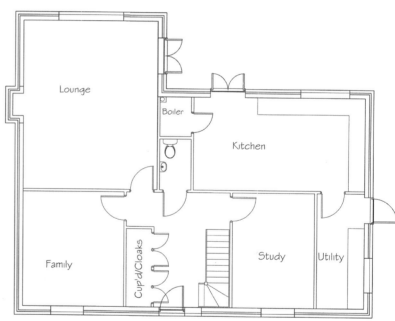

G R O U N D   F L O O R

F I R S T   F L O O R

Lounge	5.9 x 4.9m
Kitchen	6.2 x 3.3m
Family room	4.0 x 3.7m
Study	4.0 x 3.95m
Utility	4.0 x 1.7m
Bedroom 1	5.3 x 4.75m max + en-suite
Bedroom 2	3.8 x 2.8m
Bedroom 3	4.7 x 2.9m

F102

The copyright belongs to Design & Materials Ltd.

176 sq. m.

Overall dimensions 13.45 x 9.60m

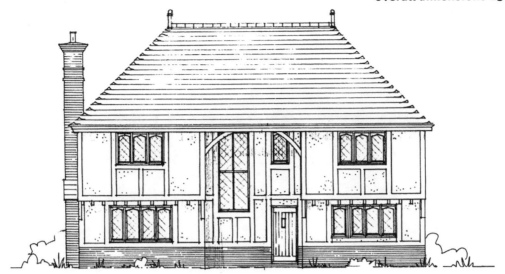

FRONT ELEVATION

Why should a home with a cottage feel be dark and cramped? No reason at all as this design ably demonstrates. The full height window over the staircase floods light into the entrance hall and gallery and this is then borrowed by the feature windows to the family room and dining area, which themselves, project into the garden with glazing on three sides. Although illustrated in the Sussex style, a few alterations and change of materials would fit it into other counties.

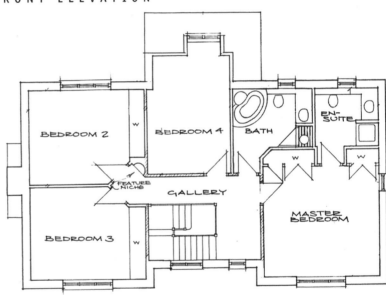

FIRST FLOOR

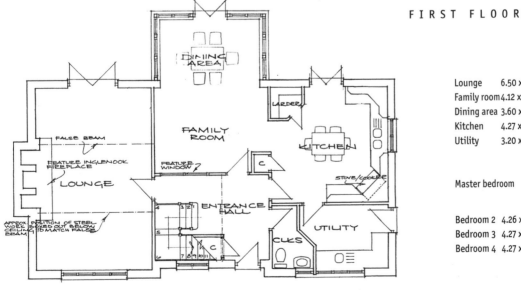

GROUND FLOOR

Lounge	6.50 x 4.27m
Family room	4.12 x 3.05m
Dining area	3.60 x 2.40m
Kitchen	4.27 x 4.15m
Utility	3.20 x 2.25m

Master bedroom	4.27 x 3.96m + wardrobes & en-suite
Bedroom 2	4.26 x 3.35m
Bedroom 3	4.27 x 3.35m
Bedroom 4	4.27 x 3.02m

BEDRULE

The copyright belongs to Designer Homes

**177 sq. m
including a garage
of 20 sq. m.**

Overall dimensions 12.54 x 10.50m

FRONT ELEVATION

Deciding where to put the fireplace is
important. Not only does this become the
focal point of the room but it impacts on just
how one is going to furnish the room. A
corner fireplace is often the answer and it can
be more efficient as there are no cold spots to
the side. The concept of family daily dining as
opposed to formal dining is espoused in the
large area adjoining the kitchen. The large
hall storage cupboard and the walk-in linen
cupboard would find favour with many.

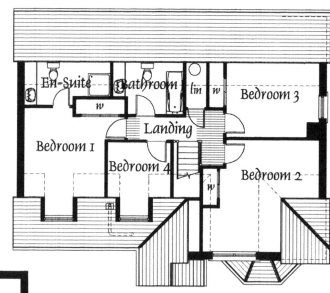

FIRST FLOOR

GROUND FLOOR

Living room 4.72 x 4.65m	
Dining room 4.04 x 3.91m	
Kitchen 3.12 x 2.90m	
Family daily dining room 3.91 x 3.10m	
Utility 2.85 x 1.60m	
Garage 5.85 x 4.00m max	

Bedroom 1 3.81 x 3.50m
+ wardrobe
& en-suite

Bedroom 2 4.19 x 4.11m
+ wardrobe

Bedroom 3 3.66 x 2.62m
+ wardrobe

Bedroom 4 3.05 x 2.29m

GREEN WARBLER

The copyright belongs to Designer Homes

**178 sq. m.
including a garage
of 16 sq. m.**

Overall dimensions 14 x 11m

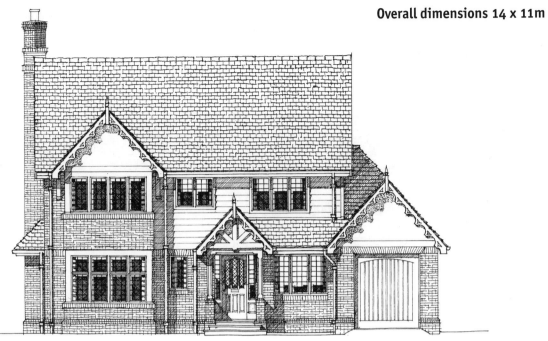

FRONT ELEVATION

What makes this home stand out is not just the wealth of accommodation but the attention to detail in the external appearance. It's not just the choice of materials, for they can be changed with ease. It is the way the roofs over, say, the garage, linking across to the porch, are pitched to run into each other. The filigree barge boards and finials do, however lend it a particular character.

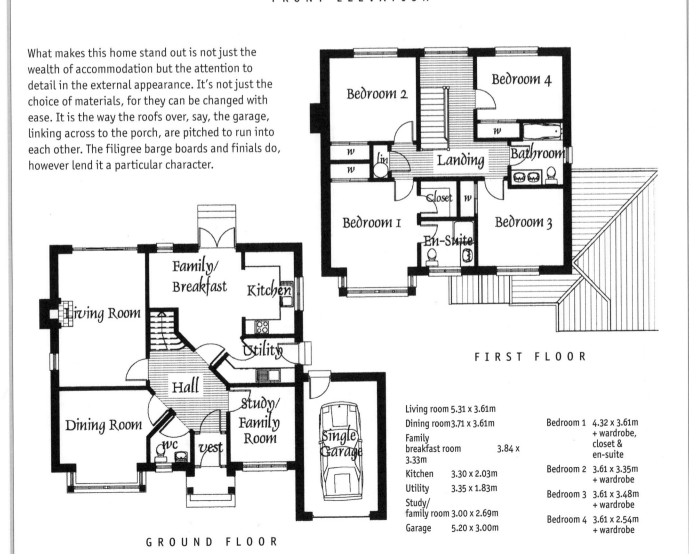

FIRST FLOOR

GROUND FLOOR

Living room 5.31 x 3.61m		
Dining room 3.71 x 3.61m	Bedroom 1	4.32 x 3.61m + wardrobe, closet & en-suite
Family breakfast room 3.84 x 3.33m		
Kitchen 3.30 x 2.03m	Bedroom 2	3.61 x 3.35m + wardrobe
Utility 3.35 x 1.83m		
Study/ family room 3.00 x 2.69m	Bedroom 3	3.61 x 3.48m + wardrobe
Garage 5.20 x 3.00m	Bedroom 4	3.61 x 2.54m + wardrobe

163

THE HOWARD

The copyright belongs to The Self-Build House Company Ltd.

178 sq. m.

Overall dimensions 11.8 x 10.1m

FRONT ELEVATION

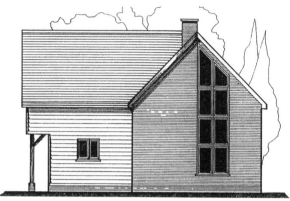

SIDE ELEVATION

There is a distinctly colonial feel to this home with its areas of clapboard, the well supported balcony and, inside, the large gallery seating area over the lounge. The garage and carport, which are shewn on the elevations are not included in the plans and have not, therefore been included in the overall size of the building. As drawn they would add around 25 square metres.

Kitchen/dining room	5.2 x 4.2m
Sitting room	6.4 x 5.0m
Bedroom 3	3.2 x 3.0m + bathroom

Master bedroom	6.3 x 4.0m + dressing room & bathroom
Bedroom 2	4.5 x 4.1m
Gallery	6.8 x 2.1m

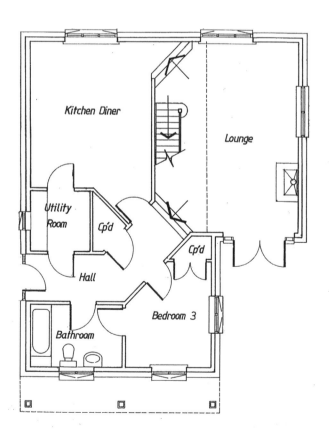

GROUND FLOOR

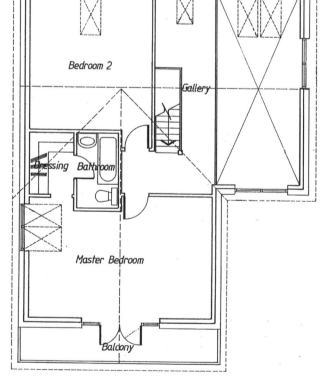

FIRST FLOOR

THE TITHE BARN

The copyright belongs to Scandia-Hus Limited

180 sq. m.

Overall dimensions 14.11 x 13.03m

R E A R   E L E V A T I O N

F R O N T   E L E V A T I O N

S I D E   E L E V A T I O N

You don't need to convert an old barn to get a home that looks and feels just like one. This design gives you all that you would want from an old barn but with a modern construction and more certain costings. Inside, whilst the atmosphere of the barn conversion is retained, the layout is of a modern family home with all of the facilities and features that one would expect.

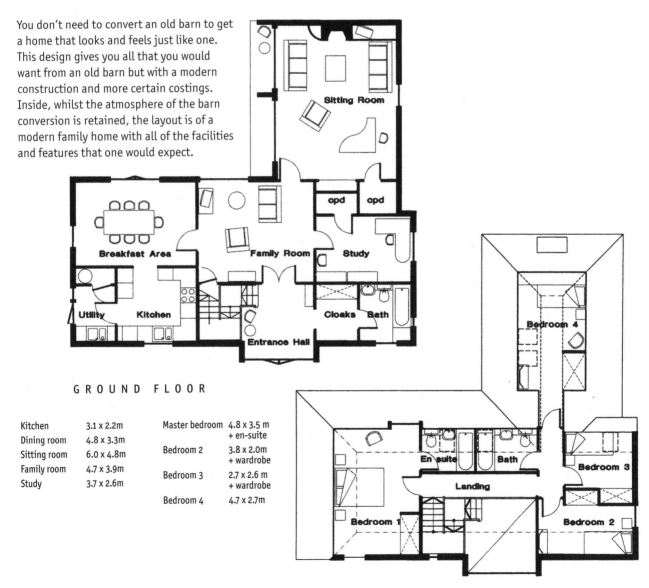

GROUND FLOOR

FIRST FLOOR

Kitchen	3.1 x 2.2m	Master bedroom	4.8 x 3.5 m + en-suite	
Dining room	4.8 x 3.3m	Bedroom 2	3.8 x 2.0m + wardrobe	
Sitting room	6.0 x 4.8m			
Family room	4.7 x 3.9m	Bedroom 3	2.7 x 2.6 m + wardrobe	
Study	3.7 x 2.6m	Bedroom 4	4.7 x 2.7m	

OAKLEY

The copyright belongs to Custom Homes Ltd.

180 sq. m.

Overall dimensions 17.3 x 8.8m

FRONT ELEVATION

SIDE ELEVATION

A house that fits onto a site with a width of less than eleven metres and yet provides five bedrooms all with an-suite facilities! Admittedly it is a deep house but not excessively so. The utility extension at the rear is interesting as it emulates the traditional additive development by being finished in differing materials.

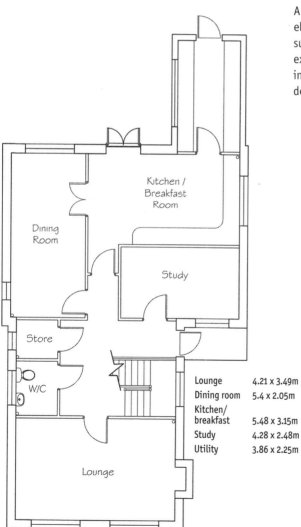

Lounge	4.21 x 3.49m
Dining room	5.4 x 2.05m
Kitchen/ breakfast	5.48 x 3.15m
Study	4.28 x 2.48m
Utility	3.86 x 2.25m

Bedroom 1	3.9 x 2.53m + en-suite
Bedroom 2	4.28 x 2.85m max + en-suite
Bedroom 3	3.0 x 2.78m + en-suite
Bedroom 4	3.49 x 2.93m + en-suite
Bedroom 5	3.08 x 2.78m + en-suite

GROUND FLOOR

FIRST FLOOR

CROWN COTTAGE

The copyright belongs to T. J. Crump OAKRIGHTS Ltd.

180 sq. m

Overall dimensions 15.05 x 6.54m

FRONT ELEVATION

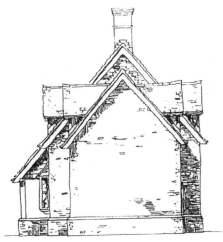

SIDE ELEVATION

Giving all of the appearance of a traditional English cottage, this is one of the smaller contributions to this book from this company. Yet one look at the wealth of accommodation provided shows that despite its quaint looks, it is, nevertheless a substantial family home.

GROUND FLOOR

FIRST FLOOR

Sitting room	6.17 x 3.73m
Breakfast room	3.38 x 3.05m
Dining Room	3.73 x 2.97m
Kitchen	3.73 x 3.05m
Utility	2.67 x 2.36m
Study	2.67 x 2.36m
Bedroom 1	3.73 x 2.95m + dressing room & en-suite
Bedroom 2	3.73 x 3.10m
Bedroom 3	3.73 x 3.05m
Bedroom 4	3.73 x 2.97m

GOLDCREST

The copyright belongs to Designer Homes

180 sq. m. including a garage of 19 sq. m.

Overall dimensions 10.85 x 10.85m

FRONT ELEVATION

Just when you think that this almost square home with an integral garage is going to be boring, the signature of this contributor shews up with the curved staircase. In fact this home is not at all boring, even without that. Note the fact that the landing goes right through to the rear wall giving it space for a window to light not only the landing, but down into the inner hallway.

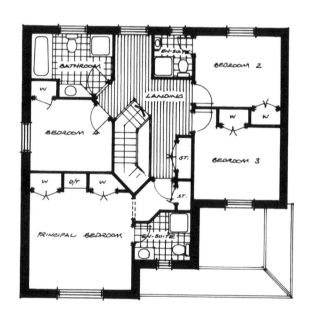

FIRST FLOOR

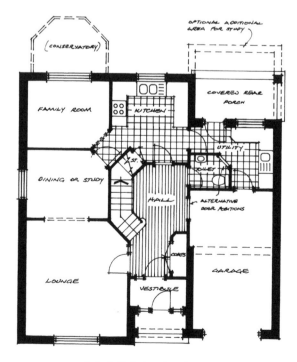

GROUND FLOOR

Lounge	4.65 x 4.19m	Principal bedroom	4.19 x 3.88m + wardrobes & en-suite
Dining room/ study	3.35 x 2.67m		
Family room	3.35 x 2.67m	Bedroom 2	3.50 x 2.90m + wardrobe & en-suite
Kitchen	3.20 x 3.12m		
Utility	3.40 x 2.35m max		
Garage	5.94 x 3.28m	Bedroom 3	3.50 x 2.90m + wardrobe
		Bedroom 4	3.35 x 2.82m + wardrobe

HAMPTON

The copyright belongs to Designer Homes

181 sq. m.

Overall dimensions 13 x 11.70m

FRONT ELEVATION

The symmetrical appearance to the front elevation, which would fit in with the local vernacular in many areas, belies the fact that this design is basically a 'T' shape. By pushing the accommodation back into this rear extension the designer is able to limit the height of the main roof. The eaves line is also dropped to halfway through the upstairs windows. This brings the ridge height down and creates sloping ceilings in the bedrooms without any loss of floor space.

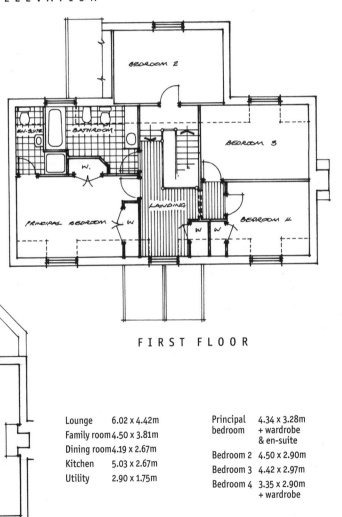

FIRST FLOOR

GROUND FLOOR

Lounge	6.02 x 4.42m	Principal bedroom	4.34 x 3.28m + wardrobe & en-suite
Family room	4.50 x 3.81m		
Dining room	4.19 x 2.67m		
Kitchen	5.03 x 2.67m	Bedroom 2	4.50 x 2.90m
Utility	2.90 x 1.75m	Bedroom 3	4.42 x 2.97m
		Bedroom 4	3.35 x 2.90m + wardrobe

CAXTON 96-033

The copyright belongs to Potton Ltd.

181 sq. m.

Overall dimensions 16.7 x 9.7m

FRONT ELEVATION

If this home was built on the minimum site width, the French doors to the sun room would have to be re-positioned or else the kitchen would have to be re-arranged for the sun room to be located at the back. The large kitchen/breakfast room would be an attraction for many.

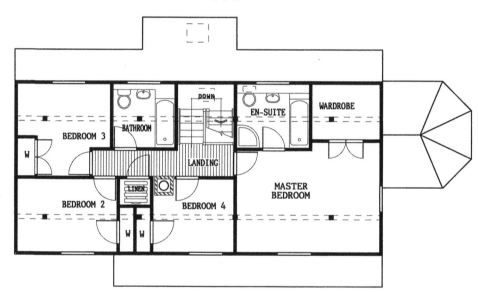

FIRST FLOOR

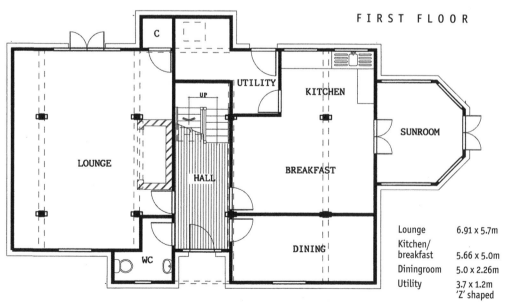

GROUND FLOOR

Lounge	6.91 x 5.7m	Bedroom 1	3.81 x 2.52m
Kitchen/ breakfast	5.66 x 5.0m	Bedroom 2	3.62 x 2.52m
Diningroom	5.0 x 2.26m	Bedroom 3	3.38 x 3.2m
Utility	3.7 x 1.2m 'Z' shaped	Bedroom 4	2.87 x 2.52m

OAKWEB- P

The copyright belongs to Potton Ltd.

181 sq. m.

Overall dimensions 14.3 x 9.7m

F R O N T   E L E V A T I O N

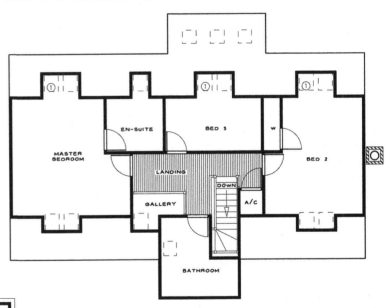

F I R S T   F L O O R

Another design that owes its conception to rural barns. This time, however, the internal arrangements follow the conventions for a modern house although the large hall would be an added feature.

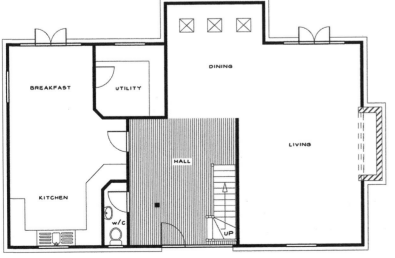

G R O U N D   F L O O R

Lounge	7.55 x 4.75m
Diningroom	4.3 x 3.6m
Kitchen/ breakfast	7.55 x 4.6m
Utility	2.7 x 2.7m
Master bedroom	4.6 x 4.4m max + en-suite
Bedroom 2	4.4 x 3.8m
Bedroom 3	3.8 x 2.0m

BALM COTTAGE

The copyright belongs to T. J. Crump OAKRIGHTS Ltd.

181 sq. m

Overall dimensions 15.04 x 8.70m

FRONT ELEVATION

SIDE ELEVATION

Another lovely cottage that within its petite exterior manages to hide a lot of accommodation. Having the main bedroom downstairs can be an asset for older or disabled people. Upstairs the large gallery can double up as an extra sitting room or even a workroom.

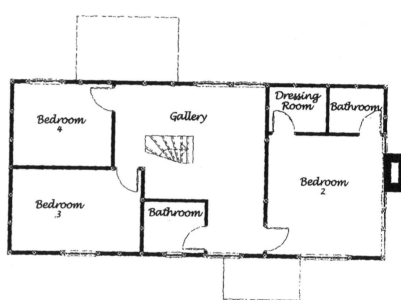

FIRST FLOOR

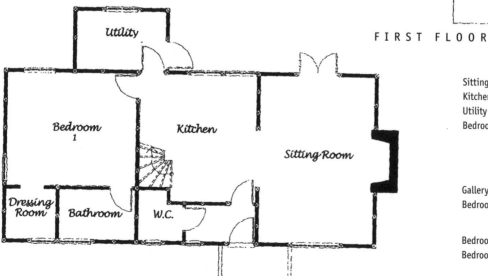

Sitting room	5.92 x 4.32m
Kitchen	4.47 x 4.45m
Utility	3.25 x 2.06m
Bedroom 1	4.88 x 4.01m + dressing room & bathroom
Gallery/sitting	5.97 x 5.61m
Bedroom 2	4.29 x 4.19m + dressing room & en-suite
Bedroom 3	4.87 x 2.87m
Bedroom 4	3.71 x 2.87m

GROUND FLOOR

LARK

The copyright belongs to Designer Homes

**181 sq. m.
including a garage
of 16 sq. m.**

Overall dimensions 15.85 x 13.15m

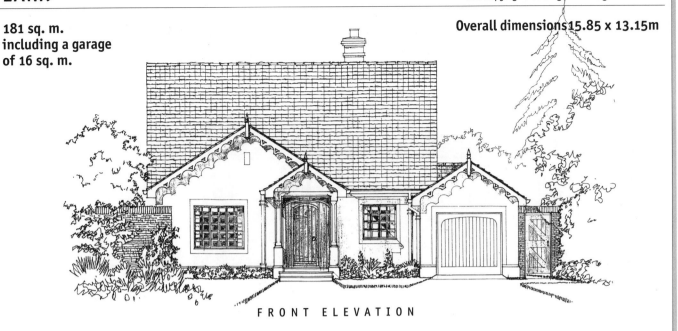

FRONT ELEVATION

Many sensitive sites have restrictions on the ridge height that one can build to. Sometimes the solution is a bungalow or a chalet bungalow or dormer style house. This is another solution to the problem. The roof is asymmetric. The slope at the front or road side is steeper than it is to the rear. From the front the house looks just like a bungalow and, if gable windows are inappropriate, sky lights can be used to light the bedrooms on the rear roof plane.

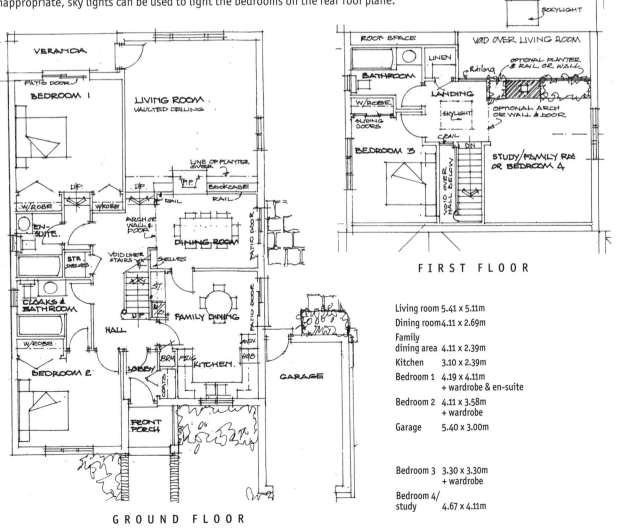

GROUND FLOOR

FIRST FLOOR

Living room 5.41 x 5.11m

Dining room 4.11 x 2.69m

Family
dining area 4.11 x 2.39m

Kitchen 3.10 x 2.39m

Bedroom 1 4.19 x 4.11m
+ wardrobe & en-suite

Bedroom 2 4.11 x 3.58m
+ wardrobe

Garage 5.40 x 3.00m

Bedroom 3 3.30 x 3.30m
+ wardrobe

Bedroom 4/
study 4.67 x 4.11m

01-262

The copyright belongs to Potton Ltd.

182 sq. m.

Overall dimensions 13 x 12.4m

FRONT ELEVATION

The sunroom is not essential to this design but it does, nevertheless, provide it with a central feature and one that cheers up the rear elevation. The master suite is generous but does not detract from the remaining three bedrooms, which are all of good size.

Lounge	6.75 x 4.7m
Kitchen/ breakfast	4.6 x 4.6m
Diningroom	4.45 x 3.7m
Sunroom	4.6 x 3.m7 max
Master bedroom	4.4 x 3.75m + wardrobe and en-suite
Bedroom 2	3.4 x 2.75m + wardrobe
Bedroom 3	3.2 x2.45m
Bedroom 4	3.4 x 3.3m

REAR ELEVATION

GROUND FLOOR

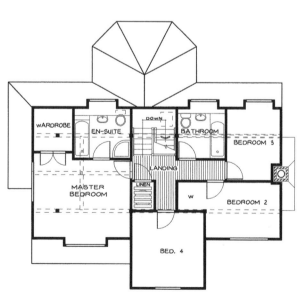

FIRST FLOOR

THE PADDOCKS

The copyright belongs to a ScAN architectural practice – S. Buttler

184 sq. m.

Overall dimensions 15.9 x 14.2m

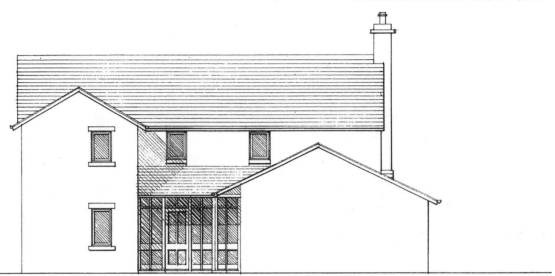

F R O N T   E L E V A T I O N

This attractive family home provides the whole range of accommodation that one would expect to find in a house of this size. The covered porch area is extended around and across the front of the garage door to allow easy access under cover, but it would not be difficult to arrange a door between the garage and the lobby if that was required.

F I R S T   F L O O R

G R O U N D   F L O O R

Lounge	6.2 x 4.4m		Bedroom 1	4.4 x 3.2m
Dining room	3.6 x 3.3m		Bedroom 2	4.4 x 3.3m
Kitchen	6.0 x 3.6m			+ dressing room
Study	3.4 x 3.4m			& en-suite
Utility	2.7 x 1.7m		Bedroom 3	3.6 x 3.3m
Garage	6.0 x 6.0m		Bedroom 4	3.4 x 3.4m

THE KUNGSVIK

The copyright belongs to Scandia-Hus Limited

185 sq. m.

Overall dimensions 13.51 x 9.01m

REAR ELEVATION

SIDE ELEVATION

It is no accident that these contributors always choose to list the kitchen first and then the dining or eating areas. They recognise that, for most families, this is the hub of their living environment. Not that this home skimps on all of the other facilities for, as well as the generous sitting room, the large landing is also utilised as further living accommodation.

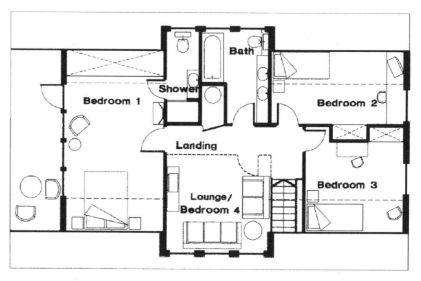

FIRST FLOOR

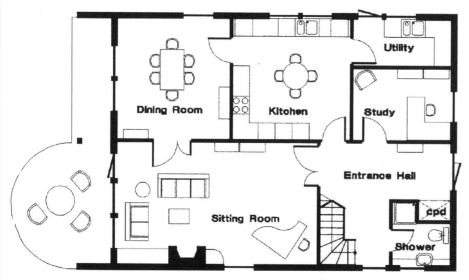

GROUND FLOOR

Kitchen	4.2 x 4.0m
Dining room	4.2 x 3.9m
Sitting room	7.0 x 4.2m
Study	3.5 x 2.5m
Master bedroom	5.2 x 3.4m + en-suite
Bedroom 2	4.6 x 2.5m
Bedroom 3	3.5 x 3.4m
TV Lounge/ Bedroom 4	3.5 x 3.1m

FURUDAL

The copyright belongs to The Swedish House Company Ltd.

185 sq. m.

Overall dimensions 13.2 x 8.55m.

As a concept in family living, this home is an interesting one with its accent on living accommodation taking centre stage. Clearly the guiding inspiration is that bedrooms are just somewhere to sleep and that they should be accessible to the lower and upper living areas with their verandahs and balconies.

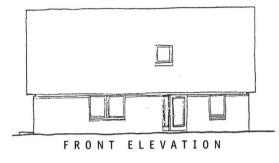

FRONT ELEVATION

NORTH ELEVATION

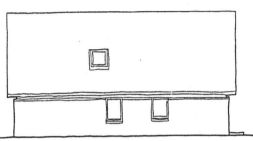

REAR ELEVATION

SOUTH ELEVATION

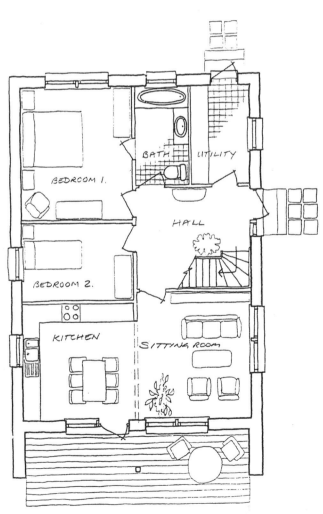

GROUND FLOOR

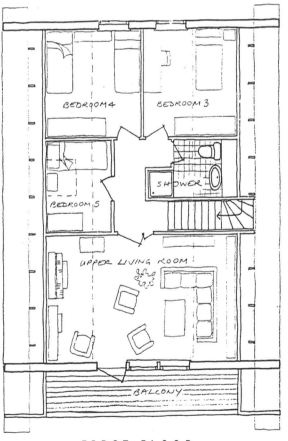

FIRST FLOOR

Sitting room	4.1 x 3.8m		Upper living room	6.6 x 4.1m
Kitchen	3.8 x 3.8m		Bedroom 3	3.5 x 3.3m
Utility	3.2 x 1.9m		Bedroom 4	3.5 x 3.2m
Bedroom 1	4.3 x 3.8m + bathroom		Bedroom 5	3.0 x 3.2m
Bedroom 2	3.8 x 2.5m			

HOUSES 186 TO 230 SQ. M.

When one gets to houses of these sizes the scope for accommodation really begins to take off. Extra rooms can be had without compromising other main rooms. If what you want is a wide and impressive entrance area then it can be had without loss. If you decide that a great or dining hall is what you want then its provision, complete with an impressive staircase, ceases to be a problem. The breakfast area no longer needs to be a part of the kitchen and it can take its place as a room in its own right. The family room is almost a standard feature without the need to let go of the idea of a separate study or office.

More than one of the bedrooms, if it stays at just four, can have en-suite facilities and all of them can be double with fully built in wardrobes. Dressing rooms also become more common at these sizes and in some designs there is scope for the number of bedrooms to increase.

At this size the building can start to assert itself and employ individualistic architectural features.

Contributors in this section:
Associated Self Build Architects
The Border Design Centre
T.J.Crump OAKWRIGHTS Ltd.
Custom Homes Ltd.
Design & Materials Ltd.
Designer Homes
Potton Ltd.
The Self Build House Company Ltd.
Scottish Architects Network
Scandia-Hus Ltd.
The Swedish House Company Ltd.

YARROW

The copyright belongs to Designer Homes

**186 sq. m.
including a garage of 22 sq. m.**

Overall dimensions 15.20 x 11.15m

FRONT ELEVATION

This design has varied roof lines that tend to draw the eye down, reducing the visual impact of what is, after all, quite a large family home. The regulations require a toilet on the entrance floor. It is positioned at the back for ease of access from the family rooms and garage.

GROUND FLOOR

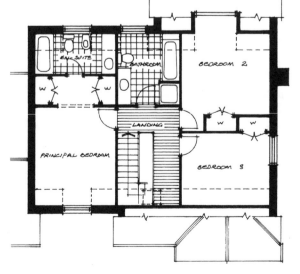

FIRST FLOOR

Lounge	4.80 x 4.72m	Principal bedroom	4.11 x 3.50m + dressing room & en-suite
Dining room	3.58 x 2.44m		
Family room	3.50 x 3.28m		
Kitchen	3.81 x 3.43m	Bedroom 2	3.81 x 3.43 + wardrobe
Utility	2.15 x 1.70m		
Study/ bedroom 4	3.58 x 3.12m	Bedroom 3	3.81 x 3.05m
Garage	6.25 x 3.60m		

02-910

186 sq. m.

Overall dimensions 17.3 x 9.8m

F R O N T   E L E V A T I O N

S I D E   E L E V A T I O N

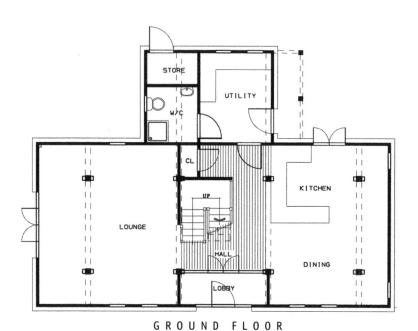

G R O U N D   F L O O R

A design that unashamedly copies a traditional country barn and which probably looks at its best when clad in timber. The large lounge and the almost equally large kitchen lie on either side of the central hall and the utility and store with showering facilities would appeal to those who favoured the outside life.

Lounge	5.75 x 5.2m
Dining/kitchen	5.75 x 4.4m
Utility	3.2 x 2.7m
Bedroom 1	5.75 x 3.3m
Bedroom 2	4.4 x 2.8m
Bedroom 3	4.4 x 2.8m
Bedroom 4	3.2 x 2.8m

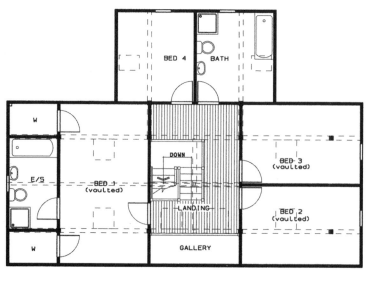

F I R S T   F L O O R

ELMLEY

The copyright belongs to T. J. Crump OAKRIGHTS Ltd.

187 sq. m.

Overall dimensions 16.10 x 7.70m

F R O N T   E L E V A T I O N

S I D E   E L E V A T I O N

So many traditional features find their way into this family home. In the past many homes evolved over the years. This was known as 'additive development' and this is apparent in the solid wall construction of the utility room. Note also the cantilevered section allowing the upper part to be larger.

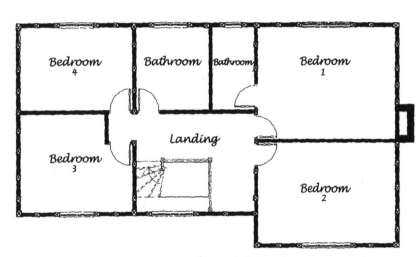

F I R S T   F L O O R

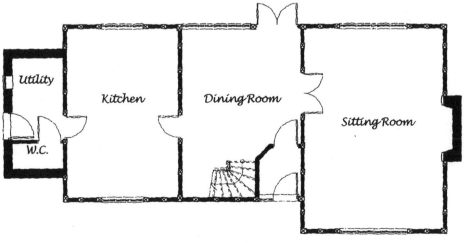

G R O U N D   F L O O R

Sitting room	6.73 x 4.93m
Dining room	5.64 x 4.14m
Kitchen	5.64 x 3.96m
Utility	2.77 x 1.75m
Bedroom 1	4.93 x 3.68m + en-suite
Bedroom 2	4.93 x 3.68m
Bedroom 3	3.96 x 3.23m
Bedroom 4	3.84 x 2.77m

PATTERDALE

The copyright belongs to Designer Homes

186 sq. m.
including a garage of 21 sq. m.

Overall dimensions 18.50 x 10.00m

F R O N T   E L E V A T I O N

Once again the trademark design quirk of this contributor shows up in the angled internal walls and the steps within and down to certain rooms. It makes for an exciting internal design that, nevertheless, conforms to the norms as far as the outside appearance is concerned. The accommodation flows nicely from room to room with the kitchen/breakfast room at the hub.

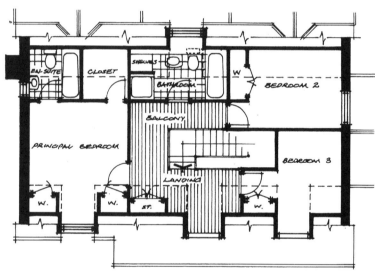

F I R S T   F L O O R

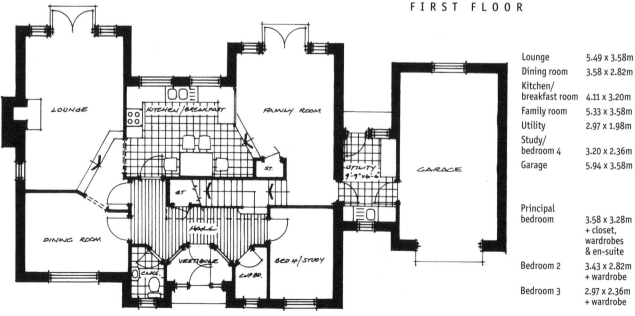

G R O U N D   F L O O R

Lounge	5.49 x 3.58m
Dining room	3.58 x 2.82m
Kitchen/ breakfast room	4.11 x 3.20m
Family room	5.33 x 3.58m
Utility	2.97 x 1.98m
Study/ bedroom 4	3.20 x 2.36m
Garage	5.94 x 3.58m
Principal bedroom	3.58 x 3.28m + closet, wardrobes & en-suite
Bedroom 2	3.43 x 2.82m + wardrobe
Bedroom 3	2.97 x 2.36m + wardrobe

TIPPERARY

The copyright belongs to Designer Homes

**188 sq. m.
including a garage of 33 sq. m.**

Overall dimensions 13.20 x 11.00m

FRONT ELEVATION

This smart four bedroom house would look good in many street scenes. It has an extremely high pitched roof which would lend itself to be tiled with some of the plain clay tiles. Once again this contributor has to show something out of the ordinary and that is done by lowering the window line in the main bedroom and introducing the arched head.

FIRST FLOOR

Living room	5.99 x 3.61m
Dining room	3.61 x 3.30m
Kitchen	3.61 x 2.69m
Breakfast room	3.02 x 2.31m
Utility	2.25 x 1.75m
Garage	6.45 x 4.75m
Bedroom 1	4.80 x 3.61m + closet & en-suite
Bedroom 2	4.80 x 3.02m + wardrobes
Bedroom 3	3.61 x 3.61m + wardrobe
Bedroom 4	3.02 x 2.69m + wardrobe

GROUND FLOOR

PASTURES VIEW

The copyright belongs to an ASBA architectural practice – S. Buttler

188 sq. m.
including a garage of 44 sq. m.

Overall dimensions 15.2 x 12.6m

FRONT ELEVATION

The garage is a fairly hefty proportion of this home's overall size and gives an adequate demonstration of the fact that its costs cannot be ignored and, indeed, in some cases should be counted in as part of the overall calculations. This garage, like so many, shares the same foundations, walling and roofing as the main house including the tabled verges. It has windows and expensive doors and the only trade not fully represented might be the plasterer.

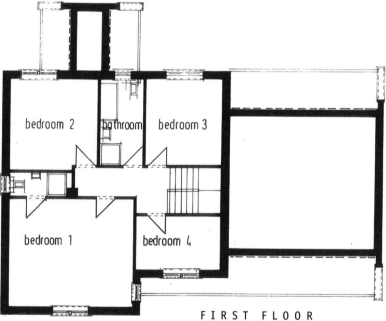

FIRST FLOOR

GROUND FLOOR

Lounge	5.0 x 4.1m
Dining room	4.5 x 3.5m
Kitchen	4.8 x 3.3m
Sun room	3.2 x 2.25m
Garage	7.9 x 5.75m
Bedroom 1	4.9 x 4.15m + en-suite
Bedroom 2	3.5 x 3.45m
Bedroom 3	3.3 x 3.0m
Bedroom 4	3.3 x 2.0m

LINDISFARNE

The copyright belongs to The Border Design Centre

190 sq. m.
including a garage of 16 sq. m.

Overall dimensions 14.3 x 13.8m

FRONT ELEVATION

This house was designed for a site in Northumberland overlooking Lindisfarne, hence the balcony off the study. With a little re-arrangement and slight change of names this could be classified as a four bedroom home or, alternatively, in a situation where the study would be better off downstairs; it could change places with bedroom 2.

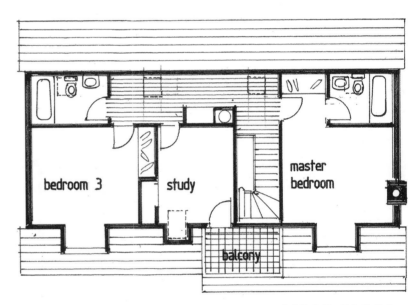

FIRST FLOOR

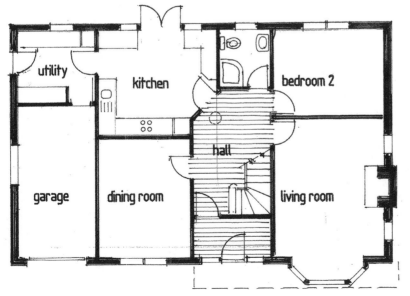

GROUND FLOOR

Living room	5.77 x 4.11m
Dining room	4.39 x 3.50m
Kitchen	4.39 x 3.81m + utility area
Bedroom 2	4.11 x 2.99m
Garage	5.5 x 2.85m
Master bedroom	4.11 x 3.50m + wardrobe & en-suite
Bedroom 3	4.11 x 3.50m + wardrobe
Study	3.50 x 2.89m

HOME FARM VIEW

The copyright belongs to an ASBA architectural practice – S.Buttler

191 sq. m.
including a garage of 40 sq. m.

Overall dimensions 21.1 x 13.9m

Why do garages have to be square to the house? The answer is that they don't and this house is a marvellous illustration of that point. Having the garage facing the road can make the garage doors into the dominant architectural feature. The usual solution to that problem is to have the garage doors facing across the plot. If, however, turning space is restricted, this design could be the answer.

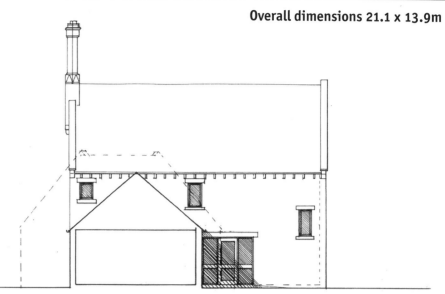

FRONT ELEVATION

Kitchen	4.7 x 3.7m
Lounge	7.1 x 4.4m
Dining room	4.6 x 3.1m
Sun room	4.5 x 2.4m
Utility	2.0 x 1.9m
Garage	6.7 x 6.0m

Bedroom 1	4.4 x 3.5m + en-suite
Bedroom 2	4.4 x 3.5m
Bedroom 3	3.5 x 3.4m
Bedroom 4	3.7 x 3.0m

GROUND FLOOR

FIRST FLOOR

BENINGTON-P

The copyright belongs to Potton Ltd.

**192 sq. m
including a garage of 29 sq. m.**

Overall dimensions 13.5 x 11.8m

FRONT ELEVATION

A comfortable suburban home which, with a slight variation on the external materials, would fit into most street scenes. The French doors at the rear give scope for the addition of a conservatory or sun room and the garage is large enough for two family sized cars.

GROUND FLOOR

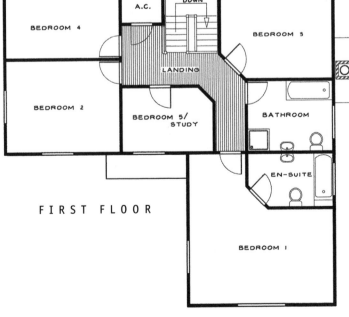

FIRST FLOOR

Lounge	5.7 x 4.1m
Kitchen	3.8 x 2.75m
Dining room	3.8 x 2.9m
Utility	1.8 x 1.75m
Garage	5.3 x 5.3m

Bedroom 1	5.3 x 5.3m including en-suite
Bedroom 2	4.2 x 3.3m
Bedroom 3	4.1 x 3.15m
Bedroom 4	4.2 x 2.4m
Bedroom 5/ study	3.3 x 2.3m

WILLOW WARBLER

The copyright belongs to Designer Homes

193 sq. m. including a garage of 18 sq. m.

Overall dimensions 15.50 x 14.25m

FRONT ELEVATION

This substantial family house has a distinctly cottage feel to it that is not entirely due to the illustration of the porch area with the climbing rose. The catslide roof coming down onto the garage draws the eye down. The hipped main roof lessens the visual impact of the house and the forward projection adds interest and complexity. Inside the signature of this contributor is shown in the offset walls and curved staircase.

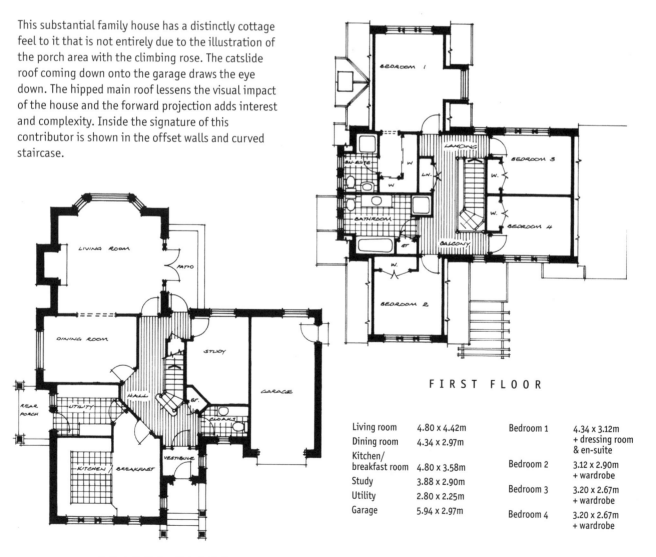

FIRST FLOOR

GROUND FLOOR

Living room	4.80 x 4.42m	Bedroom 1	4.34 x 3.12m + dressing room & en-suite
Dining room	4.34 x 2.97m		
Kitchen/ breakfast room	4.80 x 3.58m	Bedroom 2	3.12 x 2.90m + wardrobe
Study	3.88 x 2.90m		
Utility	2.80 x 2.25m	Bedroom 3	3.20 x 2.67m + wardrobe
Garage	5.94 x 2.97m	Bedroom 4	3.20 x 2.67m + wardrobe

WELWYN

The copyright belongs to Custom Homes Ltd.

194 sq. m.

Overall dimensions 15.8 x 10.5m

In some areas the ridge height of the proposed dwelling is a sensitive planning issue and steps have to be taken to bring it down. This design does that by introducing a 'flat top' to what would otherwise be the highest ridge point. By lowering the eaves line at the same time, the eye is 'drawn down'. Loss of space to the upper part is minimised by the acceptance of lower ceiling heights to certain outside walls.

FRONT ELEVATION

Lounge	6.31 x 5.11m
Dining room	3.48 x 2.72m
Kitchen	4.83 x 3.16m
Family room	4.56 x 3.16m
Study	3.68 x 2.08m

Bedroom 1	5.91 x 4.49m max + en-suite
Bedroom 2	4.67 x 3.16 + en-suite
Bedroom 3	4.48 x 3.22m max
Bedroom 4	4.48 x 3.22m max

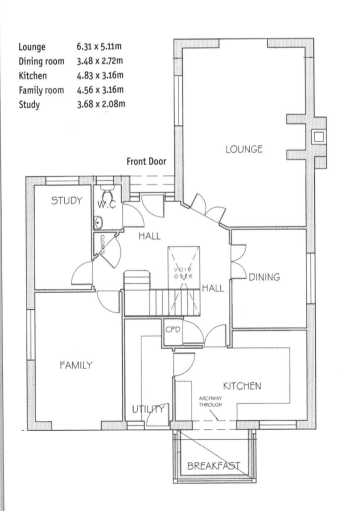

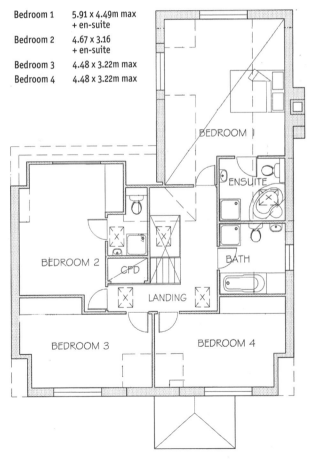

GROUND FLOOR

FIRST FLOOR

DALFORS

The copyright belongs to The Swedish House Company Ltd.

194 sq. m.   **Overall dimensions 13.95 x 8.55m**

 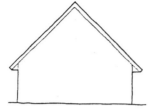 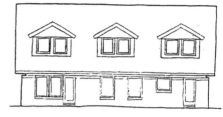

F R O N T   E L E V A T I O N   S I D E   E L E V A T I O N   R E A R   E L E V A T I O N

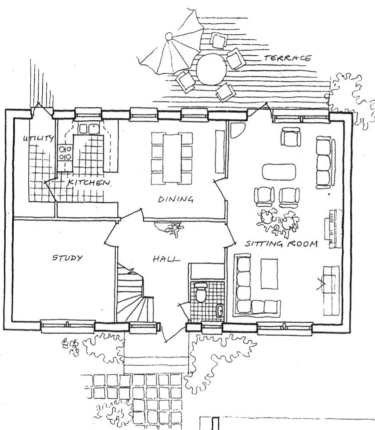

A simple name change for the study would make this lovely home into a one with five bedrooms. Alternatively, given its size, that room could be a family room or second sitting room. All the upstairs bedrooms would have sloping ceilings, offset by the generous size of the dormers.

GROUND FLOOR

Sitting room	7.8 x 4.6m
Dining room	4.3 x 3.8m
Kitchen	3.8 x 2.4m
Utility	3.8 x 1.7m
Study	4.1 x 3.9m
Bedroom 1	4.1 x 3.6m + dressing room & bathroom
Bedroom 2	4.2 x 3.4m
Bedroom 3	4.2 x 3.1m
Bedroom 4	4.2 x 2.4m

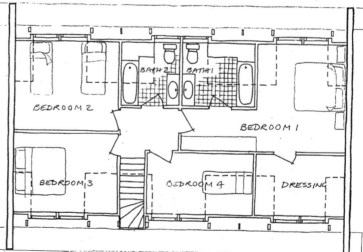

F I R S T   F L O O R

BRAMBLING

**196 sq. m.
including a garage of 30 sq. m.**

The copyright belongs to Designer Homes

Overall dimensions 17.10 x 11.95m

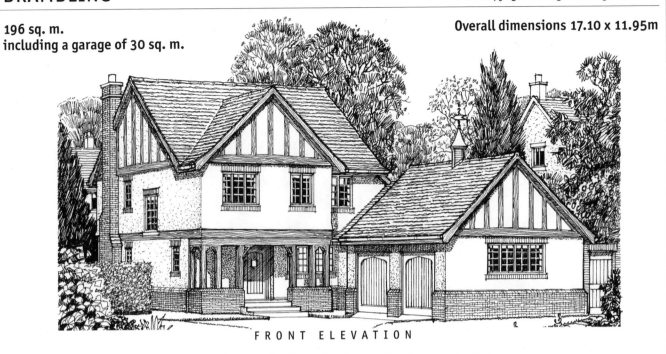

FRONT ELEVATION

Projecting the front bedroom gable extension forward and supporting it on massive timbers means that there is room underneath for the large front porch. This gives a certain grandeur to this four bedroom family home. The garage is set forward, attached to the house via the utility room and with its doors facing across the plot. The timbered upper gables mirror the porch detail.

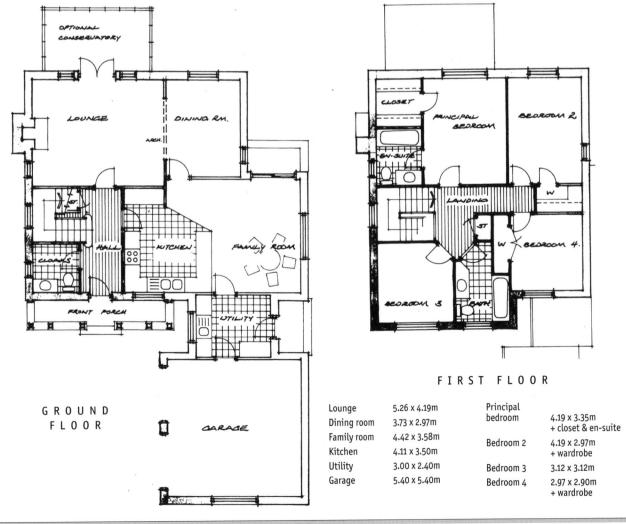

GROUND FLOOR

FIRST FLOOR

Lounge	5.26 x 4.19m		Principal bedroom	4.19 x 3.35m + closet & en-suite
Dining room	3.73 x 2.97m			
Family room	4.42 x 3.58m		Bedroom 2	4.19 x 2.97m + wardrobe
Kitchen	4.11 x 3.50m			
Utility	3.00 x 2.40m		Bedroom 3	3.12 x 3.12m
Garage	5.40 x 5.40m		Bedroom 4	2.97 x 2.90m + wardrobe

GAMLNG – P

The copyright belongs to Potton Ltd.

196 sq. m. including a 32 sq. m. garage

Overall dimensions 14.4 x 12.25m

FRONT ELEVATION

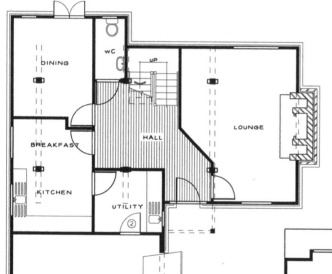

GROUND FLOOR

Positioning the garage door so that it faces across the site means that, on a narrow site, the turn in could be quite tight. Nevertheless, it means that the garage, whilst taking up almost a third of the ground floor area, does not become the dominant architectural feature.

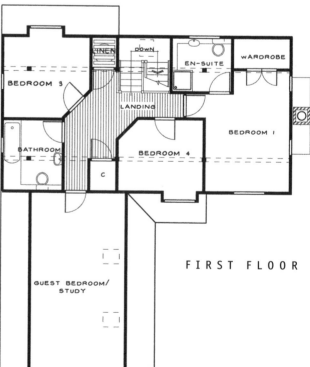

FIRST FLOOR

Lounge	5.8 x 4.5m	Bedroom 1	4.5 x 3.25m + wardrobe & en-suite	
Dining room	3.7 x 3.1m			
Kitchen/ breakfast	4.2 x 3.1m	Bedroom 2 (Guest)	6.8 x 3.6m	
Utility	3.6 x 2.3m	Bedroom 3	3.3 x 3.0m	
Garage	5.7 x 5.6m	Bedroom 4	3.3 x 2.7m	

SANDMARTIN

The copyright belongs to Designer Homes

**198 sq. m.
including a garage
of 32 sq. m.**

Overall dimensions 18.10 x 13.40m

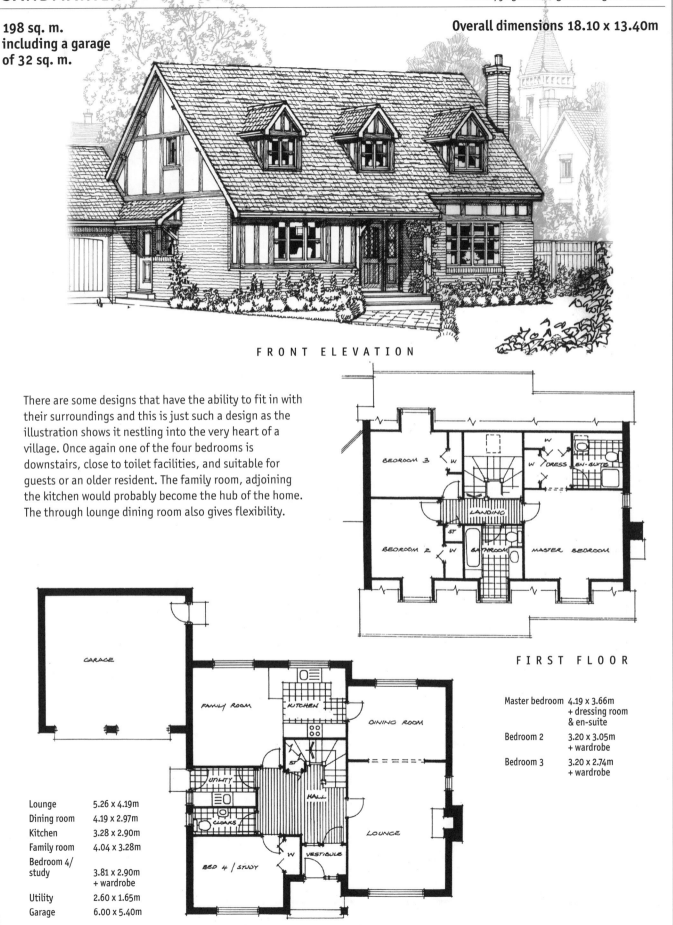

FRONT ELEVATION

There are some designs that have the ability to fit in with their surroundings and this is just such a design as the illustration shows it nestling into the very heart of a village. Once again one of the four bedrooms is downstairs, close to toilet facilities, and suitable for guests or an older resident. The family room, adjoining the kitchen would probably become the hub of the home. The through lounge dining room also gives flexibility.

FIRST FLOOR

Master bedroom 4.19 x 3.66m
+ dressing room
& en-suite

Bedroom 2   3.20 x 3.05m
+ wardrobe

Bedroom 3   3.20 x 2.74m
+ wardrobe

Lounge   5.26 x 4.19m
Dining room   4.19 x 2.97m
Kitchen   3.28 x 2.90m
Family room   4.04 x 3.28m
Bedroom 4/
study   3.81 x 2.90m
               + wardrobe
Utility   2.60 x 1.65m
Garage   6.00 x 5.40m

GROUND FLOOR

GRANSDEN 02-911

The copyright belongs to Potton Ltd.

199 sq. m.

Overall dimensions 15.8 x 9.7m

FRONT ELEVATION

A long rectangle with a lean-to extension is often the hallmark of a traditional barn and it is the simplicity of shape that gives it elegance. The vaulted ceilings to the upstairs bedrooms give extra character but, for those who would find this uncomfortable, this is something that could easily be changed.

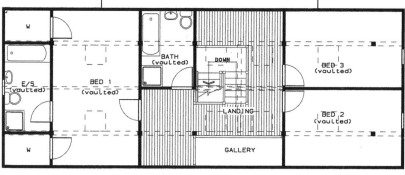

FIRST FLOOR

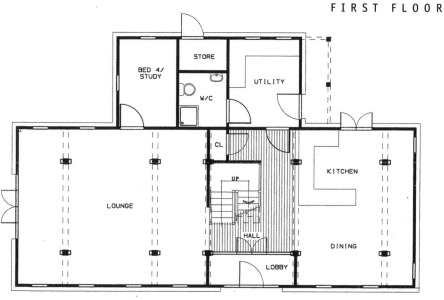

GROUND FLOOR

Lounge	7.3 x 5.25m
Dining/kitchen	5.25 x 4.4m
Utility	3.2 x 2.7m
Study/bedroom 4	3.2 x 2.25m
Bedroom 1	5.3 x 3.3m + wardrobe & en-suite
Bedroom 2	4.4 x 2.8m
Bedroom 3	4.4 x 2.8m

THE HALLAND

The copyright belongs to Scandia-Hus Limited

200 sq. m.

Overall dimensions 13.51 x 9.01m

FRONT ELEVATION

SIDE ELEVATION

This chalet bungalow has four good sized bedrooms to complement the generous ground floor living accommodation. Each bedroom has sloping ceilings, giving them a distinctive character with the large dormer windows providing cosy seating areas.

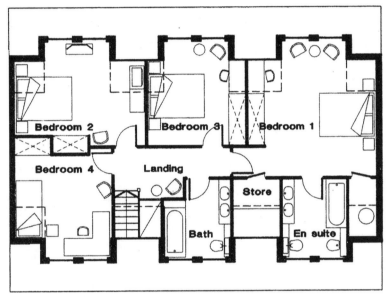

FIRST FLOOR

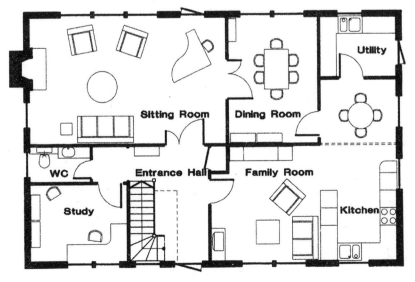

GROUND FLOOR

Kitchen	4.0 x 2.7m
Breakfast area	2.7 x 2.1m
Dining room	4.3 x 2.1m
Sitting room	6.9 x 4.3m
Family room	4.0 x 3.8m
Study	3.4 x 2.7m
Master bedroom	4.9 x 4.6 m + en-suite
Bedroom 2	4.6 x 3.8m
Bedroom 3	3.8 x 3.5m
Bedroom 4	3.4 x 3.3m

D270 – 2

The copyright belongs to Design & Materials Ltd.

**201 sq. m.
including a garage of 20 sq. m.**

Overall dimensions 16 x 13.8m

FRONT ELEVATION

Two themes stand out with this design. Light is the first with vaulted ceilings and gable head windows to the lounge and the upper part gallery sitting area. The second is flexibility of accommodation. Either there are three bedrooms upstairs with a study plus two bedrooms downstairs or there are six bedrooms. But what's in name? Maybe the downstairs bedrooms could be something entirely different.

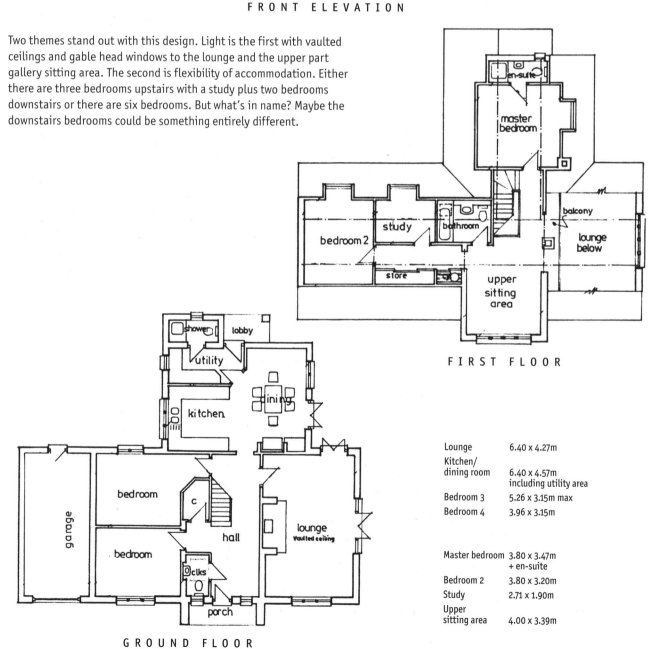

FIRST FLOOR

GROUND FLOOR

Lounge	6.40 x 4.27m
Kitchen/ dining room	6.40 x 4.57m including utility area
Bedroom 3	5.26 x 3.15m max
Bedroom 4	3.96 x 3.15m
Master bedroom	3.80 x 3.47m + en-suite
Bedroom 2	3.80 x 3.20m
Study	2.71 x 1.90m
Upper sitting area	4.00 x 3.39m

WATERFORD

The copyright belongs to Potton Ltd.

202 sq. m.

Overall dimensions 12.9 x 12.85m

FRONT ELEVATION

This is a very nice sized family house with a wealth of accommodation arranged in a compact shape that would allow it to fit comfortably on many plots. The forward projecting central gable at the front is countered by the two at the back, making both major elevations interesting.

FIRST FLOOR

GROUND FLOOR

Lounge	5.9 x 4.1m	Bedroom 1	4.4 x 4.1m + en-suite
Kitchen	4.1 x 4.1m		
Breakfast room	3.8 x 3.4m	Bedroom 2	4.1 x 3.5m + en-suite
Utility	2.7 x 1.7m		
Dining room	4.1 x 4.1m	Bedroom 3	4.1 x 3.3m max
Family room	4.0 x 3.7m max	Bedroom 4	4.2 x 2.4m
		Bedroom 5	3.7 x 3.3m max

WHITNEY

The copyright belongs to T. J. Crump OAKRIGHTS Ltd.

202 sq. m.

Overall dimensions 16.70 x 10.22m

FRONT ELEVATION

SIDE ELEVATION

What's in a name? The designers of this home have chosen to have two of the bedrooms on the ground floor whilst the sitting room and master suite are on the top floor. Maybe that's to take advantage of a view from the balcony. Maybe it just reflects the family life and requirements that were anticipated.

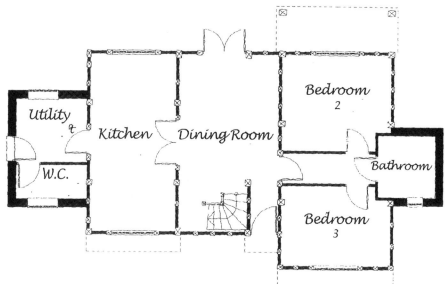

GROUND FLOOR

FIRST FLOOR

Kitchen	6.40 x 3.20m
Utility	2.74 x 2.13m
Dining room	6.40 x 3.84m
Bedroom 2	4.11 x 3,53m
Bedroom 3	4.11 x 2.87m
Sitting room	7.54 x 4.11m
Study	2.64 x 2.46m
Bedroom 1	6.96 x 3.25m + en-suite

THE WEALDEN

The copyright belongs to Scandia-Hus Limited

204 sq. m.

Overall dimensions 14.41 x 11.11m

This lovely home combines all the character of a traditional Wealden house with Scandinavian living principles. Once again, light and its conduct to within the deepest interiors of the home, is behind the thinking. So too with the idea that accommodation should, wherever possible, be flexible enough to adapt to ever changing family life.

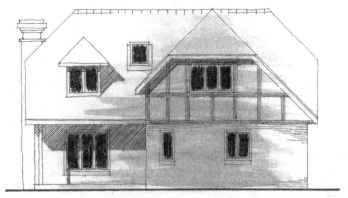

FRONT ELEVATION

SIDE ELEVATION

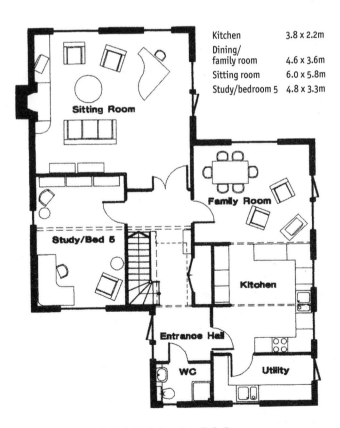

Kitchen	3.8 x 2.2m
Dining/family room	4.6 x 3.6m
Sitting room	6.0 x 5.8m
Study/bedroom 5	4.8 x 3.3m

GROUND FLOOR

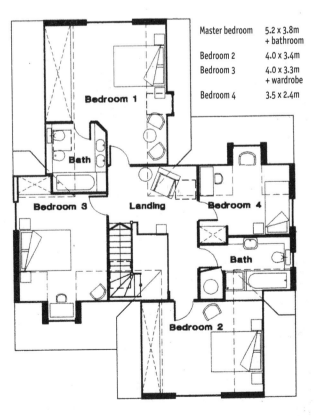

Master bedroom	5.2 x 3.8m + bathroom
Bedroom 2	4.0 x 3.4m
Bedroom 3	4.0 x 3.3m + wardrobe
Bedroom 4	3.5 x 2.4m

FIRST FLOOR

SHENMORE

The copyright belongs to T. J. Crump OAKRIGHTS Ltd.

205 sq. m.
including a carport of 36 sq. m.

Overall dimensions 15.55 x 15.13m

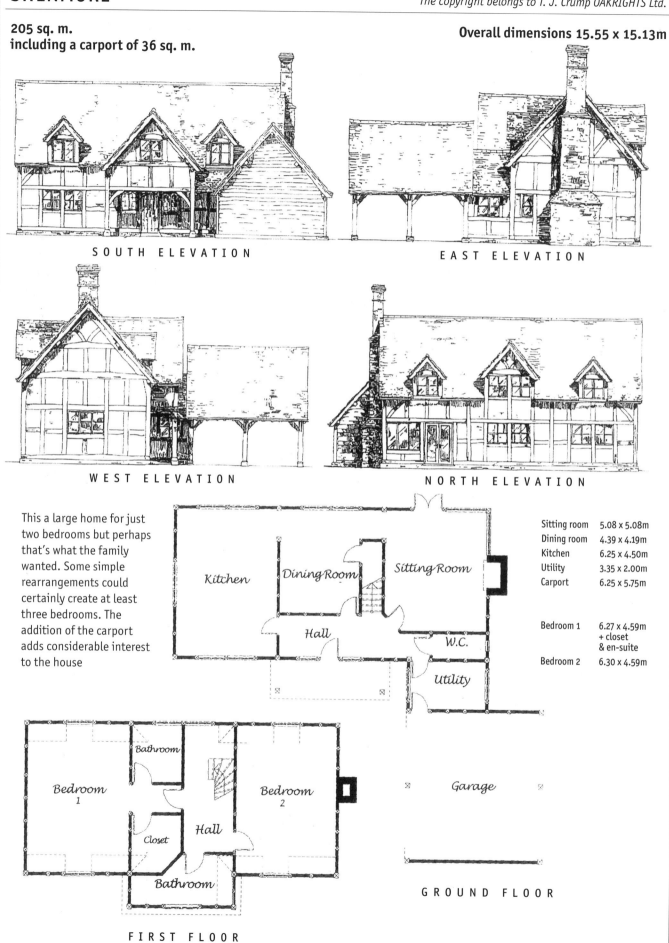

SOUTH ELEVATION

EAST ELEVATION

WEST ELEVATION

NORTH ELEVATION

This a large home for just two bedrooms but perhaps that's what the family wanted. Some simple rearrangements could certainly create at least three bedrooms. The addition of the carport adds considerable interest to the house

Sitting room	5.08 x 5.08m
Dining room	4.39 x 4.19m
Kitchen	6.25 x 4.50m
Utility	3.35 x 2.00m
Carport	6.25 x 5.75m
Bedroom 1	6.27 x 4.59m + closet & en-suite
Bedroom 2	6.30 x 4.59m

GROUND FLOOR

FIRST FLOOR

PUFFIN

207 sq. m. including a garage of 15 sq. m.

Overall dimensions 14.30 x 13.00m

F R O N T   E L E V A T I O N

One of the distinguishing features of this home is the large family/breakfast room at the rear and adjoining the kitchen. This is an idea that has become increasingly common over the past few years with busy mothers wanting to know that their young children have space to play, whilst needing to keep an eye on them. It also doubles up as the family living room leaving the lounge for 'best'.

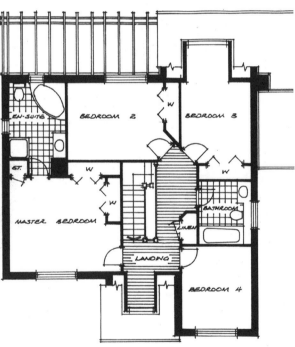

F I R S T   F L O O R

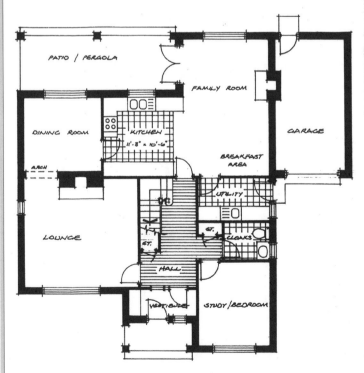

G R O U N D   F L O O R

Lounge	4.80 x 4.11m	Master bedroom	4.80 x 3.81m + en-suite & wardrobes
Dining room	3.28 x 2.97m		
Kitchen	3.43 x 3.20m	Bedroom 2	4.11 x 3.20m + wardrobe
Family room	5.94 x 3.58m		
Study/ bedroom 5	3.43 x 2.97m	Bedroom 3	4.80 x 2.97m + wardrobe
Utility	2.97 x 1.70m	Bedroom 4	3.43 x 2.97m
Garage	5.35 x 2.90m		

THE MEADOWS

The copyright belongs to an ASBA architectural practice – S. Buttler

**208 sq. m.
including a garage of 39 sq. m.**

Overall dimensions 17.8 x 14.7m

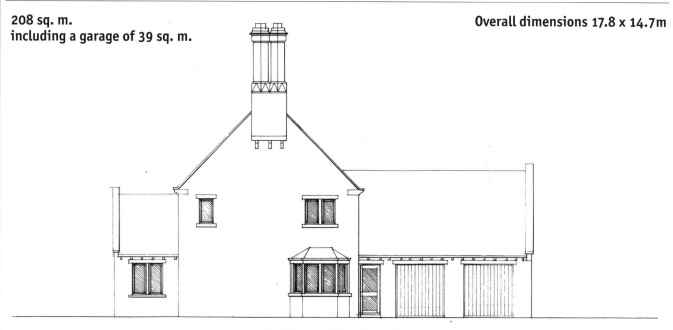

F R O N T   E L E V A T I O N

The tall chimney is a feature of this house, which was originally designed to fit in with a 'gingerbread' house that was retained within the group of homes. This is a home of solidity. It stands four square to the elements and defies them with its tabled verges and mullioned windows.

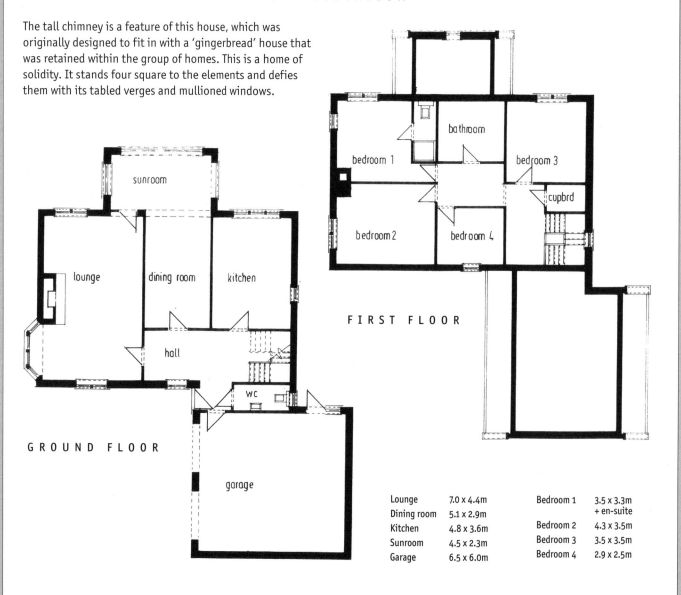

FIRST FLOOR

GROUND FLOOR

Lounge	7.0 x 4.4m		Bedroom 1	3.5 x 3.3m
Dining room	5.1 x 2.9m			+ en-suite
Kitchen	4.8 x 3.6m		Bedroom 2	4.3 x 3.5m
Sunroom	4.5 x 2.3m		Bedroom 3	3.5 x 3.5m
Garage	6.5 x 6.0m		Bedroom 4	2.9 x 2.5m

STRATHBLANE

The copyright belongs to Designer Homes

213 sq. m.

Overall dimensions 14.95 x 10.50m

FRONT ELEVATION

An 'L' or 'T' shaped house or bungalow often presents difficulties about just where to have the entrance. The answer, given in this design, is to have it in the corner at an angle and then to proclaim its presence by making it into a feature with a tower roof. Minor re-arrangements of the doors into the cloaks room could make the study into an en-suite bedroom.

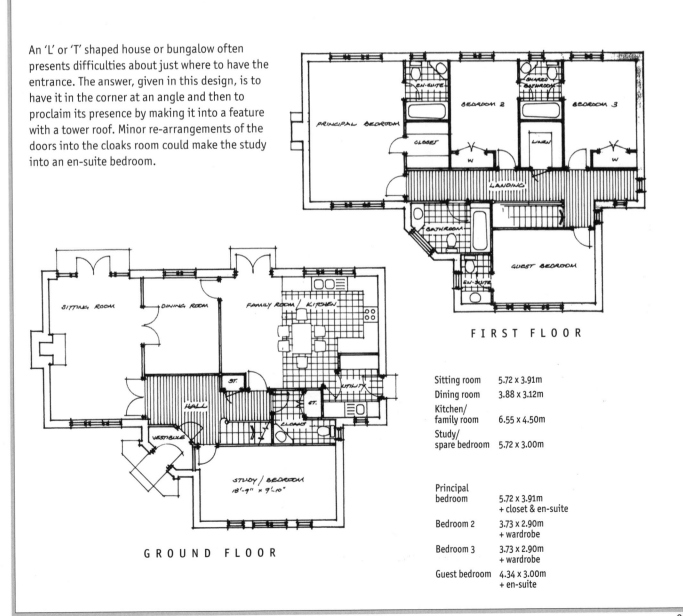

FIRST FLOOR

GROUND FLOOR

Sitting room	5.72 x 3.91m
Dining room	3.88 x 3.12m
Kitchen/ family room	6.55 x 4.50m
Study/ spare bedroom	5.72 x 3.00m
Principal bedroom	5.72 x 3.91m + closet & en-suite
Bedroom 2	3.73 x 2.90m + wardrobe
Bedroom 3	3.73 x 2.90m + wardrobe
Guest bedroom	4.34 x 3.00m + en-suite

THE ROWSTOCK

The copyright belongs to an ASBA architectural practice – Four Square Design Ltd.

215 sq. m.

Overall dimensions 15.72 x 9.38m

FRONT ELEVATION

The double bay windows to the drawing room and dining room give the frontage of this home a distinctive character. Further back and on each side, additional bay windows to the drawing room and the family room allow more light to flood into the main living areas. This is a hipped roof house but it is also a home that would look at its best on a wide site where the gardens could surround it.

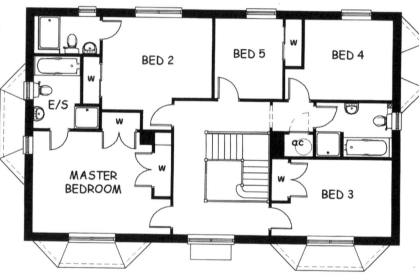

FIRST FLOOR

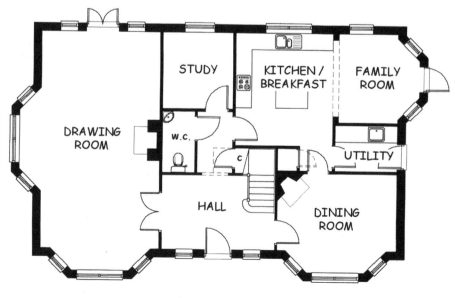

GROUND FLOOR

Drawing room	7.9 x 4.4m	
Dining room	4.4 x 2.8m	
Family room	3.2 x 2.2m	
Study	3.8 x 2.6m	
Kitchen/ breakfast room	4.1 x 3.6m	
Utility	2.3 x 1.7m	
Master bedroom	4.4 x 3.7m + wardrobes & en-suite	
Bedroom 2	3.4 x 2.9m + en-suite	
Bedroom 3	4.4 x 2.8m + wardrobe	
Bedroom 4	2.9 x 2.5m + wardrobe	

DENHOLM

The copyright belongs to Designer Homes

219 sq. m.

**Overall dimensions
13.00 x 11.95m**

FRONT ELEVATION

The frontage of this house has a certain symmetry with the equal bays on either side of the entrance doors with the projected gable above. Inside, the octagonal entrance hallway and gallery above allow unrestricted access to all rooms with the minimum of space taken up. The symmetry is deliberately lost in the rear elevation.

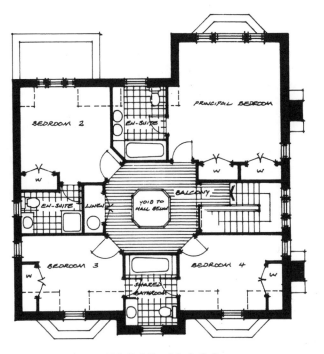

FIRST FLOOR

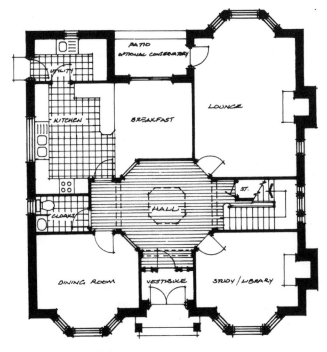

GROUND FLOOR

Lounge	5.72 x 5.56m	Principal bedroom	4.80 x 4.57m + wardrobes & en-suite
Study/library	4.19 x 2.97m + bay		
Dining room	4.19 x 2.97m + bay	Bedroom 2	3.88 x 3.73m + wardrobe & en-suite
Kitchen	4.42 x 3.28m		
Breakfast room	3.20 x 2.97m	Bedroom 3	3.50 x 2.97m + wardrobe
Utility	3.00 x 1.70m		
		Bedroom 4	3.50 x 2.97m + wardrobe

THE BARNOWL

The copyright belongs to Custom Homes Ltd.

219 sq. m.
including a garage of 29 sq. m.

Overall dimensions 19.85 x 12.35m

F R O N T   E L E V A T I O N

The vaulted ceiling of the hall with glazing running from top to bottom is an important feature of this family home. Outside the elevations are cheered up and given character by the use of different materials including rendering with brick features and stained timber boarding. This reinforces the impression that the building has evolved over time, a characteristic that applies to many country dwellings.

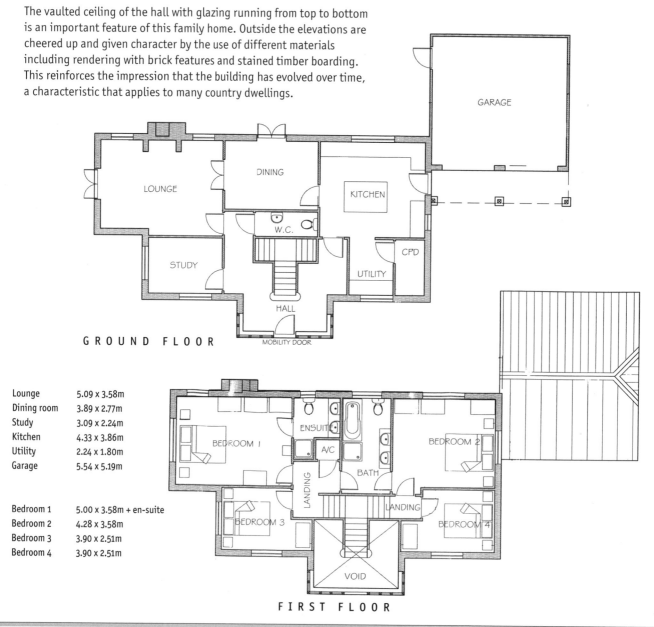

Lounge	5.09 x 3.58m
Dining room	3.89 x 2.77m
Study	3.09 x 2.24m
Kitchen	4.33 x 3.86m
Utility	2.24 x 1.80m
Garage	5.54 x 5.19m
Bedroom 1	5.00 x 3.58m + en-suite
Bedroom 2	4.28 x 3.58m
Bedroom 3	3.90 x 2.51m
Bedroom 4	3.90 x 2.51m

G R O U N D   F L O O R

F I R S T   F L O O R

LINGEN

The copyright belongs to T. J. Crump OAKRIGHTS Ltd.

223 sq. m.

Overall dimensions 17.85 x 10.24m

FRONT ELEVATION

The idea of a dining hall comes into its own with this exciting design, doing away with the 'waste of space' that a central hallway can often produce. The separation of the sitting room and study means that there will always be somewhere to escape the hurly burly of family life.

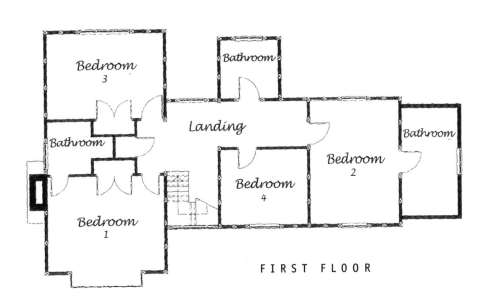

Bedroom 3

Bathroom

Landing

Bathroom

Bathroom

Bedroom 1

Bedroom 4

Bedroom 2

FIRST FLOOR

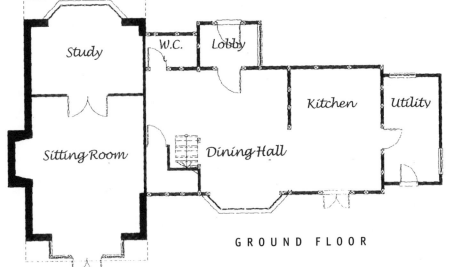

Study

W.C.

Lobby

Sitting Room

Dining Hall

Kitchen

Utility

GROUND FLOOR

Sitting room	5.28 x 4.57m
Study	4.57 x 2.59m
Dining hall	5.72 x 4.67m
Kitchen	4.72 x 3.86m
Utility	4.01 x 2.26m
Bedroom 1	4.73 x 3.73m + en-suite
Bedroom 2	4.73 x 3.25m + bathroom
Bedroom 3	4.73 x 3.58m + wardrobe
Bedroom 4	3.00 x 2.50m

DALSTUGA

The copyright belongs to The Swedish House Company Ltd.

224 sq. m.

Overall dimensions 13.95 x 9.15m.

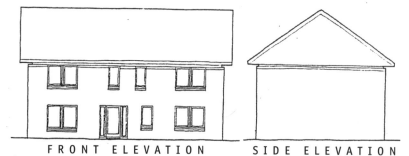

FRONT ELEVATION   SIDE ELEVATION   REAR ELEVATION

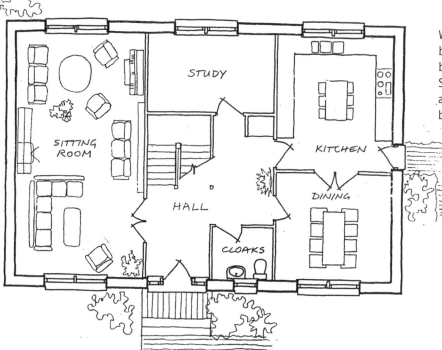

GROUND FLOOR

What would, at first, appear to be quite an ordinary four bedroom home is given Scandinavian flair with the addition of features such as a full bathroom to the master bedroom and an additional shower room to the communal bathroom. An uncomplicated shape means that this house would be extremely cost effective to build.

Sitting room	8.4 x 4.5m
Dining room	4.1 x 3.7m
Kitchen	4.6 X 4.1m
Study	4.4 x 2.7m
Bedroom 1	6.3 x 4.1 m + bathroom
Bedroom 2	4.6 x 4.2m
Bedroom 3	4.2 x 3.5m
Bedroom 4	4.1 x 3.5m

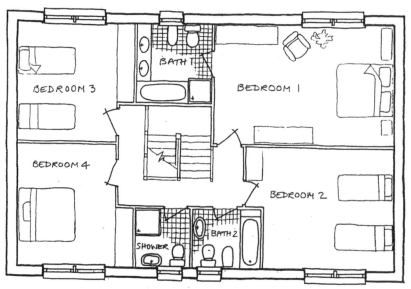

FIRST FLOOR

ALEXANDRIA

The copyright belongs to Designer Homes

225 sq. m.

Overall dimensions 14.70 x 12.70m

F R O N T   E L E V A T I O N

This is a lovely design that packs a whole lot of accommodation into a relatively modest size. The living room is detached from the rest of the living accommodation with the study having almost a separate entrance from the ground floor sun room. Upstairs this space is repeated to provide another sun room or a fifth bedroom.

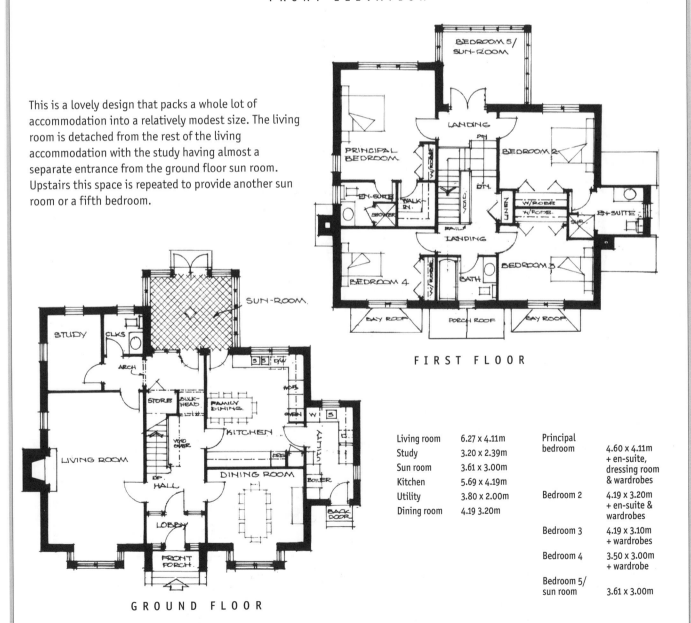

F I R S T   F L O O R

G R O U N D   F L O O R

Living room	6.27 x 4.11m	Principal bedroom	4.60 x 4.11m + en-suite, dressing room & wardrobes
Study	3.20 x 2.39m		
Sun room	3.61 x 3.00m		
Kitchen	5.69 x 4.19m		
Utility	3.80 x 2.00m	Bedroom 2	4.19 x 3.20m + en-suite & wardrobes
Dining room	4.19 3.20m		
		Bedroom 3	4.19 x 3.10m + wardrobes
		Bedroom 4	3.50 x 3.00m + wardrobe
		Bedroom 5/ sun room	3.61 x 3.00m

THE CHIDDINGSTONE

The copyright belongs to Scandia-Hus Limited

229 sq. m.

Overall dimensions 15.91 x 13.81m

F R O N T   E L E V A T I O N

Open the front door of this bungalow home and you are greeted with a view through three separate sets of double doors through the entrance hall, the dining area, the sitting room and on through the sun room to the gardens beyond. Five good bedrooms are provided in the finished state but, for those on an initially tight budget , there is the option of leaving the top floor until a later date.

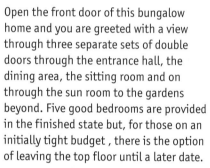

G R O U N D   F L O O R

F I R S T   F L O O R

Kitchen	3.6 x 3.1m		Bedroom 4	4.9 x 3.0m + dressing room & en-suite
Dining hall	6.6 x 3.8m			
Sitting room	5.9 x 4.8m			
Study	3.6 x 2.1m		Bedroom 5	4.9 x 3.4m
Master bedroom	4.6 x 3.3m + en-suite		Landing/ sitting area	5.2 x 2.1m
Bedroom 2	3.4 x 2.7m + dressing room			
Bedroom 3	3.4 x 2.7m			
Sun room	3.6 x 3.4m			

T210

229 sq. m.
including a garage of 30 sq. m.

Overall dimensions 18.42 x 12.38m

Although not entered in the category of homes for narrow sites, this is, nevertheless, a home that is designed to fit on a fairly restricted plot. Bringing the garage forward and setting its doors facing across the site reduces the visual impact of those doors and adds interest and depth to the elevation. Hipping the main roof means that the eye is drawn away from the boundaries. Inside, the accommodation is generous and comprehensive.

FRONT ELEVATION

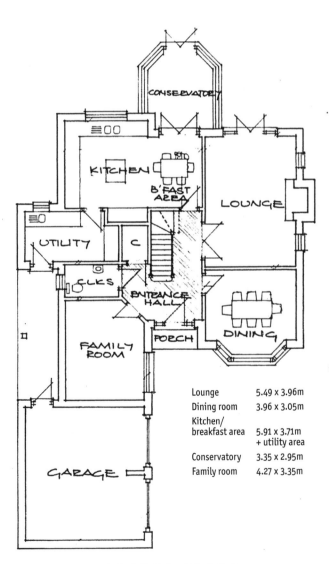

Lounge	5.49 x 3.96m
Dining room	3.96 x 3.05m
Kitchen/ breakfast area	5.91 x 3.71m + utility area
Conservatory	3.35 x 2.95m
Family room	4.27 x 3.35m

GROUND FLOOR

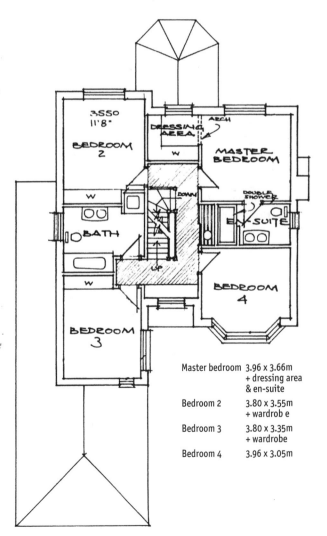

Master bedroom	3.96 x 3.66m + dressing area & en-suite
Bedroom 2	3.80 x 3.55m + wardrob e
Bedroom 3	3.80 x 3.35m + wardrobe
Bedroom 4	3.96 x 3.05m

FIRST FLOOR

HOUSES 231 TO 280 SQ. M.

W hen you get to these sizes the scope for the designer, from both an internal as well as an external point of view is greatly increased and they can really let rip with providing the things that most people would really dream of having in their new home.

Even if they have not gone to the point of providing specific annexes, offices or playroom accommodation, something that is perfectly possible at these sizes, they are able to double up on some of the living rooms. Modern family life can be stressful and noisy. Houses of these sizes can, however, provide scope for the generations to live almost separately within the same home with more than one lounge, separate eating areas and possible provision for specific activities.

Contributors in this section:
Associated Self Build Architects
The Border Design Centre
T.J.Crump OAKWRIGHTS Ltd.
Custom Homes Ltd.
Design & Materials Ltd.
Designer Homes
Potton Ltd.
The Self Build House Company Ltd.
Scottish Architects Network
Scandia-Hus Ltd.
The Swedish House Company Ltd.

THE LAPPLAND

The copyright belongs to Scandia-Hus Limited

234 sq. m.

Overall dimensions 14.41 x 12.91m

Once again, this typical Scandinavian design makes maximum use of natural light. A roof light situated in the very top of the home conducts the light onto the upper gallery and then on down into the entrance hall. Steps lead down from this hall into a sitting room that opens onto a covered deck sheltered by the balcony to the bedroom above.

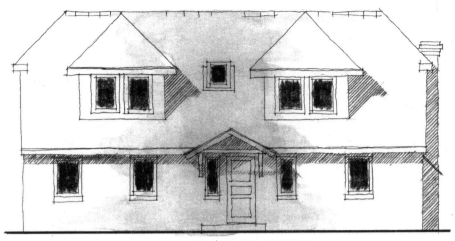

FRONT ELEVATION

REAR ELEVATION

SIDE ELEVATION

Kitchen	3.6 x 2.7m
Dining room	4.4 x 3.6m
Sitting room	7.2 x 5.3m
Family/ breakfast room	3.6 x 3.5m
Study/bedroom 5	3.5 x 3.4m

Master bedroom	4.0 x 3.9m + sauna & en-suite
Bedroom 2	4.2 x 3.4m
Bedroom 3	4.0 x 3.5m
Bedroom 4	4.0 x 2.7m
Landing/ TV lounge	4.4 x 3.0m

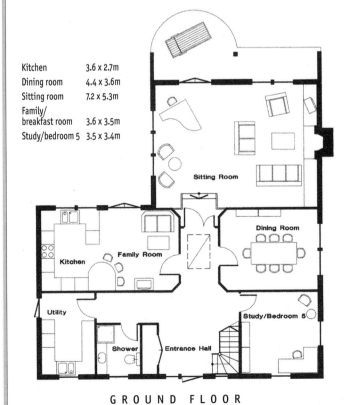

GROUND FLOOR

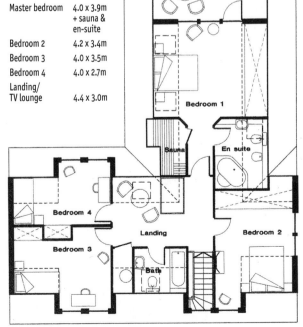

FIRST FLOOR

213

ATHOLL

The copyright belongs to Designer Homes

235 sq. m.
including a garage of 32 sq. m.

Overall dimensions 18.50 x 10.50m

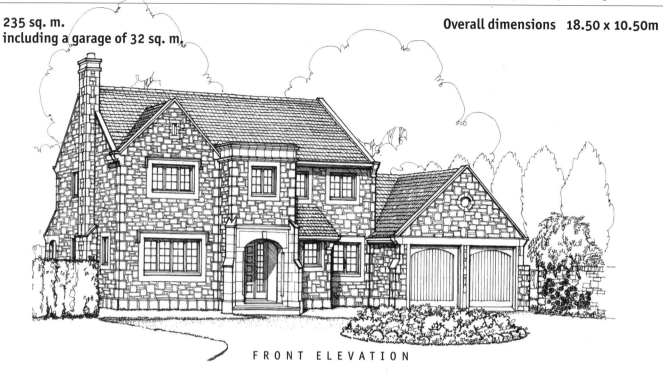

FRONT ELEVATION

A large family home with what many would regard as a small kitchen. Yet perhaps the size of the kitchen reflects modern family life and the convenience with which foods can now be prepared. All the more important then to have a reasonable space such as the breakfast/family room with the kitchen as an adjunct to it rather than being the dominant feature.

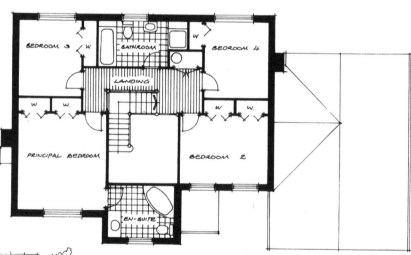

FIRST FLOOR

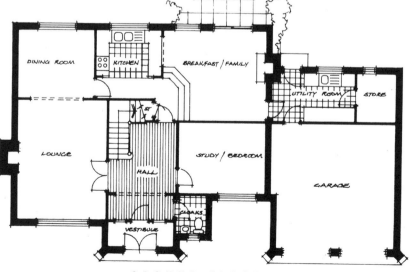

GROUND FLOOR

Lounge	5.26 x 4.11m
Dining room	3.50 x 3.05m
Kitchen	3.05 x 3.05m
Family/ breakfast room	4.72 x 3.96m
Study/ spare bedroom	4.04 x 3.12m
Utility	3.70 x 2.10m + store
Garage	5.70 x 5.50m
Principal bedroom	4.27 x 4.11m + wardrobes & en-suite
Bedroom 2	3.96 x 3.05m + wardrobes
Bedroom 3	3.35 x 2.90m + wardrobe
Bedroom 4	3.35 x 2.90m + wardrobe

THE DAIRY

The copyright belongs to an ASBA architectural practice – S. Buttler

235 sq. m.
including a garage of 40 sq. m.

Overall dimensions 18.0 x 12.7m

FRONT ELEVATION

In many homes the staircase is designed to arrive in the middle of the upper part of the house with the bedrooms grouped around the upper landing. In this house the square spiral staircase goes up in one corner of the building, leaving the entrance hallway clear. The staircase is lit by a roof light.

FIRST FLOOR

GROUND FLOOR

Kitchen	4.75 x 3.4m
Lounge	7.1 x 4.4m
Dining room	4.3 x 3.1m
Sun room	4.5 x 2.4m
Utility	2.0 x 2.0m
Garage	6.75 x 5.9m

Bedroom 1	4.4 x 3.5m + en-suite
Bedroom 2	4.4 x 3.5m
Bedroom 3	3.5 x 3.4m
Bedroom 4	3.7 x 3.0m

GRANEG-P

The copyright belongs to Potton Ltd.

235 sq. m.

Overall dimensions 14.7 x 12m

FRONT ELEVATION

If only four bedrooms were required this home could be sited on a plot that was around one metre narrower than the minimum given above. On the other hand, it is a design that would perhaps lend itself to a wider and more imposing situation.

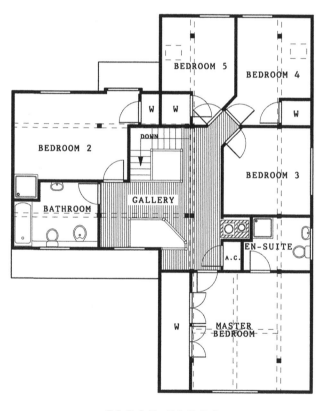

FIRST FLOOR

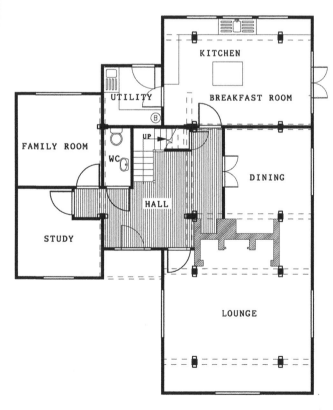

GROUND FLOOR

Lounge	5.8 x 5.7m	Master bedroom	4.6 x 4.4 m + wardrobe & en-suite
Diningroom	4.0 x 3.4m		
Kitchen/ breakfast	5.8 x 4.0m	Bedroom 2	4.4 x 3.2m + wardrobe
Utility	2.2 x 2.2m	Bedroom 3	3.3 x 3.3m
Family room	3.4 x 3.2m	Bedroom 4	4.0 x 2.8m
Study	3.3 x 3.2m	Bedroom 5	4.0 x 2.8m

ARDINGLEY

The copyright belongs to T. J. Crump OAKRIGHTS Ltd.

237 sq. m.
including a garage of 37 sq. m.

Overall dimensions 27.38 x 12.86m

FRONT ELEVATION

The more or less square sitting room to the ground floor has a vaulted ceiling and the upstairs sitting room looks down onto it through the balustrading. Once again the dining hall is the pivotal point in the design with the entrance facilities confined to a relatively small lobby and toilet.

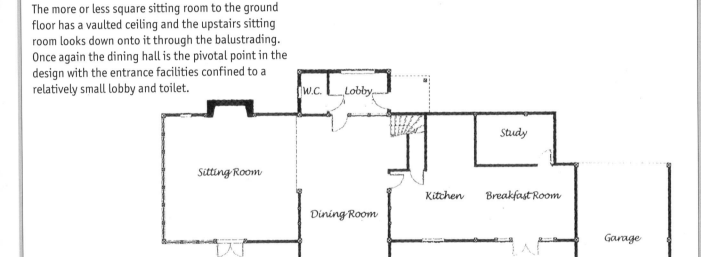

GROUND FLOOR

FIRST FLOOR

Sitting room	7.14 x 6.30m
Dining room	8.43 x 4.67m
Kitchen	6.30 x 4.62m
Breakfast room	5.54 x 3.71m
Study	4.27 x 2.44m
Garage	7.62 x 4.90m
Sitting room	5.92 x 4.62m
Bedroom 1	4.70 x 4.62m + dressing room & en-suite
Bedroom 2	4.19 x 3.17m
Bedroom 3	4.19 x 2.87m

AUCHENSKEOCH

The copyright belongs to The Border Design Centre

238 sq. m.

Overall dimensions 20.5 x 12.9m

REAR ELEVATION

Originally designed for a wooded site, this 'X' shaped building still has the trademark tower that this designer loves to employ. The approach is from the side to a cloistered corner entrance opening onto a vestibule and then to a double height hall with minstrel galleries and an open plan first floor study that could just as easily be enclosed as a fourth bedroom.

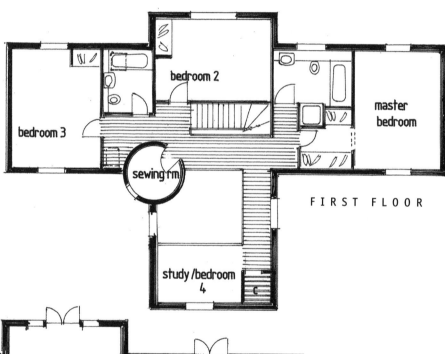

FIRST FLOOR

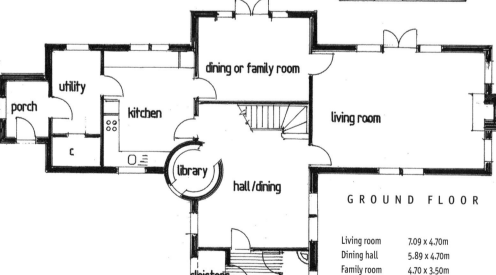

GROUND FLOOR

Living room	7.09 x 4.70m	Master bedroom	4.70 x 3.76m
Dining hall	5.89 x 4.70m		+ dressing room
Family room	4.70 x 3.50m		& en-suite
Library	2.18 diameter	Bedroom 2	4.70 x 3.81m
Kitchen	4.70 x 3.81m	Bedroom 3	4.70 x 3.20m
	+ utility area	Study/Bedroom 4	3.50 x 2.28m
		Sewing room	2.18 diameter

DENHAM 98-012

The copyright belongs to Potton Ltd.

**243 sq. m.
including a garage of 34 sq. m.**

Overall dimensions 15.2 x 14.6m

FRONT ELEVATION

Having the garage projecting from the front of the house means that it will fit onto a narrower site and, if this is possible, to have the garage doors looking across the plot means that the garage doors do not become the dominant feature. This home has most if not all of the accommodation many families would wish for. The main bedroom, above the garage has partly sloping ceilings that are vaulted and lit by roof lights.

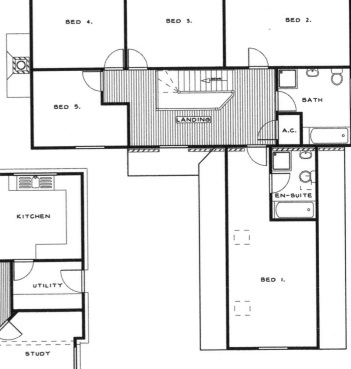

FIRST FLOOR

GROUND FLOOR

Lounge	6.5 x 4.0m	Bedroom 1	7.9 x 3.6 mincluding en-suite
Dining room	3.7 x 3.4m		
Kitchen/ breakfast	5.1 x 3.4m	Bedroom 2	5.1 x 3.4m
Utility	2.8 x 1.9m	Bedroom 3	4.0 x 3.4m
Study	3.4 x 3.0m	Bedroom 4	3.7 x 3.4m
Garage	5.8 x 5.8m	Bedroom 5	3.8 x 3.0m max

THE KIRKWOOD

The copyright belongs to The Self-Build House Company Ltd.

244 sq. m.
including a garage of 40 sq. m.

Overall dimensions 18.07 x 12.91m

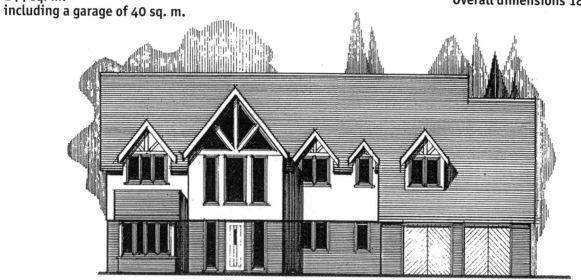

FRONT ELEVATION

This imposing new home would fit into most areas of the country but it would look particularly good on a wide plot in a leafy suburb where the accommodation and its layout would be all that was expected. The extra deep garage is sufficient to allow the car to be parked and unloaded in the dry.

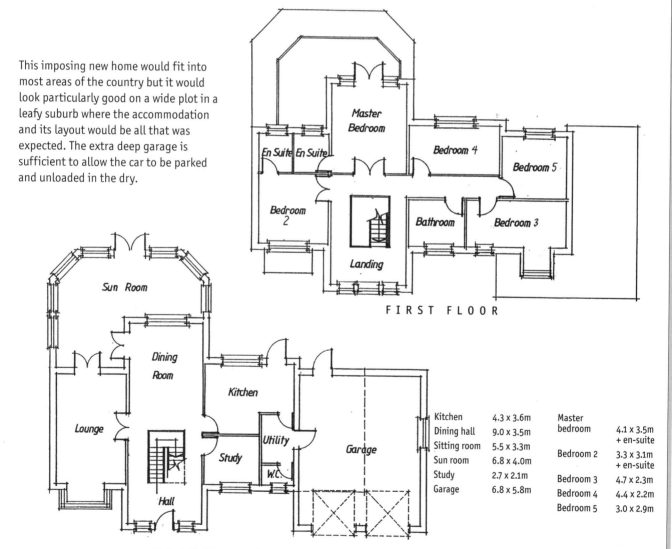

FIRST FLOOR

GROUND FLOOR

Kitchen	4.3 x 3.6m	Master bedroom	4.1 x 3.5m + en-suite
Dining hall	9.0 x 3.5m		
Sitting room	5.5 x 3.3m	Bedroom 2	3.3 x 3.1m + en-suite
Sun room	6.8 x 4.0m		
Study	2.7 x 2.1m	Bedroom 3	4.7 x 2.3m
Garage	6.8 x 5.8m	Bedroom 4	4.4 x 2.2m
		Bedroom 5	3.0 x 2.9m

THE CAMBRIDGE

The copyright belongs to The Self-Build House Company Ltd.

245 sq. m.

Overall dimensions 15.58 x 12.20m

FRONT ELEVATION

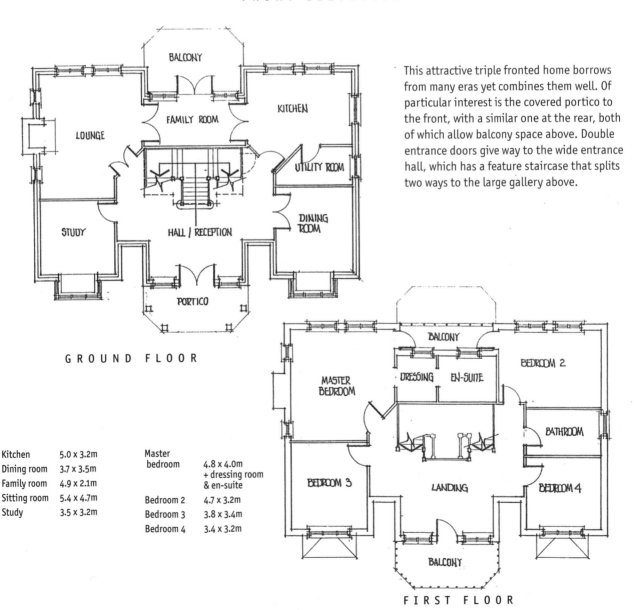

This attractive triple fronted home borrows from many eras yet combines them well. Of particular interest is the covered portico to the front, with a similar one at the rear, both of which allow balcony space above. Double entrance doors give way to the wide entrance hall, which has a feature staircase that splits two ways to the large gallery above.

GROUND FLOOR

FIRST FLOOR

Kitchen	5.0 x 3.2m	Master bedroom	4.8 x 4.0m + dressing room & en-suite	
Dining room	3.7 x 3.5m			
Family room	4.9 x 2.1m			
Sitting room	5.4 x 4.7m	Bedroom 2	4.7 x 3.2m	
Study	3.5 x 3.2m	Bedroom 3	3.8 x 3.4m	
		Bedroom 4	3.4 x 3.2m	

TURNBERRY

The copyright belongs to Designer Homes

244 sq. m.

Overall dimensions 15.90 x 15.90m

F R O N T   E L E V A T I O N

Although illustrated with a detached double garage this is not included in the plans or the dimensions. The curved staircase determines much of the layout within the home. The offset walls to the ground floor give scope for interesting shapes and an easy flow of accommodation. The kitchen layout borrows from and mirrors the curve of the staircase, utilising the resulting shape to wrap units around the island unit.

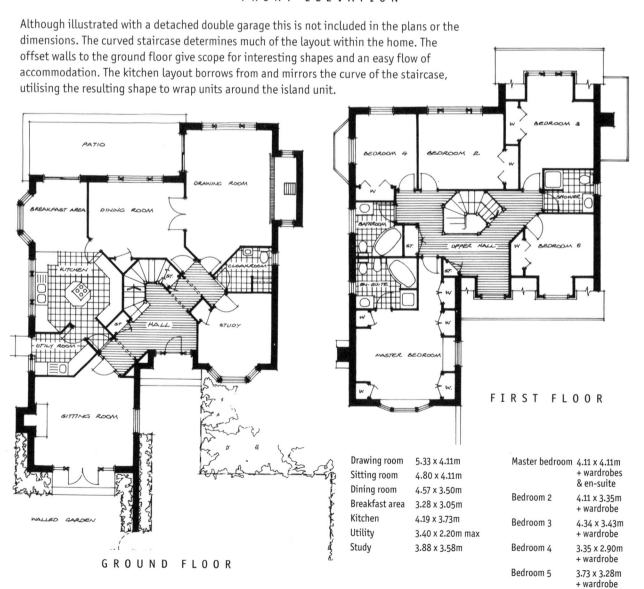

G R O U N D   F L O O R

F I R S T   F L O O R

Drawing room	5.33 x 4.11m	Master bedroom	4.11 x 4.11m + wardrobes & en-suite
Sitting room	4.80 x 4.11m		
Dining room	4.57 x 3.50m		
Breakfast area	3.28 x 3.05m	Bedroom 2	4.11 x 3.35m + wardrobe
Kitchen	4.19 x 3.73m	Bedroom 3	4.34 x 3.43m + wardrobe
Utility	3.40 x 2.20m max		
Study	3.88 x 3.58m	Bedroom 4	3.35 x 2.90m + wardrobe
		Bedroom 5	3.73 x 3.28m + wardrobe

WOODCROFT

The copyright belongs to Designer Homes

245 sq. m.
including a garage of 36 sq. m.

Overall dimensions 19.10 x 17.10m

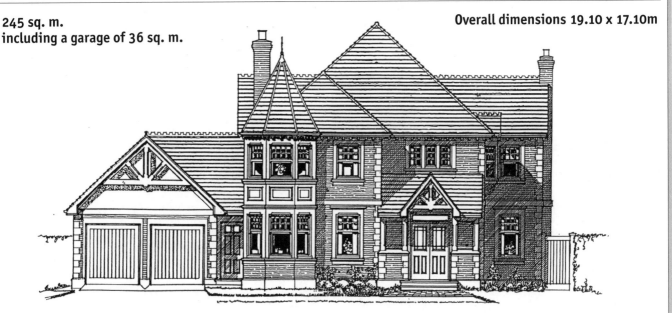

F R O N T   E L E V A T I O N

This really is an interesting design. Everywhere you look there is something exciting. The tower lends a certain character to the frontage and then provides additional sitting areas to both the drawing room and the principal bedroom. There is a large living room opening, with folding doors, onto the study. Bay windows enhance the dining, breakfast and guest bedrooms.

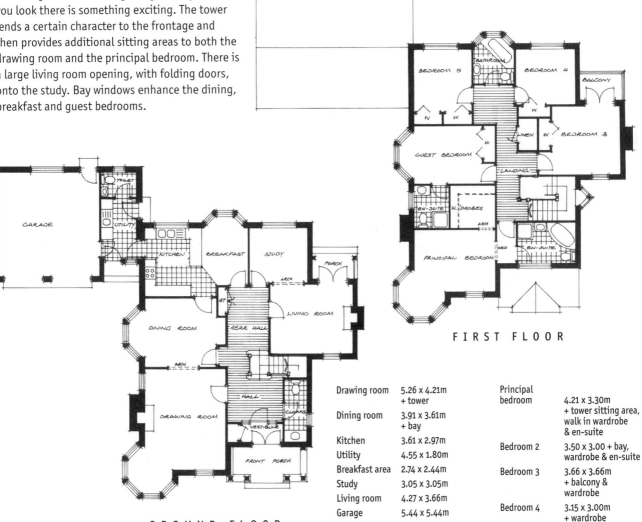

F I R S T   F L O O R

G R O U N D   F L O O R

Drawing room	5.26 x 4.21m + tower	Principal bedroom	4.21 x 3.30m + tower sitting area, walk in wardrobe & en-suite
Dining room	3.91 x 3.61m + bay		
Kitchen	3.61 x 2.97m	Bedroom 2	3.50 x 3.00 + bay, wardrobe & en-suite
Utility	4.55 x 1.80m		
Breakfast area	2.74 x 2.44m	Bedroom 3	3.66 x 3.66m + balcony & wardrobe
Study	3.05 x 3.05m		
Living room	4.27 x 3.66m	Bedroom 4	3.15 x 3.00m + wardrobe
Garage	5.44 x 5.44m		
		Bedroom 5	3.30 x 3.00m + wardrobes

TRAFFORD

The copyright belongs to Designer Homes

**245 sq. m.
including a garage of 29 sq. m.**

Overall dimensions 17.40 x 14.50m

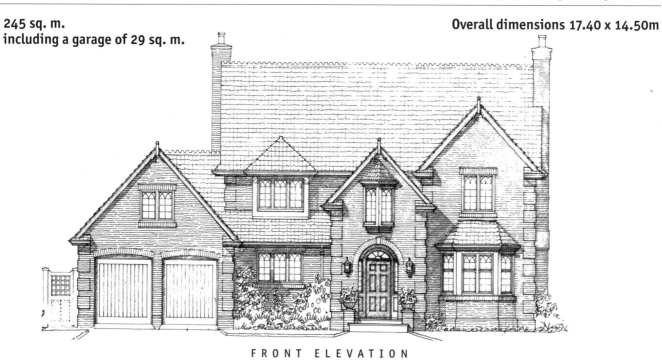

FRONT ELEVATION

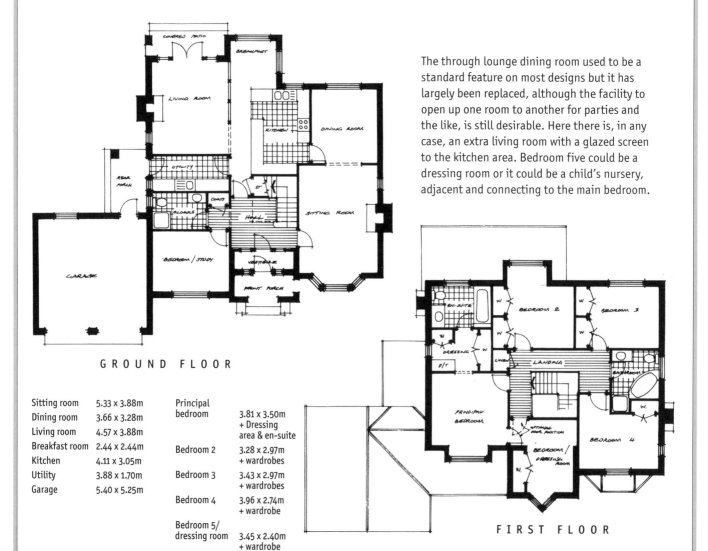

GROUND FLOOR

FIRST FLOOR

The through lounge dining room used to be a standard feature on most designs but it has largely been replaced, although the facility to open up one room to another for parties and the like, is still desirable. Here there is, in any case, an extra living room with a glazed screen to the kitchen area. Bedroom five could be a dressing room or it could be a child's nursery, adjacent and connecting to the main bedroom.

Sitting room	5.33 x 3.88m	
Dining room	3.66 x 3.28m	
Living room	4.57 x 3.88m	
Breakfast room	2.44 x 2.44m	
Kitchen	4.11 x 3.05m	
Utility	3.88 x 1.70m	
Garage	5.40 x 5.25m	

Principal bedroom	3.81 x 3.50m + Dressing area & en-suite
Bedroom 2	3.28 x 2.97m + wardrobes
Bedroom 3	3.43 x 2.97m + wardrobes
Bedroom 4	3.96 x 2.74m + wardrobe
Bedroom 5/ dressing room	3.45 x 2.40m + wardrobe

DENHAM 02-088

The copyright belongs to Potton Ltd.

246 sq. m.
including a garage of 34 sq. m.

Overall dimensions 14.5 x 15m

FRONT ELEVATION

This home is illustrated with a hipped roof and false dormers. This method of construction, which is common in many areas, tends to lower the visual impact of the house without actually changing the actual ridge height. On a tight plot such as the suggested minimum the effect of the hips would be to take the house away from its immediate neighbours and reduce the danger of 'cramming'.

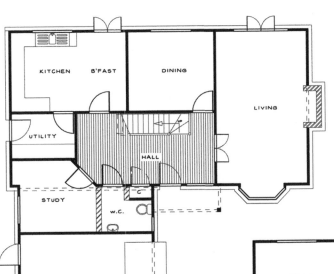

GROUND FLOOR

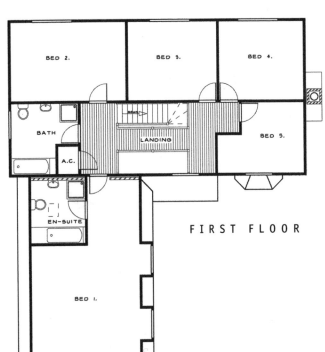

FIRST FLOOR

Lounge	6.5 x 4.0m	Bedroom 1	7.85 x 4.9m including en-suite	
Dining room	3.8 x 3.4m			
Kitchen/ breakfast	5.1 x 3.4m	Bedroom 2	5.1 x 3.4m	
Utility	2.8 x 1.75m	Bedroom 3	4.0 x 3.4m	
Study	3.4 x 3.1m	Bedroom 4	3.7 x 3.4m	
Garage	5.8 x 5.8m	Bedroom 5	3.35 x 3.0m	

COTSWOLD

The copyright belongs to Designer Homes

**246 sq. m.
including a garage
of 36 sq. m.**

Overall dimensions 19.75 x 17.50m

FRONT ELEVATION

The name gives the clue to the origins of this design. The lack of symmetry, the introduction of offset gable projections, bay windows and forward gable extensions with differing roof pitches and planes, are all typical of this area. Pulling the kitchen out of the main house and into the forward extension with the utility room gives it easy access to the garage as well as the rest of the home.

Drawing room	6.86 x 3.88m
Living room	5.11 x 3.88m
Dining room	3.43 x 3.05m
Study	2.97 x 2.82m
Kitchen/ breakfast room	4.72 x 3.81m
Utility	3.30 x 2.25m
Garage	6.00 x 6.00m

Principal bedroom	4.11 x 3.88m + closet & en-suite
Bedroom 2	3.35 x 3.05m + wardrobe
Bedroom 3	4.11 x 3.28m + wardrobe
Bedroom 4	3.88 x 3.10m + wardrobe

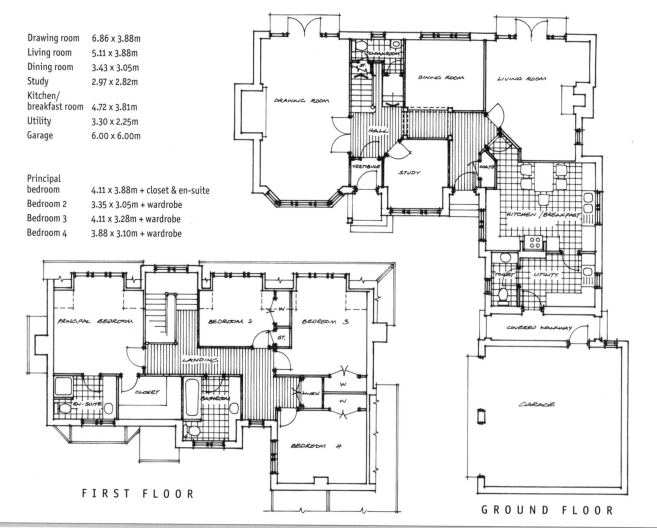

FIRST FLOOR

GROUND FLOOR

DUNNING

The copyright belongs to The Border Design Centre

246 sq. m.
including a garage of 22 sq. m.

Overall dimensions 18.5 x 17.2m

REAR ELEVATION

Having at least one bedroom on the ground floor is a feature that is often employed by this contributor. In this home, however, the ground floor is designed for occupation by a person confined to a wheelchair, with easy access to the building and comfortable circulation space. Upstairs these parameters need not apply and the accommodation is laid out for conventional occupation.

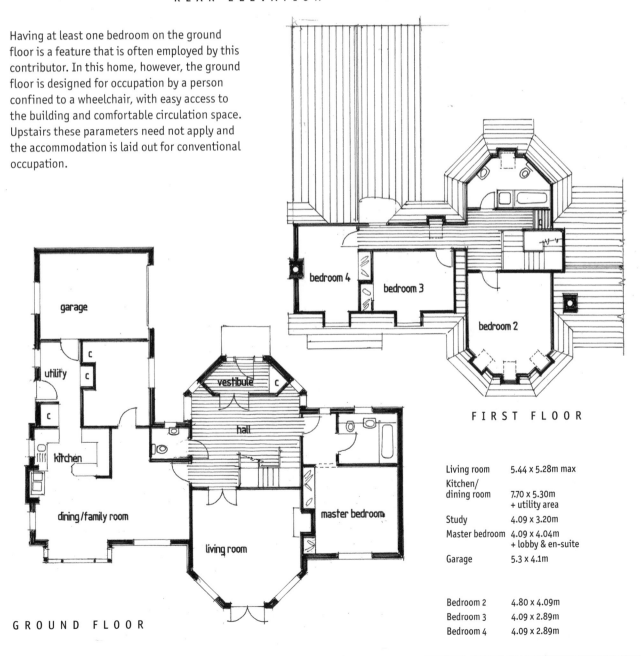

FIRST FLOOR

GROUND FLOOR

Living room	5.44 x 5.28m max
Kitchen/ dining room	7.70 x 5.30m + utility area
Study	4.09 x 3.20m
Master bedroom	4.09 x 4.04m + lobby & en-suite
Garage	5.3 x 4.1m
Bedroom 2	4.80 x 4.09m
Bedroom 3	4.09 x 2.89m
Bedroom 4	4.09 x 2.89m

HOLLYHOUSE

The copyright belongs to T. J. Crump OAKRIGHTS Ltd.

246 sq. m.

Overall dimensions 15.5 x 14.75m

F R O N T   E L E V A T I O N

With a few name changes this home could provide five bedrooms. Alternatively some might relish having a gym as well as a downstairs bedroom. The sitting room is separated from the main body of the house as an extension off the kitchen and the hall doubles up as a dining area.

Sitting room	5.96 x 4.92m
Dining room	4.36 x 3.86m
Kitchen	6.88 x 5.10m
Utility	2.33 x 2.18m
Bedroom 4	4.36 x 3.58m
Gym	3.58 x 2.31m
Bedroom 1	4.92 x 4.29m
	+ wardrobe & en-suite
Bedroom 2	3.55 x 3.27m + wardrobe
Bedroom 3	3.53 x 3.20m + wardrobe
Study	3.78 x 3.40m

R E A R   E L E V A T I O N

G R O U N D   F L O O R

F I R S T   F L O O R

PAPPLE C

The copyright belongs to Potton Ltd.

247 sq. m.

Overall dimensions 14.1 x 13.9m

FRONT ELEVATION

Extra space in the roof does not come for free but it is, nevertheless, one of the most cost effective ways to increase the accommodation. Thought must, however, be given to just how the third and additional floors are reached, as, without a proper staircase, they cannot really be thought of in terms of living space.

GROUND FLOOR

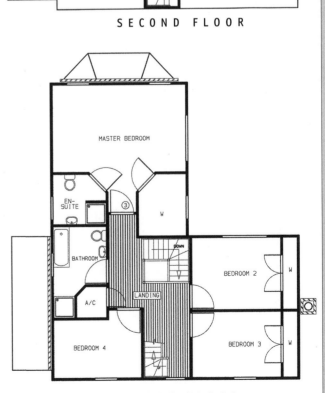

SECOND FLOOR

FIRST FLOOR

Drawing room	5.7 x 4.5m		Master bedroom	5.8 x 3.7m + wardrobe & en-suite
Dining room	5.4 x 3.4m av.			
Kitchen/diner	6.4 x 5.7m max		Bedroom 2	3.8 x 2.9m + wardrobe
Study	3.9 x 2.2m			
Utility	2.2 x 2.0m		Bedroom 3	3.8 x 2.6m + wardrobe
			Bedroom 4	3.8 x 2.3m
			1st attic room	4.0 x 3.7m
			2nd attic room	5.1 x 4.0m

WARESC-P

The copyright belongs to Potton Ltd.

247 sq. m.

Overall dimensions 16.37 x 14.26m

F R O N T   E L E V A T I O N

There are some situations where the brickwork for the inglenook can be allowed to intrude upon the necessary distance to the boundary. In others you would need a little more width to the site. Combining the kitchen, breakfast and sun room in this design gives it character.

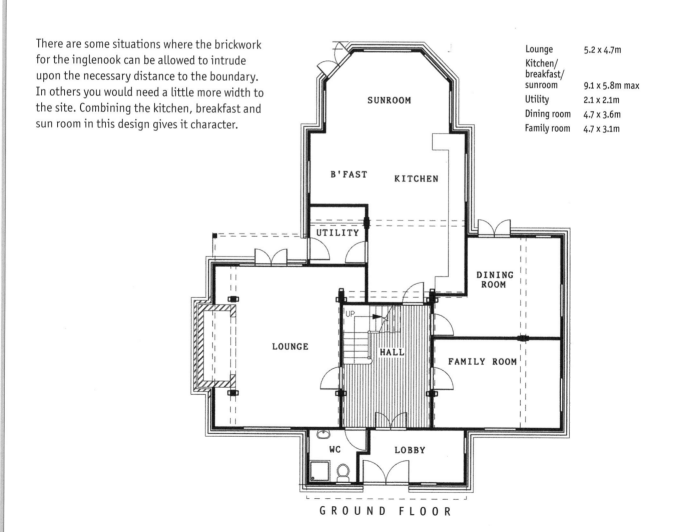

Lounge	5.2 x 4.7m
Kitchen/ breakfast/ sunroom	9.1 x 5.8m max
Utility	2.1 x 2.1m
Dining room	4.7 x 3.6m
Family room	4.7 x 3.1m

G R O U N D   F L O O R

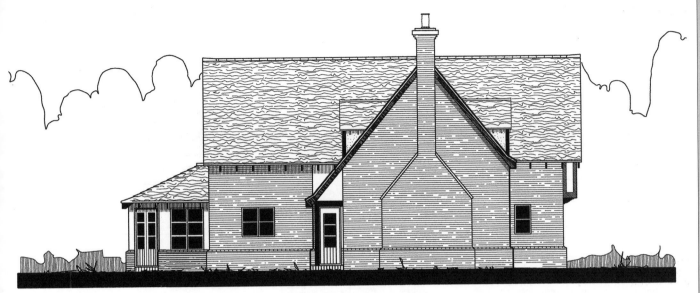

SIDE ELEVATION

Master bedroom 6.2 x 4.7m max
                    + wardrobe & en-suite

Bedroom 2   3.8 x 2.8m + wardrobe

Bedroom 3   3.8 x 2.8m + wardrobe

Bedroom 4   3.5 x 3.4m

Bedroom 5   3.8 x 3.6m
                  + wardrobe & en-suite

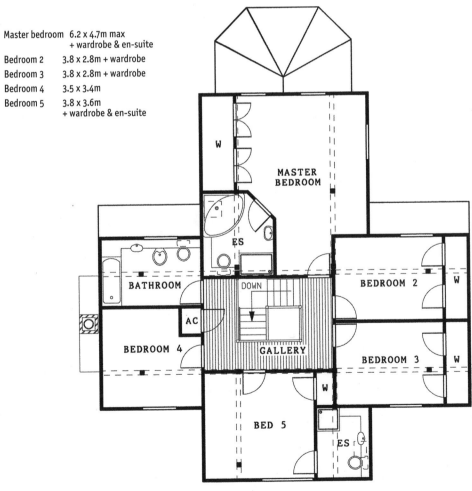

FIRST FLOOR

DALARNA

The copyright belongs to The Swedish House Company Ltd.

247 sq. m.

Overall dimensions 13.93 x 9.13m.

FRONT ELEVATION

SIDE ELEVATION – EAST

The British concept of a strict division between sleeping and living accommodation can be turned on its head by Scandinavian ideals as encompassed in this lovely home. The central feature is the verandah and the balcony off the sitting room and upper lounge. Bedroom accommodation is then divided between the ground and first floors.

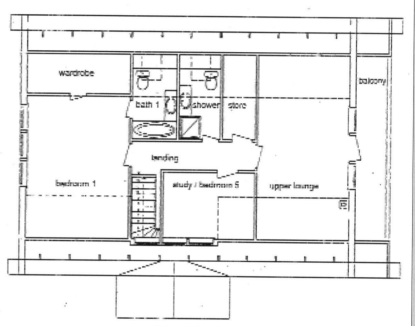

FIRST FLOOR

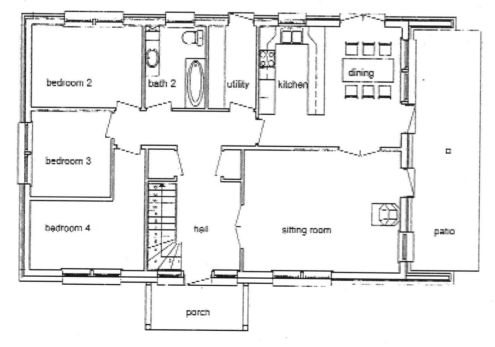

GROUND FLOOR

Sitting room	5.6 x 4.2m
Dining room	4.1 x 2.7m
Kitchen	4.1 x 2.4m
Utility	2.8 x 1.8m
Bedroom 2	4.0 x 2.8m
Bedroom 3	3.0 x 2.9m
Bedroom 4	4.1 x 2.4m
Upper lounge	7.2 x 4.0m
Bedroom 1	5.5 x 4.1m + wardrobe & bathroom
Study/ bedroom 5	3.6 x 2.6m

MERLIN

The copyright belongs to Designer Homes

**250 sq. m.
including a garage
of 27 sq. m.**

Overall dimensions 14.80 x 11.60m

FRONT ELEVATION

A solid and dependable house design providing five good sized bedrooms, two of them en-suite. The large family room, adjoining the kitchen, with access to the patio might be where much of the day to day family activity takes place. The living room, accessed by double glazed doors from the hall could then be left for 'best'. The dining room, divorced from the kitchen but easily accessible, could just as well be called a study or provide an office for someone working from home.

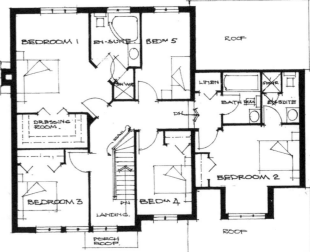

FIRST FLOOR

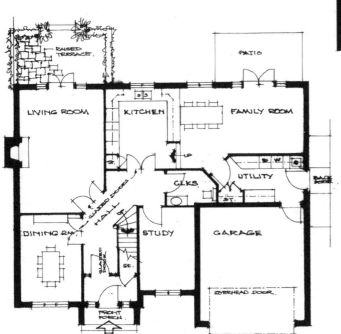

GROUND FLOOR

Living room	5.89 x 4.11m	Bedroom 1	4.67 x 3.50m + dressing room & en-suite
Dining room	4.1 9x 3.00m		
Kitchen	3.81 x 3.61m	Bedroom 2	4.39 x 3.66m av. + en-suite
Family room	6.02 x 3.10m		
Study	3.88 x 2.69m	Bedroom 3	3.40 x 3.00m + wardrobe
Garage	5.41 x 5.11m		
		Bedroom 4	3.88 x 2.69m + wardrobe
		Bedroom 5	4.11 x 2.41m

233

THE LINDEN

The copyright belongs to Scandia-Hus Limited

250 sq. m.

Overall dimensions 17.41 x 13.51m

FRONT ELEVATION

Banks of skylights flood light down from the vaulted ceiling of the upper landing into the ground floor dining room. Rows of deep and wide windows and patio doors let in further light to this and many of the other living rooms. The full height gable projection housing the staircase adds interest to the front elevation whilst its gable head windows light up the top landing even further.

SIDE ELEVATION

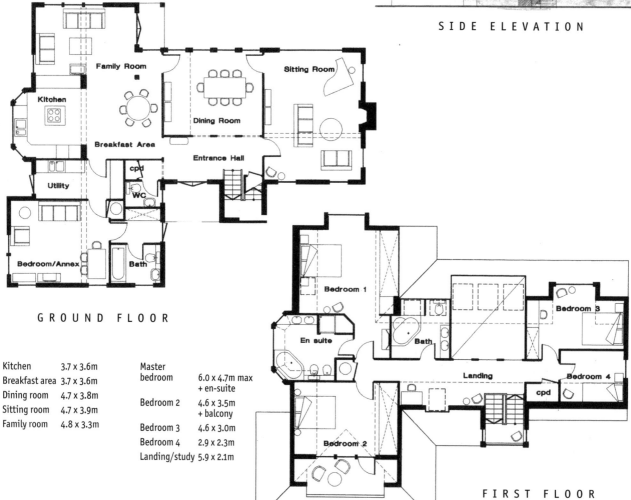

GROUND FLOOR

FIRST FLOOR

Kitchen	3.7 x 3.6m	Master bedroom	6.0 x 4.7m max + en-suite
Breakfast area	3.7 x 3.6m		
Dining room	4.7 x 3.8m	Bedroom 2	4.6 x 3.5m + balcony
Sitting room	4.7 x 3.9m		
Family room	4.8 x 3.3m	Bedroom 3	4.6 x 3.0m
		Bedroom 4	2.9 x 2.3m
		Landing/study	5.9 x 2.1m

DUNANS

250 sq. m.

Overall dimensions 16.4 x 9.6m

FRONT ELEVATION

Seven bedrooms, three of them with en-suite facilities. Four reception rooms plus a large kitchen dining room. This is a house that simply abounds in accommodation and all within a fairly reasonable size. The designers have gone for room numbers in most cases rather than large dimensions and that probably reflects their client's lifestyle. The full height windows to the staircase projection add considerable interest.

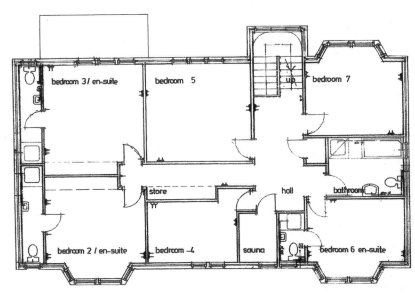

FIRST FLOOR

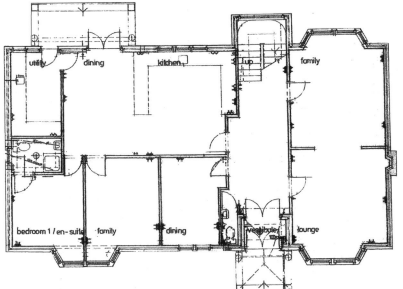

GROUND FLOOR

Lounge	4.0 x 4.0m + bay
Family room	4.0 x 4.0m + bay
Kitchen/ dining room	7.2 x 4.2m
Dining room	3.6 x 2.4m
2nd Family room	3.6 x 3.0m + bay
Utility	3.4 x 2.1m
Bedroom 1	3.0 x 2.9m + en-suite & bay
Bedroom 2	4.0 x 3.4m + bay & en-suite
Bedroom 3	4.3 x 4.0m + en-suite
Bedroom 4	3.6 x 2.4m
Sauna	1.9 x 1.5m
Bedroom 5	4.3 x 3.9m
Bedroom 6	3.9 x 2.4m + bay
Bedroom 7	3.9 x 2.9m + bay

THE SWAVESEY

The copyright belongs to The Self-Build House Company Ltd.

253 sq. m.
including a garage of 40 sq. m.

Overall dimensions 17.71 x 12.35m

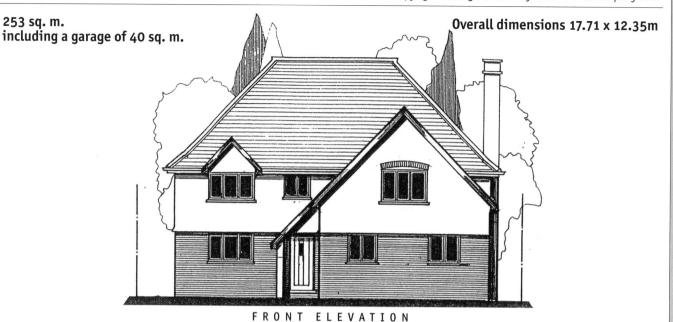

FRONT ELEVATION

There was a temptation to place this home in the section dealing with homes for narrow sites because, although it is quite a big house, it is capable of being sited on a fairly restricted plot. The use of the hipped roof to the main section brings the eye away from the boundaries and the lower eave line of the forward projection, added to the false dormer, gives the illusion of a lower roof height.

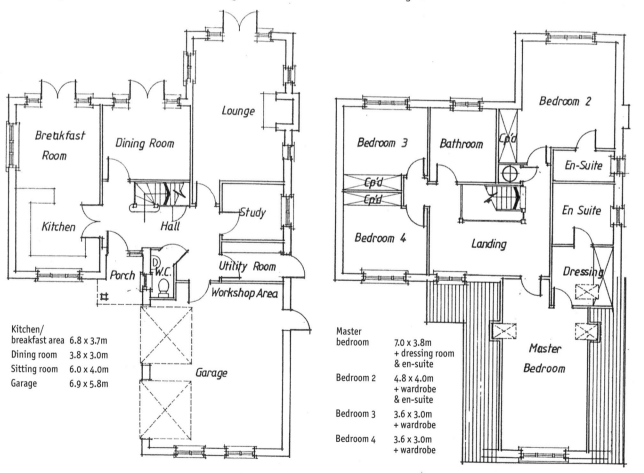

Kitchen/
breakfast area   6.8 x 3.7m
Dining room   3.8 x 3.0m
Sitting room   6.0 x 4.0m
Garage   6.9 x 5.8m

Master
bedroom   7.0 x 3.8m
                 + dressing room
                 & en-suite

Bedroom 2   4.8 x 4.0m
                 + wardrobe
                 & en-suite

Bedroom 3   3.6 x 3.0m
                 + wardrobe

Bedroom 4   3.6 x 3.0m
                 + wardrobe

GROUND FLOOR   FIRST FLOOR

THE CHADDLEWORTH

The copyright belongs to an ASBA architectural practice – Four Square Design Ltd.

253 sq. m.
including a garage of 33 sq. m.

Overall dimensions 21.85 x 8.71m

F R O N T   E L E V A T I O N

The wonder is that so much accommodation has been packed into what is, after all, not a huge house. A double garage, four reception rooms, a kitchen/breakfast room and utility plus five bedrooms, two of which are en-suite. Very clever use has been made of the roof voids of the bungalow sections to provide dressing room and en-suite facilities to the two major bedrooms.

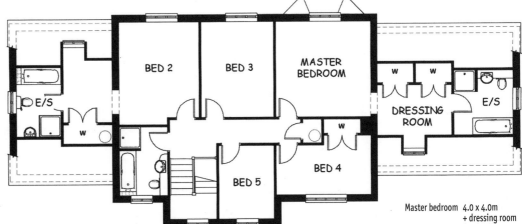

F I R S T   F L O O R

Master bedroom	4.0 x 4.0m + dressing room & en-suite
Bedroom 2	4.3 x 3.4m + dressing room & en-suite
Bedroom 3	4.0 x 3.1m
Bedroom 4	4.0 x 2.4m + wardrobe
Bedroom 5	3.0 x 2.4m
Drawing room	7.1 x 4.0m
Dining room	4.0 x 3.1m
Family room	4.0 x 3.4m
Study	3.1 x 2.0m
Kitchen/ breakfast room	4.1 x 3.9m
Utility	2.5 x 2.0m
Garage	5.8 x 5.7m

G R O U N D   F L O O R

237

CORRA LINN

The copyright belongs to The Border Design Centre

258 sq. m.

Overall dimensions 20.3 x 10.4m

FRONT ELEVATION

This large house avoids being over high by means of relatively narrow spans. This was useful and instrumental in its original conception where it was built in the grounds of a country house, which it was important not to overshadow. It has a double height dining hall with a gallery and all the major rooms are designed to overlook the front of the house.

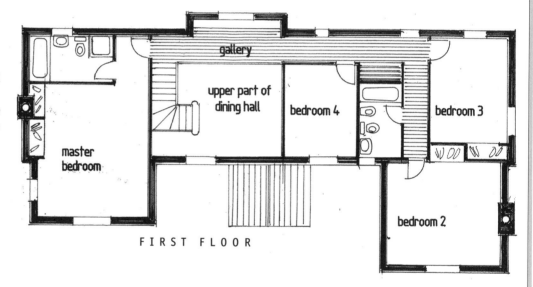

FIRST FLOOR

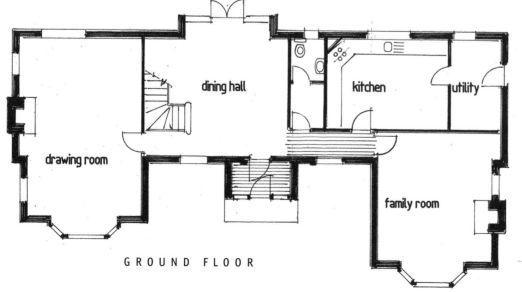

GROUND FLOOR

Drawing room	7.10 x 5.00m
Dining hall	5.89 x 5.31m
Kitchen/ breakfast room	5.21 x 3.50m + utility area
Family room	5.1 x 4.6m
Master bedroom	5.21 x 5.00m + lobby & en-suite
Bedroom 2	4.70 x 4.11m + wardrobe
Bedroom 3	4.70 x 3.40m + wardrobe
Bedroom 4	3.60 x 2.99m

THE STABLES

The copyright belongs to a ScAN architectural practice – S.Buttler

258 sq. m.
including a garage of 41 sq. m.

Overall dimensions 17.9 x 10.6m

F R O N T   E L E V A T I O N

It is quite usual to have two single garage doors to a double garage. Not only does that mean that the architectural influence of the garage doors are lessened but it also means that the whole of the garage does not have to be opened up in inclement weather. Here that principle is taken one step further with the garages being entirely separate, whilst still having access to the main house.

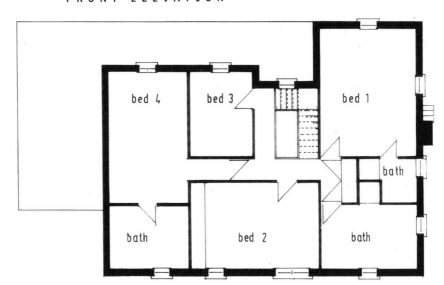

F I R S T   F L O O R

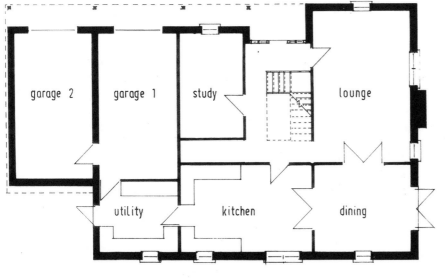

G R O U N D   F L O O R

Lounge	6.25 x 4.2m
Dining room	4.2 x 3.6m
Kitchen	5.6 x 3.6m
Study	4.3 x 2.7m
Utility	3.3 x 2.9m
Garage 1	6.9 x 3.3m
Garage 2	6.9 x 3.3m
Bedroom 1	5.3 x 4.2m + en-suite
Bedroom 2	5.6 x 3.6m
Bedroom 3	3.5 x 2.7m
Bedroom 4	5.5 x 3.35m + bathroom

EASTBOURNE

The copyright belongs to Designer Homes

260 sq. m.
including a garage of 29 sq. m.

Overall dimensions 18.70 x 13.60m

FRONT ELEVATION

There are quite a few 'wow' factors with this design, starting with the impressive entrance. The octagonal area in the family room, set aside for eating, would keep the rest of the room clear for other family activities. The principal bedroom has a large en-suite bathroom, but it doesn't stop there. It also has a dressing room and a wardrobe and then there is the large walk in clothes closet.

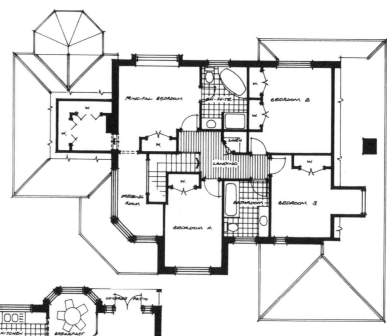

FIRST FLOOR

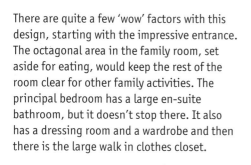

GROUND FLOOR

Sitting room	6.02 x 4.50m
Dining room	4.11 x 2.97m
Kitchen	3.43 x 2.97m
Family/ breakfast room	5.41 x 4.19m + bay
Utility	2.60 x 2.20m
Study/library	4.11 x 3.43m
Garage	5.40 x 5.40m

Principal bedroom	4.19 x 3.58m + dressing room, clothes closet, wardrobes & en-suite
Bedroom 2	4.19 x 3.50m + wardrobes
Bedroom 3	3.43 x 3.05m + wardrobe
Bedroom 4	3.88 x 2.90m + wardrobe

THE SAND SCHOOL

The copyright belongs to a ScAN architectural practice – S. Buttler

263 sq. m.
including a garage of 35 sq. m.

Overall dimensions 20.7 x 14.1m

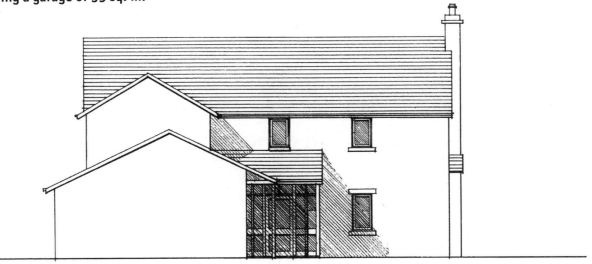

F R O N T   E L E V A T I O N

This modern family home has the garage and utility sections situated in a forward projecting single storey section. Having the garage doors looking across the plot means that they do not become the dominant architectural feature, but care must be taken to ensure that there is sufficient site width for cars to turn into the garage. The massive kitchen has room for a breakfast or casual dining section.

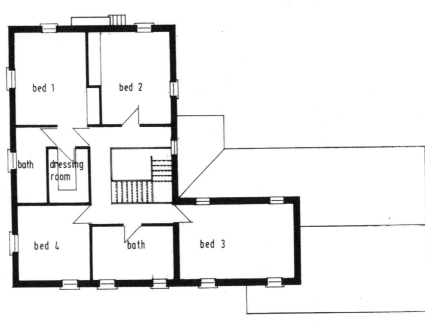

F I R S T   F L O O R

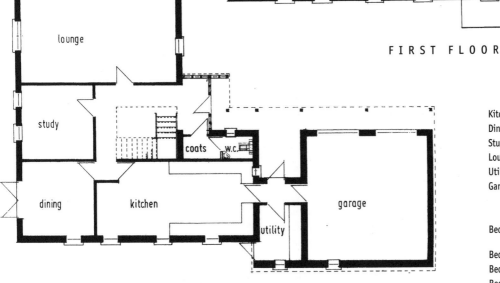

Kitchen	7.7 x 3.5m
Dining room	3.6 x 3.5m
Study	3.6 x 3.5m
Lounge	7.1 x 4.5m
Utility	2.6 x 2.0m
Garage	5.9 x 5.9m
Bedroom 1	4.4 x 3.5m + wardrobe, dressing room & en-suite
Bedroom 2	4.4 x 3.4m + wardrobe
Bedroom 3	5.75 x 3.55m
Bedroom 4	3.6 x 3.5m

G R O U N D   F L O O R

CHALFONT

The copyright belongs to Designer Homes

**263 sq. m.
including a garage
of 39 sq. m.**

Overall dimensions 19.50 x 15.60m

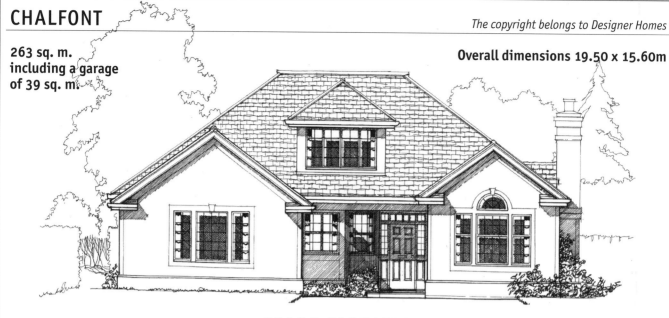

FRONT ELEVATION

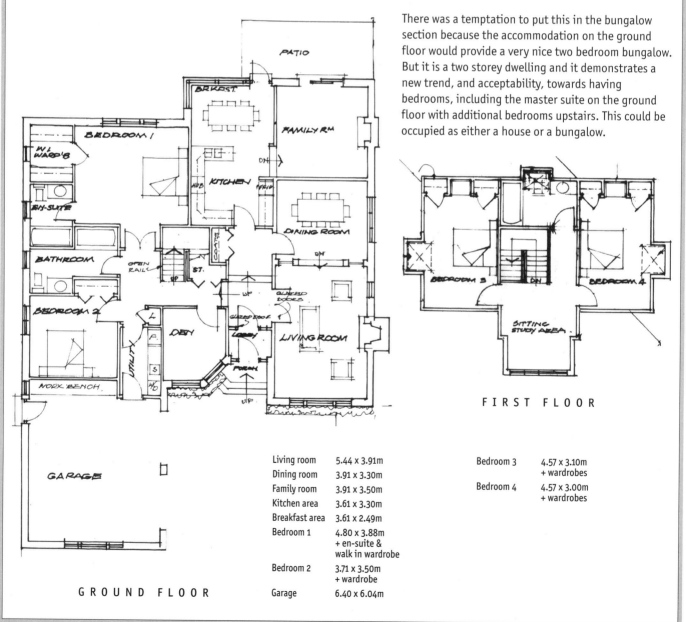

There was a temptation to put this in the bungalow section because the accommodation on the ground floor would provide a very nice two bedroom bungalow. But it is a two storey dwelling and it demonstrates a new trend, and acceptability, towards having bedrooms, including the master suite on the ground floor with additional bedrooms upstairs. This could be occupied as either a house or a bungalow.

FIRST FLOOR

GROUND FLOOR

Living room	5.44 x 3.91m
Dining room	3.91 x 3.30m
Family room	3.91 x 3.50m
Kitchen area	3.61 x 3.30m
Breakfast area	3.61 x 2.49m
Bedroom 1	4.80 x 3.88m + en-suite & walk in wardrobe
Bedroom 2	3.71 x 3.50m + wardrobe
Garage	6.40 x 6.04m

Bedroom 3	4.57 x 3.10m + wardrobes
Bedroom 4	4.57 x 3.00m + wardrobes

THE STONEHURST

The copyright belongs to Scandia-Hus Limited

267 sq. m.

Overall dimensions 18.29 x 11.93m

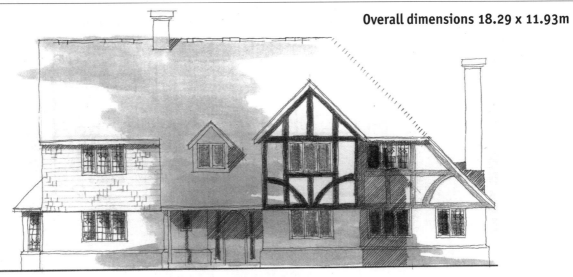

FRONT ELEVATION

This traditional design with its catslide roof at one end contains everything most families would want including five double bedrooms, two with en-suite facilities and a landing, which can double up as a sitting area. Downstairs features a large sitting room with inglenook fireplace, a family room with a fireplace, plus a study, dining room and a large kitchen and breakfast room.

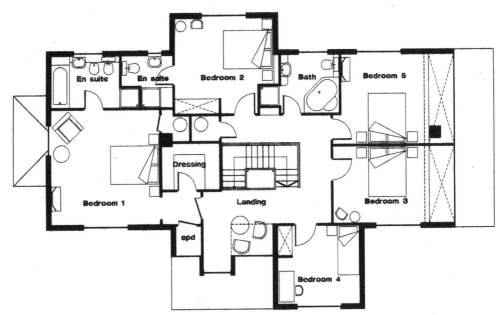

FIRST FLOOR

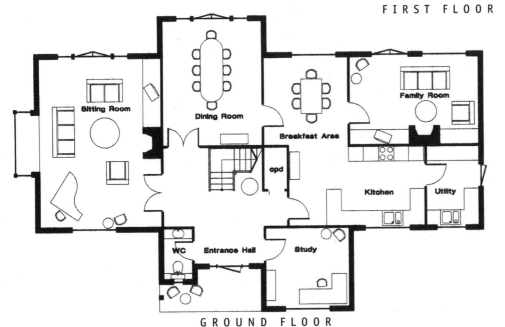

GROUND FLOOR

Kitchen	5.4 x 3.1m
Breakfast area	3.4 x 3.4m
Dining room	4.9 x 4.0m
Sitting room	6.7 x 4.9m
Family room	5.1 x 3.4m
Study	3.4 x 3.0m
Master bedroom	4.5 x 4.4m + dressing room & en-suite
Bedroom 2	3.8 x 3.3m
Bedroom 3	3.9 x 3.0m
Bedroom 4	3.4 x 3.1m
Bedroom 5	3.5 x 2.3m
Landing/sitting room	5.5 x 5.1m

P317

The copyright belongs to Design & Materials Ltd.

272 sq. m.

Overall dimensions 19.33 x 13.29m

FRONT ELEVATION

This double fronted family home was obviously conceived for those for whom the garden and activities in and around the house, are important. The garden room as an extension off the lounge could be the summer lounge or it could become the sunroom. The utility with its wet room or shower room would act as a barrier to dirt being brought into the home and the glazed bay projections and full height glazed walls in the breakfast area and the dining room propel the living space into the garden.

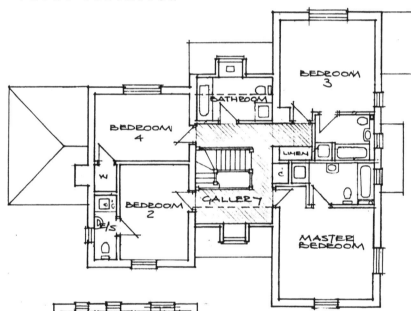

FIRST FLOOR

GROUND FLOOR

Lounge	7.67 x 4.50m
Dining room	4.42 x 3.66m
Garden room	4.72 x 3.50m
Kitchen/ breakfast room	5.80 x 4.50m + bay & larder
Utility	3.35 x 2.13m + shower room
Master bedroom	4.50 x 4.27m + en-suite
Bedroom 2	4.52 x 3.40m + en-suite
Bedroom 3	4.55 x 4.08m
Bedroom 4	4.50 x 3.05m

HARDWICK OO-179

The copyright belongs to Potton Ltd.

272 sq. m.

Overall dimensions 17.9 x 15.2m

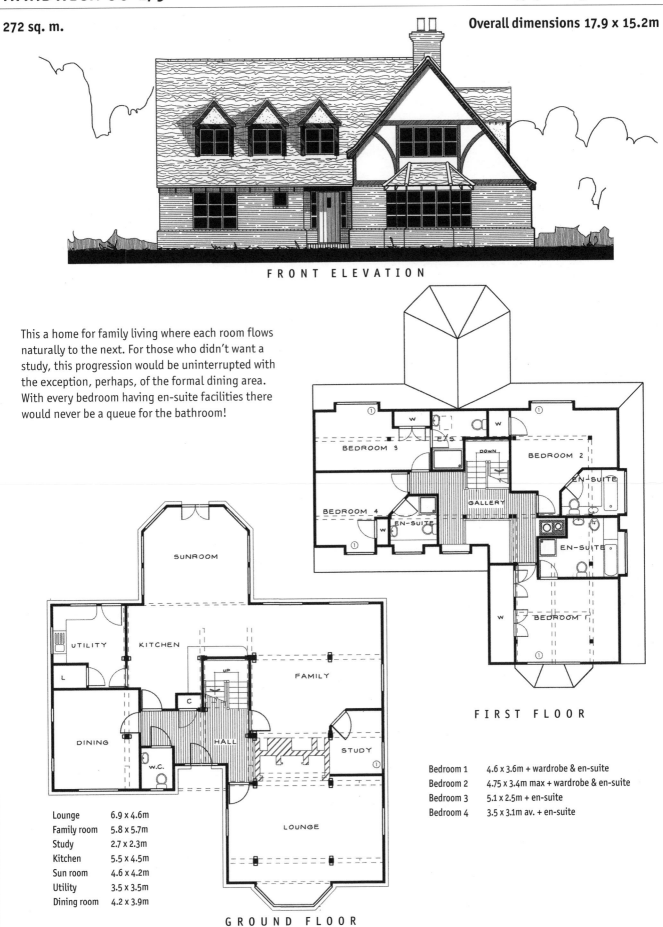

FRONT ELEVATION

This a home for family living where each room flows naturally to the next. For those who didn't want a study, this progression would be uninterrupted with the exception, perhaps, of the formal dining area. With every bedroom having en-suite facilities there would never be a queue for the bathroom!

FIRST FLOOR

GROUND FLOOR

Lounge	6.9 x 4.6m
Family room	5.8 x 5.7m
Study	2.7 x 2.3m
Kitchen	5.5 x 4.5m
Sun room	4.6 x 4.2m
Utility	3.5 x 3.5m
Dining room	4.2 x 3.9m

Bedroom 1	4.6 x 3.6m + wardrobe & en-suite
Bedroom 2	4.75 x 3.4m max + wardrobe & en-suite
Bedroom 3	5.1 x 2.5m + en-suite
Bedroom 4	3.5 x 3.1m av. + en-suite

245

SELKIRK

The copyright belongs to Designer Homes

277 sq. m. including a garage of 35 sq. m.

Overall dimensions 22.60 x 17.20m

FRONT ELEVATION

This attractive design has so many features. The dining hall, divided from the main walkway by posts and beams is an important use of space. If it had been walled in, the resulting dining room would have been very much smaller and would have been divorced from the kitchen and the rest of the reception rooms. The large dressing room for the en-suite with cupboards, shelves and wardrobes built into it, is something that many would love.

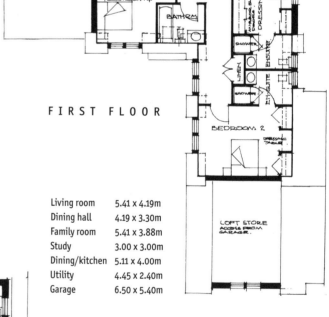

FIRST FLOOR

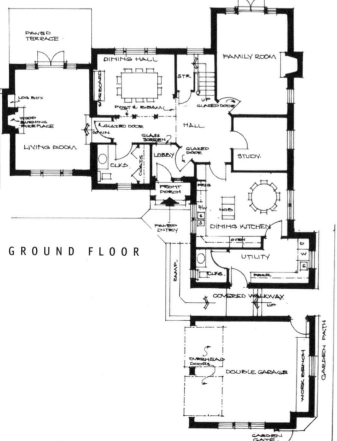

GROUND FLOOR

Living room	5.41 x 4.19m
Dining hall	4.19 x 3.30m
Family room	5.41 x 3.88m
Study	3.00 x 3.00m
Dining/kitchen	5.11 x 4.00m
Utility	4.45 x 2.40m
Garage	6.50 x 5.40m
Bedroom 1	5.28 x 3.91m + dressing room & en-suite
Bedroom 2	4.42 x 3.71m + wardrobes + en-suite
Bedroom 3	3.61 x 3.50m + wardrobe
Bedroom 4	3.20 x 2.74m + wardrobe

SOMMERVILLE HOUSE

The copyright belongs to T. J. Crump OAKRIGHTS Ltd.

278 sq. m.

Overall dimensions 17.98 x 10.60m

FRONT ELEVATION

SIDE ELEVATION

A very traditional family home that combines a brick or stone exterior with the oak framing. Once again the idea of a dining hall is employed with the entrance facilities confined to a relatively small lobby and toilet. The study would suit someone working from home.

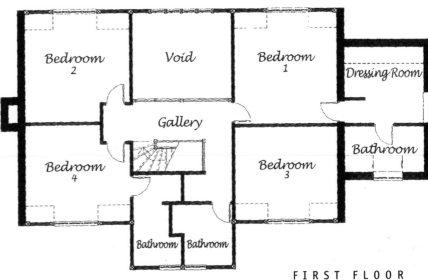

FIRST FLOOR

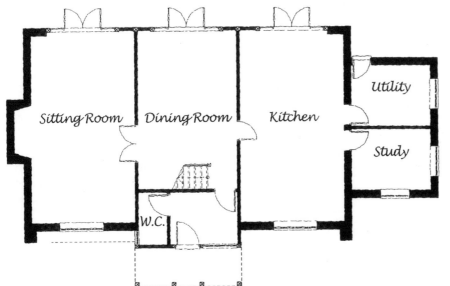

GROUND FLOOR

Sitting room	7.47 x 4.42m
Dining room	6.20 x 4.09m
Study	3.20 x 2.34m
Kitchen	7.34 x 4.32m
Utility	3.20 x 2.34m
Bedroom 1	4.37 x 4.32m + dressing room & en-suite
Bedroom 2	4.32 x 3.58m
Bedroom 3	4.29 x 3.76m
Bedroom 4	4.32 x 3.48m & en-suite

KEMPLEY

The copyright belongs to T. J. Crump OAKRIGHTS Ltd.

278 sq.m.

Overall dimensions 21.38 x 10.25m

F R O N T E L E V A T I O N

A fine example of a house where the top floor is cantilevered out over
the ground floor to gain extra space and add interest to the elevations.
Once again the idea of a dining hall is employed with an open gallery to
the top landing overlooking this feature.

FIRST FLOOR

GROUND FLOOR

Sitting room	8.46 x 5.38m
Dining hall	5.26 x 4.57m
Kitchen	5.26 x 4.27m
Utility	4.98 x 4.70m
Bedroom 1	5.97 x 5.59m + en-suite
Bedroom 2	5.66 x 3.68m
Bedroom 3	4.62 x 3.99m + en-suite

HUNTLEY

The copyright belongs to T. J. Crump OAKRIGHTS Ltd.

278 sq. m.

Overall dimensions 16.0 x 11.66m

FRONT ELEVATION

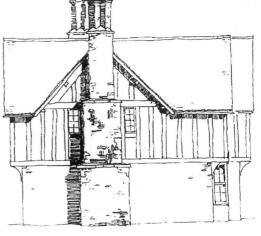

SIDE ELEVATION

The layout of this home is very modern and follows the same pattern as is found in many new houses. But there the similarity ends for this house takes that modern layout and lends a character to it with features that one would only expect in a traditional house.

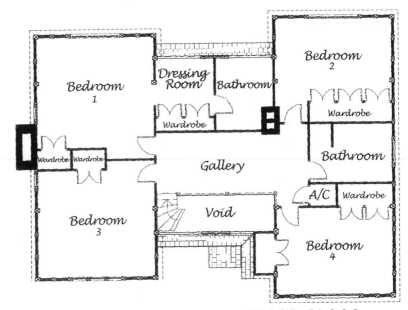

FIRST FLOOR

Sitting room	8.10 x 4.75m
Dining room	4.95 x 4.04m
Study	4.77 x 2.84m
Kitchen	5.00 x 4.65m
Utility	2.50 x 1.70m
Bedroom 1	4.87 x 4.80m + dressing room & en-suite
Bedroom 2	4.87 x 4.19m + wardrobe
Bedroom 3	4.87 x 4.26m + wardrobe
Bedroom 4	4.90 x 4.11m + wardrobe

GROUND FLOOR

THE CARLISLE

The copyright belongs to Custom Homes Ltd.

279 sq. m.
including a garage of 37 sq. m.

Overall dimensions 24.38 x 14.60m

FRONT ELEVATION

Linking and offsetting the garage with the main house via the utility area is a clever way to bring interest to the frontage. Apart from its triple garage this home provides extremely generous accommodation including five good sized bedrooms, two of which are en-suite. Linking one bedroom to the main bathroom is also a good idea if there is enough wall space.

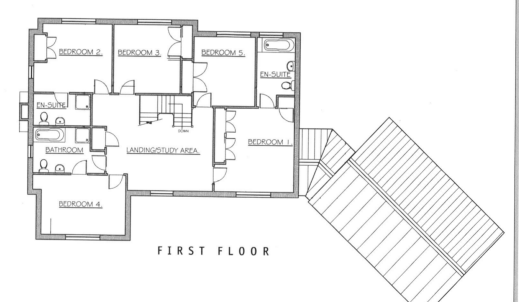

FIRST FLOOR

GROUND FLOOR

Living room	6.90 x 4.10m
Study	3.60 x 4.50m
Dining room	4.06 x 3.45m
Kitchen/ family room	7.73 x 5.19m + utility
Garage	7.80 x 5.40m
Bedroom 1	4.23 x 4.08m + en-suite
Bedroom 2	4.08 x 3.45m + en-suite
Bedroom 3	3.48 x 3.45m + wardrobe
Bedroom 4	4.50 x 3.00m
Bedroom 5	3.76 x 3.48m
Landing/study	4.40 x 3.23m

E116

**280 sq. m.
including a garage
of 39 sq. m.**

Overall dimensions 18.45 x 16.45m

FRONT ELEVATION

The dining hall is the hub of this home. The octagonal conservatory is, of course, optional but it does lend character to the building and its position, off the lounge, is interesting. The downstairs bedroom could always be called and used as something else. Upstairs there are three good sized bedrooms with the gallery landing open to the dining hall below.

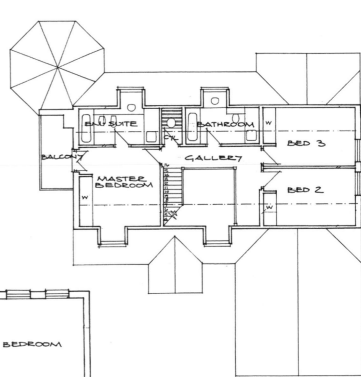

FIRST FLOOR

GROUND FLOOR

Lounge	5.49 x 4.52m + conservatory	Master bedroom	4.27 x 4.20m + en-suite & balcony
Kitchen	4.57 x 4.27m		
Utility	2.57 x 2.14m	Bedroom 2	4.88 x 3.05m
Dining hall	5.12 x 4.57m	Bedroom 3	4.88 x 3.05m
Study	4.88 x 3.05m		
Bedroom	5.47 x 4.88m		
Garage	6.71 x 5.49m		

HOUSES OVER 280 SQ. M.

For many would be self builders the houses of this size are only a distant dream. However, for quite a lucky few they are only too real. These sizes allow the designers full flow to their creative ambitions. Although they often have to conform to local styles and choice of external materials many of the bigger ones are starting to be architectural units in their own right, dictating, to an extent, their own environment. The larger houses in this section are getting to be six or more times the size of the three bedroom semi detached estate house. That's a theoretical capability of eighteen bedrooms – almost the size of a hotel!

Whilst many will only look enviously at these designs, knowing they are, for the time being, beyond their means, the free expressions of design that they employ can often be translated downwards into much smaller houses.

Contributors in this section:
Associated Self Build Architects
The Border Design Centre
T.J.Crump OAKWRIGHTS Ltd.
Custom Homes Ltd.
Design & Materials Ltd.
Designer Homes
Potton Ltd.
The Self Build House Company Ltd.
Scottish Architects Network
Scandia-Hus Ltd.
The Swedish House Company Ltd.

THE FOSDYKE

The copyright belongs to an ASBA architectural practice – Julian Owen Associates

281 sq. m.

Overall dimensions 22.8 x16.6m

SIDE (WEST) ELEVATION

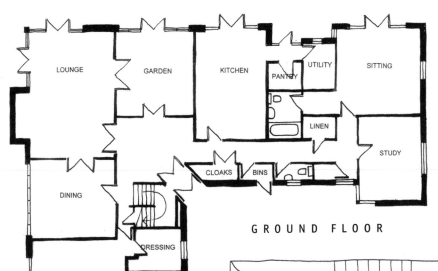

GROUND FLOOR

This contribution could easily have found its way into the section on 'Homes with a granny flat' or even 'Homes with an office/playroom or special accommodation'. If the study became a bedroom and the utility room was re-arranged to serve as small kitchenette this end of the home could be a granny flat. Just as easily these rooms could be self contained as office accommodation for someone working from home.

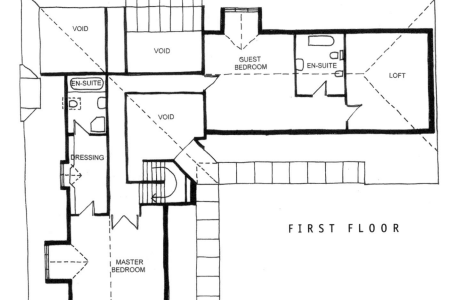

FIRST FLOOR

Lounge	6.0 x 4.5m
Dining room	4.5 x 4.0m
Kitchen	5.8 x 3.8m
Utility	2.3 x 1.7m
Sitting room	4.5 x 4.5m
Study	4.2 x 3.5m
Guest bedroom	5.0 x 4.8m + dressing room & en-suite
Garden room	4.5 x 4.0m
Master bedroom	5.5 x 5.0m + dressing room & en-suite
2nd guest bedroom	5.0 x 5.0m + en-suite

HEREFORD

The copyright belongs to Designer Homes

284 sq. m.

Overall dimensions 18.10 x 15.70m

FRONT ELEVATION

The staircase tower with its arched high level window gives a sort of Gothic feel to this home, especially when taken together with the illustrated filigree bargeboards. The breakfast room, though protruding to the rear, is the only direct link between the kitchen and the family room. This device mitigates against the family room being used for eating and retains its use as a second lounge or true family room.

GROUND FLOOR

FIRST FLOOR

Living room	5.64 x 4.47m	Principal bedroom	4.21 x 4.17m + wardrobe, dressing room & en-suite	
Study	3.10 x 3.05m			
Dining room	4.17 x 3.61m			
Kitchen	4.57 x 4.21m			
Family room	5.38 x 4.21m	Guest bedroom	4.21 x 4.17m + wardrobe & en-suite	
Breakfast room	3.66 x 3.05m			
Utility	2.85 x 2.10m			
		Bedroom 3	3.96 x 3.35m + wardrobe	
		Bedroom 4	4.17 x 3.20m + wardrobes	
		Bedroom 5	3.96 x 2.90m + wardrobe	

THE COPTHORNE

The copyright belongs to Scandia-Hus Limited

285 sq. m.

Overall dimensions 18.4 x 11.6m

FRONT ELEVATION

A graceful manor house with a double fronted aspect and a catslide roof to one end that gives it a distinctive style. If the music room was not wanted as such, it could just as easily be the sixth bedroom and it is the versatility of this design that makes it so attractive.

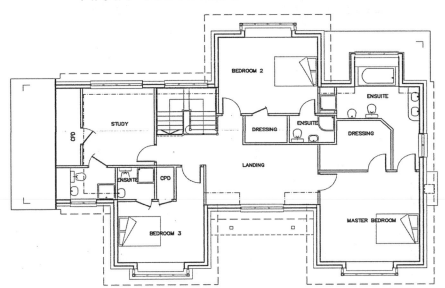

FIRST FLOOR

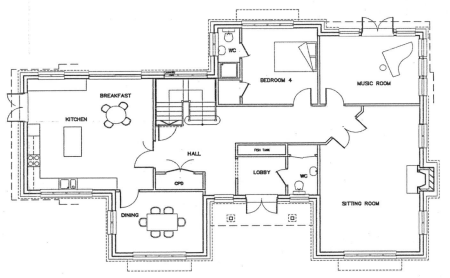

GROUND FLOOR

Kitchen/ breakfast room	5.7 x 5.6m
Dining room	3.9 x 3.1m
Sitting room	7.4 x 4.5m
Music room	4.5 x 3.5m
Bedroom 4	3.9 x 3.5m
Master bedroom	4.6 x 4.5m + dressing area & en-suite
Bedroom 2	4.6 x 3.9m + dressing area & en-suite
Bedroom 3	3.9 x 3.1m + en-suite
Study/bedroom 5	3.9 x 3.3m

ALTRINGHAM

The copyright belongs to The Border Design Centre

286 sq. m.
including a garage complex of 34 sq. m.

Overall dimensions 19.3 x 13.7m

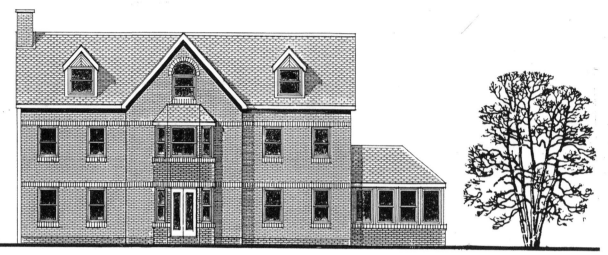

FRONT ELEVATION

In order to preserve an unobstructed main view, the driveway is led up the side of the house, keeping motor cars out of sight. To maximise the area of garden the home was designed on three storeys, with the children's rooms on the upper floor and first floor drawing room. The tower spiral staircase also helps to reduce the footprint and preserve garden space.

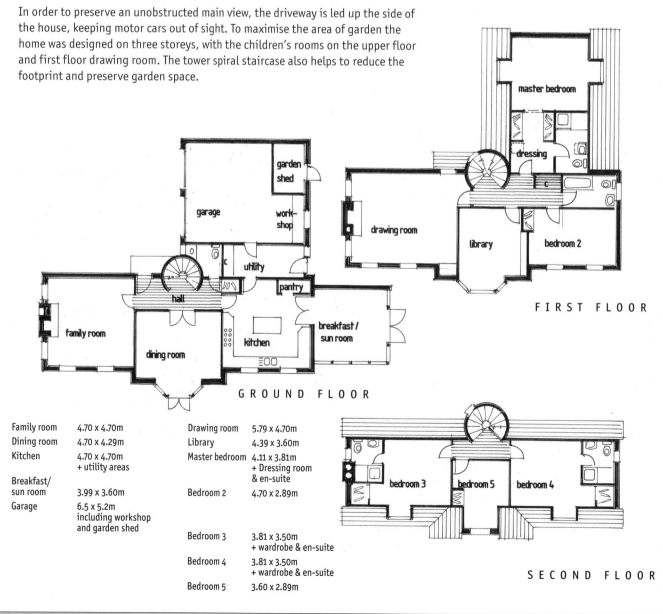

Family room	4.70 x 4.70m	Drawing room	5.79 x 4.70m	
Dining room	4.70 x 4.29m	Library	4.39 x 3.60m	
Kitchen	4.70 x 4.70m + utility areas	Master bedroom	4.11 x 3.81m + Dressing room & en-suite	
Breakfast/ sun room	3.99 x 3.60m	Bedroom 2	4.70 x 2.89m	
Garage	6.5 x 5.2m including workshop and garden shed	Bedroom 3	3.81 x 3.50m + wardrobe & en-suite	
		Bedroom 4	3.81 x 3.50m + wardrobe & en-suite	
		Bedroom 5	3.60 x 2.89m	

ABERDOVEY

The copyright belongs to The Border Design Centre

289 sq. m.
including a garage of 26 sq. m.

Overall dimensions 20.2 x 11.2m

There is a distinctly nautical feel to this lovely home, which is hardly surprising when one learns that it was designed for the entrance of a boatyard where the owner wanted to take advantage of the views and keep an eye on the comings and goings in the marina. For those who like the design but prefer the living room on the ground floor, whilst it is an 'upside down' house, it could easily be reversed.

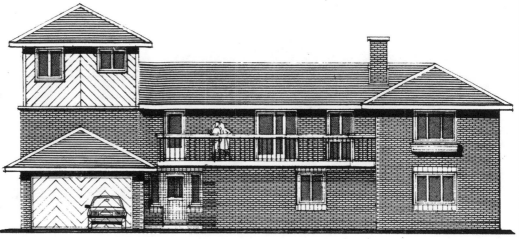

FRONT ELEVATION

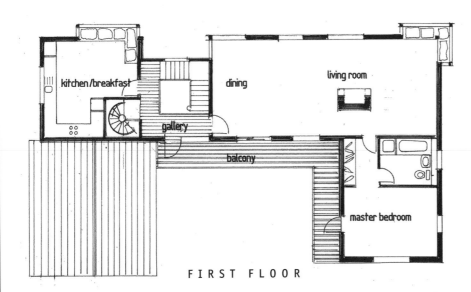

FIRST FLOOR

Bedroom 2	4.70 x 3.81m
Bedroom 3	4.70 x 3.50m + wardrobe
Bedroom 4	3.50 x 3.20m + wardrobe
Bedroom 5	3.50 x 3.20m + wardrobe
Utility	3.50 x 2.70m
Workshop	4.60 x 1.9m
Garage	5.5 x 4.7m

Living/ dining room	11.30 x 4.70m
Kitchen/ breakfast room	4.70 x 4.70m
Master bedroom	4.70 x 3.50m + Dressing area & en-suite

| Crow's nest study | 4.70 x 4.70m |

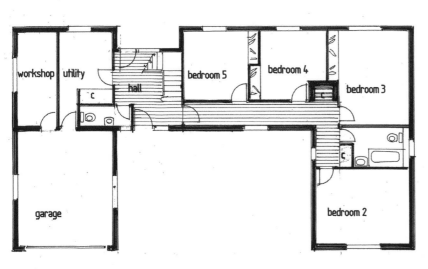

GROUND FLOOR

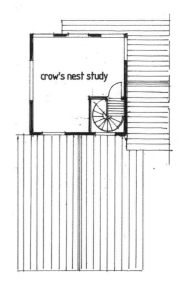

SECOND FLOOR

257

HATTON CASTLE

The copyright belongs to The Border Design Centre

290 sq. m.

Overall dimensions 22.2 x 12.5m

REAR ELEVATION

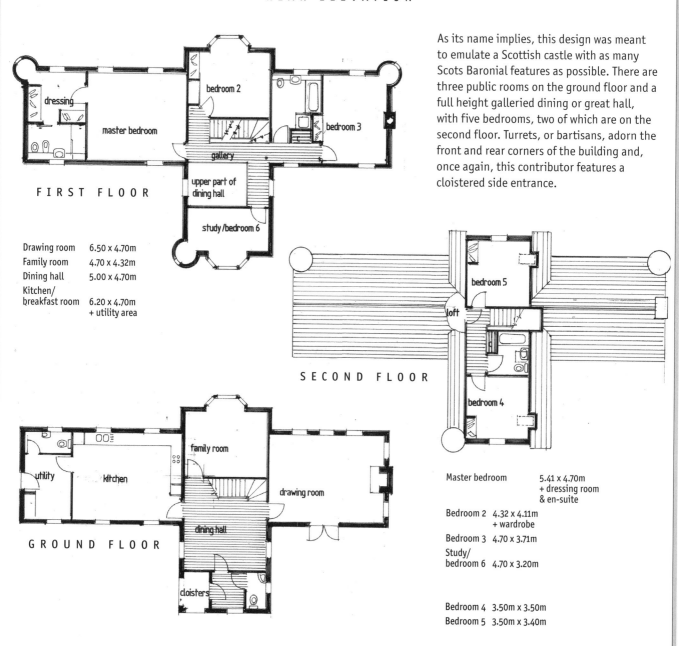

As its name implies, this design was meant to emulate a Scottish castle with as many Scots Baronial features as possible. There are three public rooms on the ground floor and a full height galleried dining or great hall, with five bedrooms, two of which are on the second floor. Turrets, or bartisans, adorn the front and rear corners of the building and, once again, this contributor features a cloistered side entrance.

FIRST FLOOR

Drawing room	6.50 x 4.70m
Family room	4.70 x 4.32m
Dining hall	5.00 x 4.70m
Kitchen/ breakfast room	6.20 x 4.70m + utility area

SECOND FLOOR

GROUND FLOOR

Master bedroom	5.41 x 4.70m + dressing room & en-suite
Bedroom 2	4.32 x 4.11m + wardrobe
Bedroom 3	4.70 x 3.71m
Study/ bedroom 6	4.70 x 3.20m
Bedroom 4	3.50m x 3.50m
Bedroom 5	3.50m x 3.40m

97-301

290 sq. m.

Overall dimensions 21.1 x 13.7m

F R O N T   E L E V A T I O N

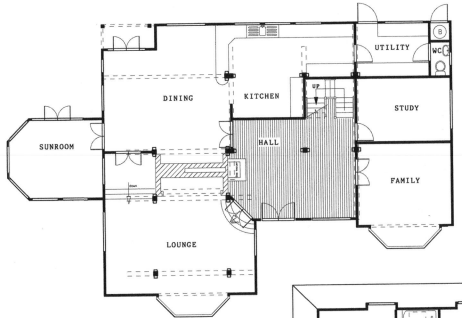

G R O U N D   F L O O R

The change of level indicated between the lounge and dining room around the side of the inglenook would create a very interesting living space, especially when combined with the walk through to the kitchen. Four of the bedrooms have en-suite facilities and the fifth has the ability to share.

Lounge	6.9 x 5.2m
Dining room	6.2 x 5.9m
Kitchen	5.7 x 4.2m max
Utility	3.4 X 2.4m
Study	4.3 x 2.9m
Family room	4.35 x 3.6m
Sun room	4.3 x 3.5m

Bedroom 1	4.6 x 4.2m + wardrobe & en-suite
Bedroom2	3.4 x 3.3m + wardrobe & en-suite
Bedroom 3	3.5 x 2.5m + wardrobe & shared en-suite
Bedroom 4	3.5 x 3.4m + wardrobe & shared en-suite
Bedroom 5	4.4 x 2.2m

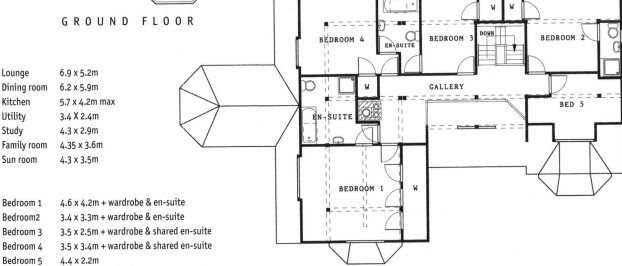

F I R S T   F L O O R

THE MILLSTONE

The copyright belongs to Scandia-Hus Limited

291 sq. m.
including a garage of 42 sq. m.

Overall dimensions 18.21 x 12.6m

FRONT ELEVATION

The design of this rambling family home caters for the varied and numerous interests of a busy family, providing space for every activity. The large farmhouse kitchen has a cosy fire at one end and the cathedral roofed sitting room, the snug and the dining room all benefit from a three way fireplace, whilst maintaining their separate status.

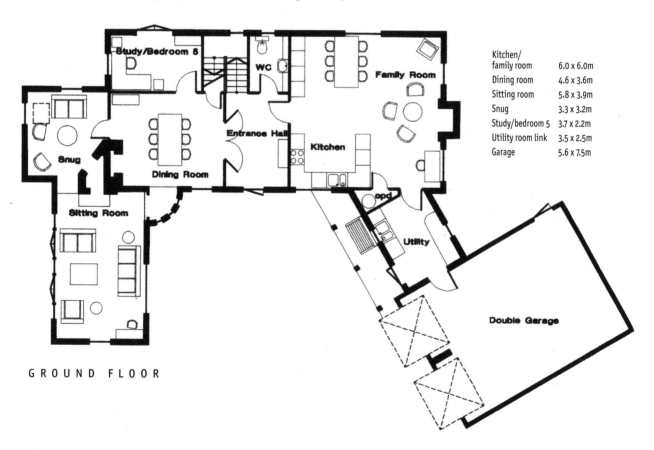

GROUND FLOOR

Kitchen/family room	6.0 x 6.0m
Dining room	4.6 x 3.6m
Sitting room	5.8 x 3.9m
Snug	3.3 x 3.2m
Study/bedroom 5	3.7 x 2.2m
Utility room link	3.5 x 2.5m
Garage	5.6 x 7.5m

R E A R   E L E V A T I O N

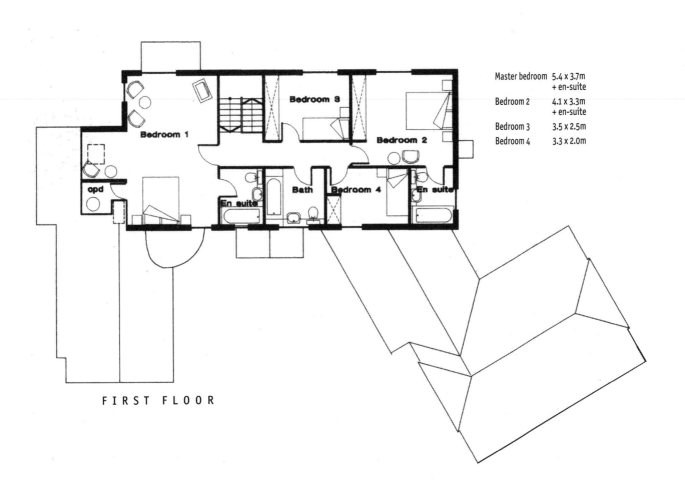

Master bedroom	5.4 x 3.7m + en-suite
Bedroom 2	4.1 x 3.3m + en-suite
Bedroom 3	3.5 x 2.5m
Bedroom 4	3.3 x 2.0m

F I R S T   F L O O R

SKELLINGTHORPE

The copyright belongs to an ASBA architectural practice - John Woodward

291 sq. m

Overall dimensions 13.9 x 12.2m

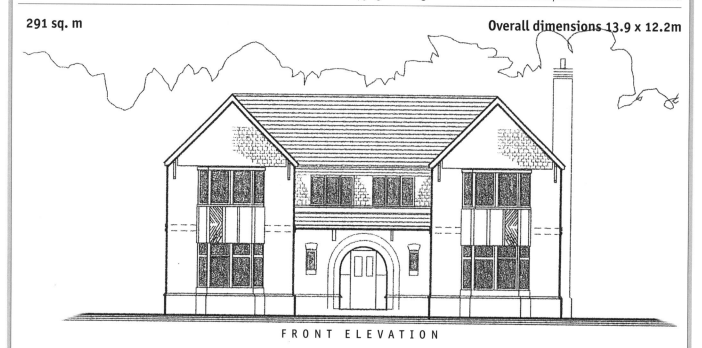

FRONT ELEVATION

A unique double fronted house designed originally for a plot in Lincolnshire. This is a solid and tested design that manages to group all of the major rooms around a central hallway and staircase. The open gallery and void above the kitchen is a feature but it could be utilised as an additional bedroom.

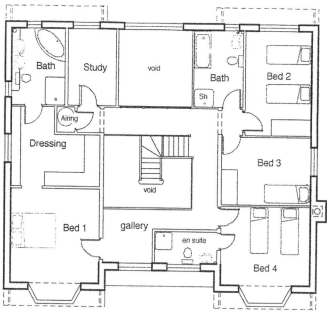

FIRST FLOOR

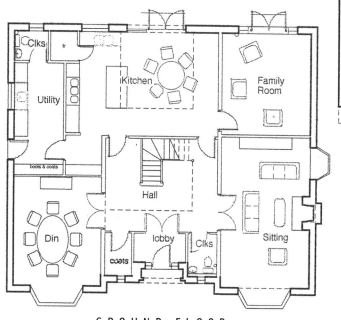

GROUND FLOOR

Sitting room	6.5 x 4.0m		Bedroom 1	4.1 x 4.0m + dressing room & en-suite
Dining room	4.7 x 4.0m			
Family room	4.4 x 4.0m		Bedroom 2	4.5 x 3.0m
Kitchen/ breakfast room	6.9 x 4.4m		Bedroom 3	4.0 x 2.9m
Utility	4.45 x 2.25m		Bedroom 4	4.0 x 3.4m + en-suite
			Study/ bedroom 5	3.3 x 2.5m

RUBIES BARN

The copyright belongs to T. J. Crump OAKRIGHTS Ltd.

294 sq. m.
including a garage of 30 sq. m.

Overall dimensions 22.25 x 21.33m

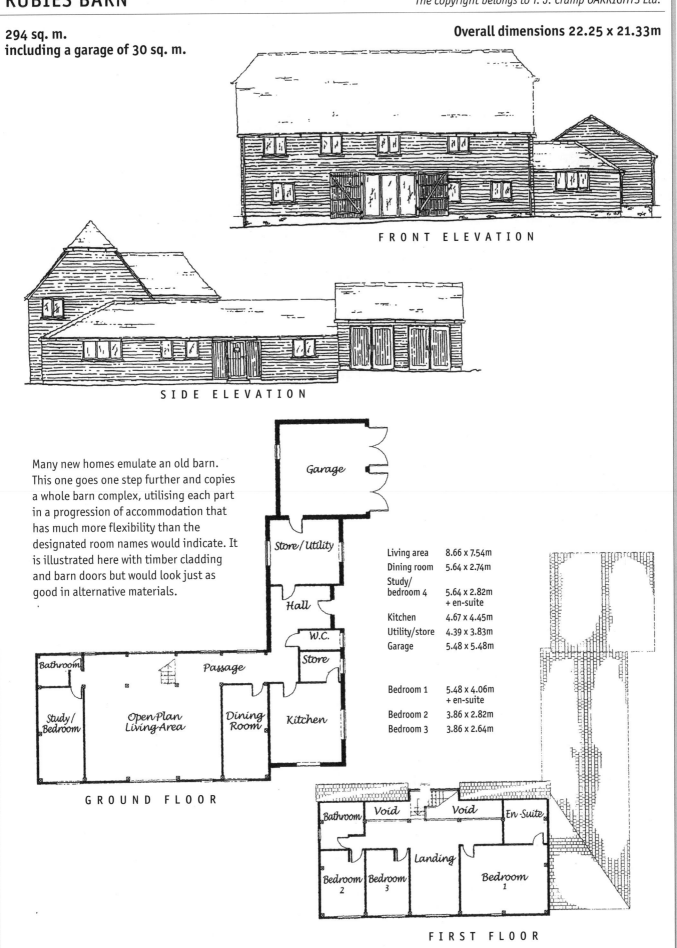

FRONT ELEVATION

SIDE ELEVATION

Many new homes emulate an old barn. This one goes one step further and copies a whole barn complex, utilising each part in a progression of accommodation that has much more flexibility than the designated room names would indicate. It is illustrated here with timber cladding and barn doors but would look just as good in alternative materials.

Living area	8.66 x 7.54m
Dining room	5.64 x 2.74m
Study/ bedroom 4	5.64 x 2.82m + en-suite
Kitchen	4.67 x 4.45m
Utility/store	4.39 x 3.83m
Garage	5.48 x 5.48m
Bedroom 1	5.48 x 4.06m + en-suite
Bedroom 2	3.86 x 2.82m
Bedroom 3	3.86 x 2.64m

GROUND FLOOR

FIRST FLOOR

THE CORLIONE

The copyright belongs to Scandia-Hus Limited

292 sq. m.

Overall dimensions 17.31 x 17.16m

This is a stunning design, reminiscent of an Italian palazzio or a Greek island villa. It is built on three floors plus a mezzanine floor to the lower level and is brim full of interesting features with columns, arches, a courtyard and a tower room. A concept home that is, nevertheless real and achievable and which provides superb accommodation, the sum of which is far greater than the simple description above.

FRONT ELEVATION

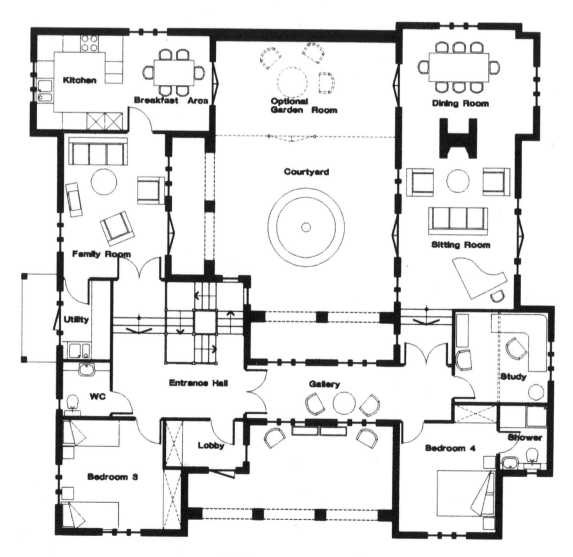

GROUND FLOOR

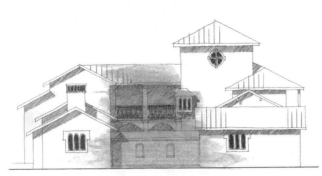

REAR ELEVATION

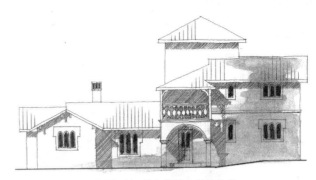

SIDE ELEVATION

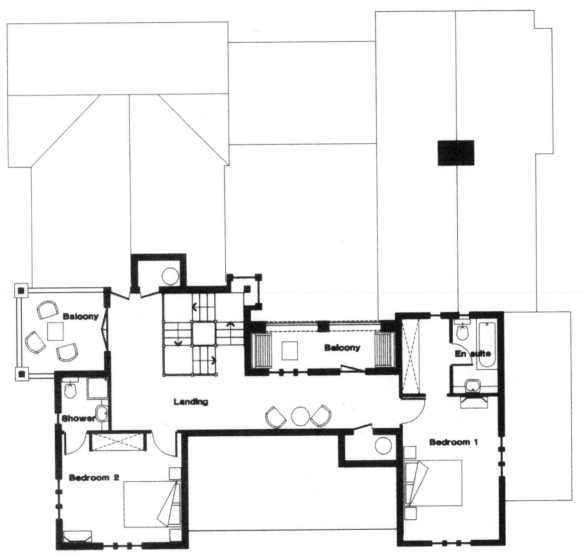

FIRST FLOOR

SECOND FLOOR

Kitchen/breakfast area	5.9 x 3.6m	Master bedroom	4.8 x 3.3m + dressing area & en-suite
Dining room	4.7 x 3.5m		
Sitting room	5.6 x 3.9m	Bedroom 2	4.1 x 3.6m + en-suite
Family room	3.9 x 3.5m		
Bedroom 3	3.6 x 3.4m		
Bedroom 4	4.2 x 3.3m + en-suite	Tower room	4.5 x 4.5m
Study	3.2 x 3.0m		

98-216

The copyright belongs to Potton Ltd.

294 sq. m.

Overall dimensions 18.9 x 12.6m

FRONT ELEVATION

GROUND FLOOR

House		Annex	
Lounge	5.8 x 5.7m	Living room	5.7 x 3.5m
Kitchen	6.5 x 5.0m	Kitchen	3.5 x 2.3m
Utility	2.8 x 2.0m	Bedroom	3.9 x 3.5m
Study	3.1 x 2.8m		+ wardrobe
Dining hall	6.7 x 5.8m		& en-suite

Bedroom 1	4.7 x 3.9m
	+ wardrobe & en-suite
Bedroom 2	4.8 x 4.1m
	+ wardrobe & en-suite
Bedroom 3	4.7 x 2.8m
Bedroom 4	4.7 x 2.8m

This is an interesting design for a home, which provides a more or less self-contained annex with the bedroom upstairs. This would be suitable for a more active older family member or a semi-detached youngster. The use of the hall as 'great hall' or dining area is an exciting and fashionable idea.

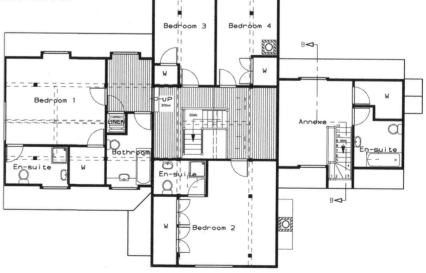

FIRST FLOOR

97-272

300 sq. m. including a 51 sq. m. garage

Overall dimensions 29.03 x 12.7m

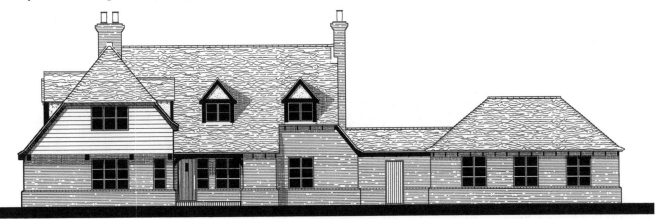

FRONT ELEVATION

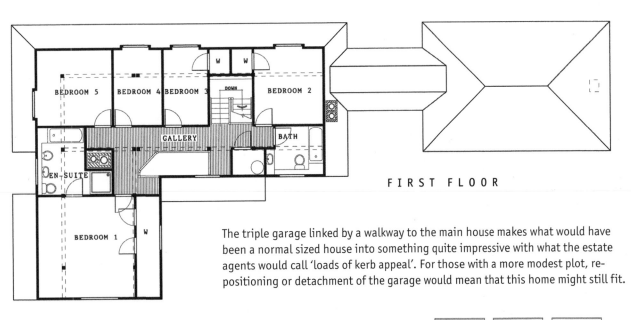

FIRST FLOOR

The triple garage linked by a walkway to the main house makes what would have been a normal sized house into something quite impressive with what the estate agents would call 'loads of kerb appeal'. For those with a more modest plot, re-positioning or detachment of the garage would mean that this home might still fit.

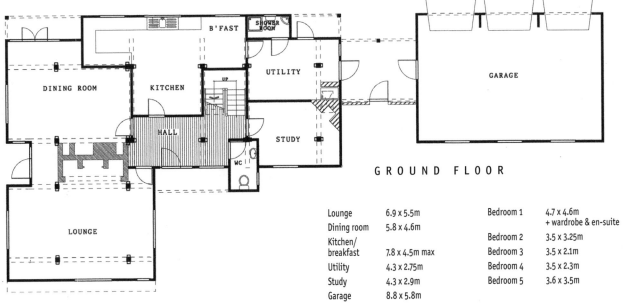

GROUND FLOOR

Lounge	6.9 x 5.5m	Bedroom 1	4.7 x 4.6m + wardrobe & en-suite
Dining room	5.8 x 4.6m		
Kitchen/ breakfast	7.8 x 4.5m max	Bedroom 2	3.5 x 3.25m
Utility	4.3 x 2.75m	Bedroom 3	3.5 x 2.1m
Study	4.3 x 2.9m	Bedroom 4	3.5 x 2.3m
Garage	8.8 x 5.8m	Bedroom 5	3.6 x 3.5m

KNIGHTSBRIDGE

The copyright belongs to Designer Homes

303 sq. m.
including a garage of 36 sq. m.

Overall dimensions 21.40 x 14.30m

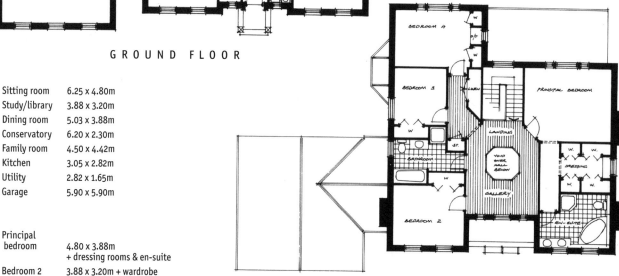

FRONT ELEVATION

GROUND FLOOR

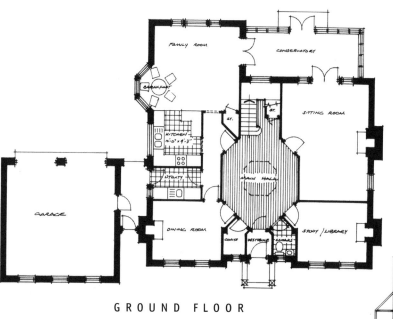

Almost half of the available top floor space is taken up with the master suite! Such a lavish arrangement might not find favour with everybody and indeed if it were not required, the design would not be compromised if the upper part were re-arranged to provide five bedrooms. Once again this contributor demonstrates the versatility of a central octagonal hallway and landing with all rooms having easy access.

Sitting room	6.25 x 4.80m
Study/library	3.88 x 3.20m
Dining room	5.03 x 3.88m
Conservatory	6.20 x 2.30m
Family room	4.50 x 4.42m
Kitchen	3.05 x 2.82m
Utility	2.82 x 1.65m
Garage	5.90 x 5.90m

Principal bedroom	4.80 x 3.88m + dressing rooms & en-suite
Bedroom 2	3.88 x 3.20m + wardrobe
Bedroom 3	3.05 x 2.82m + wardrobe
Bedroom 4	4.11 x 3.05m + wardrobes

FIRST FLOOR

GALWAY

The copyright belongs to T. J. Crump OAKRIGHTS Ltd.

306 sq. m.
including a garage of 36 sq. m.

Overall dimensions 22.0 x 12.71m

FRONT ELEVATION

This exciting design of a family home is centred on the great hall and the galleried area above it. The closets to the minor bedrooms could just as well be en-suite shower rooms whilst the master suite enjoys a full sized bathroom.

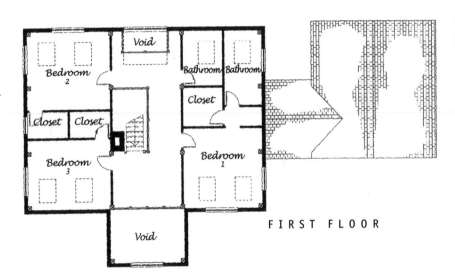

FIRST FLOOR

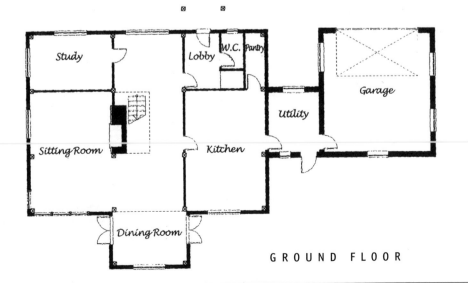

GROUND FLOOR

Great hall	9.19 x 3.78m
Sitting room	6.22 x 4.42m
Dining area	4.09 x 2.82m
Study	4.42 x 2.92m
Kitchen	6.17 x 4.37m
Utility	4.37 x 3.07m
Garage	6.07 x 5.87m
Bedroom 1	4.37 x 4.08m + closet & en-suite
Bedroom 2	4.45 x 4.01m + closet
Bedroom 3	4.45 x 3.53m + closet

PRESTON

The copyright belongs to T. J. Crump OAKRIGHTS Ltd.

322 sq. m.

Overall dimensions 22.22 x 13.19m

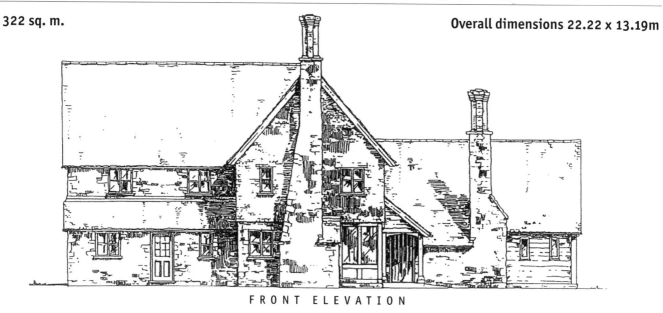

FRONT ELEVATION

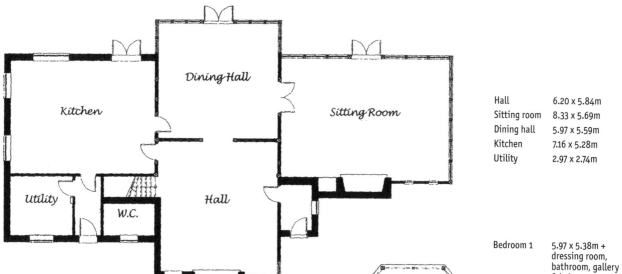

GROUND FLOOR

Hall	6.20 x 5.84m
Sitting room	8.33 x 5.69m
Dining hall	5.97 x 5.59m
Kitchen	7.16 x 5.28m
Utility	2.97 x 2.74m

Bedroom 1	5.97 x 5.38m + dressing room, bathroom, gallery & balcony
Bedroom 2	4.47 x 3.07m
Bedroom 3	4.47 x 3.07m

This is a big home and if four bedrooms were required then all that would be needed would be to make the gallery area, off the main bedroom overlooking the sitting room, into an en-suite, thus freeing up the dressing room area to act as a fourth bedroom. The entrance hall is huge and would be a room in its own right but, combined with the dining hall, would be magnificent.

FIRST FLOOR

95-046

324 sq. m.

The copyright belongs to Potton Ltd.

Overall dimensions 24.9 x 14.5m

F R O N T   E L E V A T I O N

In common with many of the larger houses illustrated within this book, although I have indicated a minimum site width, this is a home that really deserves a much larger plot. The impressive hall would provide a 'wow' factor upon entrance and that would only increase as you move from room to room.

Lounge	6.75 x 6.5m
Kitchen/ breakfast	6.7 x 6.6m max
Dining room	6.7 x 4.2m max
Utility	4.5 x 3.25m
Study	6.9 x 3.0m
Store	2.55 x 1.8m

G R O U N D   F L O O R

Master bedroom	6.4 x 4.6m + dressing room & en-suite
Bedroom 2	3.4 x 2.9m + walk-in wardrobe
Bedroom 3	3.6 x 3.5m
Bedroom 4	4.0 x 3.5m

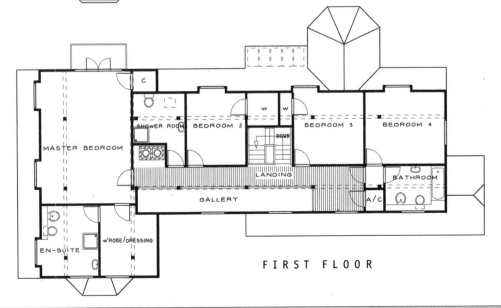

F I R S T   F L O O R

THE VENNEL

The copyright belongs to a ScAN architectural practice – Walter Wood Associates

326 sq. m.   **Overall dimensions 23.25 x 10.0m**

FRONT ELEVATION   SIDE ELEVATION

Is it a church conversion or is it a new build? Although this is primarily a book for new plans this one bears inclusion simply because it could actually be built as a new building in a situation where the planners wanted it to emulate a church. It might also give some good ideas to those who have toyed with the idea of converting one of the many redundant churches.

Living/ dining area	7.85 x 7.7m max
Kitchen/ breakfast room	5.6 x 3.6m max
Office/study	4.2 x 2.7m + cupboard
Bedroom 2	4.2 x 2.9m + wardrobe
Master bedroom	3.6 x 3.5m + wardrobe & en-suite
Bedroom 1	4.4 x 2.8m + wardrobe
Bedroom 3	4.2 x 2.8m
Gallery/ sitting area	7.7 x 2.3m max
Evening room	5.1 x 2.7m

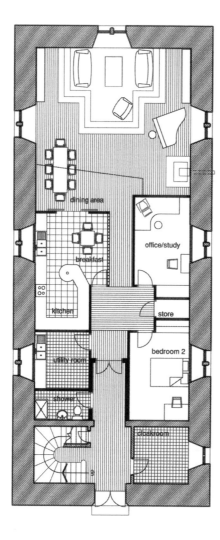

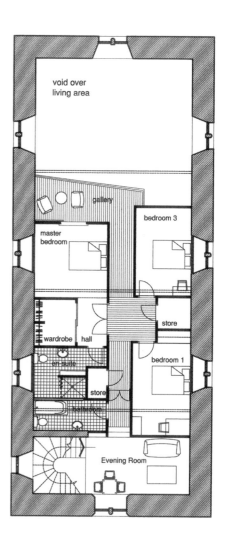

GROUND FLOOR   FIRST FLOOR

THE CLIFFORD

The copyright belongs to an ASBA architectural practice - Reed Architects

327 sq. m.

Overall dimensions 17.3 x 10.4m

FRONT ELEVATION

This house was designed for a sensitive site on the Welsh borders and its design reflects the defensive nature of the location with the round stair tower and massive walls. The garden room and dining room have full height glazing and this is reflected in the projecting bay of the master bedroom. With two attic bedrooms there is a total of five bedrooms and three bathrooms.

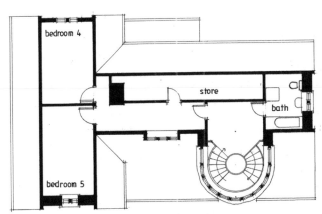

SECOND FLOOR

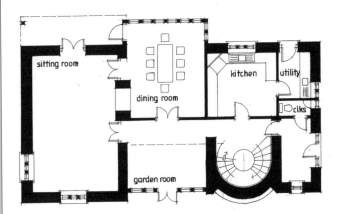

GROUND FLOOR

Sitting room	7.8 x 5.0m	Bedroom 1	6.5 x 5.0m + en-suite
Dining room	5.5 x 4.5m		
Kitchen	4.0 x 3.7m	Bedroom 2	5.0 x 3.3m
Utility	2.7 x 1.9m	Bedroom 3	3.7 x 2.5m
Garden room	4.5 x 3.9m	Study	3.7 x 3.3m
		Bedroom 4	4.7 x 3.0m
		Bedroom 5	5.2 x 3.0m
		Store	8.8 x 1.4m

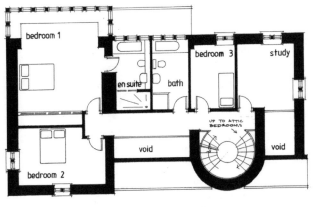

FIRST FLOOR

WATERFORD B

The copyright belongs to Potton Ltd.

327 sq. m.
including a garage and lobby
with storage over of 53.5 sq. m.

Overall dimensions 19.8 x 15m

FRONT ELEVATION

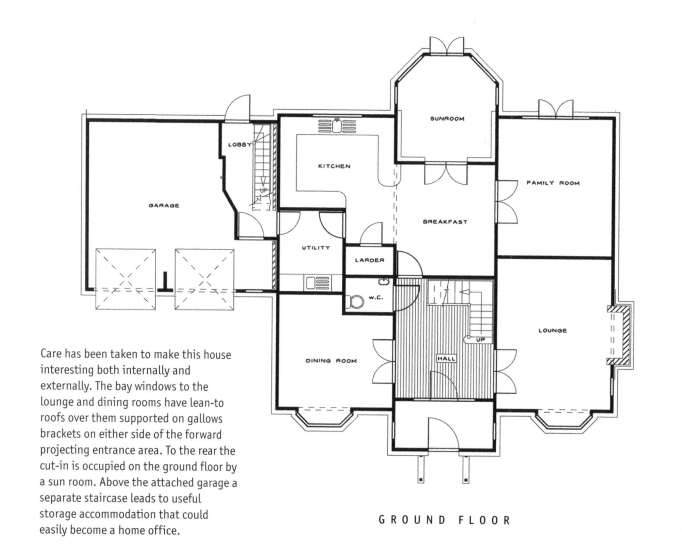

Care has been taken to make this house interesting both internally and externally. The bay windows to the lounge and dining rooms have lean-to roofs over them supported on gallows brackets on either side of the forward projecting entrance area. To the rear the cut-in is occupied on the ground floor by a sun room. Above the attached garage a separate staircase leads to useful storage accommodation that could easily become a home office.

GROUND FLOOR

REAR ELEVATION

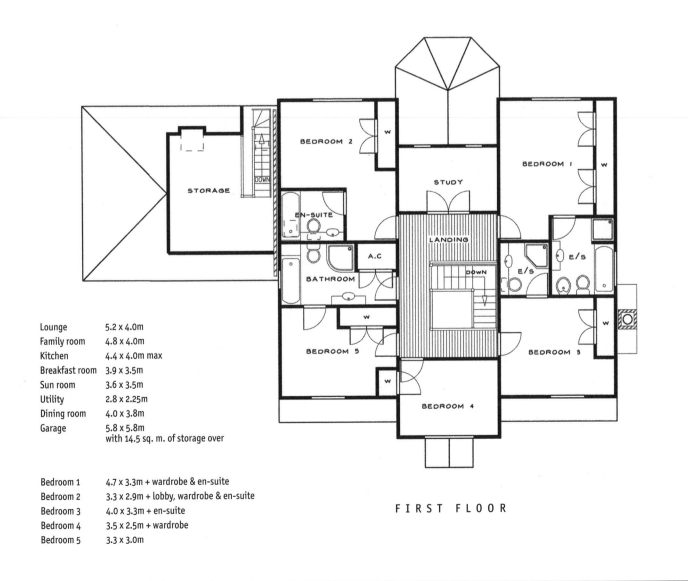

Lounge	5.2 x 4.0m
Family room	4.8 x 4.0m
Kitchen	4.4 x 4.0m max
Breakfast room	3.9 x 3.5m
Sun room	3.6 x 3.5m
Utility	2.8 x 2.25m
Dining room	4.0 x 3.8m
Garage	5.8 x 5.8m with 14.5 sq. m. of storage over

Bedroom 1	4.7 x 3.3m + wardrobe & en-suite
Bedroom 2	3.3 x 2.9m + lobby, wardrobe & en-suite
Bedroom 3	4.0 x 3.3m + en-suite
Bedroom 4	3.5 x 2.5m + wardrobe
Bedroom 5	3.3 x 3.0m

FIRST FLOOR

FORRESTERS

The copyright belongs to The Swedish House Company Ltd.

329 sq. m.

Overall dimensions 16.33 x 13.93m

FRONT ELEVATION

SIDE ELEVATION – WEST

This imposing family home boasts six bedrooms on two floors. Also, in a feature that is a trademark of this contributor's designs, it has a second lounge to the upper part with access to a balcony that is above the patio area to the downstairs sitting room. This mixture of accommodation would allow separate family activities to take place on each floor.

FIRST FLOOR

GROUND FLOOR

Sitting room	8.4 x 5.3m		Family room	7.2 x 4.2m
Dining area	4.1 x 3.7m		Bedroom 1	4.7 x 4.7m + bathroom
Kitchen	5.1 x 4.7m			
Utility	3.0 x 2.0m		Bedroom 2	3.6 x 3.4m max
Bedroom 5	3.4 x 2.9m		Bedroom 3	3.6 x 3.4m
Bedroom 6	4.1 x 2.9m		Bedroom 4	3.6 x 3.6m

THE EWELL

The copyright belongs to The Self-Build House Company Ltd.

331 sq. m.

Overall dimensions 15.57 x 14.42m

This is a well proportioned home on three floors providing six double bedrooms, three of which have en-suite facilities. Bedrooms 2 & 3 are drawn as having access to the communal bathroom but that does mean that there are three doors to this room. The large entrance hall with the gallery above is also useful space that could double up as a dining hall.

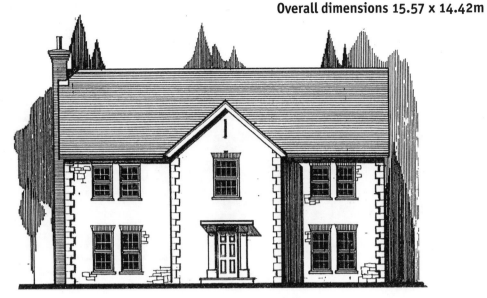

FRONT ELEVATION

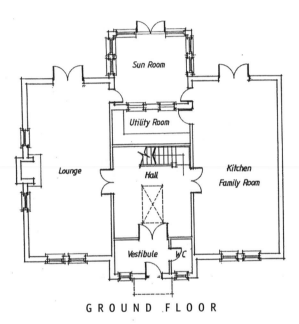

GROUND FLOOR

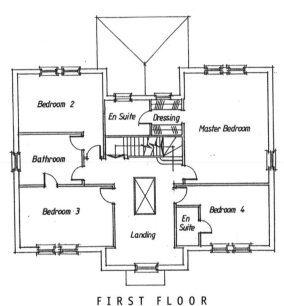

FIRST FLOOR

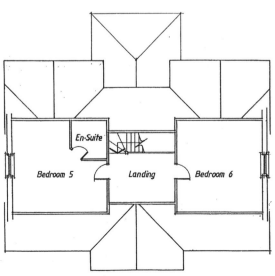

SECOND FLOOR

Kitchen/ family room	10.0 x 5.0m	Master bedroom	6.4 x 5.0m + dressing room & en-suite
Sitting room	10.0 x 5.0m		
Sun room	4.4 x 3.7m	Bedroom 2	5.0 x 3.3m
Utility	4.64 x 1.86m	Bedroom 3	5.5 x 3.4m
		Bedroom 4	4.1 x 3.4m + en-suite
		Bedroom 5	5.6 x 5.4m including en-suite
		Bedroom 6	5.35 x 5.07m.

INVER ALMOND

The copyright belongs to The Border Design Centre

333 sq. m.

Overall dimensions 17.3 x 16.1m

FRONT ELEVATION

This design originates with a Scottish castle where a level plinth has been carved out of the hillside and entrance is made by means of a bridge to the upper ground floor level. The central part of the house is a two storey dining hall overlooked by a gallery at main entrance level, on which is the magnificent drawing room with its large round bay window. A further wing could be added opposite the drawing room. There is also provision for a lift between floors.

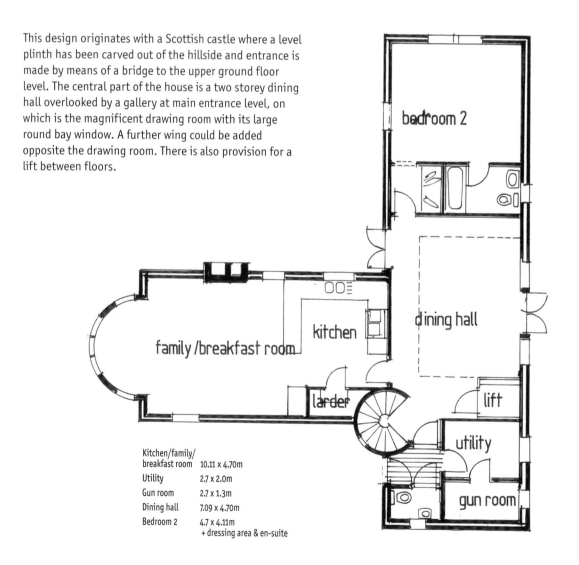

Kitchen/family/ breakfast room	10.11 x 4.70m
Utility	2.7 x 2.0m
Gun room	2.7 x 1.3m
Dining hall	7.09 x 4.70m
Bedroom 2	4.7 x 4.11m + dressing area & en-suite

LOWER GROUND FLOOR

SIDE ELEVATION

Drawing room   7.90 x 4.70m
Study   2.89 x 2.49m
Bedroom 3   4.70 x 3.50m
                + wardrobe
Bedroom 4   3.20 x 2.89m
                + wardrobe

Master bedroom 5.00 x 3.50m
                + dressing room
                & en-suite
Bedroom 5   3.20 x 2.89m
                + en-suite

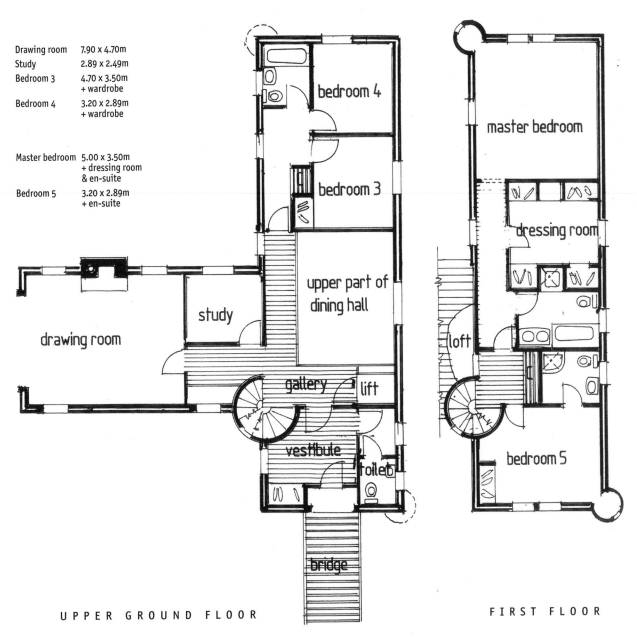

UPPER GROUND FLOOR   FIRST FLOOR

WOODHALL SPA

The copyright belongs to an ASBA architectural practice – John Woodward

333 sq. m.

Overall dimensions 15.9 x 15.2m

FRONT ELEVATION

A simple name change makes this handsome home into a six bedroom house with three bathrooms. The playroom is open to the kitchen so that mother can keep an eye on the children whilst she's busy. The utility room also has that most prized of possessions, even in this age of the fitted kitchen, a pantry!

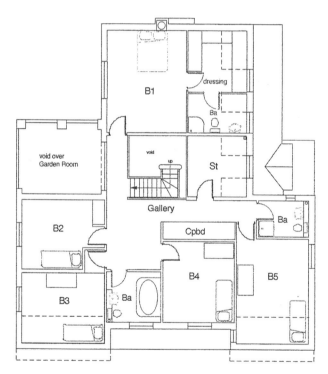

FIRST FLOOR

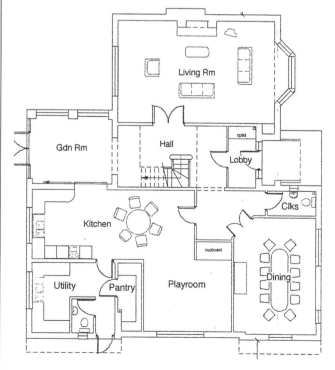

GROUND FLOOR

Living room	8.0 x 5.0m	Bedroom 1	5.0 x 4.0m + dressing room & en-suite	
Dining room	5.6 x 4.2m			
Kitchen	8.2 x 3.4m			
Playroom	4.5 x 3.5m	Bedroom 2	4.2 x 3.4m	
Utility	3.4 x 1.9m + pantry	Bedroom 3	4.2 x 3.4m	
		Bedroom 4	4.1 x 3.5m	
Garden room	4.4 x 3.3m	Bedroom 5	5.1 x 3.6m	
		Study	3.0 x 3.0m	

ROCHESTER

The copyright belongs to Potton Ltd.

336 sq. m.

Overall dimensions 19.1 x 18.5m

FRONT ELEVATION

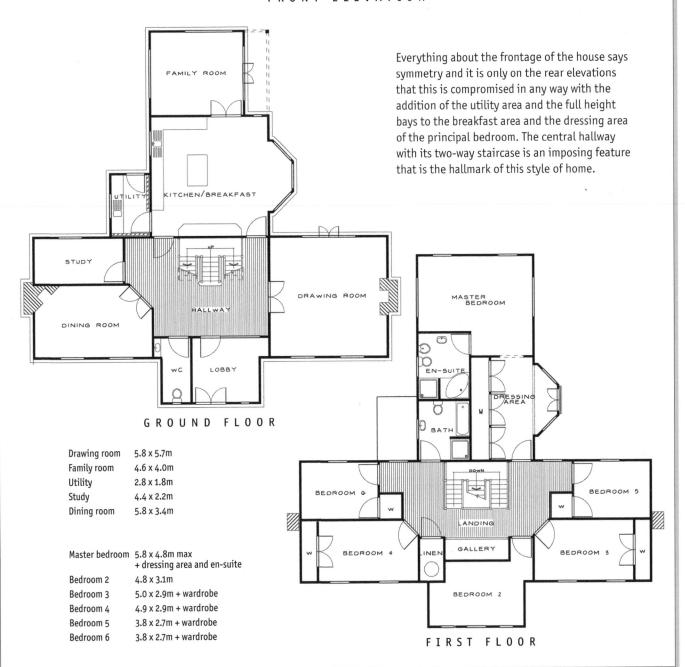

Everything about the frontage of the house says symmetry and it is only on the rear elevations that this is compromised in any way with the addition of the utility area and the full height bays to the breakfast area and the dressing area of the principal bedroom. The central hallway with its two-way staircase is an imposing feature that is the hallmark of this style of home.

GROUND FLOOR

FIRST FLOOR

Drawing room	5.8 x 5.7m
Family room	4.6 x 4.0m
Utility	2.8 x 1.8m
Study	4.4 x 2.2m
Dining room	5.8 x 3.4m
Master bedroom	5.8 x 4.8m max + dressing area and en-suite
Bedroom 2	4.8 x 3.1m
Bedroom 3	5.0 x 2.9m + wardrobe
Bedroom 4	4.9 x 2.9m + wardrobe
Bedroom 5	3.8 x 2.7m + wardrobe
Bedroom 6	3.8 x 2.7m + wardrobe

MARSTOW

The copyright belongs to T. J. Crump OAKRIGHTS Ltd.

337 sq. m.
including a garage of 34 sq. m.

Overall dimensions 20.96 x 19.35m

FRONT ELEVATION

REAR ELEVATION

This lovely home unashamedly copies a traditional barn, right down to the stone or brick plinth, the timber cladding and the heavy full height barn doors to the full height and vaulted ceiling of the entrance hall. So too with the internal accommodation where areas are given a designation rather than rigid divisions.

Entrance hall	5.33 x 3.86m
Dining area	4.14 x 3.81m
Family area	3.81 x 1.88m
Snug	3.58 x 3.53m
Kitchen	4.29 x 3.83m
Utility	3.83 x 1.73m
Bedroom 2	4.80 x 3.73m + en-suite
Bedroom 3	3.88 x 3.73m + wardrobe
Bedroom 4	3.88 x 2.84m
Garage	6.25 x 5.38m
Bedroom 1	6.02 x 3.58m + bathroom & dressing room
Living room	7.98 x 5.94m

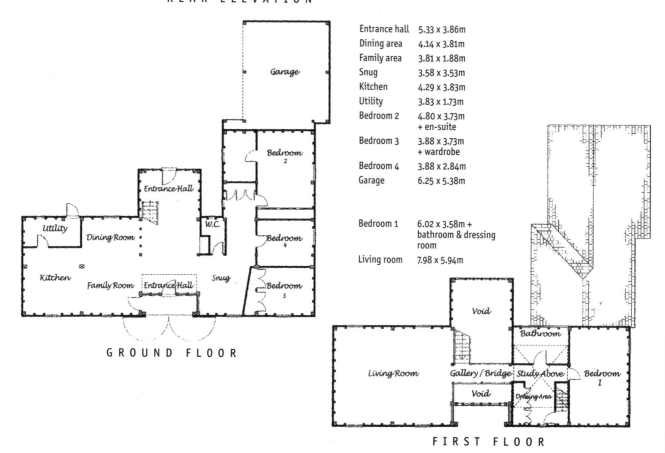

GROUND FLOOR

FIRST FLOOR

SADDLEWOODS

The copyright belongs to an ASBA architectural practice – Julian Owen Associates

338 sq. m.
including a garage of 43 sq. m.

Overall dimensions 26.2 x 17.4m

S I D E   E L E V A T I O N

Whole walls of glazing greet the garden and invite it into the home. Full height gable head windows form one end wall of the master bedroom, which shares access to a balcony with the other bedrooms. This architect has rightly identified that laundry originates upstairs and should therefore be dealt with on that level in the drying/laundry room.

FIRST FLOOR

GROUND FLOOR

Living room	6.3 x 6.0m
Family room	5.0 x 3.0m
Sunroom	5.5 x 2.5m
Kitchen/ dining room	7.0 x 6.0m
Study	5.0 x 4.5m
Utility	6.5 x 2.3m
Master bedroom	6.0 x 5.5m + en-suite
Bedroom 2	7.0 x 3.0m
Bedroom 3	7.0 x 3.0m
Bedroom 4	5.0 x 1.5m
Bedroom 5	7.0 x 5.0m
Drying room	3.0 x 1.5m

STOCKS BARN

The copyright belongs to T. J. Crump OAKRIGHTS Ltd.

341 sq. m.

Overall dimensions 20.93 x 18.0m

FRONT ELEVATION

Looking just like a barn conversion rather than a new home, this design would allow light to flood in to most of the living/reception areas and the principal bedroom. The living room with its vaulted ceiling is separated from the main body of the home. On the other hand, the combination of kitchen, breakfast room and family dining would probably be where most family activities take place.

Great hall	6.63 x 4.67m
Living room	6.78 x 5.49m
Dining room	4.98 x 3.12m
Study	4.98 x 2.31m
Family dining	5.54 x 5.20m
Kitchen	5.54 x 4.06m
Breakfast room	7.39 x 3.68m
Utility/ mud room	4.98 x 3.12m

Living Room

Dining Room

Hall

Breakfast Room

Utility / Mudroom

Pantry

Entrance Lobby   W.C.

Study

Kitchen

Family Dining
307,79 sq ft

GROUND FLOOR

Bedroom 3

En-Suite   Bathroom

En - Suite

Bedroom 1

Bedroom 2

Upper Hall

Bedroom 4

Closet

Bedroom 1	7.47 x 4.34m + closet & en-suite
Bedroom 2	4.98 x 3.86m
Bedroom 3	3.53 x 3.48m + en-suite
Bedroom 4	4.60 x 2.74m

FIRST FLOOR

BENENDEN

The copyright belongs to T. J. Crump OAKRIGHTS Ltd.

348 sq. m.

Overall dimensions 21.43 x 12.42m

FRONT ELEVATION

Those rooms that need to be private and separated from the hustle and bustle of family life are indeed separate, including, to an extent, the kitchen. As for the rest, they are shown in this illustration as being open to each other, although that could quite easily be changed.

SIDE ELEVATION

Hall	4.75 x 4.57m
Dining hall	5.03 x 4.77m
Sitting room	9.37 x 5.21m
Study	4.67 x 2.46m
Kitchen	5.94 x 3.66m
Utility	4.29 x 1.37m
Bedroom 1	4.98 x 4.72m + en-suite
Bedroom 2	4.75 x 4.50m
Bedroom 3	3.89 x 2.79m
Bedroom 4	2.64 x 2.54m

GROUND FLOOR

FIRST FLOOR

D150

345 sq. m.
including a garage of 38 sq. m.

Overall dimensions 23.58 x 12.50m

FRONT ELEVATION

Although they fell out of favour for a while, three storey houses have a long tradition in both town and country. There are knock on effects such as the need for fire doors and/or escapes but other than that, the structural implications are minimal. The footprint is, of course reduced and, if the top floor rooms are in the roof, the ridge height is not necessarily higher.

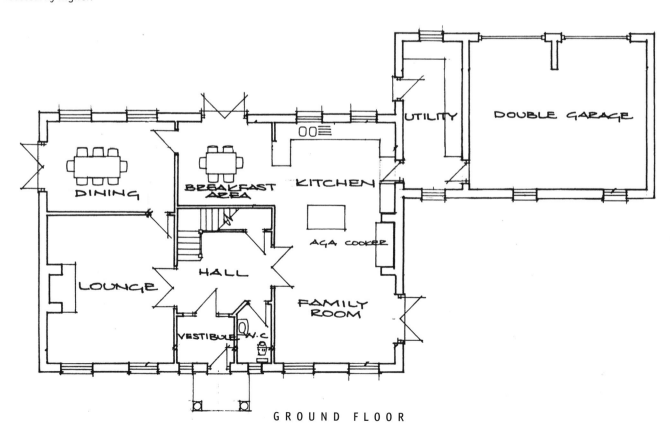

GROUND FLOOR

ALTERNATIVE SINGLE STOREY SECTION

Lounge	5.45 x 4.90m
Kitchen/ family room	8.90 x 4.60m
Breakfast area	3.70 x 3.20m
Dining room	4.90 x 3.35m
Utility	5.49 x 2.13m
Garage	6.84 x 5.49m
Master bedroom	4.69 x 4.60m + lobby, dressing area & en-suite
Bedroom 2	4.40 x 4.40m
Bedroom 3	4.90 x 4.40m
Bedroom 4	4.69 x 4.33m
Bedroom 5	4.89 x 4.33m

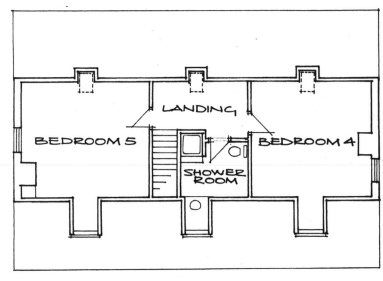

ATTIC FLOOR

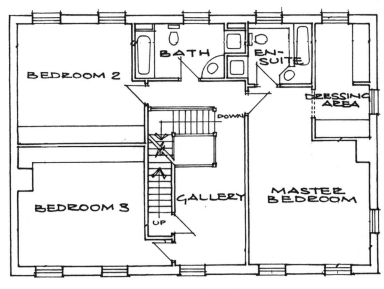

FIRST FLOOR

96-140

The copyright belongs to Potton Ltd.

349 sq. m.

Overall dimensions 18.5 x 17.2m

FRONT ELEVATION

There is a serious amount of accommodation in this home with six reception rooms and five bedrooms. The double fronted or 'H' shape makes for an interesting design and helps it fit on a relatively modest plot. In the original concept a double garage was linked to one end at an angle, providing even greater interest.

GROUND FLOOR

FIRST FLOOR

Lounge	7.4 x 6.5m
Dining room	6.7 x 5.7m
Family room	4.5 x 3.4m
Study	3.1 x 2.4m
Sun lounge	5.8 x 3.7m
Utility	3.6 x 2.2m
Master bedroom	4.7 x 4.6m
	+ wardrobe & en-suite
Bedroom 2	4.6 x 4.2m
	+ wardrobe & en-suite
Bedroom 3	3.5 x 2.9m + wardrobe
Bedroom 4	3.5 x 3.4m + wardrobe
Bedroom 5	4.9 x 4.5m

THE RUSPER

The copyright belongs to The Self-Build House Company Ltd.

**350 sq. m.
including a garage of 67 sq. m.**

Overall dimensions 26.7 x 16.34m

It is good to see that we are now beginning to repatriate some of the best design ideals from the colonial era. It is not just the clapboarding that gives this house its New England feel. Every element of the external design is characteristic of that period, including the long outbuildings section with its cupola and the 'hayloft' doors. The roof of the main house looks ripe for exploitation as extra accommodation.

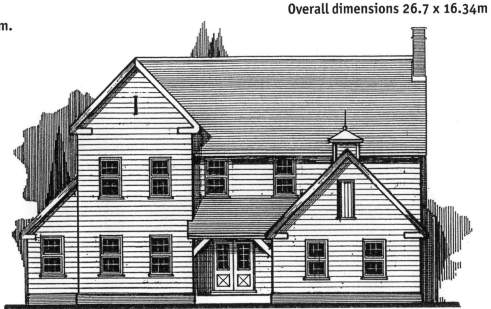

FRONT ELEVATION

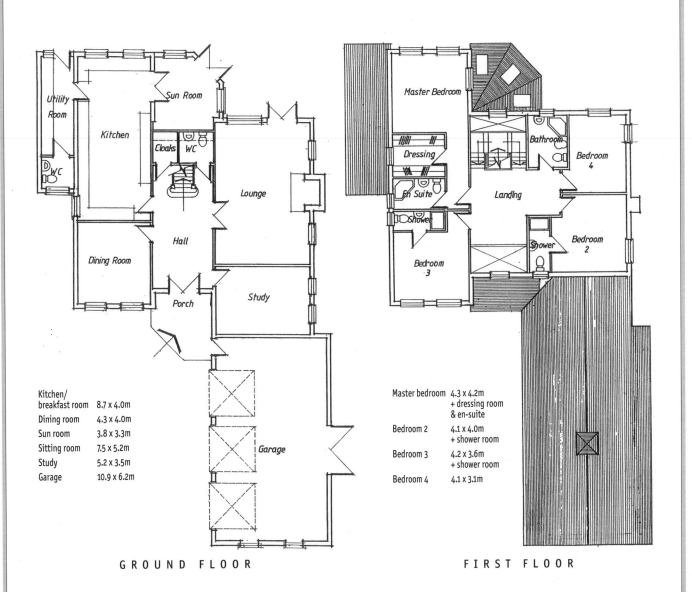

Kitchen/ breakfast room	8.7 x 4.0m
Dining room	4.3 x 4.0m
Sun room	3.8 x 3.3m
Sitting room	7.5 x 5.2m
Study	5.2 x 3.5m
Garage	10.9 x 6.2m

Master bedroom	4.3 x 4.2m + dressing room & en-suite
Bedroom 2	4.1 x 4.0m + shower room
Bedroom 3	4.2 x 3.6m + shower room
Bedroom 4	4.1 x 3.1m

GROUND FLOOR

FIRST FLOOR

THE DENYON

The copyright belongs to Scandia-Hus Limited

363 sq. m.

Overall dimensions 17.1 x 11.9m

FRONT ELEVATION

A truly magnificent modern family home that finds its roots in grander times. Some might not like the tandem garage but, if the site permitted, this could always be changed to a traditional double with a lesser depth leaving space at the rear for another room. The rooms in the top floor make proper use of the roof and increase the feeling of well being that this design engenders.

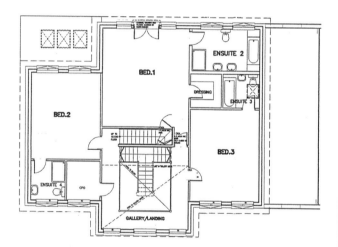

FIRST FLOOR

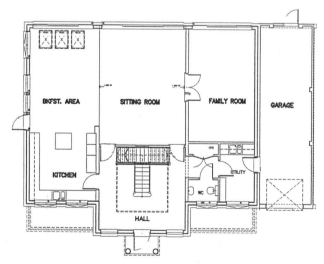

GROUND FLOOR

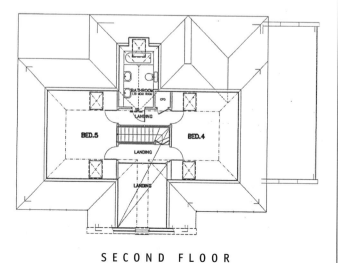

SECOND FLOOR

		Master bedroom	5.4 x 5.0m + dressing room & en-suite
Kitchen/ breakfast room	9.5 x 4.0m		
Sitting room	6.3 x 5.0m		
Family room	6.2 x 3.0m	Bedroom 2	4.9 x 4.0m + en-suite
Utility	3.4 x 2.0m		
Garage	9.8 x 3.1m	Bedroom 3	5.0 x 4.0m + en-suite
		Bedroom 4	4.8 x 3.8m
		Bedroom 5	4.9 x 4.0m

THE ETON

The copyright belongs to Custom Homes Ltd.

363 sq. m.

Overall dimensions 20.70 x 11.78m

F R O N T   E L E V A T I O N

This large family home has its accommodation grouped around a feature hallway and gallery, which opens onto a balcony. The symmetry is deliberately broken up by the addition of further forward projections and gables together with a two storey side extension. The breakfast room is, unusually, featured as a self-contained room that has links with both the kitchen and the dining room.

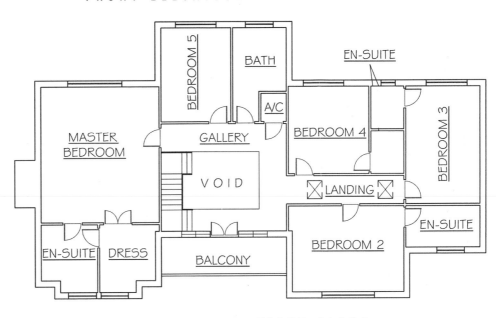

F I R S T   F L O O R

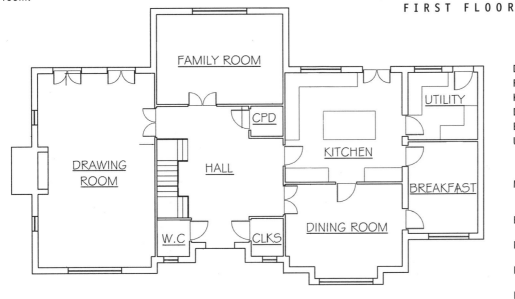

G R O U N D   F L O O R

Drawing room	8.27 x 5.21m
Family room	5.49 x 3.84m
Kitchen	5.12 x 4.67m
Dining room	5.12 x 3.51m
Breakfast room	3.91 x 3.05m
Utility	3.05 x 2.88m
Master bedroom	5.78 x 5.10m + dressing room & en-suite
Bedroom 2	4.95 x 3.60m + en-suite
Bedroom 3	5.03 x 3.23m + wardrobe
Bedroom 4	3.75 x 3.60m + wardrobe
Bedroom 5	3.98 x 3.00m

96-074

The copyright belongs to Potton Ltd.

364 sq. m.

Overall dimensions 19.2 x 16.1m

FRONT ELEVATION

Many would prefer, in a home of this size, an en-suite bathroom for the master bedroom, perhaps at the expense of bedroom five. However, with free standing roll top baths coming back into fashion, perhaps there is no need to formally enclose the bathing facilities with a room as big as this.

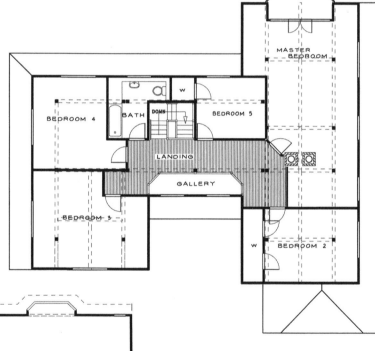

GROUND FLOOR

FIRST FLOOR

Lounge	7.0 x 5.6m
Kitchen/breakfast	5.5 x 5.5m
Utility	5.8 x 2.3m
Study	4.5 x 4.0m 'L' shaped
Dining room	6.9 x 4.9m
Family room	5.0 x 4.9m
Master bedroom	10.0 x 5.8m + balcony
Bedroom 2	4.7 x 3.5m + wardrobe
Bedroom 3	5.8 x 4.7m
Bedroom 4	4.5 x 3.7m
Bedroom 5	3.4 x 3.0m

THOMPSON HOUSE

The copyright belongs to an ASBA architectural practice – John Woodward

364 sq. m.
including a garage
and sheds of 45 sq. m.

Overall dimensions 25.45 x 15.31m

FRONT ELEVATION

The garden room, this time with a vaulted ceiling, is an important feature in many of this contributor's designs. It is a light filled room that can be used as a day room whilst enjoying the garden. That means being able to keep the rest of the house tidy. Upstairs two of the bedrooms share an en-suite bathroom, the master bedroom has its own en-suite and the other bedroom and exercise room share a joint lobby to the communal bathroom.

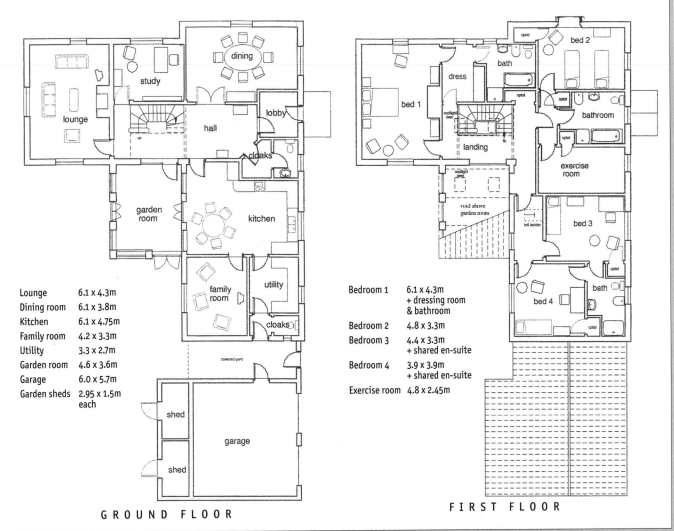

Lounge	6.1 x 4.3m
Dining room	6.1 x 3.8m
Kitchen	6.1 x 4.75m
Family room	4.2 x 3.3m
Utility	3.3 x 2.7m
Garden room	4.6 x 3.6m
Garage	6.0 x 5.7m
Garden sheds	2.95 x 1.5m each

Bedroom 1	6.1 x 4.3m + dressing room & bathroom
Bedroom 2	4.8 x 3.3m
Bedroom 3	4.4 x 3.3m + shared en-suite
Bedroom 4	3.9 x 3.9m + shared en-suite
Exercise room	4.8 x 2.45m

GROUND FLOOR

FIRST FLOOR

01-168

375 sq. m. including garage of 34.8 sq. m.

Overall dimensions 20.2 x 16.3m

FRONT ELEVATION

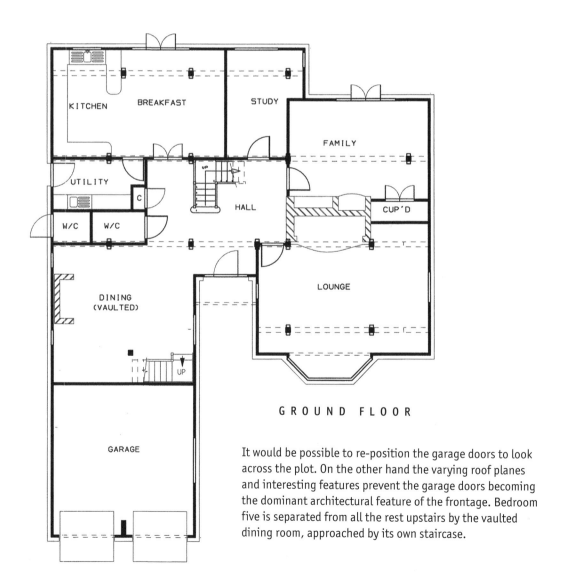

GROUND FLOOR

It would be possible to re-position the garage doors to look across the plot. On the other hand the varying roof planes and interesting features prevent the garage doors becoming the dominant architectural feature of the frontage. Bedroom five is separated from all the rest upstairs by the vaulted dining room, approached by its own staircase.

REAR ELEVATION

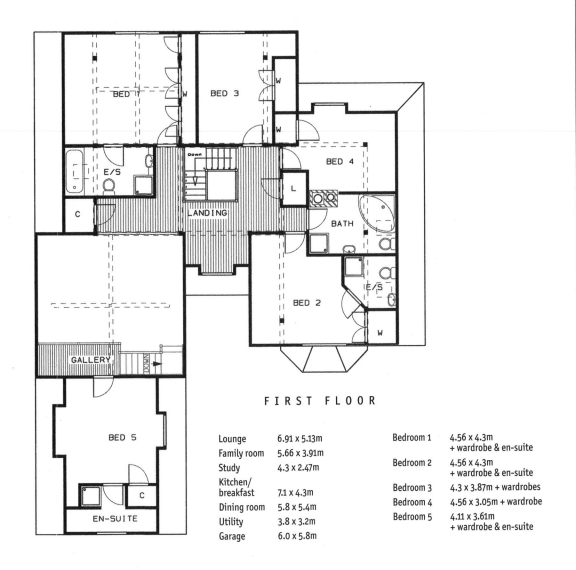

FIRST FLOOR

Lounge	6.91 x 5.13m		Bedroom 1	4.56 x 4.3m + wardrobe & en-suite
Family room	5.66 x 3.91m		Bedroom 2	4.56 x 4.3m + wardrobe & en-suite
Study	4.3 x 2.47m		Bedroom 3	4.3 x 3.87m + wardrobes
Kitchen/ breakfast	7.1 x 4.3m		Bedroom 4	4.56 x 3.05m + wardrobe
Dining room	5.8 x 5.4m		Bedroom 5	4.11 x 3.61m + wardrobe & en-suite
Utility	3.8 x 3.2m			
Garage	6.0 x 5.8m			

PENTRIDGE

The copyright belongs to T. J. Crump OAKRIGHTS Ltd.

376 sq. m.
including a garage of 34 sq. m.

Overall dimensions 18.96 x 18.62m

FRONT ELEVATION   SIDE ELEVATION

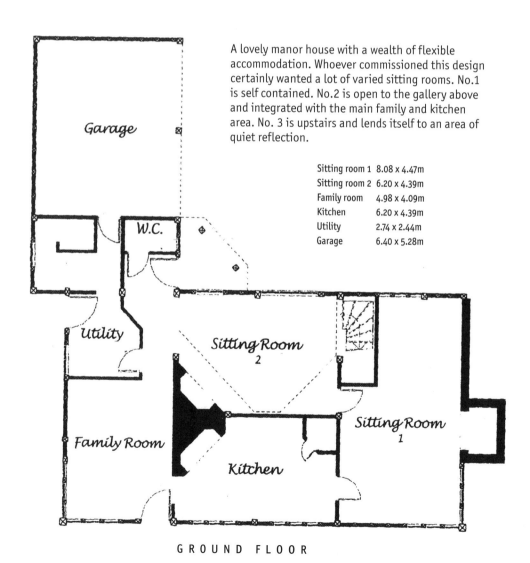

A lovely manor house with a wealth of flexible accommodation. Whoever commissioned this design certainly wanted a lot of varied sitting rooms. No.1 is self contained. No.2 is open to the gallery above and integrated with the main family and kitchen area. No. 3 is upstairs and lends itself to an area of quiet reflection.

Sitting room 1	8.08 x 4.47m
Sitting room 2	6.20 x 4.39m
Family room	4.98 x 4.09m
Kitchen	6.20 x 4.39m
Utility	2.74 x 2.44m
Garage	6.40 x 5.28m

GROUND FLOOR

REAR ELEVATION

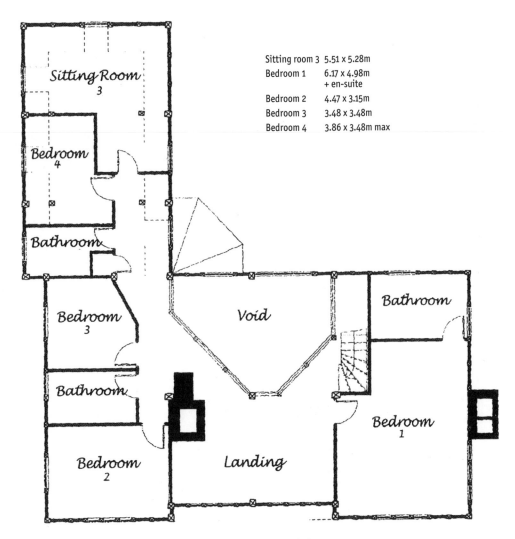

Sitting room 3	5.51 x 5.28m
Bedroom 1	6.17 x 4.98m + en-suite
Bedroom 2	4.47 x 3.15m
Bedroom 3	3.48 x 3.48m
Bedroom 4	3.86 x 3.48m max

FIRST FLOOR

R102

372 sq. m.

Overall dimensions 20.12 x 14.00m

FRONT ELEVATION

The sunroom provides a link between the family room, the kitchen/breakfast room, the sitting room and the garden. Some people like the dining room to be divorced from the other living rooms whilst others prefer it to adjoin the kitchen of the lounge. A simple name change would make this a family room and what is now called the family room could easily become the dining room.

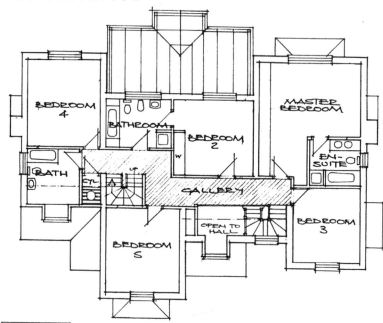

FIRST FLOOR

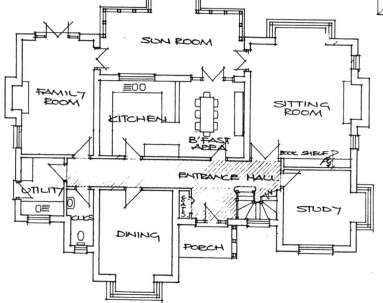

GROUND FLOOR

Sitting room	6.10 x 5.49m
Kitchen/ breakfast room	7.93 x 3.96m
Sunroom	7.93 x 4.09m max
Utility	2.97 x 2.26m
Family room	6.10 x 3.96m
Dining room	4.57 x 3.96m
Study	3.96 x 3.50m

Master bedroom	5.49 x 3.96m + lobby & en-suite
Bedroom 2	4.42 x 3.96m
Bedroom 3	3.96 x 3.60m
Bedroom 4	4.57 x 3.96m
Bedroom 5	4.67 x 3.96m

ARKLEY

The copyright belongs to Custom Homes Ltd.

387 sq. m.
including a garage of 41.5 sq. m.

Overall dimensions 20 x 12.9m

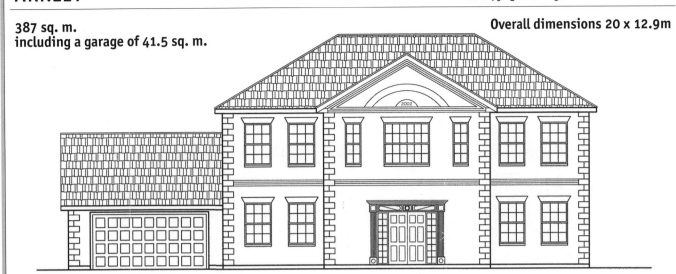

FRONT ELEVATION

The measurement that is not given above is that of the hallway and landing which measures a whopping 44 square metres on each floor including 16 square metres allocated to the staircase. To give you an idea of just how grand that is, it is nearly as big as an average semi-detached home and bigger than the smallest bungalow that this same company has contributed to this book!

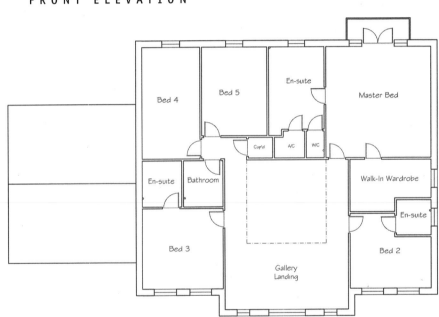

FIRST FLOOR

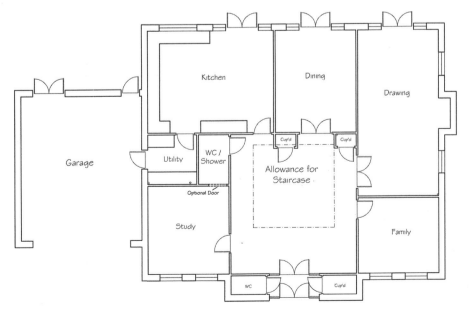

GROUND FLOOR

Drawing room	8.0 x 4.0m
Family room	4.0 x 3.6m
Dining room	4.9 x 4.0m
Kitchen	6.2 x 4.9m
Study	4.2 x 4.0m
Utility	2.4 x 2.4m
Garage	7.0 x 6.0m
Master bedroom	5.4 x 5.2m + walk-in wardrobe & en-suite
Bedroom 2	4.0 x 3.6m + en-suite
Bedroom 3	4.0 x 3.9m + en-suite
Bedroom 4	5.4 x 2.9m
Bedroom 5	4.3 x 3.2m

THE SANDHAMN

The copyright belongs to Scandia-Hus Limited

389 sq. m.

Overall dimensions 21.31 x 16.21m

F R O N T   E L E V A T I O N

Employing an 'H' shape allows this large home to provide two very distinct areas for living in each wing, linked by the entrance/dining hall which is lit from the skylights in the vaulted ceiling of the gallery above. The separation of the two living areas is continued with the provision of two staircases to the upper part and the four upstairs bedrooms, so that this home could be suitable for either a loose association within a family or some stricter division.

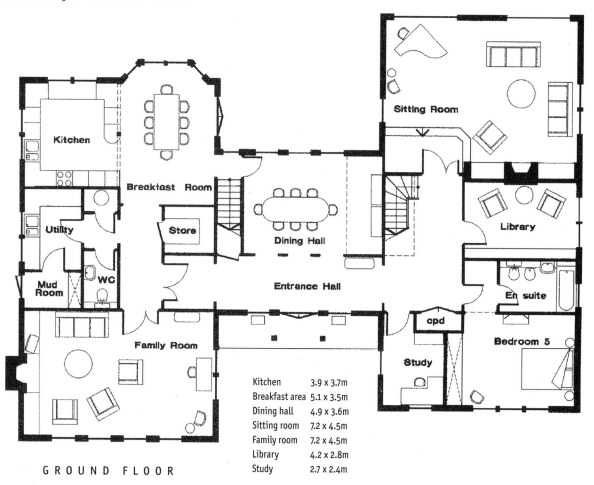

Kitchen	3.9 x 3.7m
Breakfast area	5.1 x 3.5m
Dining hall	4.9 x 3.6m
Sitting room	7.2 x 4.5m
Family room	7.2 x 4.5m
Library	4.2 x 2.8m
Study	2.7 x 2.4m

G R O U N D   F L O O R

REAR ELEVATION

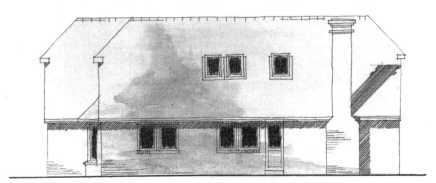

SIDE ELEVATION

Master bedroom 5.1 x 5.0m
+ wardrobe & en-suite

Bedroom 2   4.0 x 4.0 m
+ en-suite

Bedroom 3   4.0 x 4.0m

Bedroom 4   4.6 x 4.1m

Bedroom 5   4.7 x 3.4m

Relax/
exercise area 3.8 x 3.0m

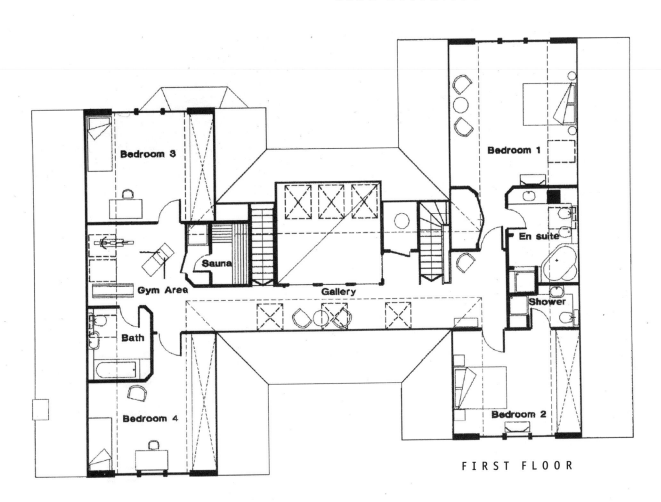

FIRST FLOOR

CRANBOURNE

The copyright belongs to T. J. Crump OAKRIGHTS Ltd.

392 sq. m.

Overall dimensions 21.14 x 16.21m

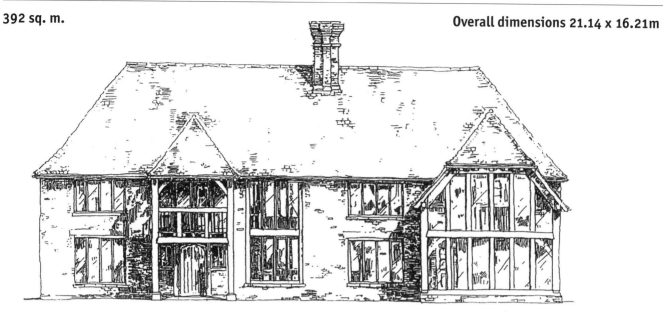

FRONT ELEVATION

Some might wonder at the lack of a formal lounge area to the ground floor. But look at the accommodation. There is a great hall that could double as a living area. There is a conservatory that goes full height and integrates the bedroom above and there is the sitting room on the first floor.

GROUND FLOOR

FIRST FLOOR

Great hall	6.60 x 6.20m
Kitchen	6.88 x 6.20m
Utility	2.46 x 2.67m
Study	3.68 x 2.46m
Office	4.14 x 3.86m
Conservatory	5.18 x 5.18m

Sitting room	6.25 x 6.17m
Bedroom 1	5.03 x 3.78m + bathroom
Bedroom 2	4.29 x 3.68m + en-suite
Bedroom 3	4.14 x 3.76m
Bedroom 4	3.50 x 3.38m + en-suite

THE MYRTLES

The copyright belongs to T. J. Crump OAKRIGHTS Ltd.

401 sq. m.
including a garage of 36 sq. m.

Overall dimensions 26.9 x 25.0m

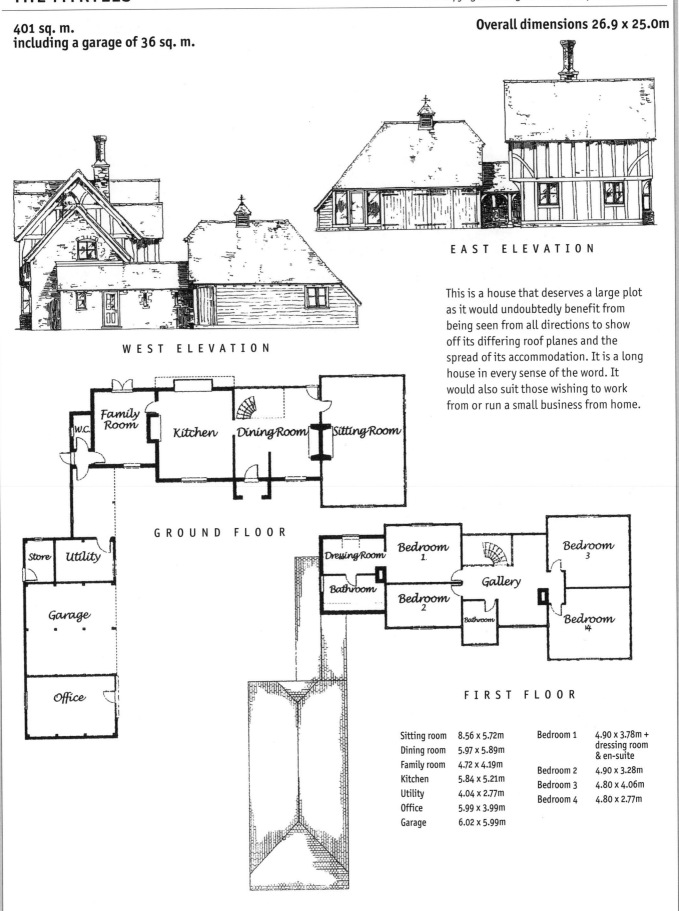

WEST ELEVATION

EAST ELEVATION

This is a house that deserves a large plot as it would undoubtedly benefit from being seen from all directions to show off its differing roof planes and the spread of its accommodation. It is a long house in every sense of the word. It would also suit those wishing to work from or run a small business from home.

GROUND FLOOR

FIRST FLOOR

Sitting room	8.56 x 5.72m		Bedroom 1	4.90 x 3.78m + dressing room & en-suite
Dining room	5.97 x 5.89m			
Family room	4.72 x 4.19m			
Kitchen	5.84 x 5.21m		Bedroom 2	4.90 x 3.28m
Utility	4.04 x 2.77m		Bedroom 3	4.80 x 4.06m
Office	5.99 x 3.99m		Bedroom 4	4.80 x 2.77m
Garage	6.02 x 5.99m			

303

HEMINC-P

The copyright belongs to Potton Ltd.

402 sq. m.

Overall dimensions 19 x 17m

FRONT ELEVATION

This is a truly imposing looking home that manages to provide all and more of the accommodation that one would expect in a property of this size within a compact but impressive shape. The great hall would provide a feature in its own right and with basically three lounges, all tastes in entertainment could be satisfied without interfearing with others.

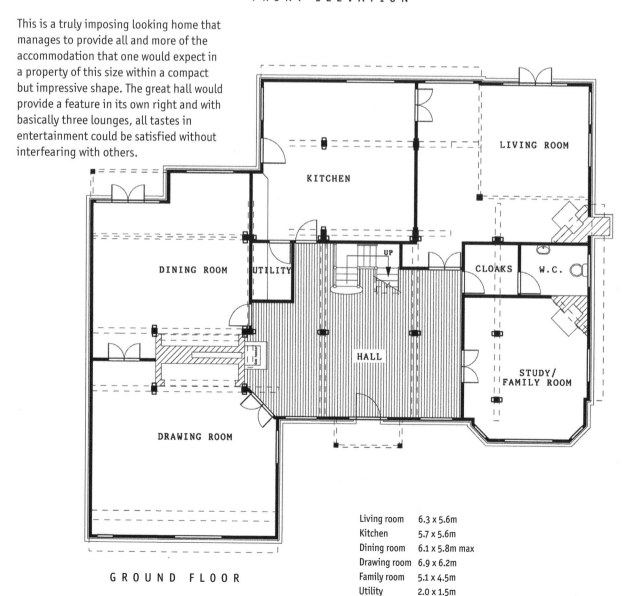

GROUND FLOOR

Living room	6.3 x 5.6m
Kitchen	5.7 x 5.6m
Dining room	6.1 x 5.8m max
Drawing room	6.9 x 6.2m
Family room	5.1 x 4.5m
Utility	2.0 x 1.5m

REAR ELEVATION

Bedroom 1	4.7 x 4.5m + wardrobe & en-suite
Bedroom 2	4.5 x 3.9m + wardrobe & en-suite
Bedroom 3	4.8 x 3.5m + en-suite
Bedroom 4	4.3 x 3.5m max + en-suite
Bedroom 5	3.7 x 3.5m + wardrobe & en-suite

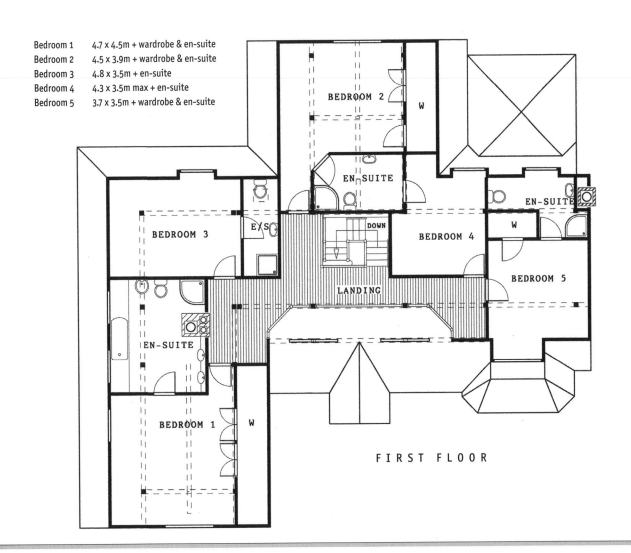

FIRST FLOOR

00-146

The copyright belongs to Potton Ltd.

405 sq. m.

Overall dimensions 25.3 x 21.2m

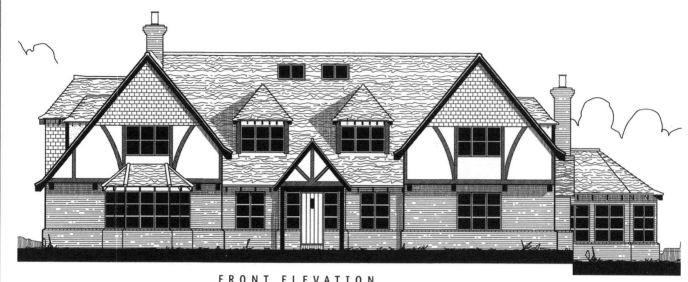

FRONT ELEVATION

This a home of shapes. From the great hall, the reception accommodation flows from room to room with each area, except the lounge accessed from the previous one. Level changes add to the interest and are reflected in the external appearance where multiple roof planes and differing shapes serve to make this a truly wonderful home.

Living room	6.9 x 5.5m
Dining room	7.0 x 6.5m
Kitchen	5.6 x 5.3m
Utility	3.5 x 2.2m
Breakfast room	4.6 x 3.9m
Family room	7.9 x 4.2m
Lounge	7.1 x 5.8m
Sun room	4.6 x 4.2m

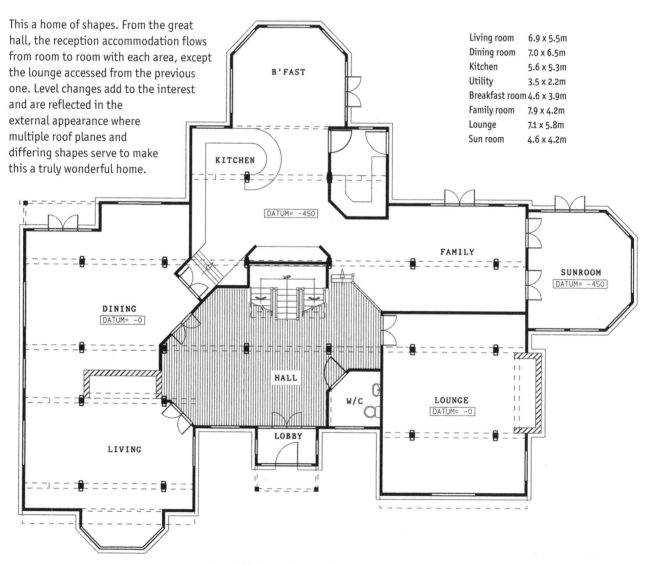

GROUND FLOOR

REAR ELEVATION

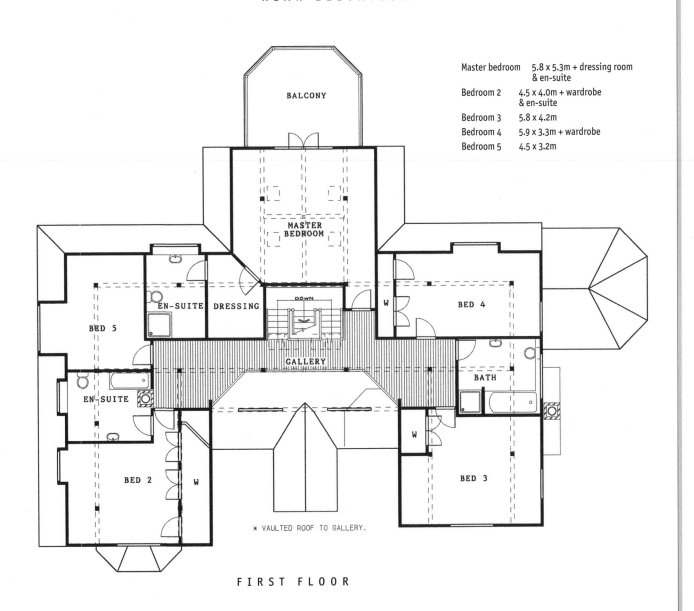

Master bedroom	5.8 x 5.3m + dressing room & en-suite
Bedroom 2	4.5 x 4.0m + wardrobe & en-suite
Bedroom 3	5.8 x 4.2m
Bedroom 4	5.9 x 3.3m + wardrobe
Bedroom 5	4.5 x 3.2m

BALCONY

MASTER BEDROOM

EN-SUITE DRESSING

DOWN

W

BED 4

BED 5

GALLERY

EN-SUITE

BATH

BED 2

W

W

BED 3

* VAULTED ROOF TO GALLERY.

FIRST FLOOR

THE HALLCROFT

The copyright belongs to an ASBA architectural practice – Julian Owen Associates

**425 sq. m.
including a garage of 50 sq. m.**

Overall dimensions 25.7 x 21.5m

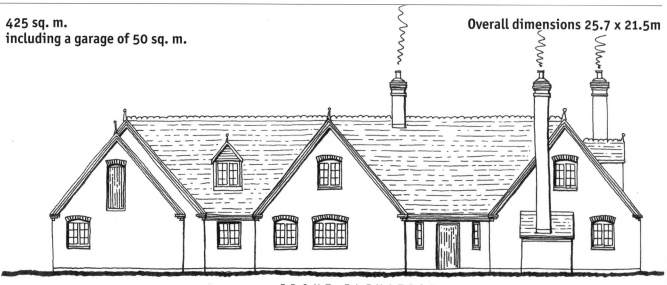

FRONT ELEVATION

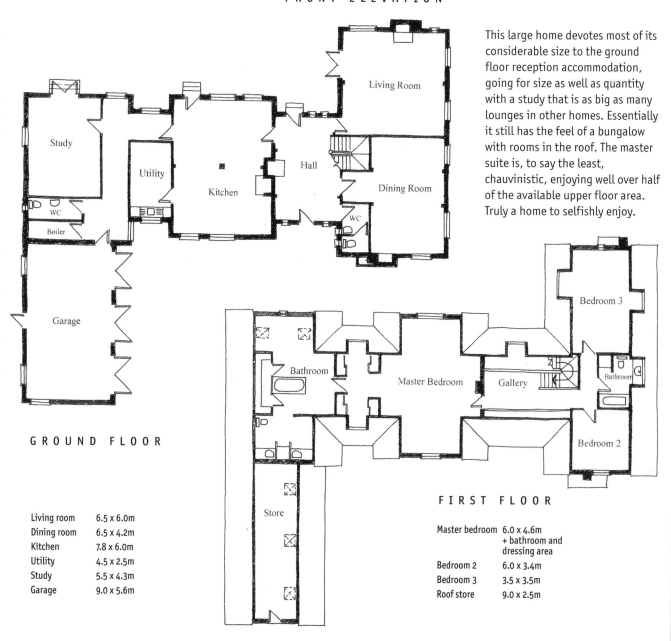

GROUND FLOOR

FIRST FLOOR

This large home devotes most of its considerable size to the ground floor reception accommodation, going for size as well as quantity with a study that is as big as many lounges in other homes. Essentially it still has the feel of a bungalow with rooms in the roof. The master suite is, to say the least, chauvinistic, enjoying well over half of the available upper floor area. Truly a home to selfishly enjoy.

Living room	6.5 x 6.0m
Dining room	6.5 x 4.2m
Kitchen	7.8 x 6.0m
Utility	4.5 x 2.5m
Study	5.5 x 4.3m
Garage	9.0 x 5.6m

Master bedroom	6.0 x 4.6m + bathroom and dressing area
Bedroom 2	6.0 x 3.4m
Bedroom 3	3.5 x 3.5m
Roof store	9.0 x 2.5m

98-020

The copyright belongs to Potton Ltd.

435 sq. m.

Overall dimensions 24.1 x 14.5m

FRONT ELEVATION

The fact that one of the downstairs rooms is designated 'changing room' indicates that this design may have been conceived to go with either a swimming pool or a tennis court or something similar. Either way, this a house for the enthusiastic and active family with a hobbies room upstairs and plenty of storage and washing facilities.

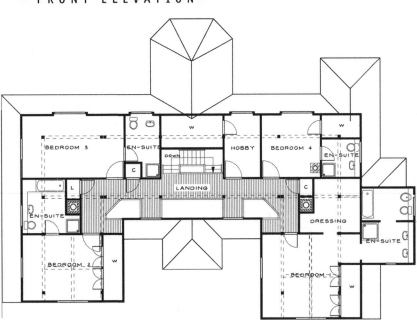

FIRST FLOOR

GROUND FLOOR

Lounge	8.35 x 6.3m
Dining room	6.5 x 5.8m
Kitchen/family room	12.0 x 4.3m
Sun room	4.6 x 4.2m
Study	5.0 x 4.9m
Changing room	4.8 x 2.2m
Utility	5.4 x 3.3m
Bedroom 1	4.7 x 4.m + dressing area & en-suite
Bedroom 2	4.6 x 3.7m + wardrobe & en-suite
Bedroom 3	5.9 x 3.4m + en-suite
Bedroom 4	3.5 x 3.5m + wardrobe & en-suite
Hobbies room	3.5 x 2.1m

D170A

The copyright belongs to Design & Materials Ltd.

442 sq. m.
including a garage of 33 sq. m.

Overall dimensions 20.96 x 16.51m

F R O N T   E L E V A T I O N

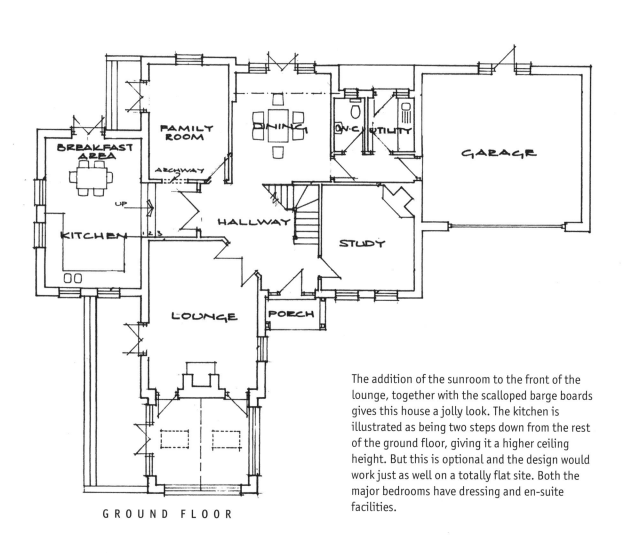

G R O U N D   F L O O R

The addition of the sunroom to the front of the lounge, together with the scalloped barge boards gives this house a jolly look. The kitchen is illustrated as being two steps down from the rest of the ground floor, giving it a higher ceiling height. But this is optional and the design would work just as well on a totally flat site. Both the major bedrooms have dressing and en-suite facilities.

REAR ELEVATION

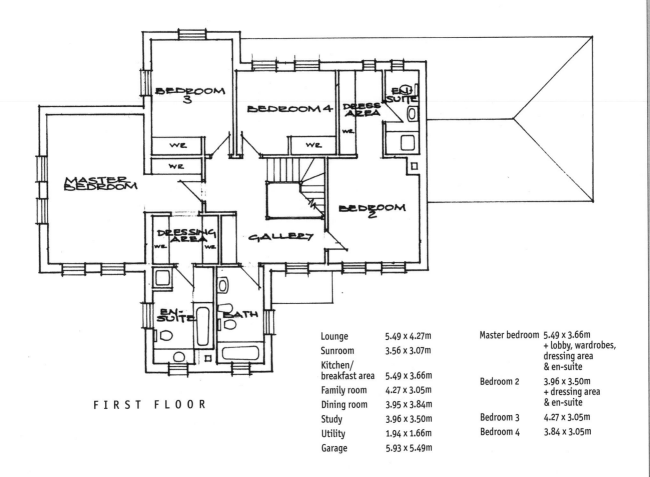

FIRST FLOOR

Lounge	5.49 x 4.27m	
Sunroom	3.56 x 3.07m	
Kitchen/ breakfast area	5.49 x 3.66m	
Family room	4.27 x 3.05m	
Dining room	3.95 x 3.84m	
Study	3.96 x 3.50m	
Utility	1.94 x 1.66m	
Garage	5.93 x 5.49m	

Master bedroom	5.49 x 3.66m + lobby, wardrobes, dressing area & en-suite
Bedroom 2	3.96 x 3.50m + dressing area & en-suite
Bedroom 3	4.27 x 3.05m
Bedroom 4	3.84 x 3.05m

97-172

The copyright belongs to Potton Ltd.

446 sq. m.

Overall dimensions 21.9 x 22m

FRONT ELEVATION

Just reading through the list and the sizes of the ground floor rooms makes one realise that this a big house, the heart of which, as with so many of these designs, is the great hall. This combined kitchen and sun room makes for a magnificent space within which a family would tend to congregate.

Lounge	6.9 x 6.8m
Dining room	6.4 x 6.3m
Kitchen/ sun room	7.3 x 9.1m
Family room	7.0 x 4.9m
Study	6.9 x 5.3m

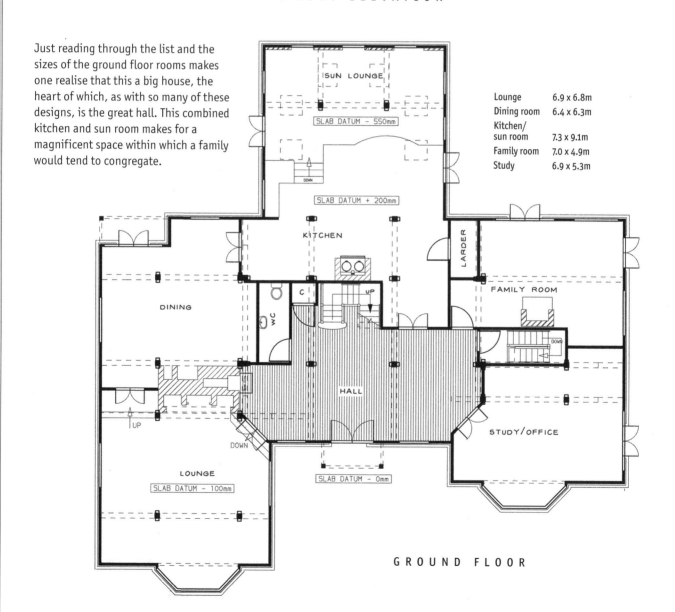

GROUND FLOOR

REAR ELEVATION

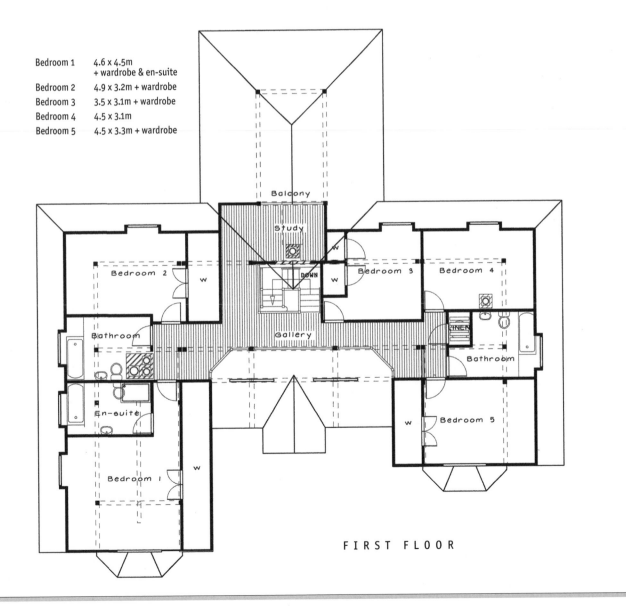

Bedroom 1   4.6 x 4.5m
             + wardrobe & en-suite
Bedroom 2   4.9 x 3.2m + wardrobe
Bedroom 3   3.5 x 3.1m + wardrobe
Bedroom 4   4.5 x 3.1m
Bedroom 5   4.5 x 3.3m + wardrobe

FIRST FLOOR

HENHAM

The copyright belongs to Custom Homes Ltd.

460 sq. m.

Overall dimensions 12.1 x 9.8m

FRONT ELEVATION

The two way staircase rising from the centre of the large inner hall and opening onto a galleried landing is just the start of this large home. Six reception rooms plus all of the usual accompaniments and a utility area with a boot room are matched on the first floor by six bedrooms, all of which have wardrobes and en-suite facilities.

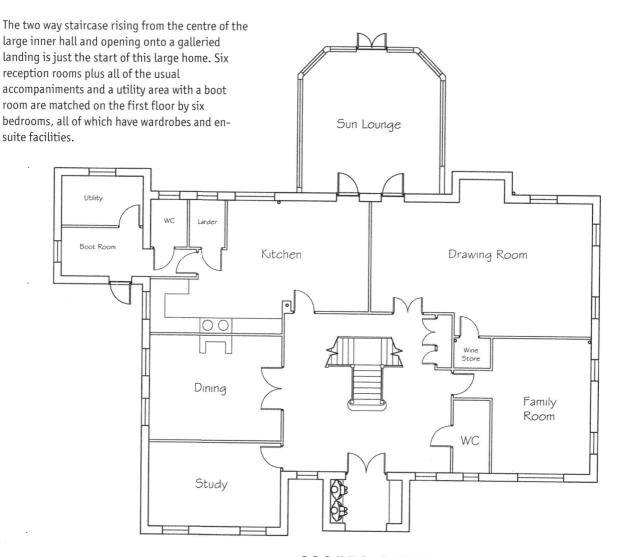

Sun Lounge

Utility

WC   Larder

Boot Room

Kitchen

Drawing Room

Wine Store

Dining

Family Room

WC

Study

GROUND FLOOR

S I D E   E L E V A T I O N

Drawing room	9.0 x 5.3m max	Bedroom 1	5.45 x 4.8m + dressing room & en-suite
Family room	5.3 x 4.0m	Bedroom 2	5.3 x 3.65m + wardrobe & en-suite
Kitchen	9.0 x 5.3m max including larder	Bedroom 3	3.6 x 3.55m + wardrobe & en-suite
Dining room	5.45 x 4.15m	Bedroom 4	4.2 x 4.0m + wardrobe & en-suite
Study	5.45 x 3.25m	Bedroom 5	4.7 x 3.45m + wardrobe & en-suite
Utility/ boot room	3.9 x 3.3m	Bedroom 6	5.0 x 3.45m + wardrobe & en-suite
Sun lounge	5.6 x 5.6m		

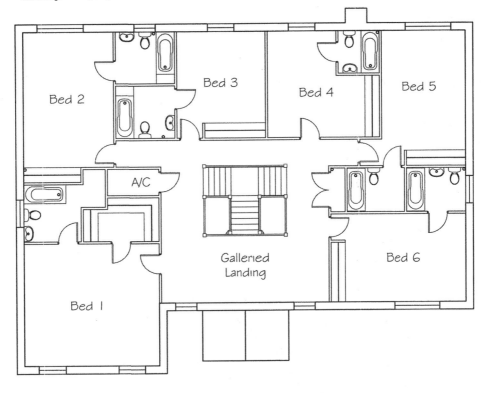

F I R S T   F L O O R

THE FAIRHURST

The copyright belongs to an ASBA architectural practice – Julian Owen Associates

483 sq. m.
including a garage of 58 sq. m.

Overall dimensions 30.5 x 27.0m

FRONT ELEVATION

GROUND FLOOR

What can one say about such a stunning design? Externally the 'kerb appeal' is instant. They say that a fine whisky is all in the blending and this house demonstrates that architecture can borrow mix and match from various periods to marvellous effect. Internally every thought has been given to comfort living. Truly a home to value and enjoy.

FIRST FLOOR

Sitting room	8.5 x 6.0m	Master bedroom	6.0 x 5.5m + dressing room & en-suite
Vaulted room	8.5 x 6.0m		
Dining hall	7.0 x 6.0m	Bedroom 1	6.0 x 4.5m including en-suite
Family room	6.0 x 4.5m		
Kitchen	6.0 x 4.0m	Bedroom 2	6.0 x 3.5m including en-suite
Breakfast room	5.0 x 3.5m		
Study	4.5 x 3.0m	Bedroom 3	4.0 x 3.5m
Utility	3.0 x 2.5m	Bedroom 4	4.0 x 3.5m
Garage	9.3 x 6.3m	Sitting room	9.0 x 4.5m

RUNNYMEDE

The copyright belongs to Designer Homes

488 sq. m.

Overall dimensions 21.60 x 20.10m

FRONT ELEVATION

This large family home is arranged around a double curved staircase lading up, in two directions from the entrance hall to the upper landing and gallery. The symmetry of the front elevation is only slightly broken by the bay to the living room. If the study was not required upstairs then this would be a true six bedroom house with three of those bedroom en-suite.

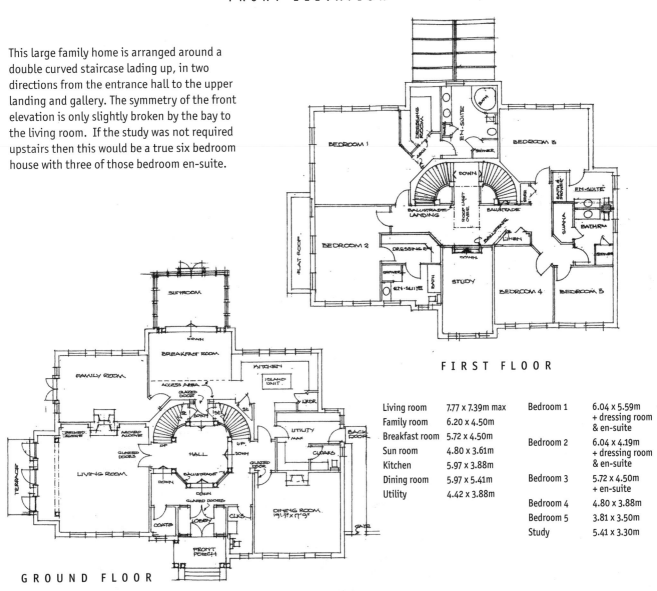

FIRST FLOOR

GROUND FLOOR

Living room	7.77 x 7.39m max	Bedroom 1	6.04 x 5.59m + dressing room & en-suite
Family room	6.20 x 4.50m		
Breakfast room	5.72 x 4.50m	Bedroom 2	6.04 x 4.19m + dressing room & en-suite
Sun room	4.80 x 3.61m		
Kitchen	5.97 x 3.88m		
Dining room	5.97 x 5.41m	Bedroom 3	5.72 x 4.50m + en-suite
Utility	4.42 x 3.88m		
		Bedroom 4	4.80 x 3.88m
		Bedroom 5	3.81 x 3.50m
		Study	5.41 x 3.30m

CRAIGLARACH

The copyright belongs to The Border Design Centre

493 sq. m.
including a garage of 37 sq. m.

Overall dimensions 25.6 x 17.2m

FRONT ELEVATION

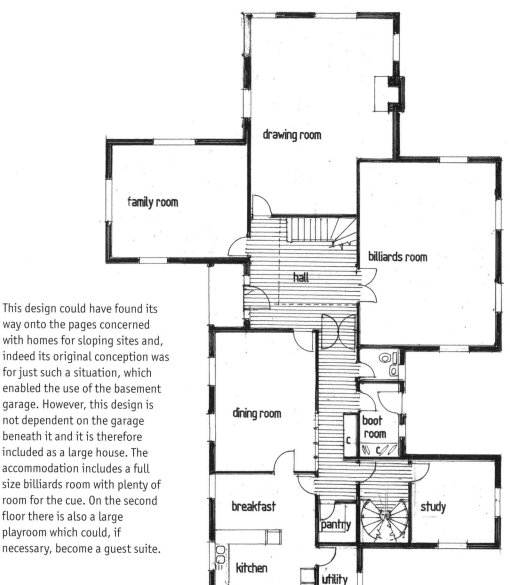

This design could have found its way onto the pages concerned with homes for sloping sites and, indeed its original conception was for just such a situation, which enabled the use of the basement garage. However, this design is not dependent on the garage beneath it and it is therefore included as a large house. The accommodation includes a full size billiards room with plenty of room for the cue. On the second floor there is also a large playroom which could, if necessary, become a guest suite.

GROUND FLOOR

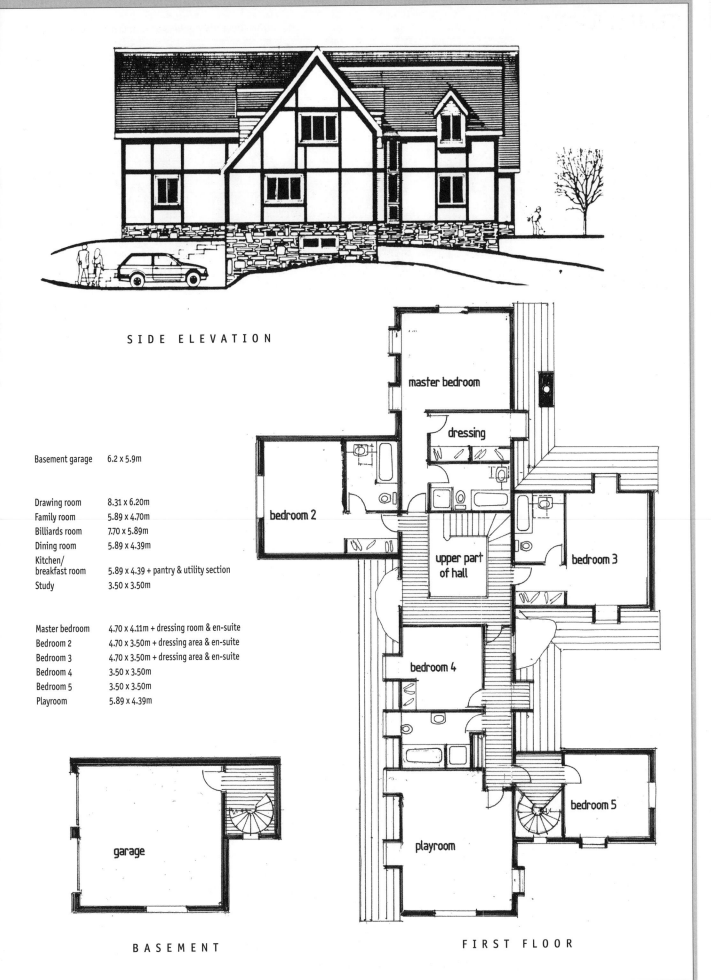

SIDE ELEVATION

Basement garage	6.2 x 5.9m
Drawing room	8.31 x 6.20m
Family room	5.89 x 4.70m
Billiards room	7.70 x 5.89m
Dining room	5.89 x 4.39m
Kitchen/breakfast room	5.89 x 4.39 + pantry & utility section
Study	3.50 x 3.50m
Master bedroom	4.70 x 4.11m + dressing room & en-suite
Bedroom 2	4.70 x 3.50m + dressing area & en-suite
Bedroom 3	4.70 x 3.50m + dressing area & en-suite
Bedroom 4	3.50 x 3.50m
Bedroom 5	3.50 x 3.50m
Playroom	5.89 x 4.39m

master bedroom

dressing

bedroom 2

bedroom 3

upper part of hall

bedroom 4

bedroom 5

playroom

garage

BASEMENT

FIRST FLOOR

FERNHILL COURT

The copyright belongs to T. J. Crump OAKRIGHTS Ltd.

529 sq. m.

Overall dimensions 26.45 x 14.84m

FRONT ELEVATION

This would be a marvellous home to live in. The accommodation is arranged to provide the maximum privacy to each room whilst existing within the flow of normal family life. Whatever activity you wanted to engage in, it would not have to interfere with other family members. Once again the large entrance is the hub of the house

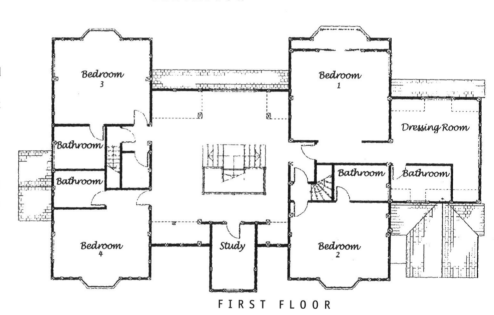

FIRST FLOOR

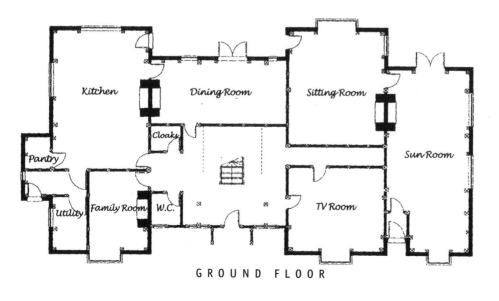

GROUND FLOOR

Kitchen	7.49 x 5.48m
Utility	2.31 x 1.96m
Hall	5.94 x 5.36m
Family room	4.29 x 3.35m
Dining room	7.85 x 3.45m
TV room	5.56 x 4.50m
Sun room	9.86 x 4.67m
Bedroom 1	5.49 x 4.70m + dressing room & en-suite
Bedroom 2	5.56 x 5.49m + en-suite
Study	3.48 x 2.46m
Bedroom 3	5.61 x 4.80m + en-suite
Bedroom 4	5.59 x 3.99m + en-suite

GLEBE MANOR

The copyright belongs to T. J. Crump OAKRIGHTS Ltd.

539 sq. m.

Overall dimensions 25.54 x 16.34m

FRONT ELEVATION

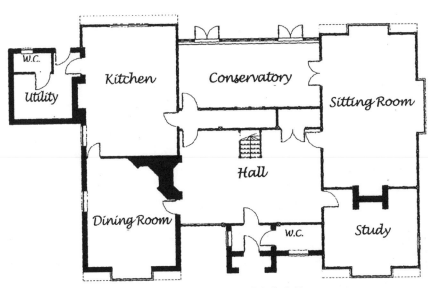

GROUND FLOOR

Such a lot of accommodation within a relatively compact shape is achieved by means of a double fronted design where the basic shape is an 'H'. The huge entrance hall opens onto each one of the ground floor reception rooms and the galleried landing above it divides the two wings of the upper part.

Great hall	8.59 x 5.33m
Sitting room	8.73 x 5.69m
Study	5.66 x 4.37m
Dining room	6.12 x 5.36m
Kitchen	7.47 x 5.21m
Utility	3.57 x 2.59m
Conservatory	8.58 x 3.78m
Bedroom 1	7.98 x 5.69m + en-suite
Bedroom 2	6.15 x 5.69m + en-suite
Bedroom 3	5.69 x 4.95m + w.c.
Bedroom 4	5.69 x 4.59m + en-suite

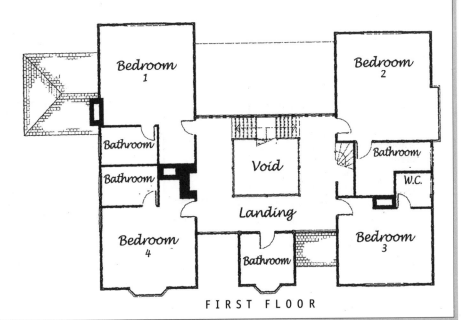

FIRST FLOOR

DENTON BARN

The copyright belongs to T. J. Crump OAKRIGHTS Ltd.

584 sq. m.
including a garage of 27 sq. m.

Overall dimensions 30.25 x 29.63m

FRONT ELEVATION

This home is illustrated at a smaller scale to many others and a casual glance might lead one to think that this is quite a small house. However, a quick look at the overall size and room dimensions will tell you that this is a seriously large home.

SIDE ELEVATION

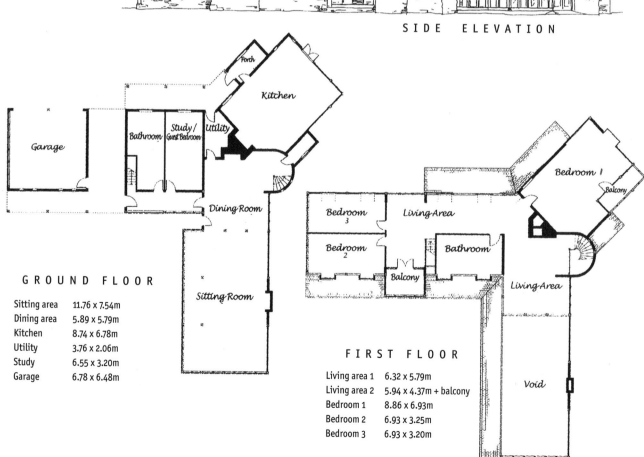

GROUND FLOOR

Sitting area	11.76 x 7.54m
Dining area	5.89 x 5.79m
Kitchen	8.74 x 6.78m
Utility	3.76 x 2.06m
Study	6.55 x 3.20m
Garage	6.78 x 6.48m

FIRST FLOOR

Living area 1	6.32 x 5.79m
Living area 2	5.94 x 4.37m + balcony
Bedroom 1	8.86 x 6.93m
Bedroom 2	6.93 x 3.25m
Bedroom 3	6.93 x 3.20m

HOMES FOR NARROW SITES

Adversity, in the form of restrictions on site, can tax the ingenuity of the designer. Happily, as is demonstrated within these pages, many of the contributors rise to the challenge to produce designs that are inventive and exciting.

The temptation will always be to build right up to the boundary but, quite apart from the fact that the planners will be concerned to see that you don't do that, it isn't always the best solution. Most people will want to ensure that there is a pathway down at least one side of the house.

The garage, if there is to be one, presents the most problems. With a narrow frontage the idea of putting it so that the doors face across the plot simply isn't possible in many cases. Clever design then moves to lessen the impact of the forward facing door and 'drag' it back or away from the focal point of the house frontage. An alternative might be to detach the garage and dress up the frontage with walling and paving to create a mews effect.

Contributors in this section:
Associated Self Build Architects
The Border Design Centre
T.J.Crump OAKWRIGHTS Ltd.
Custom Homes Ltd.
Design & Materials Ltd.
Designer Homes
Potton Ltd.
The Self Build House Company Ltd.
Scottish Architects Network
Scandia-Hus Ltd.
The Swedish House Company Ltd.

FELL VIEW

The copyright belongs to a ScAN architectural practice - S. Buttler

66 sq. m.

Overall dimensions 8.1 x 6.75m

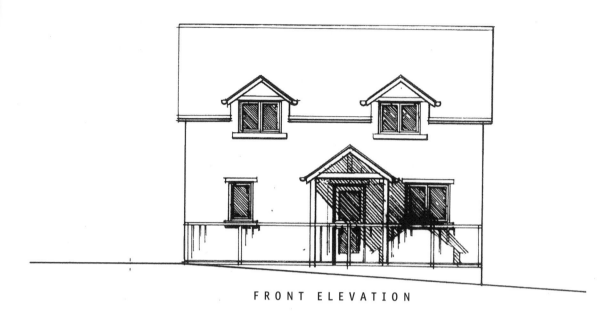

FRONT ELEVATION

With no living or bedroom windows to one side and only secondary windows to two of the other sides, this house could fit on a plot that was either narrow or lacked depth. The generous accommodation is extremely flexible. The lounge could be sub-divided if a separate dining room was required. On some sites the accommodation could be reversed to put the living rooms on the first floor.

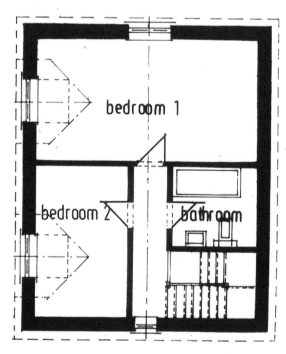

FIRST FLOOR

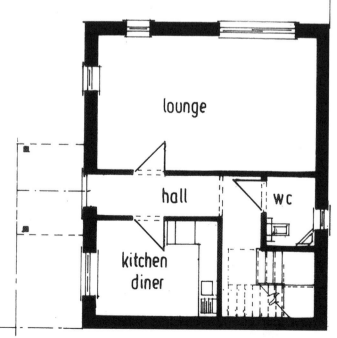

GROUND FLOOR

Kitchen/ dining room	3.3 x 2.5m	Bedroom 1	6.1 x 3.2m
Lounge	6.1 x 3.5m	Bedroom 2	4.0 x 2.5m

GAVINGTON LODGE

82 sq. m.

Overall dimensions 10.0 x 6.3m

SIDE ELEVATION

As the name implies this design was originally conceived as a gatehouse to a much larger property. Nevertheless it stands alone in design terms and is proof that small does not have to be boring and that features usually associated with larger houses can be successfully employed. If only all designers of houses would learn these lessons.

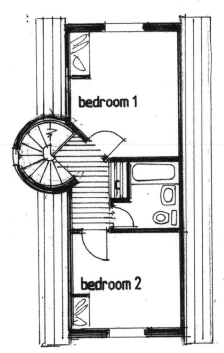

FIRST FLOOR

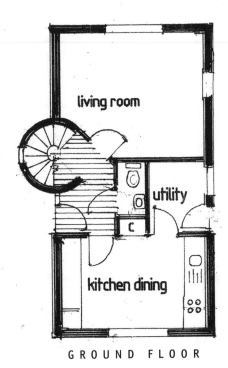

GROUND FLOOR

Living room	4.70 x 4.11m
Kitchen/ dining room	4.70 x 2.99m + utility area
Bedroom 1	4.11 x 3.50m
Bedroom 2	3.50 x 2.99m

OUZEL

The copyright belongs to Designer Homes

104 sq. m.

Overall dimensions 15.90 x 11.00m

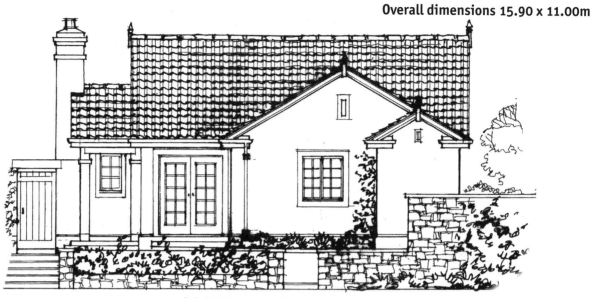

F R O N T   E L E V A T I O N

This smart little bungalow would fit onto a relatively narrow plot. All of the living accommodation is situated at the back of the bungalow with the bedrooms at the front and on one side. It would perhaps be best suited to an elevated plot where the differences in level gained some privacy for the bedrooms. If a garage were required this could go at the front of the home, preferably with its doors looking across the plot, if it was wide enough.

Living room	5.49 x 3.91m
Dining room	3.66 x 3.05m max
Kitchen	3.66 x 2.59m max
Bedroom 1	3.96 x 3.81m + wardrobe & en-suite
Bedroom 2	3.61 x 3.05m + wardrobe
Bedroom 3	3.05 x 2.74m + wardrobe

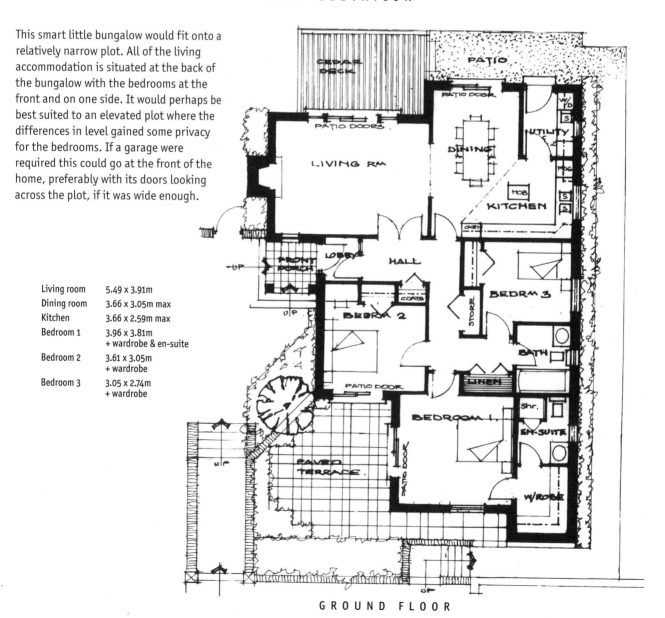

G R O U N D   F L O O R

THE BEVVY

The copyright belongs to The Self-Build House Company Ltd.

114 sq. m

Overall dimensions 14.76 x 6.3m

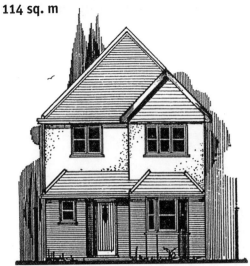

FRONT ELEVATION

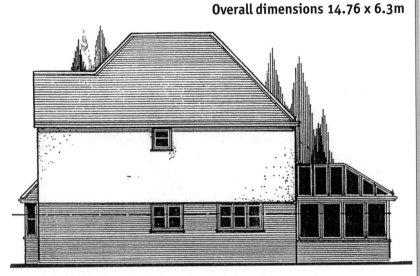

SIDE ELEVATION

REAR ELEVATION

In certain circumstances this house could fit onto a plot that was only just over eight metres wide, although consideration would have to be given to garaging or parking. Every aspect of the design, which harks back in feel to the 1930's, is intended to satisfy the demands of a narrow site. The lines on either side are clean and the roof is hipped to draw the eye away from the boundaries.

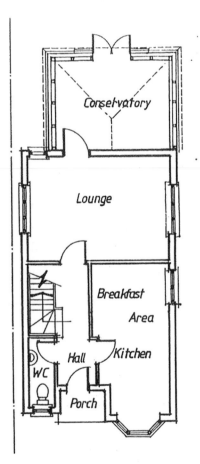

GROUND FLOOR

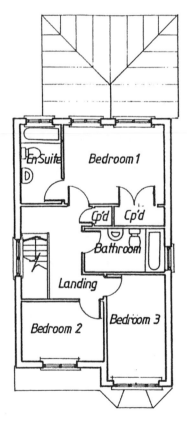

FIRST FLOOR

Kitchen/dining area	6.0 x 2.7m
Sitting room	5.5 x 3.8m
Conservatory	4.5 x 3.3m

Master bedroom	3.8 x 2.9m + wardrobe & en-suite
Bedroom 2	3.2 x 2.2m
Bedroom 3	4.0 x 2.2m

BIRCHGROVE-P

The copyright belongs to Potton Ltd.

114 sq. m.

Overall dimensions 16.16 x 9.82m

With the main entrance at the side, this bungalow could be fitted onto a relatively narrow site although, if a garage was required, some thought would have to be given to just how and where it was positioned. The comfortable entrance hall gives access to most rooms, negating the necessity for long corridors.

FRONT ELEVATION

Lounge diner   6.3 x 6.2m
Kitchen   4.8 x 2.9m
Sun room   4.1 x 2.5m
Bedroom 1   4.7 x 4.2m
                + en-suite
Bedroom 2   4.0 x 3.0m

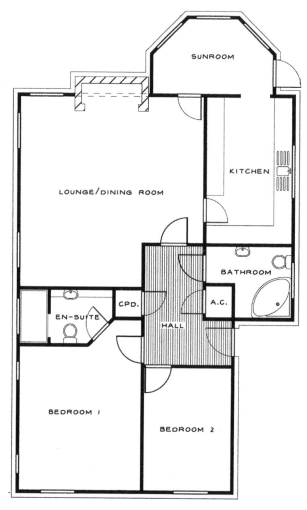

GROUND FLOOR

REAR ELEVATION

SIDE ELEVATION

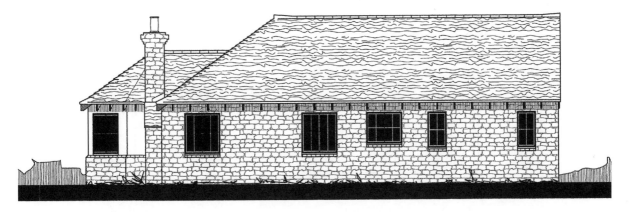

SIDE ELEVATION

D149

116 sq. m.

Overall dimensions 13.70 x 5.14m

A home with three reception rooms and three bedrooms, one of which is en-suite on a site of just over seven metres? Well this proves that it can be done and that the room sizes can remain sensible if not generous. The use of the ding hall is one of the keys because that frees up space that would otherwise be wasted in internal circulation. The other trick is the side entrance, which once again frees up space and allows important rooms to have a view.

Lounge	4.57 x 4.54m
Dining hall	4.54 x 2.85m
Kitchen/ breakfast room	4.57 x 4.54m max
Master bedroom	4.57 x 3.44m + en-suite
Bedroom 2	3.35 x 3.20m
Bedroom 3	3.05 x 2.86m

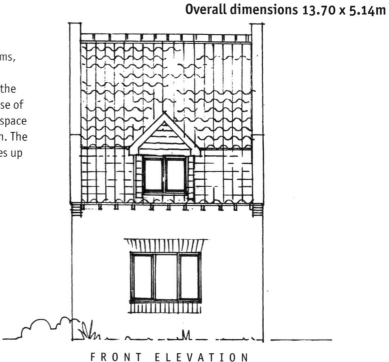

FRONT ELEVATION

FIRST FLOOR

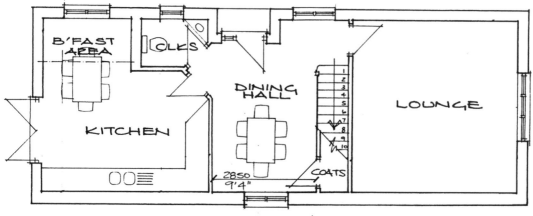

GROUND FLOOR

F122

123 sq. m. including a garage of 16 sq. m.

Overall dimensions 12.74 x 9.07m

FRONT ELEVATION

Definitely a home for a narrow site when you look at the dimensions and the layout. But this design proves that you don't necessarily have to compromise on accommodation for there are three reception rooms plus a garage and utility room and there are three good sized bedrooms one of them en-suite. Outside it doesn't look like a camped design and it still manages to have good kerb appeal.

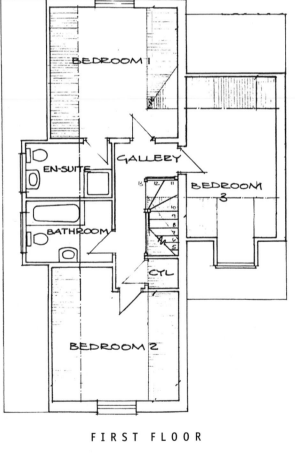

FIRST FLOOR

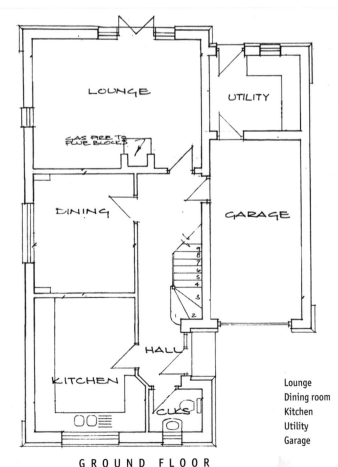

GROUND FLOOR

Lounge	5.27 x 3.96m		Bedroom 1	4.00 x 3.96m + en-suite
Dining room	3.66 x 3.17m		Bedroom 2	4.00 x 3.35m
Kitchen	4.24 x 3.50m		Bedroom 3	4.95 x 2.90m
Utility	2.90 x 2.34m			
Garage	5.59 x 2.90m			

ROSEBANK

The copyright belongs to The Border Design Centre

129 sq. m.

Overall dimensions 12.4 x 8.3m

FRONT ELEVATION

The tower stair is an imposing feature of this design, but it achieves more than that. By taking the staircase out of the main body of the home, it frees up space so that this relatively small house is able to provide quite generous accommodation. It could be positioned across the plot, but to fit into this category it would be positioned down the plot where the interest provided by the tower would create an exciting elevation.

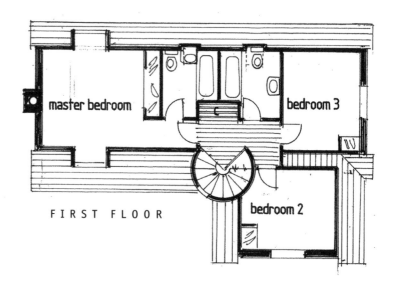

FIRST FLOOR

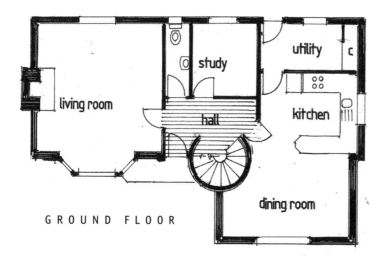

GROUND FLOOR

Living room	5.38 x 4.70m
Kitchen/ dining room	7.70 x 4.70m + utility area
Study	2.59 x 2.49m
Master bedroom	3.81 x 3.50m + wardrobe & en-suite
Bedroom 2	3.50 x 2.89m
Bedroom 3	3.50 x 2.89m

KILLIECRANKIE

The copyright belongs to The Border Design Centre

129 sq. m.

Overall dimensions 12.4 x 6.4m

FRONT ELEVATION

With three bedrooms and a study that could always become a fourth bedroom, this is an attractive country cottage. If it were positioned across the plot it would not qualify for this section. However, if it were positioned down the plot, with the driveway running down the side of the land in front of the entrance door it would fit onto a very narrow plot.

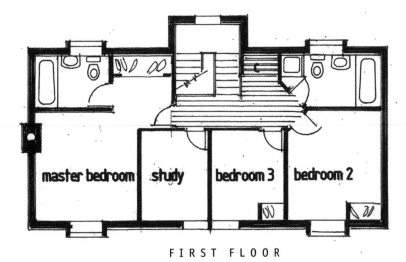

FIRST FLOOR

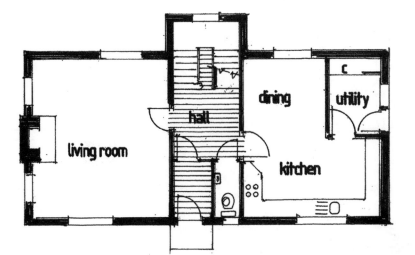

GROUND FLOOR

Living room	5.31 x 4.11m
Kitchen/ dining room	5.31 x 4.70m + utility area
Study	2.79 x 2.59m
Master bedroom	3.50 x 3.50m + dressing lobby & en-suite
Bedroom 2	3.50 x 3.20m
Bedroom 3	2.89 x 2.79m

D180

The copyright belongs to Design & Materials Ltd.

131 sq. m.

Overall dimensions 11.60 x 8.52m

FRONT ELEVATION

A lovely family home that could fit onto many of the smaller sites that are coming onto the market. It is illustrated with the roof and eaves line lowered but, if height is not a a problem, the roof could go back up and the bedrooms would not then have sloping ceilings. The wide hallway and the staircase with the half landing and the window over would prevent the feeling of being cramped.

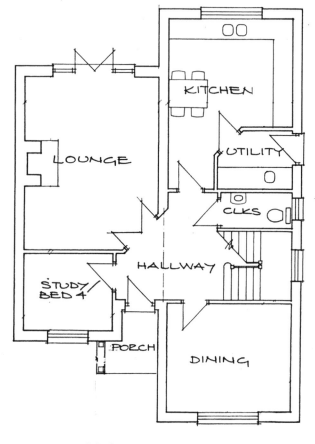

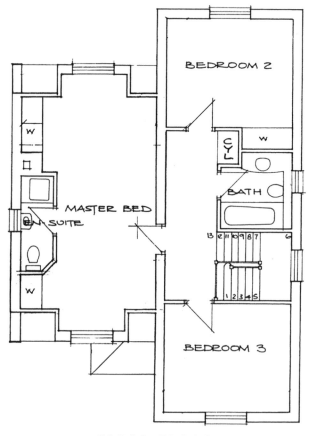

FIRST FLOOR

		Master bedroom	5.91 x 3.96m
Lounge	4.88 x 3.96m		including en-suite
Kitchen	3.66 x 3.05m		& wardrobes
Utility	2.20 x 1.60m	Bedroom 2	3.66 x 3.05m
Dining room	3.66 x 3.05m	Bedroom 3	3.66 x 3.05m
Study/			
bedroom 4	2.54 x 2.13m		

GROUND FLOOR

LOCHGAIR

The copyright belongs to The Border Design Centre

132 sq. m.

Overall dimensions 15.9 x 6.0m

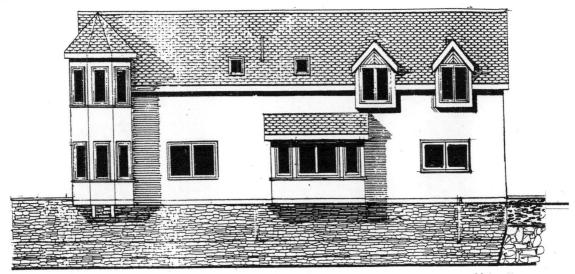

F R O N T   E L E V A T I O N

This house was built on the edge of a sea loch on a plot that is only 5 metres deep situated between the road and the sea! The views suggested a corner bay window and this was provided by cantilevering this section out over the sea as part of the dining hall. So too with the turret section giving extra space and character to the living room and master bedroom. The stairwell projects to the front as far as the road, protecting the entrance.

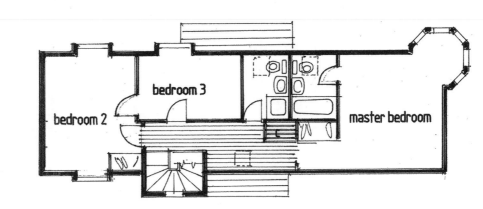

F I R S T   F L O O R

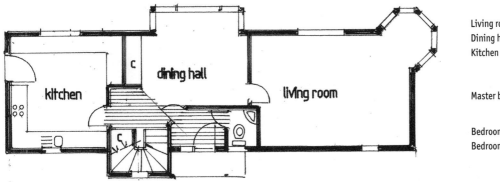

G R O U N D   F L O O R

Living room	5.74 x 4.09m
Dining hall	4.29 x 3.30m into bay
Kitchen	4.09 x 3.81m
Master bedroom	4.70 x 3.81m + dressing lobby & en-suite
Bedroom 2	4.09 x 3.20m
Bedroom 3	3.50 x 3.50m

BARLEY 02-075

The copyright belongs to Potton Ltd.

135 sq. m.

Overall dimensions 9.8 x 6.86m

FRONT ELEVATION

REAR ELEVATION

How do you get four bedrooms, two of which have en-suite facilities, on a plot that is less than nine metres wide? The answer is this town house design on three floors that does not have a significantly different ridge height to many two storey houses, as it utilises the roof space to the full.

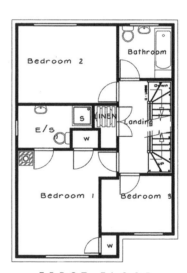

FIRST FLOOR

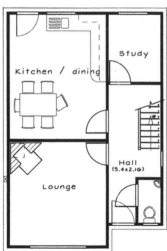

GROUND FLOOR

SECOND FLOOR

Lounge	4.2 x 4.0m	Bedroom 1	4.17 x 3.28m + en-suite & wardrobe
Kitchen/diner	4.85 x 4.0m		
Study	2.66 x 2.16m	Bedroom 2	4.0 x 3.12m
		Bedroom 3	2.88 x 2.27m
		Bedroom 4	4.3 x 4.0m + en-suite & storage

SKYLARK

The copyright belongs to Designer Homes

140 sq. m.

Overall dimensions 18.60 x 9.00m

FRONT ELEVATION

This good sized bungalow would fit onto a very narrow plot although the need for a garage might complicate the issue. The design mixes the living with the sleeping accommodation but what's in a name? Depending on the needs of the occupant, the bedrooms could be redesignated and the living room could become the master bedroom.

Living room	6.04 x 5.72m
Family room	5.72 x 3.61m
Kitchen/ dining room	4.80 x 4.65m max
Utility	2.69 x 2.69m
Bedroom 1	4.39 x 3.10m + wardrobes & en-suite
Bedroom 2	3.05 x 3.05m
Bedroom 3	2.69 x 2.69m

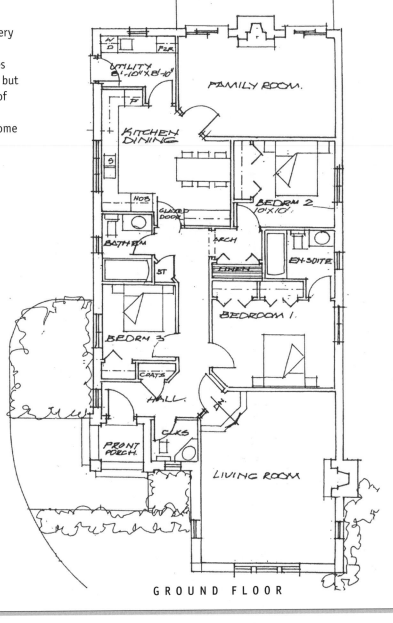

GROUND FLOOR

THE TRENT

The copyright belongs to an ASBA architectural practice - Julian Owen Associates

150 sq. m.

Overall dimensions 13.4 x 8.3m

REAR ELEVATION

This comfortable family house would fit on a plot that was just less than 10¹/₂ metres wide, if adequate parking is available. The rear elevation, which is shewn, has an interesting turret roof to one of the projections, which is matched, at lower level by the balcony on the other extension.

Living room	4.3 x 4.0m
Dining room	4.0 x 3.0m
Study	4.0 x 3.2m
Kitchen	4.7 x 3.2m
Conservatory	3.5 x 2.2mm
Bedroom 1	4.5 x 3.7m + en-suite
Bedroom 2	4.5 x 3.7m
Bedroom 3	3.7 x 2.5m

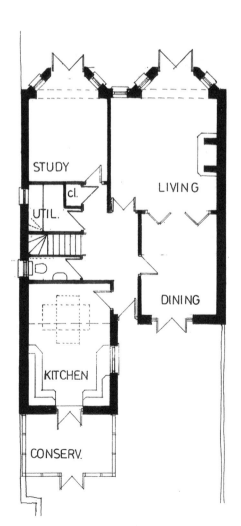

GROUND FLOOR

FIRST FLOOR

THE VINGA

The copyright belongs to The Self-Build House Company Ltd.

**150 sq. m.
including a garage of 28 sq. m.**

Overall dimensions 10.3 x 6.5m

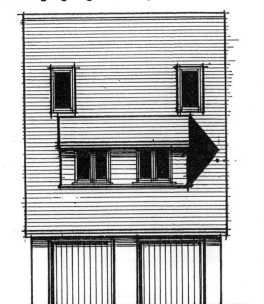

FRONT ELEVATION

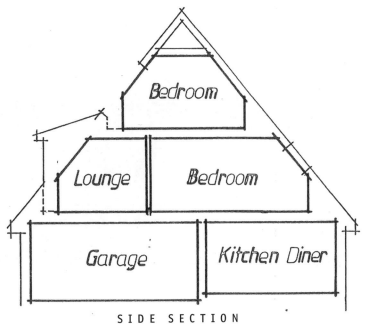

SIDE SECTION

This town house could fit on a site that was just 8.5 metres wide! The accommodation is laid out on three floors with much of the ground floor taken up by the double garage. If only one garage was required there would be scope to enlarge the kitchen or perhaps, use the space for a separate room.

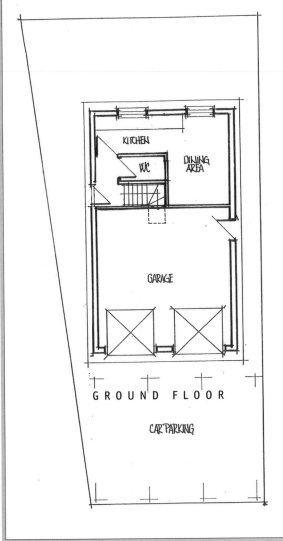

GROUND FLOOR

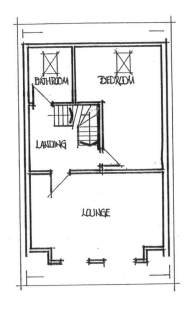

FIRST FLOOR

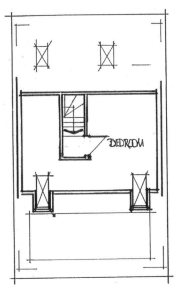

SECOND FLOOR

| Kitchen/ dining room | 5.8 x 3.4m |
| Garage | 5.8 x 4.9m |

Sitting room	5.8 x 4.3m
Master bedroom	4.3 x 3.0m
Bedroom 2	5.8 x 4.2m

FAVERSHAM

The copyright belongs to The Border Design Centre

**150 sq. m.
including a garage of 14 sq. m.**

Overall dimensions 10.6 x 10.3m

A design for a narrow sloping site. Originally conceived for a left-over site of just over ten metres wide with a drop of over four metres from the road to the back garden building line. The entrance and garage are at the middle level with the living room in the basement with direct access to the garden. The top floor provides four good bedrooms, one of which is en-suite.

FRONT ELEVATION

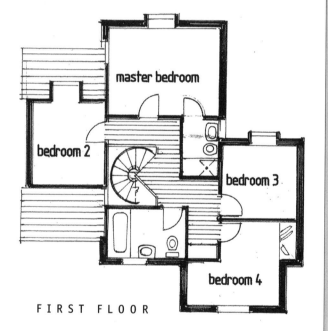

FIRST FLOOR

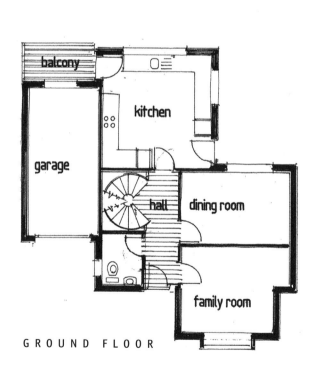

GROUND FLOOR

LOWER GROUND FLOOR

Living room	6.80 x 4.70m	Master bedroom	4.11 x 3.20m + en-suite	
Dining room	4.11 x 2.59m	Bedroom 2	2.89 x 2.59m	
Family room	4.11 x 3.20m	Bedroom 3	2.89 x 2.59m	
Kitchen/ breakfast room	4.11 x 4.11m	Bedroom 4	3.50 x 3.20m + wardrobe	
Garage	5.3 x 2.6m			

KELSO

**160 sq. m.
including a garage of 16 sq. m.**

Overall dimensions 13.10 x 10.30m

F R O N T   E L E V A T I O N

This home packs a whole lot of accommodation into a format that would fit onto quite a narrow site, yet nothing seems to be compromised, including and especially room sizes. The master suite not only has en-suite facilities but also has the advantage of a proper dressing room, something that much larger houses often fail to provide.

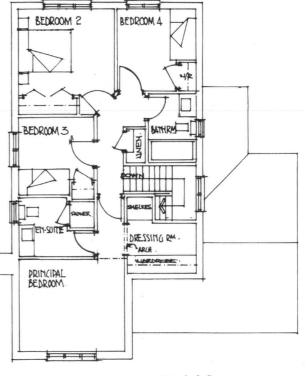

F I R S T   F L O O R

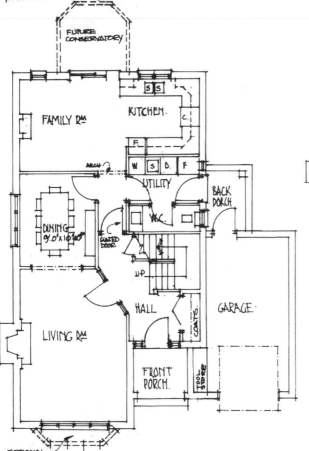

G R O U N D   F L O O R

Living room	5.44 x 3.91m	Principal bedroom	3.91 x 3.20m + dressing room & en-suite
Dining room	3.30 x 2.74m		
Family room	3.91 x 3.20m		
Kitchen	2.74 x 2.59m	Bedroom 2	3.50 x 3.00m + wardrobe
Utility	2.74 x 1.65m	Bedroom 3	3.00 x 2.74m
Garage	5.44 x 3.00m	Bedroom 4	2.92 x 2.84m

BERWICK

The copyright belongs to Designer Homes

180 sq. m.
including a garage of 25 sq. m.

Overall dimensions 14.40 x 10.20m

FRONT ELEVATION

This is one of the very few designs that have been repeated from the last book. It is a fabulous design that packs such a lot into a relatively small frontage without in any way compromising on visual attractiveness. Setting the garage back on the building and giving it just one single door despite its width reduces its visual impact. The reception accommodation is exemplary and upstairs there are four good sized bedrooms with the master bedroom having en-suite and dressing room facilities.

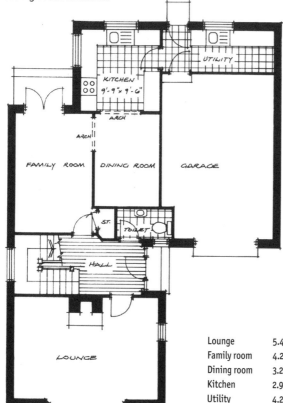

GROUND FLOOR

FIRST FLOOR

Lounge	5.41 x 4.19m	
Family room	4.27 x 2.90m	
Dining room	3.28 x 2.36m	
Kitchen	2.97 x 2.90m	
Utility	4.20 x 1.50m	
Garage	5.90 x 4.20m max	

Master bedroom	4.72 x 3.28m + en-suite, dressing room & wardrobes
Bedroom 2	3.58 x 3.28m + wardrobes
Bedroom 3	3.12 x 2.90m + wardrobe
Bedroom 4	3.58 x 2.36m + wardrobe

FLYCATCHER

The copyright belongs to Designer Homes

183 sq. m.
including a garage of 16 sq. m.

Overall dimensions 15.1 x 10.50m

FRONT ELEVATION

It was felt that this design had to be included in this book because it really gives a master class in just how to design for a narrow site. The garage does not become the dominant feature as attention is distracted from it by the run-over roof and the bay. On top of the generous living accommodation there are four bedrooms, one of them en-suite and all with fitted wardrobes.

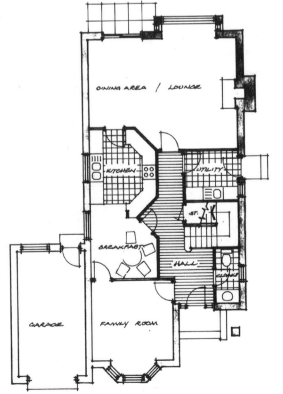

GROUND FLOOR

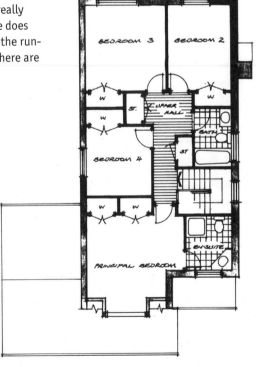

FIRST FLOOR

Lounge/ dining area	6.63 x 4.72m + bay		Principal bedroom	4.42 x 3.50m + en-suite & wardrobes
Kitchen	3.81 x 2.97m			
Breakfast area	2.97 x 2.59m		Bedroom 2	3.66 x 2.84m + wardrobe
Utility	2.30 x 2.20m			
Family room	3.58 x 3.43m		Bedroom 3	3.66 x 3.66m + wardrobe
Garage	5.40 x 3.00m		Bedroom 4	2.97 x 2.97m + wardrobe

343

BENDERLOCH

The copyright belongs to The Border Design Centre

189 sq. m.

Overall dimensions 17.3 x 10.7m

This home was designed for a narrow infill site that, nevertheless, had good views to the rear. These were exploited by the octagonal living room and master bedroom, to give all-round views. The two storey dining hall is arranged to the side of the living room so that it too can enjoy the views to the rear. To the front the cloistered entrance and the turret are the trademarks of this designer.

FRONT ELEVATION

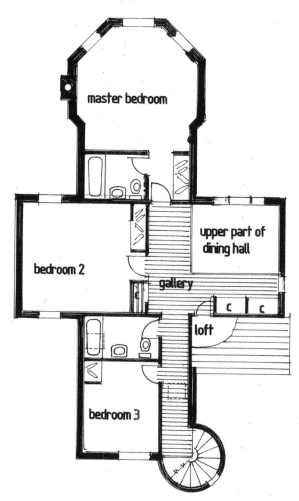

FIRST FLOOR

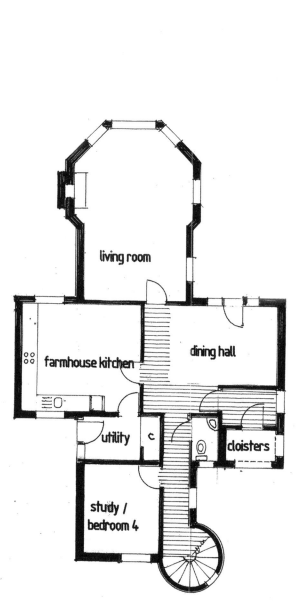

GROUND FLOOR

Living room	6.50 x 4.70m		Master bedroom	4.70 x 4.70m
Dining hall	5.31 x 4.11m			+ dressing lobby & en-suite
Kitchen	4.70 x 4.11m + utility area		Bedroom 2	4.11 x 4.11m + wardrobe
Study/ bedroom 4	3.50 x 2.99m		Bedroom 3	3.50 x 2.99m

ROYSTON

The copyright belongs to Custom Homes Ltd.

205 sq. m.

Overall dimensions 16.5 x 10.8m

This a home for a long narrow site where the shape of the building allows all of the major rooms to have principal windows to either the front or the rear. The drawing room has a double aspect. All of the bedrooms are comfortably sized and the master bedroom has a useful dressing area as well as en-suite facilities.

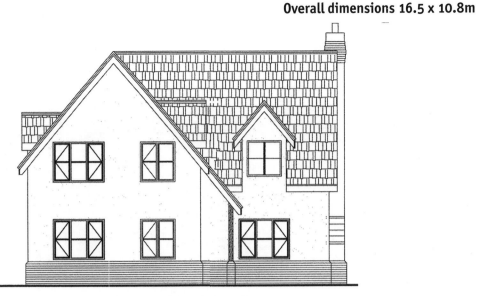

SIDE ELEVATION

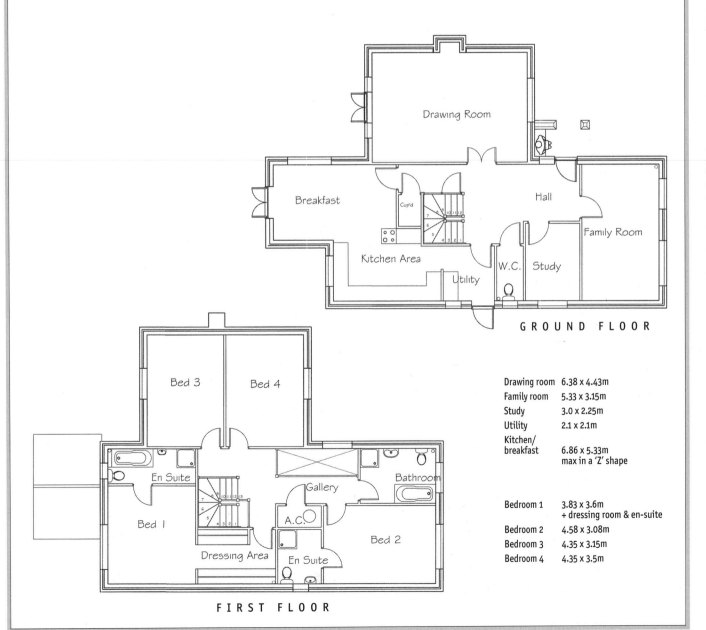

GROUND FLOOR

FIRST FLOOR

Drawing room	6.38 x 4.43m
Family room	5.33 x 3.15m
Study	3.0 x 2.25m
Utility	2.1 x 2.1m
Kitchen/ breakfast	6.86 x 5.33m max in a 'Z' shape
Bedroom 1	3.83 x 3.6m + dressing room & en-suite
Bedroom 2	4.58 x 3.08m
Bedroom 3	4.35 x 3.15m
Bedroom 4	4.35 x 3.5m

LIMERICK

The copyright belongs to Designer Homes

220 sq. m.

Overall dimensions 17.50 x 12.25m

FRONT ELEVATION

No compromise is sought with this design for a narrow site. It has four really good sized bedrooms, two of which have en-suite facilities and all of which, as is common with this contributor, have built in wardrobes. The fairly narrow spans for each section of the home prevent the ridge getting too high and the trick of having a dining hall means that there is no waste of space downstairs to get to the rooms in the rear projection.

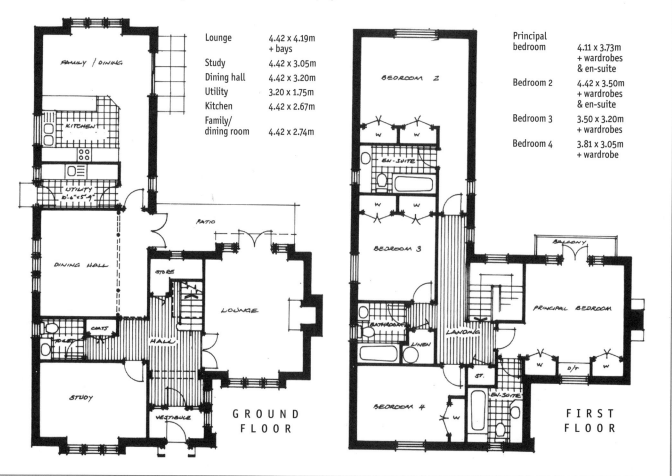

Lounge	4.42 x 4.19m + bays
Study	4.42 x 3.05m
Dining hall	4.42 x 3.20m
Utility	3.20 x 1.75m
Kitchen	4.42 x 2.67m
Family/ dining room	4.42 x 2.74m

Principal bedroom	4.11 x 3.73m + wardrobes & en-suite
Bedroom 2	4.42 x 3.50m + wardrobes & en-suite
Bedroom 3	3.50 x 3.20m + wardrobes
Bedroom 4	3.81 x 3.05m + wardrobe

GROUND FLOOR

FIRST FLOOR

THE KIMPTON

The copyright belongs to Custom Homes Ltd.

253 sq. m.

Overall dimensions 12.42 x 8.80m

The most interesting feature of this house is the fact that almost half of the available space to the upper part is taken up with the master bedroom and its dressing room and en-suite. If that selfish arrangement is not wanted, there would be a space for a fourth bedroom. The side views are interesting in that they give the impression of a church or chapel.

FRONT ELEVATION

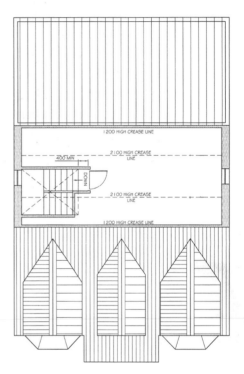

ATTIC FLOOR

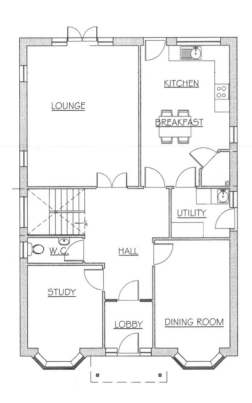

GROUND FLOOR

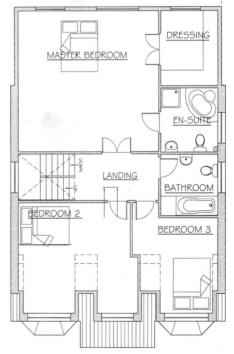

FIRST FLOOR

Lounge	5.50 x 4.50m		Master bedroom	5.78 x 5.50m + dressing room & en-suite
Kitchen/ breakfast room	5.50 x 3.59m		Bedroom 2	4.63 x 4.05m
Utility	2.37 x 1.92m		Bedroom 3	3.70 x 3.47m
Dining room	4.20 x 3.04m			
Study	3.04 x 3.22m			

HOMES FOR SLOPING SITES

Almost invariably a full levels survey will be required before any design that is to fit into a sloping site is commenced. There are several ways of approaching the 'problem' of a sloping site. The first is to engineer a level plinth upon which the home can be built in the normal way with retaining walls to hold back any bank or retain any spill over. In some cases this cut and fill arrangement can mean that a home from one of the other categories in this book can be employed but in others, as is demonstrated here, it may mean that the entrance and garage levels have to be on an upper floor. Another way is to build the house into the plot with the side on the higher end of the slope constructed as a basement or partial basement. Yet another is to build a series of blocks down the slope, partially overlapping each other.

Building on a sloping site, especially if there is a lot of underbuilding or if there is a need for expensive retaining walling either within the main structure or surrounding it, can be expensive. But the very nature of the sites and the excitement that the design solutions create mean that the resulting buildings become flagships for the flair and imagination of their originators.

Contributors in this section:
Associated Self Build Architects
The Border Design Centre
T.J.Crump OAKWRIGHTS Ltd.
Custom Homes Ltd.
Design & Materials Ltd.
Designer Homes
Potton Ltd.
The Self Build House Company Ltd.
Scottish Architects Network
Scandia-Hus Ltd.
The Swedish House Company Ltd.

MONKHILL

The copyright belongs to an ASBA architectural practice – S. Buttler

**121 sq. m.
including a garage of 24 sq. m.**

Overall dimensions 14.5 x 8.7m

FRONT ELEVATION

Although it is not shewn on a steeply sloping site, this home has been designed on three levels, following the lie of the land. As little as possible is given over to circulation space with square spiral staircases linking the garage, mezzanine and upper levels. The garage door is sheltered and made less intrusive by the supports and balcony to the lounge above.

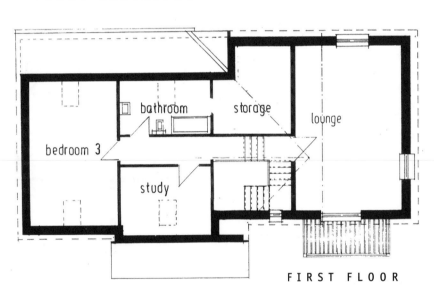

FIRST FLOOR

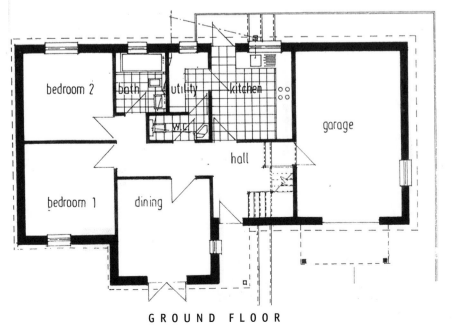

GROUND FLOOR

Kitchen	3.2 x 3.0m
Dining room	3.5 x 3.4m
Bedroom 1	3.3 x 3.1m
Bedroom 2	3.3 x 3.3m
Lounge	6.0 x 4.0m
Bedroom 3	5.2 x 3.3m
Study	3.3 x 2.4m

THE BRIGWORTH

The copyright belongs to Scandia-Hus Limited

152 sq. m.

Overall dimensions 13.56 x 10.37m

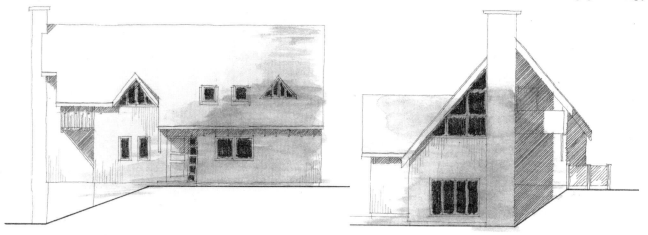

FRONT ELEVATION

SIDE ELEVATION

Light is the main feature of this wonderful split level design with triangular gable head windows to most elevations as well as timber upper balcony decks. The dining room is situated below the upper gallery, which has vaulted ceilings. Truly a home of many facets.

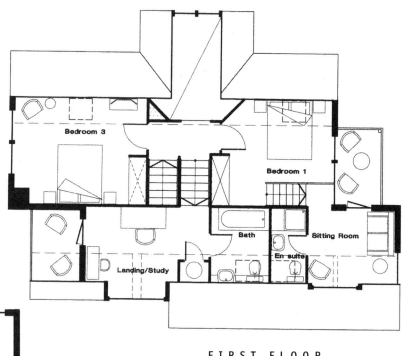

FIRST FLOOR

GROUND FLOOR

Kitchen/ breakfast area	5.5 x 3.3m
Dining room	3.7 x 3.2m
Sitting room	4.5 x 4.5m
Bedroom 2	4.5 x 3.7m
Master bedroom	4.0 x 3.6m
Dressing/ sitting area	3.0 x 2.5m
Bedroom 3	4.5 x 3.6m
Landing/study	3.2 x 2.4m

TARBERT

159 sq. m.

The copyright belongs to The Border Design Centre

Overall dimensions 14.7 x 11.1m

A home for a steep site. Entrance is via a bridge to a mezzanine floor. The tower provides a generous dropped floor en-suite to the master bedroom, a sun room off the main living room and a crows nest study to the top floor. A careful look at the plans will also reveal that there are cupboards everywhere, something that is lacking in many homes.

FRONT ELEVATION

Master bedroom 4.70 x 4.29 + wardrobe + en-suite
Bedroom 2 3.50 x 2.89m
Bedroom 3 3.50 x 2.89m

Living room 5.79 x 4.70m
Sun room 3.90 diameter
Kitchen/ dining room 6.09 x 4.70m + utility area

Crows nest study 3.90m diameter

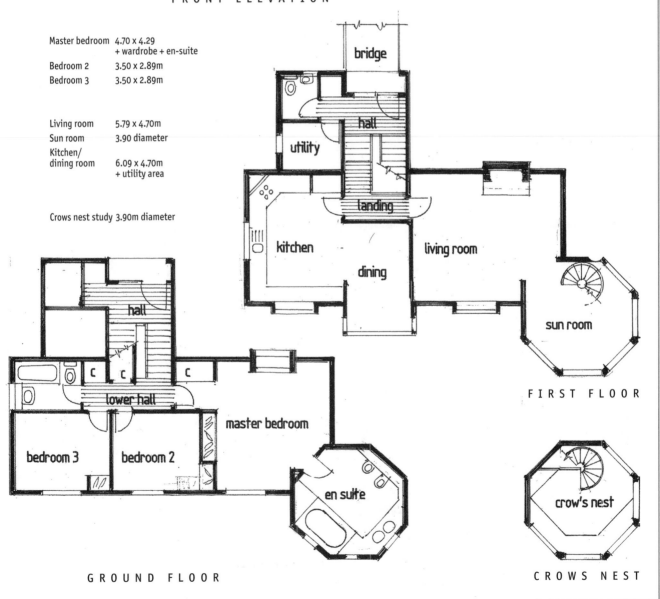

FIRST FLOOR

GROUND FLOOR

CROWS NEST

THE WATERDINE

The copyright belongs to an ASBA architectural practice - Reed Architects

179 sq. m.

Overall dimensions 17.5 x 14.1m

The house is shewn on a steep slope and the level change has been used to provide a guest bedroom to the lower floor with access to the garden. The living area is open plan with a central hearth overlooked by the gallery in the roof space. It would not take much to realise the gallery sitting area and storage areas as additional sleeping and bathroom accommodation.

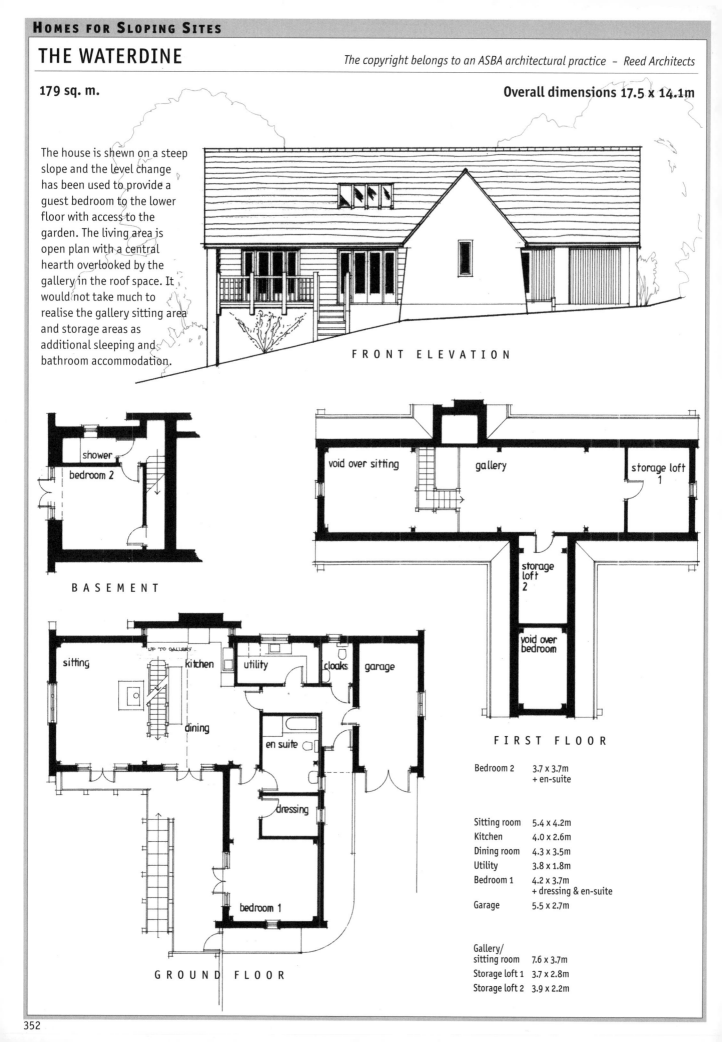

F R O N T   E L E V A T I O N

shower
bedroom 2

B A S E M E N T

void over sitting
gallery
storage loft 1

storage loft 2

void over bedroom

F I R S T   F L O O R

sitting
UP TO GALLERY
kitchen
utility
cloaks
garage
dining
en suite
dressing
bedroom 1

G R O U N D   F L O O R

Bedroom 2	3.7 x 3.7m + en-suite
Sitting room	5.4 x 4.2m
Kitchen	4.0 x 2.6m
Dining room	4.3 x 3.5m
Utility	3.8 x 1.8m
Bedroom 1	4.2 x 3.7m + dressing & en-suite
Garage	5.5 x 2.7m
Gallery/ sitting room	7.6 x 3.7m
Storage loft 1	3.7 x 2.8m
Storage loft 2	3.9 x 2.2m

CALLY

The copyright belongs to The Border Design Centre

187 sq. m.

Overall dimensions 19.6 x 9.7m

FRONT ELEVATION

One way of dealing with a steeply sloping site is to build down the slope of the land with underbuilding and extra costs. Whilst that can sometimes be the correct design solution, this home employs another, namely to run with the contours of the site. It does mean that the spans of the building have to be kept narrow but that does not mean that in certain circumstances, as here, projections cannot be taken out.

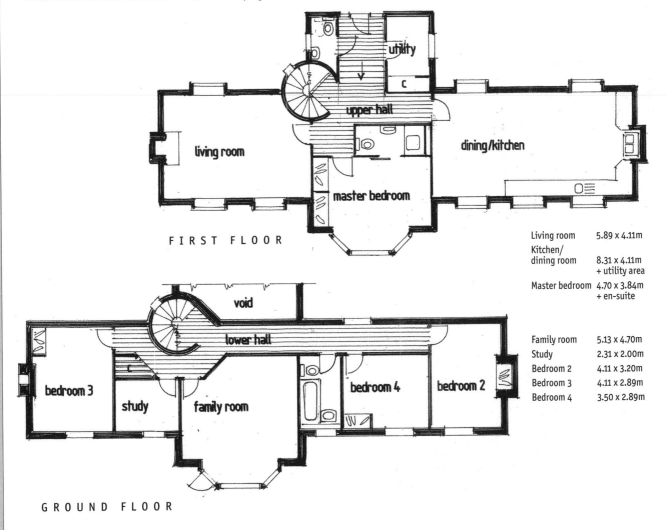

FIRST FLOOR

GROUND FLOOR

Living room	5.89 x 4.11m
Kitchen/ dining room	8.31 x 4.11m + utility area
Master bedroom	4.70 x 3.84m + en-suite
Family room	5.13 x 4.70m
Study	2.31 x 2.00m
Bedroom 2	4.11 x 3.20m
Bedroom 3	4.11 x 2.89m
Bedroom 4	3.50 x 2.89m

D272

The design belongs to Design & Materials Ltd.

**234 sq. m
including a garage of 14 sq. m.**

Overall dimensions 11.90 x 9.40m

FRONT ELEVATION

Sloping sites often bring out the best in designers and this is an example. The ground floor is the entrance floor with the garage at that level. Below that there is a basement with a garden room. The first floor contains the three major bedrooms, including the master suite, and there is a gallery overlooking the dining area below whilst, in the roof, there are two further bedrooms.

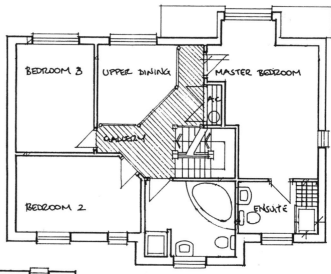

FIRST FLOOR

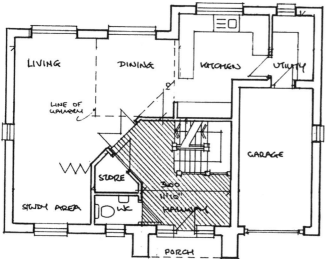

GROUND FLOOR

Living/dining/ study area	7.00 x 6.40m max
Kitchen	3.95 x 3.50m
Utility	2.40 x 1.60m
Garage	5.20 x 2.74m

Master bedroom	5.05 x 4.20m max + en-suite
Bedroom 2	4.86 x 2.75m
Bedroom 3	4.15 x 3.05m

REAR ELEVATION

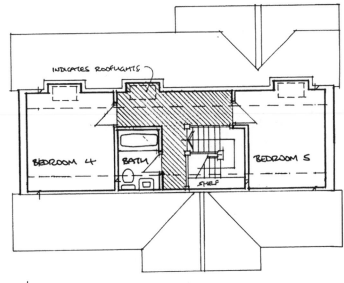

SECOND FLOOR

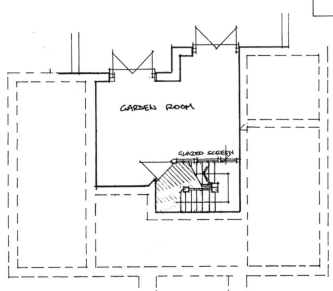

LOWER GROUND FLOOR

Garden room   5.41 x 4.95 max

Bedroom 4   3.66 x 3.40m
Bedroom 5   3.66 x 2.94m

WINDY GOWL FARM

The copyright belongs to a ScAN architectural practice – Walter Wood Associates

249 sq. m.
including a garage of 21 sq. m.

Overall dimensions 22.1 x 13.5m

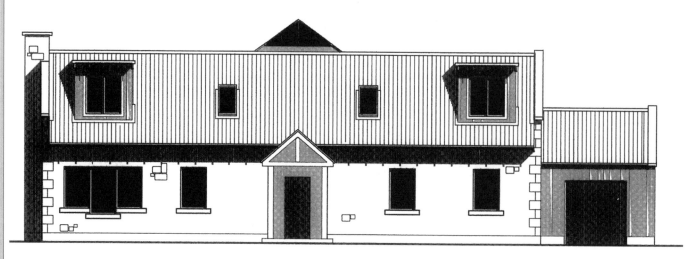

FRONT ELEVATION

From the road this home looks like a bungalow with rooms in the roof. The clue to its real identity is the glazed gable head window to the rear projection. Wide steps lead up from the entrance hall into a lobby and then on up to the lounge/dining and kitchen areas from where more steps lead back to the upper part. A modern design to suit a site that rises up from the frontage.

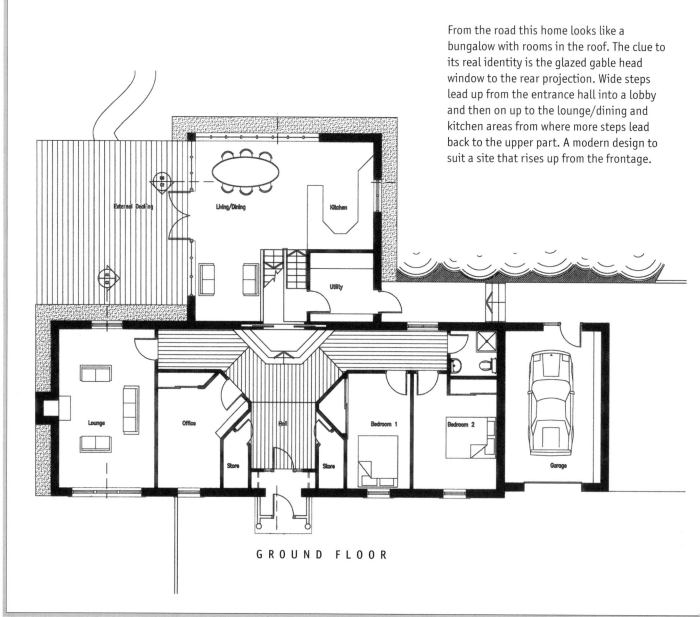

GROUND FLOOR

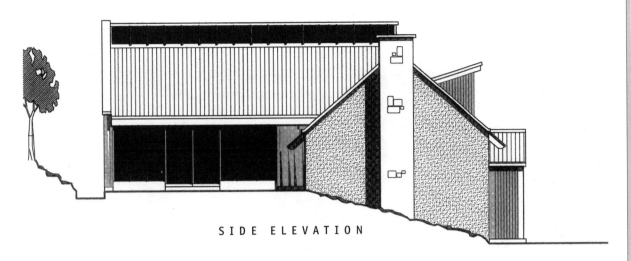

SIDE ELEVATION

Lounge	5.85 x 3.65m
Kitchen area	4.0 x 3.4m
Utility	2.5 x 2.4m
Dining/ living area	6.7 x 3.7m max
Office	4.25 x 2.4m
Bedroom 1	4.2 x 2.4m + wardrobe
Bedroom 2	4.2 x 3.2m
Garage	5.65 x 3.7m
Bedroom 3	4.7 x 4.0m
Bedroom 4	4.0 x 3.2m + lobby, dressing room & en-suite

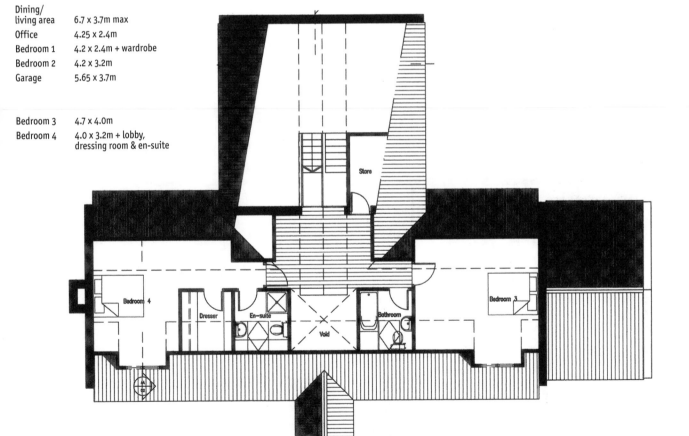

FIRST FLOOR

LEDCAMEROCH

The copyright belongs to The Border Design Centre

249 sq. m.

Overall dimensions 15.5 x 8.3m

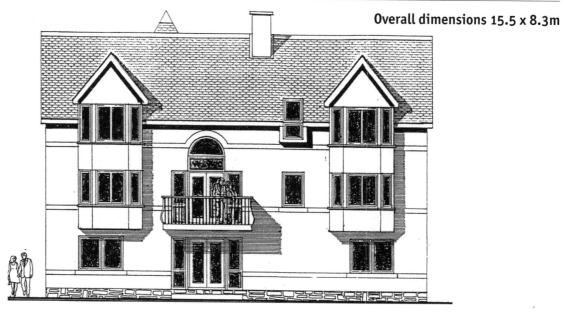

FRONT ELEVATION

This design was formulated for a site that was a left-over parcel of land that was some six metres below street level. The home is entered via a bridge to the top floor with the drawing room and family room at this level, connected by a gallery that overlooks the dining hall on the middle floor. The master bedroom is also at this middle level, as is the kitchen, whilst the remaining bedrooms are on the lower level.

SECOND FLOOR

FIRST FLOOR

GROUND FLOOR

Bedroom 2	4.70 x 4.11m	Kitchen	5.61 x 3.71m + utility area	
Bedroom 3	4.70 x 3.50m	Dining hall	4.70 x 4.22m	
Garden room	4.19 x 4.11m	Master bedroom	5.61 x 3.81m + Dressing room & en-suite	
		Drawing room	6.80 x 5.61m	
		Family room	5.61 x 3.50m	

SWHS5

The copyright belongs to The Swedish House Company Ltd.

368 sq. m.

Overall dimensions 18.5 x 14.8m

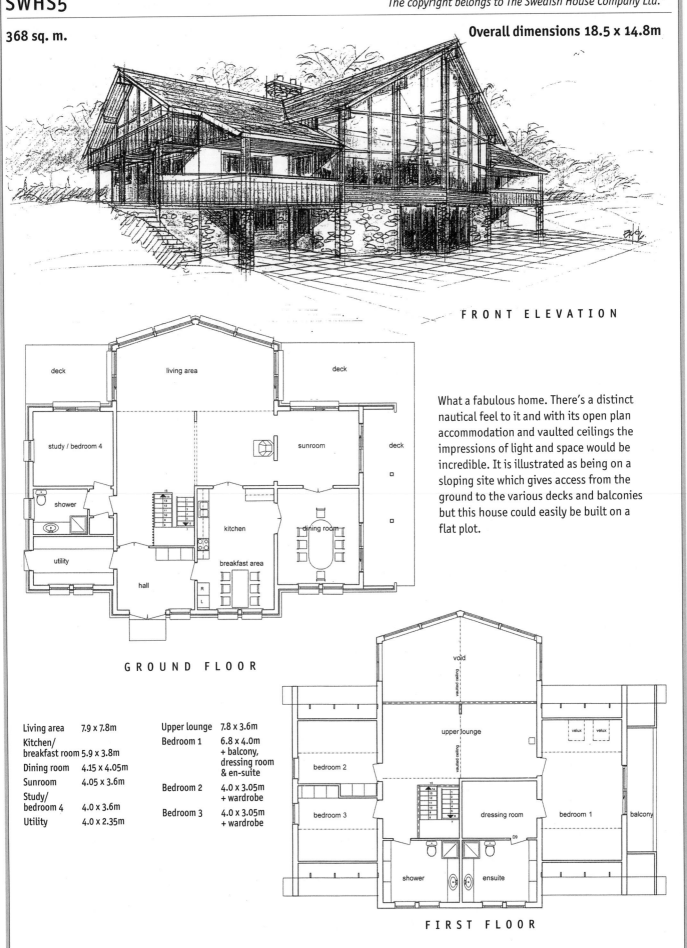

FRONT ELEVATION

GROUND FLOOR

FIRST FLOOR

What a fabulous home. There's a distinct nautical feel to it and with its open plan accommodation and vaulted ceilings the impressions of light and space would be incredible. It is illustrated as being on a sloping site which gives access from the ground to the various decks and balconies but this house could easily be built on a flat plot.

Living area	7.9 x 7.8m	Upper lounge	7.8 x 3.6m
Kitchen/ breakfast room	5.9 x 3.8m	Bedroom 1	6.8 x 4.0m + balcony, dressing room & en-suite
Dining room	4.15 x 4.05m		
Sunroom	4.05 x 3.6m	Bedroom 2	4.0 x 3.05m + wardrobe
Study/ bedroom 4	4.0 x 3.6m	Bedroom 3	4.0 x 3.05m + wardrobe
Utility	4.0 x 2.35m		

97-194

260 sq. m.

Overall dimensions 19.3 x 16m

FRONT ELEVATION

With its dining/sun room at the front and several changes of level throughout the home, this is a design that lends itself to the larger and more private plot, although with some adaptation it could be made to fit on the minimum. Having the master suite on the ground floor could suit couples who only have to think of occasional visitors.

Bedroom 1

Dressing   En-suite

WC

Study

UP

Lounge

Hall

Cloaks

Balcony

UP

Utility

Sunroom / Dining

Kitchen / B'fast

GROUND FLOOR

REAR ELEVATION

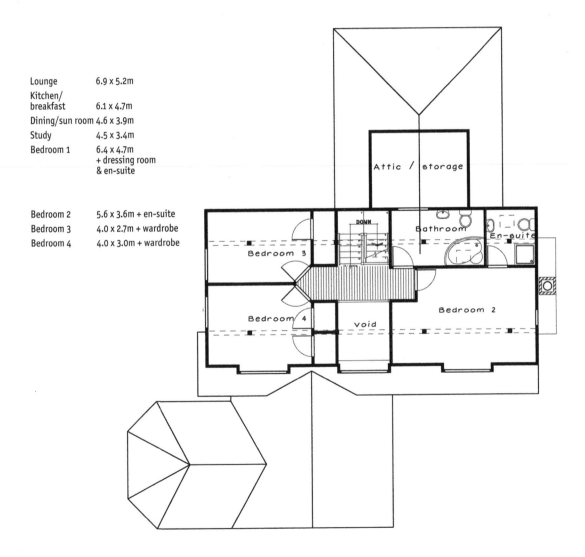

Lounge	6.9 x 5.2m
Kitchen/breakfast	6.1 x 4.7m
Dining/sun room	4.6 x 3.9m
Study	4.5 x 3.4m
Bedroom 1	6.4 x 4.7m + dressing room & en-suite
Bedroom 2	5.6 x 3.6m + en-suite
Bedroom 3	4.0 x 2.7m + wardrobe
Bedroom 4	4.0 x 3.0m + wardrobe

FIRST FLOOR

0205

273 sq. m.
including a garage of 37 sq. m.

Overall dimensions 20.5 x 17.3m

F R O N T   E L E V A T I O N   –   N O R T H

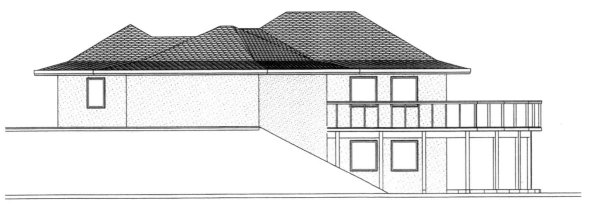

W E S T   E L E V A T I O N

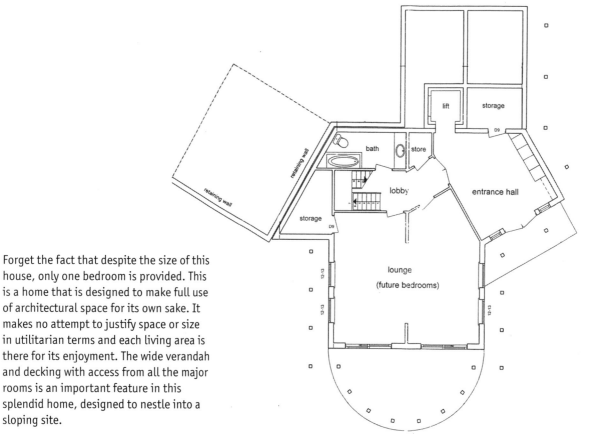

Forget the fact that despite the size of this house, only one bedroom is provided. This is a home that is designed to make full use of architectural space for its own sake. It makes no attempt to justify space or size in utilitarian terms and each living area is there for its enjoyment. The wide verandah and decking with access from all the major rooms is an important feature in this splendid home, designed to nestle into a sloping site.

L O W E R   F L O O R

S O U T H   E L E V A T I O N

E A S T   E L E V A T I O N

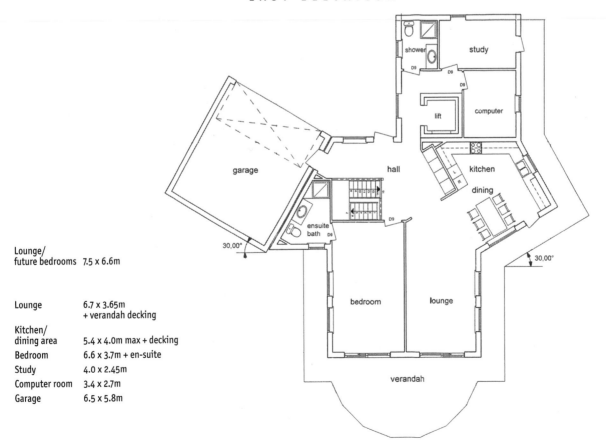

Lounge/
future bedrooms 7.5 x 6.6m

Lounge	6.7 x 3.65m + verandah decking
Kitchen/ dining area	5.4 x 4.0m max + decking
Bedroom	6.6 x 3.7m + en-suite
Study	4.0 x 2.45m
Computer room	3.4 x 2.7m
Garage	6.5 x 5.8m

U P P E R   F L O O R

T218

The copyright belongs to Design & Materials Ltd.

**523 sq. m.
including garages
of 61 sq. m.**

Overall dimensions 23.50 x 16.00m

REAR (SEA VIEW) ELEVATION

Why should homes be rectangular if the plot dictates a curve? The upside of having a sloping site is that the views are often spectacular so it makes sense to have the living accommodation on the upper floors. Having the master suite on the very top floor makes it separate and very private.

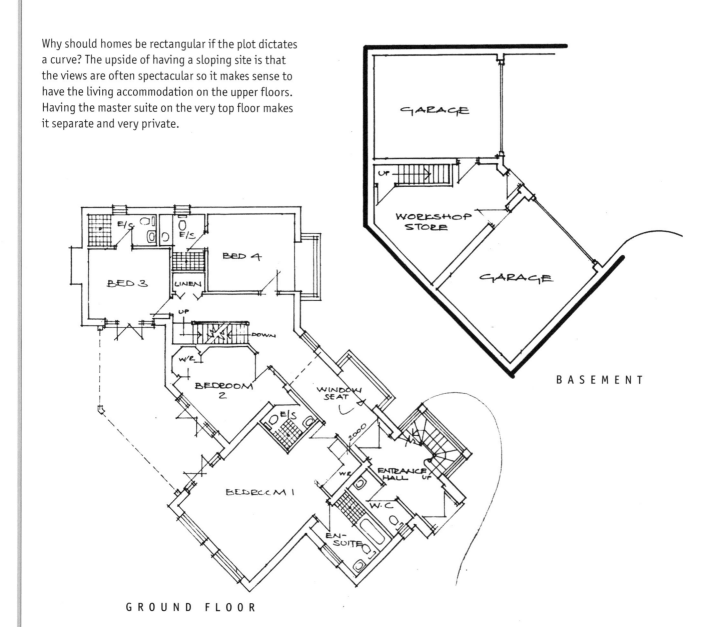

GROUND FLOOR

BASEMENT

Garage 1   6.10 x 5.15m
Workshop   6.10 x 5.15m max
Garage 2   6.10 x 4.90m

Bedroom 1   5.49 x 5.15m
              + en-suite
Bedroom 2   4.00 x 4.00m
              + wardrobe
              & en-suite
Bedroom 3   3.96 x 3.35m
              + en-suite
Bedroom 4   4.27 x 3.80m
              + en-suite & bay

Lounge   6.97 x 5.15m
Dining room   5.20 x 3.90m
Family room   4.90 x 3.96m
Kitchen   4.90 x 4.90m
Study   4.00 x 3.05m

Master bedroom 5.18 x 5.15m
              + sitting area,
              dressing room
              & en-suite

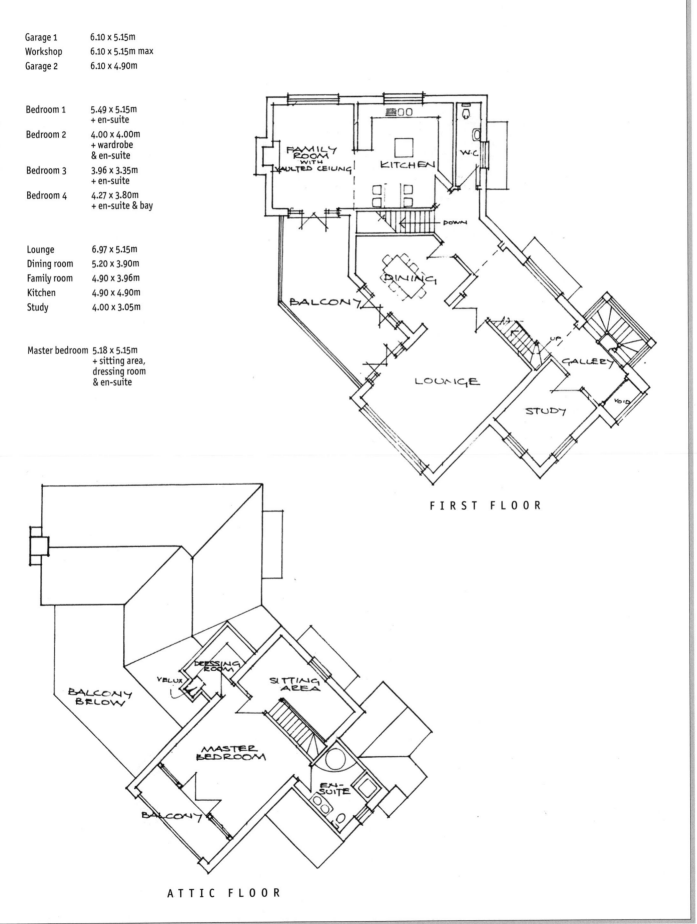

FIRST FLOOR

ATTIC FLOOR

GLENSHIELS

The copyright belongs to T. J. Crump OAKRIGHTS Ltd.

443 sq. m.
including a garage and workshop of 67 sq. m.

Overall dimensions 27.42 x 11.94m

F R O N T   E L E V A T I O N

The home is illustrated here as having been built on a sloping site, which gives it the added advantage of having decking around the main living accommodation plus the possibility of storage facilities underneath. The huge studio could just as easily be designated as a bedroom or even as two further bedrooms.

S I D E   E L E V A T I O N

G R O U N D   F L O O R

Sitting room	7.44 x 4.67m
Dining room	7.31 x 4.67m
Study	4.88 x 3.55m
Kitchen	4.74 x 3.75m
Utility/lobby	4.90 x 2.79m
Conservatory	4.14 x 2.20m
Garage	7.44 x 5.86m
Workshop	7.44 x 3.15m

Studio	9.24 x 5.79m
Bedroom 1	7.44 x 4.80m + en-suite
Bedroom 2	4.87 x 4.74m
Bedroom 3	4.80 3.68m incl. wardrobe

F I R S T   F L O O R

HOMES WITH GRANNY FLATS

First of all these annexes are not always for a granny or granddad. Sometimes they provide separate accommodation for staff or guests and sometimes they are necessary because there is a multi generational occupation. As previewed in the earlier text of this book and in Building Your Own Home there are many considerations to be made, not least the satisfaction of the planners. Planners may well be concerned to see that the annex is always going to remain an integral part of the home and not be subdivided and sold or let off. They will want to see some linkage at the very least and in many cases will insist that there is no separate entrance. Entrance can be via a shared rear lobby or utility. It can be by means of a door between the two house sections or it can be by means of an external door or French doors to one of the annex rooms. In the last analysis a new entrance door can often be created after the dwelling is occupied under Permitted Development Rights, also discussed in Building Your Own Home.

If the annex is to be an older person's home, think about how they can enjoy the gardens. Think about their easy access to those gardens and, if and when they are unable to get out into them, think about their view of them from their rooms. If an annex is to house staff, think about positioning it such that the two sections of the house can enjoy privacy from each other.

Contributors in this section:
Associated Self Build Architects
The Border Design Centre
T.J.Crump OAKWRIGHTS Ltd.
Custom Homes Ltd.
Design & Materials Ltd.
Designer Homes
Potton Ltd.
The Self Build House Company Ltd.
Scottish Architects Network
Scandia-Hus Ltd.
The Swedish House Company Ltd.

MELKINTHORPE

The copyright belongs to an ASBA architectural practice – S. Buttler

161 sq. m.

Overall dimensions 15.0 x 12.7m

F R O N T   E L E V A T I O N

Granny doesn't always join onto a nuclear family. The ground floor layout is designed for wheelchair dependent living with easy access to the outside via wide verandahs. The first floor accommodation is generously laid out for flexible use by the family, with roof lights located to maximise the views.

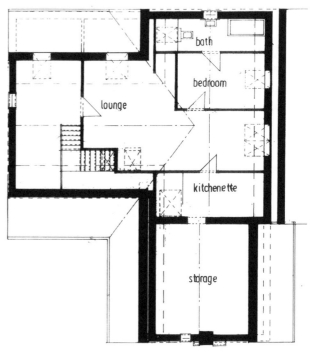

F I R S T   F L O O R

G R O U N D   F L O O R

Kitchen/living room	5.0 x 5.0m
Lounge	5.0 x 5.0m
Utility	2.0 x 1.8m
Bedroom 1	5.0 x 3.4m + dressing room & en-suite
Bedroom 2	3.4 x 3.0m + en-suite

Kitchenette	5.0 x 2.0m
Lounge	8.0 x 4.9m
Upper bedroom	4.0 x 2.4m

PEACEHAVEN

The copyright belongs to The Border Design Centre

203 sq. m.

Overall dimensions 13.9 x 13.2m

FRONT ELEVATION

Many local authorities insist that a granny flat should provide only ground floor accommodation and that it should be integrated within the main household, so as to prevent division of properties. That does not mean that an individual entrance is not allowed but some connection should be shown. Whilst well within the house, the separating corridor with this design would give each section privacy.

FIRST FLOOR

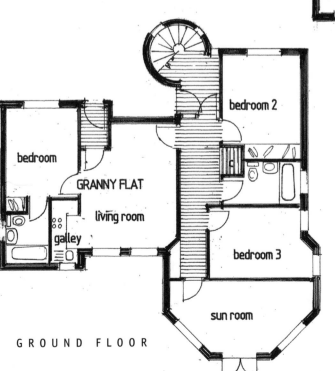

GROUND FLOOR

Bedroom 2	3.50 x 2.89m + wardrobe		Living room	5.99 x 5.89m
Bedroom 3	4.29 x 2.89m		Kitchen/ dining room	5.98 x 4.98m
Sun room	5.89 x 2.89m		Master bedroom	6.20 x 4.11m + dressing room & en-suite
Annex				
living room	4.98 x 4.11m			
Annex galley	2.49 x 1.32m			
Annex bedroom	3.50 x 2.89m + wardrobe & en-suite			

GLEN KINGLAS

The copyright belongs to a ScAN architectural practice – Design Practice

259 sq. m.

Overall dimensions 17.0 x 15.1m

FRONT ELEVATION

The sitting room and downstairs bedroom, together with the separate shower room would be well suited to an older member of the family who wants to live with the family whilst retaining some independence. The dividing hall with its entrances to both front and back would mean that they could come and go without disturbing the rest of the household. If the lack of kitchen facilities for the annex was a problem, this could be easily sorted out by a re-arrangement of the utility section.

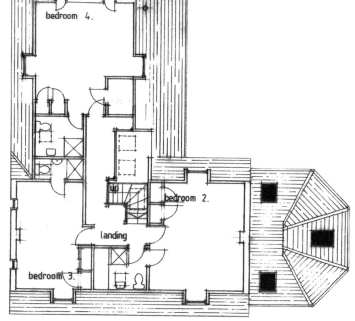

FIRST FLOOR

GROUND FLOOR

Lounge	7.0 x 4.7m
Sun room	6.2 x 4.7m max
Sitting room	6.7 x 3.4m
Kitchen/ dining room	6.5 x 4.9m max
Utility	2.4 x 2.2m
Bedroom 1	4.1 x 2.7m
Bedroom 2	5.2 x 4.7m + en-suite
Bedroom 3	5.2 x 3.3m + en-suite
Bedroom 4	5.4 x 4.8m + en-suite

THE TATTERSHALL

The copyright belongs to The Self-Build House Company Ltd.

272 sq. m.

Overall dimensions 17.0 x 14.15m

FRONT ELEVATION

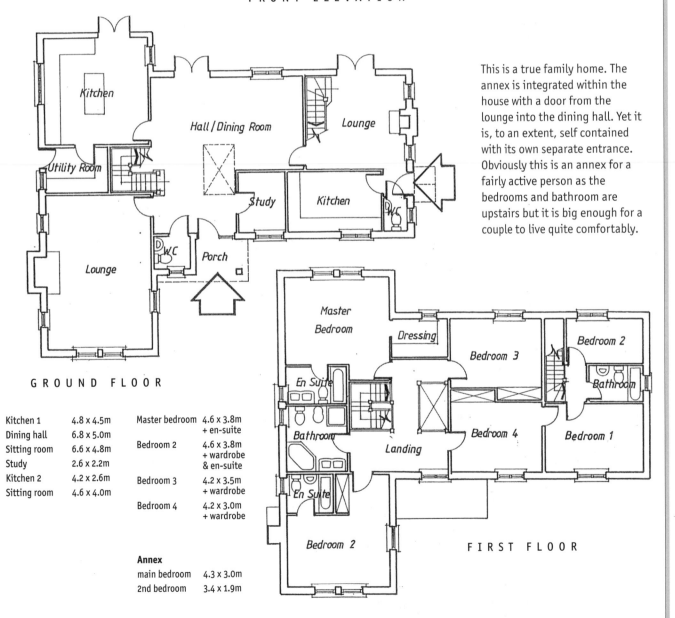

This is a true family home. The annex is integrated within the house with a door from the lounge into the dining hall. Yet it is, to an extent, self contained with its own separate entrance. Obviously this is an annex for a fairly active person as the bedrooms and bathroom are upstairs but it is big enough for a couple to live quite comfortably.

GROUND FLOOR

FIRST FLOOR

Kitchen 1	4.8 x 4.5m	Master bedroom	4.6 x 3.8m + en-suite
Dining hall	6.8 x 5.0m	Bedroom 2	4.6 x 3.8m + wardrobe & en-suite
Sitting room	6.6 x 4.8m		
Study	2.6 x 2.2m		
Kitchen 2	4.2 x 2.6m	Bedroom 3	4.2 x 3.5m + wardrobe
Sitting room	4.6 x 4.0m	Bedroom 4	4.2 x 3.0m + wardrobe

Annex

main bedroom	4.3 x 3.0m
2nd bedroom	3.4 x 1.9m

WARMINSTER

The copyright belongs to Designer Homes

314 sq. m.

Overall dimensions 22.20 x 19.50m

F R O N T   E L E V A T I O N

If the annex were not required then this would be a six bedroom house. As it is the annex provides two good bedrooms and a study/lounge with its own bathroom. It doesn't, as drawn, provide cooking facilities but they are not always required if 'granny' is going to live and eat within the family. If more separation was required, one of the bedrooms could always become the annex kitchen.

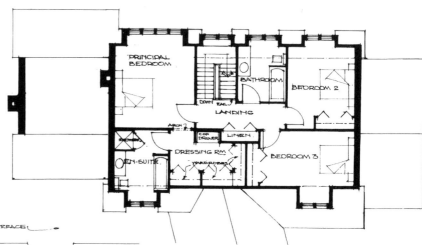

F I R S T   F L O O R

G R O U N D   F L O O R

Living room	5.99 x 4.42m
Family room	5.26 x 4.19m
Kitchen/ breakfast room	6.20 x 4.42m
Dining room	3.96 x 3.20m
Utility	4.67 x 2.69m
Annex study/ lounge	3.81 x 3.00m
1st annex bedroom	3.00 x 3.00m
2nd annex bedroom	3.20 x 3.00m
Principal bedroom	4.88m x 4.19m + dressing room & en-suite
Bedroom 2	4.19m x 3.61m + wardrobe
Bedroom 3	4.80m x 2.90m + wardrobes

BALLACHULISH

The copyright belongs to The Border Design Centre

332 sq. m.

Overall dimensions 28.7 x 11.3m

FRONT ELEVATION

It might be an old fashioned idea but this home provides a 'children's wing' capable of being shut off from the main house on both levels. Perhaps it would be better to describe the ground floor annex that is provided as a 'nanny flat', for it allows nanny and the children to live a virtually separate existence whilst remaining within the main body of the home. It is all in the naming but the flexibility provided by this design is impressive.

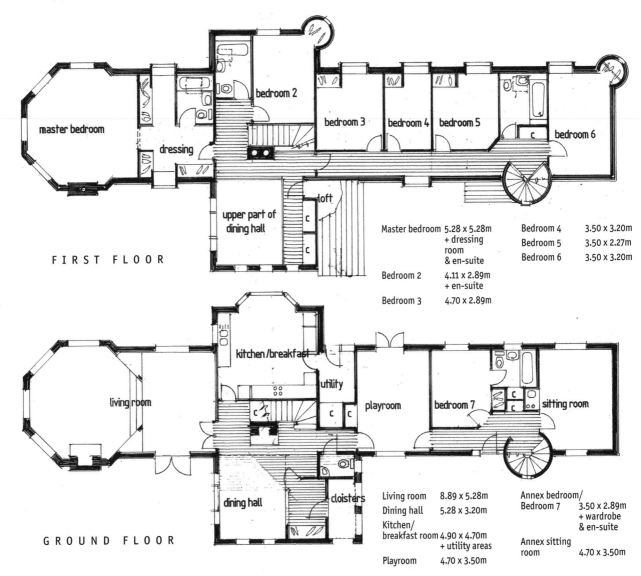

FIRST FLOOR

Master bedroom	5.28 x 5.28m + dressing room & en-suite	Bedroom 4	3.50 x 3.20m
		Bedroom 5	3.50 x 2.27m
		Bedroom 6	3.50 x 3.20m
Bedroom 2	4.11 x 2.89m + en-suite		
Bedroom 3	4.70 x 2.89m		

GROUND FLOOR

Living room	8.89 x 5.28m	Annex bedroom/	
Dining hall	5.28 x 3.20m	Bedroom 7	3.50 x 2.89m + wardrobe & en-suite
Kitchen/ breakfast room	4.90 x 4.70m + utility areas		
		Annex sitting room	4.70 x 3.50m
Playroom	4.70 x 3.50m		

SANDVIKEN

The copyright belongs to The Swedish House Company Ltd.

333 sq. m.

Overall dimensions 21.73 x 12.73m

FRONT ELEVATION

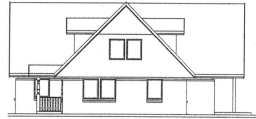

SIDE ELEVATION

REAR ELEVATION

A second entrance and hall to this home together with the door in the central passageway means that this lovely home can quite easily be divided to provide either a ground floor granny annex or self contained holiday letting accommodation. Once again, the idea that most major living rooms and the master bedroom should open onto a patio or balcony is employed.

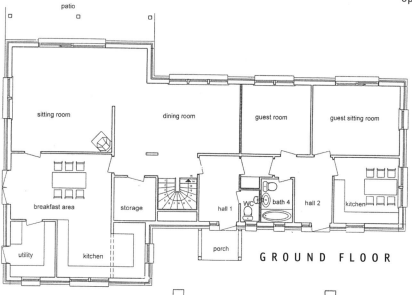

GROUND FLOOR

Sitting room	5.4 x 5.4m
Dining room	6.8 x 3.6m
Breakfast area	5.4 x 3.5m
Kitchen 1	4.7 x 2.9m
Utility	2.9 x 2.4m
Guest room	3.7 x 3.6m
Guest sitting room	4.8 x 3.6m
Kitchen 2	3.6 x 3.5m

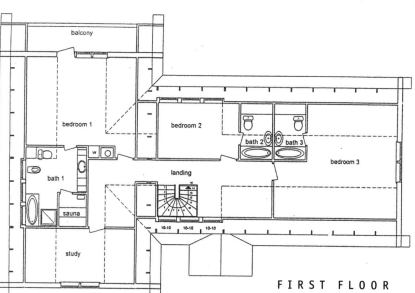

FIRST FLOOR

Bedroom 1	6.0 x 4.7m + bathroom & sauna
Bedroom 2	4.4 x 3.0 + bathroom
Bedroom 3	6.9 x 6.0m max + bathroom
Study/ bedroom 4	6.0 x 3.0m

R104

The copyright belongs to Design & Materials Ltd.

520 sq. m.
including a garage of 55 sq. m.

Overall dimensions 25.51 x 15.67m

FRONT ELEVATION

If granny flats are on the ground floor they will find better favour with the planners. If they are integrated within the main home they will find even more favour. This lovely family home could comfortably house several generations yet still allow privacy. All of the bedrooms are en-suite. Note the linen room upstairs that could also double up as a laundry. Outside, the clever reduction of the ridge height of the two end wings reduces the visual impact of this large house. Dormers in the roof void give away the fact that there is more space to take advantage of.

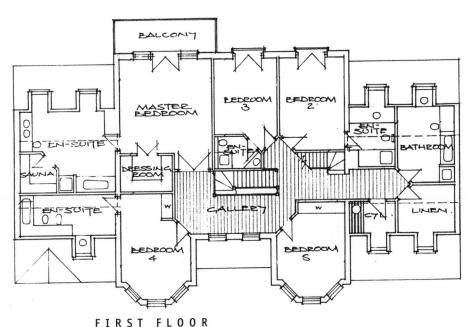

FIRST FLOOR

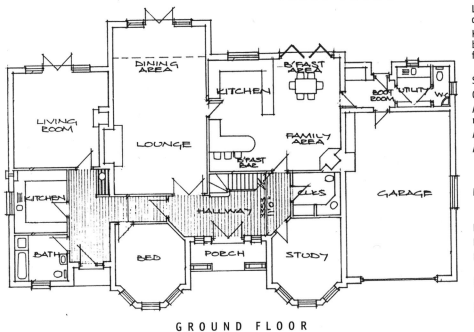

GROUND FLOOR

Lounge/dining room	9.14 x 5.18m
Kitchen/breakfast/family room	7.47 x 6.10m + boot room and utility area
Study	3.96 x 3.50m
Garage	9.00 x 6.10m
Annex living room	5.45 x 5.18m
Annex kitchen	3.50 x 3.05m
Annex bedroom	3.96 x 3.50m
Master bedroom	5.18 x 5.18m + dressing room, en-suite & sauna
Bedroom 2	5.10 x 3.68m + en-suite
Bedroom 3	4.19 x 3.68m + en-suite
Bedroom 4	4.88 x 3.96m max + en-suite
Bedroom 5	4.27 x 3.96m + en-suite
Linen room	

F108

**538 sq. m.
including a garage of 35 sq. m.**

Overall dimensions 29.63 x 26.29m

FRONT ELEVATION

A home that could have fitted into many categories because as well as a granny flat it also has an office, a playroom and a pool house. Each of the six bedrooms is en-suite. The master bedroom has stairs out of it to provide a sitting/deck area within its vaulted ceiling. The utility is shared between the two parts of the home. Truly a multi generation, multi occupational home!

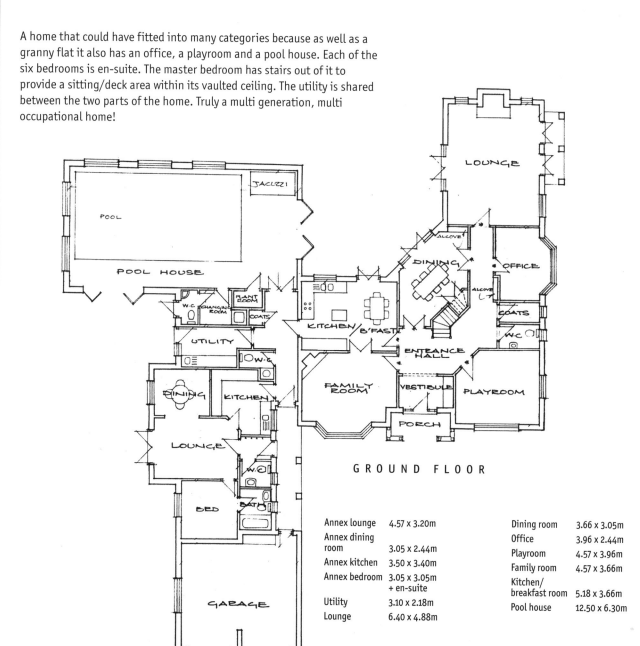

GROUND FLOOR

Annex lounge	4.57 x 3.20m	Dining room	3.66 x 3.05m
Annex dining room	3.05 x 2.44m	Office	3.96 x 2.44m
Annex kitchen	3.50 x 3.40m	Playroom	4.57 x 3.96m
Annex bedroom	3.05 x 3.05m + en-suite	Family room	4.57 x 3.66m
Utility	3.10 x 2.18m	Kitchen/ breakfast room	5.18 x 3.66m
Lounge	6.40 x 4.88m	Pool house	12.50 x 6.30m

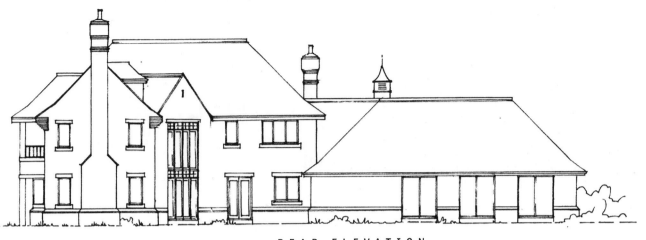

REAR ELEVATION

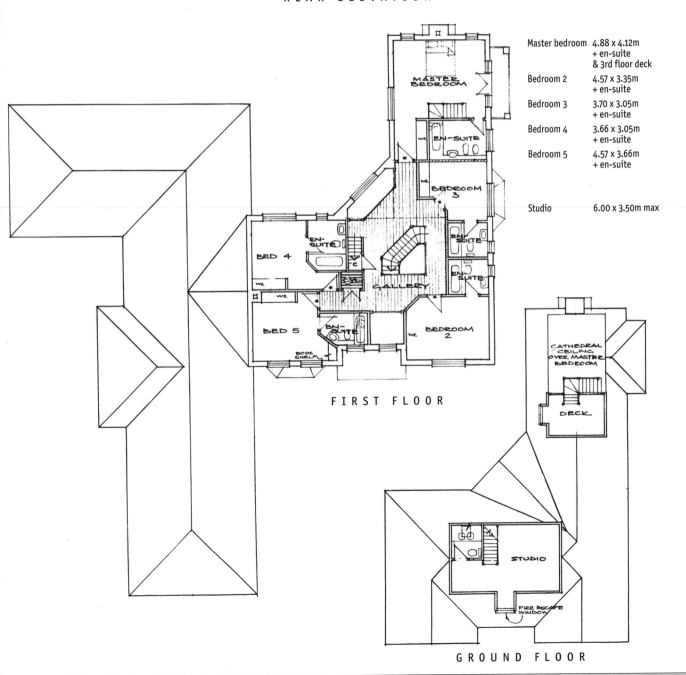

Master bedroom 4.88 x 4.12m
+ en-suite
& 3rd floor deck

Bedroom 2 4.57 x 3.35m
+ en-suite

Bedroom 3 3.70 x 3.05m
+ en-suite

Bedroom 4 3.66 x 3.05m
+ en-suite

Bedroom 5 4.57 x 3.66m
+ en-suite

Studio 6.00 x 3.50m max

FIRST FLOOR

GROUND FLOOR

HOMES WITH AN OFFICE/ PLAYROOM OR SPECIAL ACCOMMODATION

Many of the designs shewn in this section could have been placed in other categories because the playroom or office could easily have been named as a bedroom or living room. However, the idea of a playroom is becoming increasingly popular and I wanted to demonstrate how, without compromising the accepted provision of accommodation, a room could be set aside for play or other leisure activities including a gym.

The homes that have a swimming pool or pool house attached to them need no excuse to fit into this category. Having the poolroom attached to and integral with the home can mean that extra care has to be taken with things like ventilation and the temptation might be to detach it. Be aware though that although VAT is recoverable for an attached or integral pool house, it is not recoverable if it is detached, unless it is linked to the home by a substantial corridor or a covered walkway that the Excise is prepared to accept as a permanent structure.

Working from home is increasingly common. An office for a representative might just be a small room. An office for someone like a writer might have to be bigger and an office for a person running a sales organisation might need separate entrances and toilet facilities if the business is not going to impinge upon the privacy of family life.

If the roof void is to be used as a games or hobbies room, make sure that the trusses and floor joists are capable of supporting a billiard table if that's what you're planning to have up there. Make sure also that the access is wide enough to get the thing up there in the first place.

Contributors in this section:
Associated Self Build Architects
The Border Design Centre
T.J.Crump OAKWRIGHTS Ltd.
Custom Homes Ltd.
Design & Materials Ltd.
Designer Homes
Potton Ltd.
The Self Build House Company Ltd.
Scottish Architects Network
Scandia-Hus Ltd.
The Swedish House Company Ltd.

D248

The copyright belongs to Design & Materials Ltd.

162 sq. m.

Overall dimensions 14.62 x 11.82m

FRONT ELEVATION

REAR ELEVATION

Not all homes with an office need to be grand sprawling designs. Many people with fairly modest accommodation requirements work from home and simply need proper working space that is accessible to toilet facilities for visitors and is capable of being used without compromising the rest of the family activities. The larder off the kitchen would please many a cook. The balcony off the master bedroom, which has a vaulted ceiling, is another thing that makes this home special.

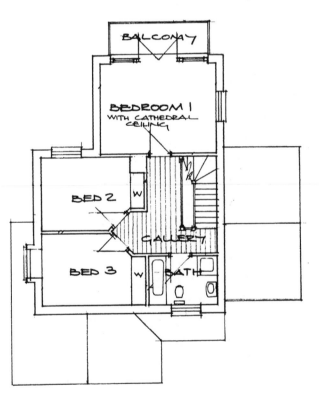

FIRST FLOOR

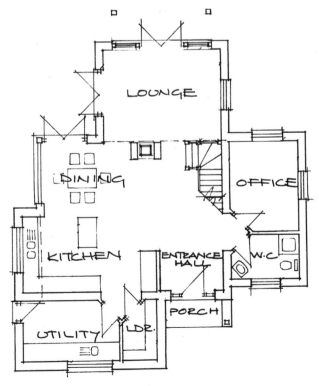

GROUND FLOOR

Lounge	4.88 x 3.66m
Kitchen/ dining room	7.28 x 5.90m
Utility	3.96 x 2.44m
Office	3.50 x 2.74m
Bedroom 1	4.88 x 3.56m + balcony
Bedroom 2	3.66 x 2.90m
Bedroom 3	3.66 x 2.90m

CALLANDER

The copyright belongs to a ScAN architectural practice - Design Practice

167 sq. m.   **Overall dimensions 21.0 x 10.2m**

FRONT ELEVATION

The games room could have been nominated as a family room but what makes the difference here, and what allows it to be in this category, is the fact that the games room has a dedicated shower room and toilet. As for the rest, it is a standard three bedroom bungalow providing generous family accommodation. The inner hall is quite big. Some might want to trim it a little in favour of, say, the kitchen.

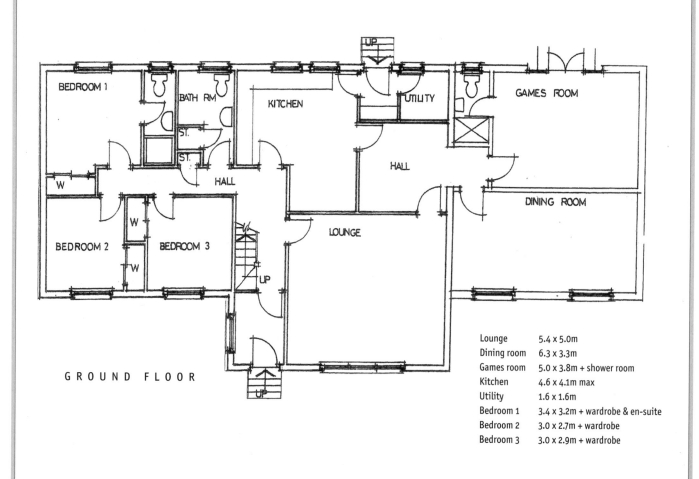

GROUND FLOOR

Lounge	5.4 x 5.0m
Dining room	6.3 x 3.3m
Games room	5.0 x 3.8m + shower room
Kitchen	4.6 x 4.1m max
Utility	1.6 x 1.6m
Bedroom 1	3.4 x 3.2m + wardrobe & en-suite
Bedroom 2	3.0 x 2.7m + wardrobe
Bedroom 3	3.0 x 2.9m + wardrobe

REDPOLL

The copyright belongs to Designer Homes

**233 sq. m.
including a garage of 28 sq. m.**

Overall dimensions 18.50 x 12.40m

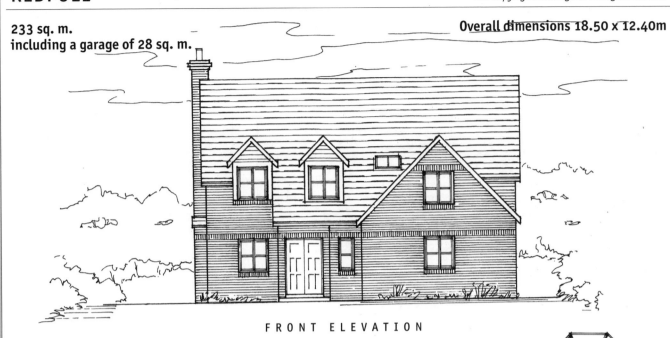

FRONT ELEVATION

This home has six reception rooms on the ground floor. The master suite, one of four designated bedrooms, has a huge dressing room, plus storage facilities and a full sized en-suite bathroom. Add to that the playroom, which could always be a fifth bedroom, and this house, despite its relatively modest size and the fact that it could fit onto quite a narrow plot, provides some serious accommodation.

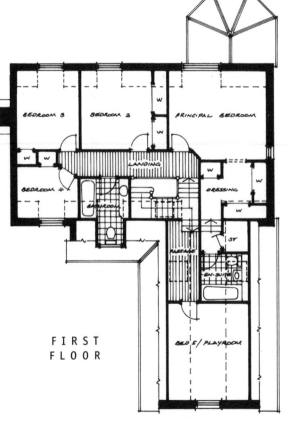

FIRST FLOOR

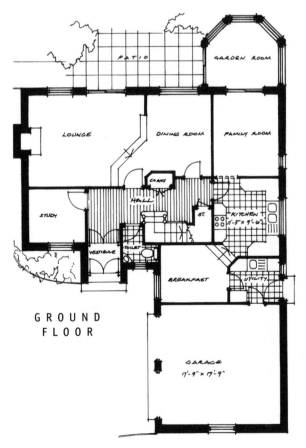

GROUND FLOOR

Lounge	5.33 x 4.11m	Principal bedroom	4.42 x 3.96m + dressing room, storage cupboard & en-suite
Dining room	4.11 x 3.05m		
Family room	4.11 x 2.90m		
Garden room	3.20 x 2.90m		
Kitchen	3.43 x 2.90m	Bedroom 2	3.43 x 3.28m + wardrobes
Breakfast room	3.05 x 2.59m		
Utility	2.20 x 1.90m	Bedroom 3	3.43 x 2.87m + wardrobe
Garage	5.35 x 5.25m		
		Bedroom 4	2.67 x 2.29m
		Playroom/ bedroom 5	4.34 x 3.58m

381

TEVIOT

The copyright belongs to Designer Homes

**237 sq. m.
including a garage of 35 sq. m.**

Overall dimensions 18.30 x 11.40m

FRONT ELEVATION

If you've decided to make the entrance into a feature tower then why not utilise the space as much as possible? Bedroom one gets to have its own walk-in closet and dressing area together with an interestingly shaped en-suite. The family room above the garage could be many things – a playroom, an office or a gym, but with its own entrance from the garage or the rear lobby, the choice is yours.

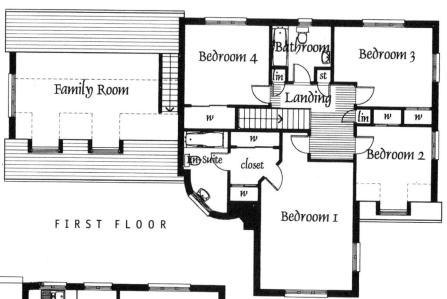

FIRST FLOOR

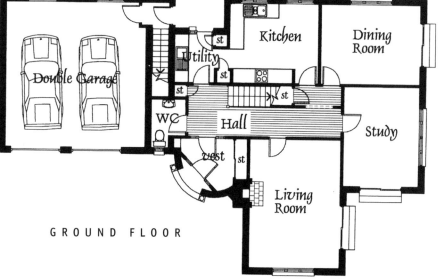

GROUND FLOOR

Living room	5.31 x 3.88m
Dining room	4.19 x 3.30m
Study	3.71 x 3.30m
Kitchen	3.81 x 3.30m
Utility	1.90 x 1.70m
Garage	5.90 x 5.90m
Bedroom 1	5.31 x 3.81m + closet & en-suite
Bedroom 2	3.45 x 3.30m + wardrobe
Bedroom 3	4.19 x 3.30m + wardrobe
Bedroom 4	3.61 x 3.30m + wardrobe
Family room	6.90 x 3.60m

D156

278 sq. m.
including a garage of 30 sq. m.

Overall dimensions 21.01 x 11.27m

Just the simple expedient of utilising the space above the garage takes this home into a different league. The playroom could in fact be anything. It could be just another bedroom. It could be an office with stairs down into the garage making it almost self contained. The master bedroom is greatly enhanced by its spectacular balcony.

FRONT ELEVATION

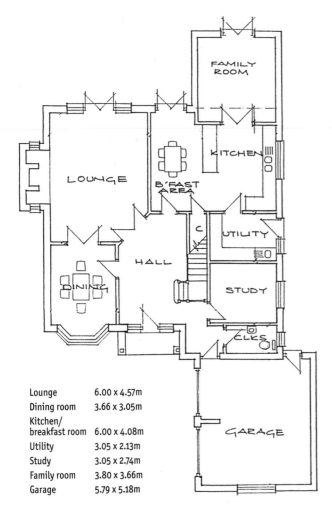

Lounge	6.00 x 4.57m
Dining room	3.66 x 3.05m
Kitchen/ breakfast room	6.00 x 4.08m
Utility	3.05 x 2.13m
Study	3.05 x 2.74m
Family room	3.80 x 3.66m
Garage	5.79 x 5.18m

GROUND FLOOR

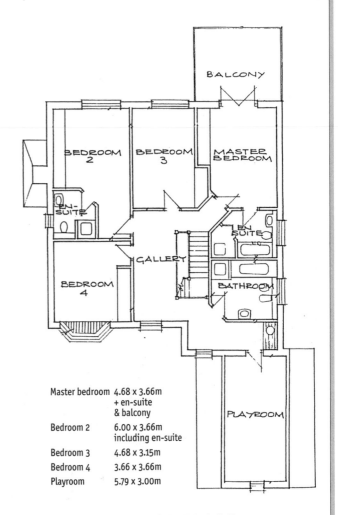

Master bedroom	4.68 x 3.66m + en-suite & balcony
Bedroom 2	6.00 x 3.66m including en-suite
Bedroom 3	4.68 x 3.15m
Bedroom 4	3.66 x 3.66m
Playroom	5.79 x 3.00m

FIRST FLOOR

PORT APPIN

The copyright belongs to The Border Design Centre

**289 sq. m.
including basement**

Overall dimensions 17.2 x 11.2m

FRONT ELEVATION

This home was built on a steeply sloping site on the edge of a harbour. The lower level is a basement that houses the boat and garden sheds plus a useful workshop area. The entrance level makes the best use of the views with a corner bay window set into the tower section that repeats in the master bedroom on the next level. Stone arches support a terrace across most of the house frontage and around the side to the utility with steps to the entrance level.

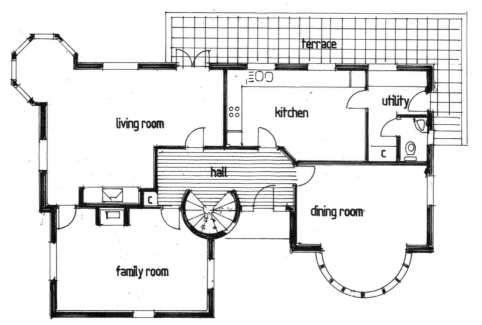

Living room	7.29 x 5.31m + corner bay
Family room	6.20 x 4.09m
Dining room	5.31 x 5.10m into bay
Kitchen	5.74 x 3.35m + utility area

GROUND FLOOR

SIDE ELEVATION

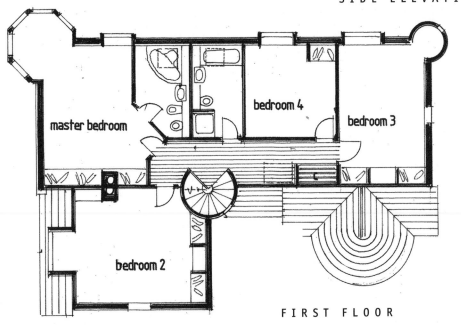

FIRST FLOOR

Boat shed   4.6 x 4.4m
               + tower section

Garden shed   4.8 x 3.0m

Workshop   5.9 x 3.6m

Master bedroom 4.62 x 4.11m
                + wardrobes & en-suite

Bedroom 2   4.70 x 4.11m
                + wardrobes

Bedroom 3   4.60 x 3.50m
                + wardrobes

Bedroom 4   3.50 x 3.50m

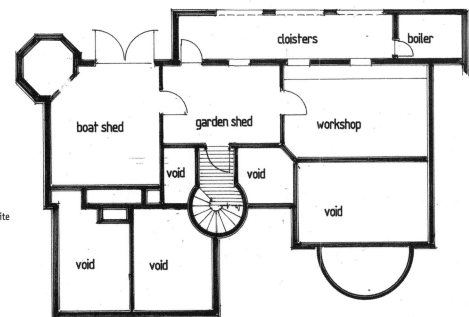

BASEMENT

SONNING

The copyright belongs to Designer Homes

**284 sq. m.
including a garage
of 30 sq. m.**

Overall dimensions 16.50 x 14.10m

FRONT ELEVATION

What could this additional room be used for? It could just be another bedroom with its own en-suite facilities. It could be an office for someone working from home. It could be a gym or a playroom. It could even have its own access via a staircase from the garage or an external staircase at the rear.

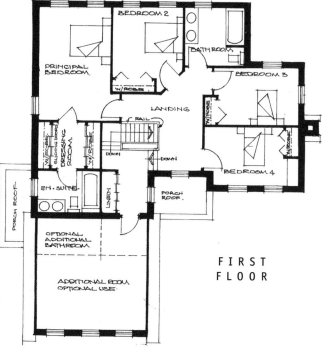

FIRST FLOOR

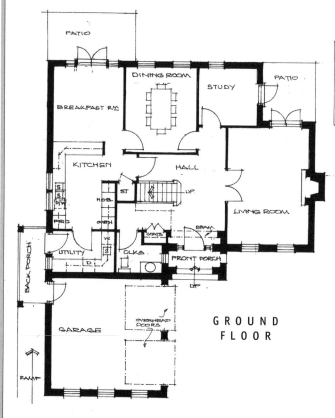

GROUND FLOOR

Living room	5.72m x 4.11m	Principal bedroom	5.49m x 3.50m + dressing room & en-suite
Study	3.00m x 2.79m		
Dining room	4.11m x 3.50m		
Breakfast room	3.61m x 3.50m	Bedroom 2	3.50m x 3.10m + wardrobe
Kitchen	4.19m x 3.10m		
Utility	3.10m x 2.00m	Bedroom 3	4.01m x 2.84m + wardrobe
Garage	5.41m x 5.41m		
		Bedroom 4	4.01m x 2.84m + wardrobe
		Additional room	5.41m x 5.41m

88-223

The copyright belongs to Potton Ltd.

330 sq. m. including a 36 sq. m. garage, a 36 sq. m. games room and a further 70 sq. m. of undesignated upper floor space.

Overall dimensions 36.4 x 13.3m

FRONT ELEVATION

Essentially this a relatively modest four bedroom house that has been extended on both sides to provide the triple garage and games room with additional accommodation over.

SIDE ELEVATION

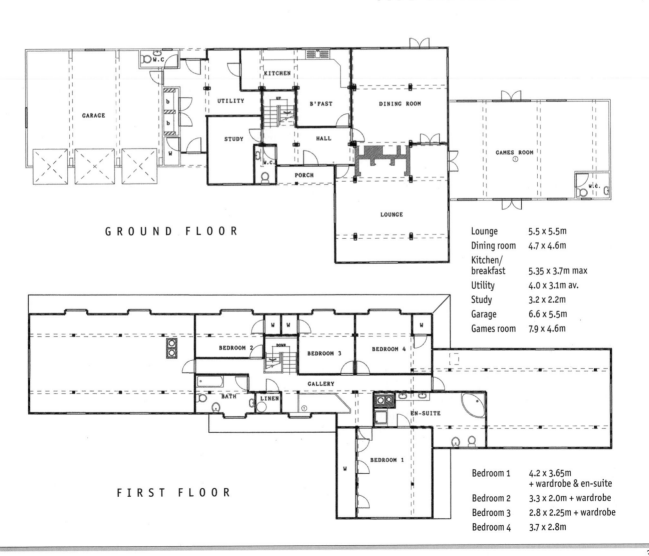

GROUND FLOOR

FIRST FLOOR

Lounge	5.5 x 5.5m
Dining room	4.7 x 4.6m
Kitchen/breakfast	5.35 x 3.7m max
Utility	4.0 x 3.1m av.
Study	3.2 x 2.2m
Garage	6.6 x 5.5m
Games room	7.9 x 4.6m

Bedroom 1	4.2 x 3.65m + wardrobe & en-suite
Bedroom 2	3.3 x 2.0m + wardrobe
Bedroom 3	2.8 x 2.25m + wardrobe
Bedroom 4	3.7 x 2.8m

P303

316 sq. m.
including a garage of 32 sq. m.

Overall dimensions 27.20 x 16.76m

FRONT ELEVATION

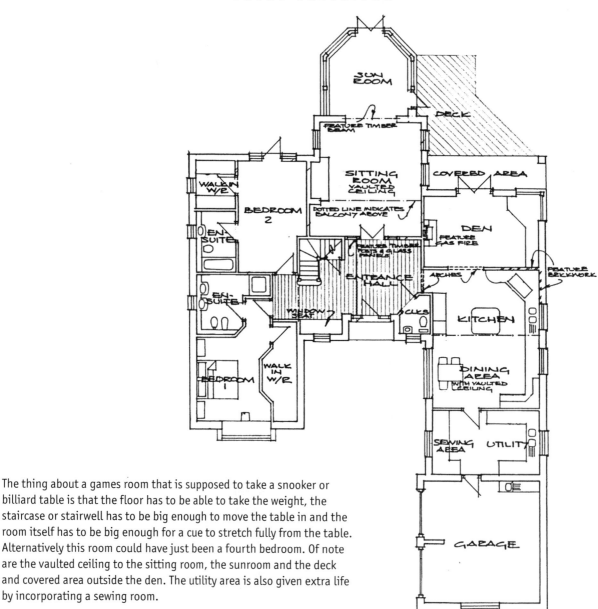

The thing about a games room that is supposed to take a snooker or billiard table is that the floor has to be able to take the weight, the staircase or stairwell has to be big enough to move the table in and the room itself has to be big enough for a cue to stretch fully from the table. Alternatively this room could have just been a fourth bedroom. Of note are the vaulted ceiling to the sitting room, the sunroom and the deck and covered area outside the den. The utility area is also given extra life by incorporating a sewing room.

GROUND FLOOR

SIDE ELEVATION

REAR ELEVATION

Sitting room	5.49 x 4.72m
Sunroom	3.64 x 3.64m
Den	5.28 x 3.35m
Kitchen/ dining room	6.50 x 4.98m
Utility/ sewing area	4.98 x 3.00m
Bedroom 1	3.96 x 3.60m + walk in wardrobe & en-suite
Bedroom 2	5.26 x 3.35m + walk in wardrobe & en-suite
Guest bedroom	5.29 x 4.80m including walk in shower
Games room	4.80 x 4.80m

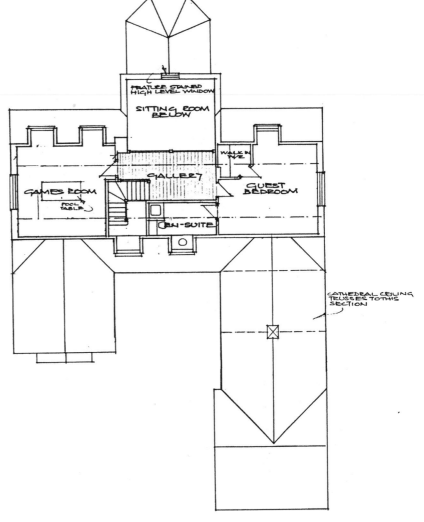

FIRST FLOOR

THE CEDAR

The copyright belongs to an ASBA architectural practice – Julian Owen Associates

349 sq. m.
including a garage of 48 sq. m.

Overall dimensions 21.6 x 20.5m

FRONT ELEVATION

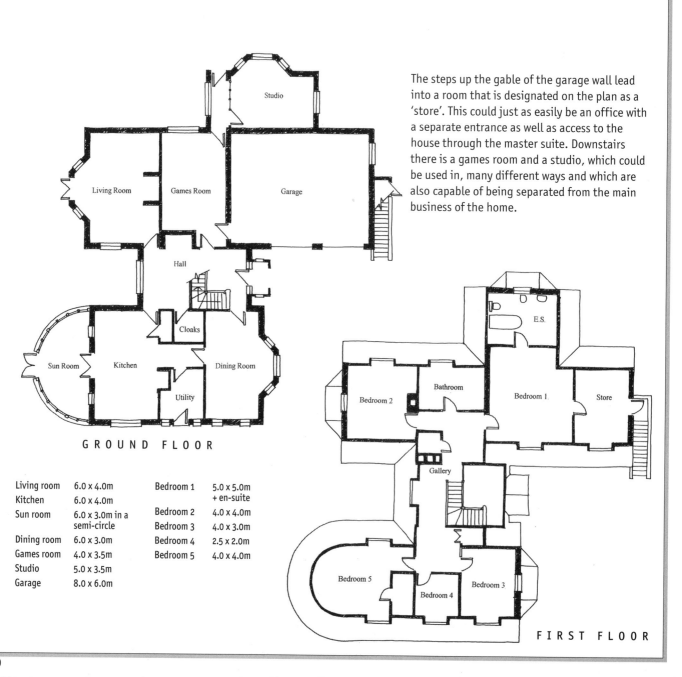

The steps up the gable of the garage wall lead into a room that is designated on the plan as a 'store'. This could just as easily be an office with a separate entrance as well as access to the house through the master suite. Downstairs there is a games room and a studio, which could be used in, many different ways and which are also capable of being separated from the main business of the home.

GROUND FLOOR

FIRST FLOOR

Living room	6.0 x 4.0m	Bedroom 1	5.0 x 5.0m + en-suite
Kitchen	6.0 x 4.0m		
Sun room	6.0 x 3.0m in a semi-circle	Bedroom 2	4.0 x 4.0m
		Bedroom 3	4.0 x 3.0m
Dining room	6.0 x 3.0m	Bedroom 4	2.5 x 2.0m
Games room	4.0 x 3.5m	Bedroom 5	4.0 x 4.0m
Studio	5.0 x 3.5m		
Garage	8.0 x 6.0m		

96-333

The copyright belongs to Potton Ltd.

405 sq. m. including a 39 sq. m. garage and an 85 sq. m. swimming pool

Overall dimensions 22.1 x 20.1m

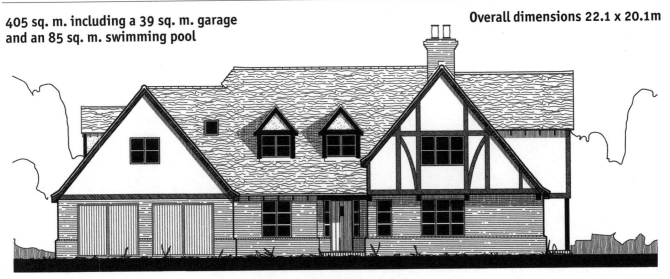

FRONT ELEVATION

A lot of this house is given over to the garage and swimming pool areas but, even with those taken off, this is still a fairly big five bedroom house with all the trimmings. So often the addition of a pool house looks like an afterthought but here, it fits in and looks as if it belongs. For those who don't like swimming there are many other uses such as gym or games room for which this space could be used.

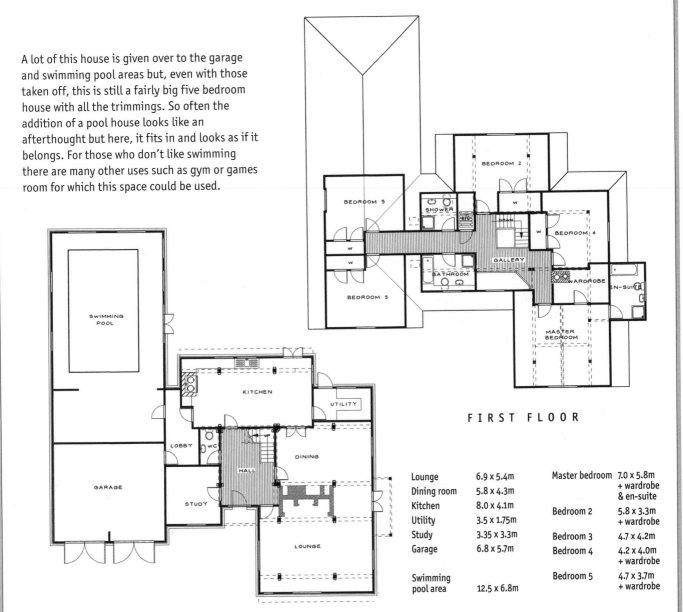

FIRST FLOOR

GROUND FLOOR

Lounge	6.9 x 5.4m	Master bedroom	7.0 x 5.8m + wardrobe & en-suite
Dining room	5.8 x 4.3m		
Kitchen	8.0 x 4.1m	Bedroom 2	5.8 x 3.3m + wardrobe
Utility	3.5 x 1.75m		
Study	3.35 x 3.3m	Bedroom 3	4.7 x 4.2m
Garage	6.8 x 5.7m	Bedroom 4	4.2 x 4.0m + wardrobe
Swimming pool area	12.5 x 6.8m	Bedroom 5	4.7 x 3.7m + wardrobe

MARLOW

The copyright belongs to Designer Homes

**398 sq. m.
including a garage
of 32 sq. m.**

Overall dimensions 23.60 x 22.20m

FRONT ELEVATION

Although it has four good sized bedrooms on the upper floor, one of which is en-suite, the designers have chosen to have the principal bedroom suite on the ground floor. This would fit into the pattern of many family lives but, in any event, the ground floor suite would certainly be useful for an older person living within the family. The recreation room, with its own access from the garage would find many different uses.

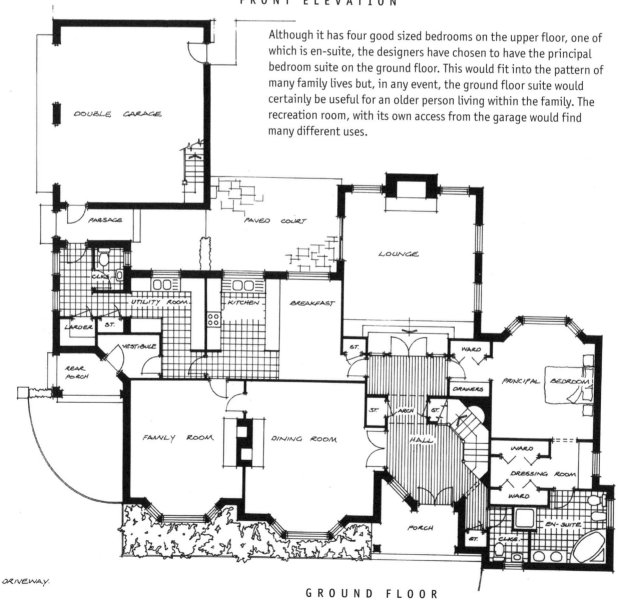

GROUND FLOOR

Lounge	5.87 x 5.41m		Guest bedroom	4.19 x 3.28m
Dining room	5.41 x 5.10m			+ dressing area & en-suite
Family room	4.50 x 4.42m		Upper hall/	
Breakfast room	4.04 x 2.59m		study	4.20 x 2.20m max
Kitchen	4.04 x 3.05m		Bedroom 3	4.80 x 3.58m + wardrobe
Utility	4.10 x 3.10m max		Bedroom 4	4.27 x 2.74m + wardrobe
Principal			Bedroom 5	4.42 x 2.74m
bedroom	4.27 x 3.88m		Recreation room	5.94 x 4.11m
	+ dressing room & en-suite			
Garage	7.16 x 5.14m			

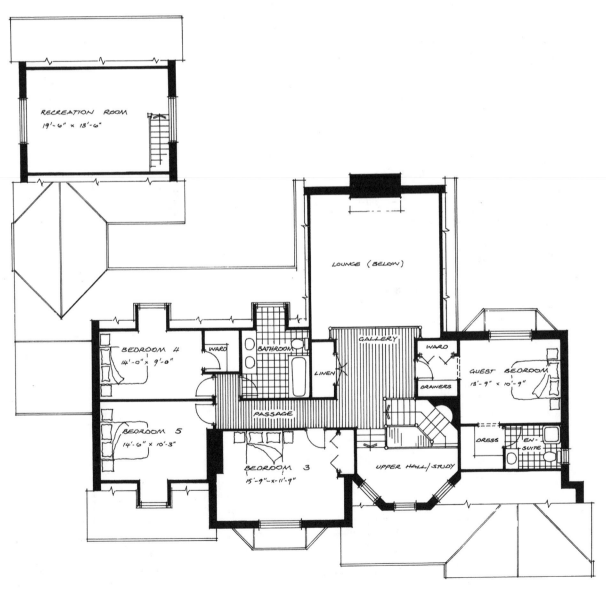

RECREATION ROOM
19'-6" x 13'-6"

LOUNGE (BELOW)

GALLERY

BEDROOM 4
14'-0" x 9'-0"

WARD

BATHROOM

LINEN

WARD

DRAWERS

GUEST BEDROOM
13'-9" x 10'-9"

PASSAGE

BEDROOM 5
14'-6" x 10'-3"

BEDROOM 3
15'-9" x 11'-9"

UPPER HALL/STUDY

DRESS

EN-SUITE

FIRST FLOOR

LITCHAM

The copyright belongs to Custom Homes Ltd.

423 sq. m.

Overall dimensions 19.3 x 15m

FRONT ELEVATION

Once again the simplicity of a symmetric design is enhanced rather than spoiled by well planned extensions to the living area. The accommodation is laid out on three floors with the roof space utilised as a playroom with a bathroom that would keep the kids out of trouble or provide the ideal hobbies or home working area.

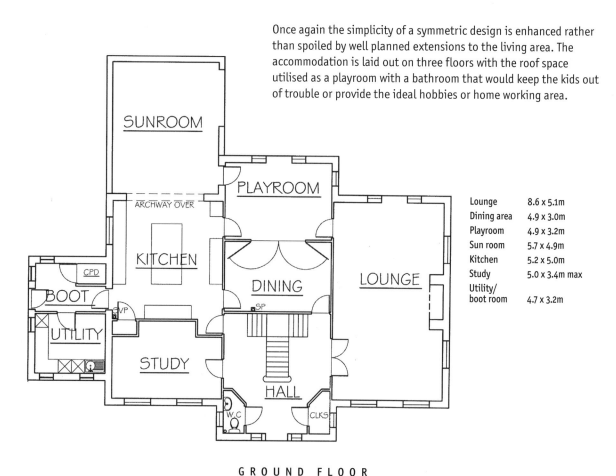

Lounge	8.6 x 5.1m
Dining area	4.9 x 3.0m
Playroom	4.9 x 3.2m
Sun room	5.7 x 4.9m
Kitchen	5.2 x 5.0m
Study	5.0 x 3.4m max
Utility/ boot room	4.7 x 3.2m

GROUND FLOOR

S I D E   E L E V A T I O N

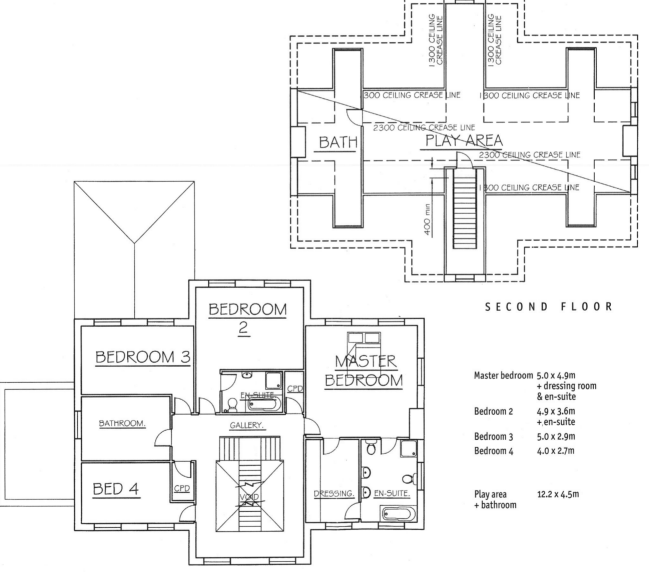

S E C O N D   F L O O R

BATH

PLAY AREA

1300 CEILING CREASE LINE
1300 CEILING CREASE LINE
1300 CEILING CREASE LINE
1300 CEILING CREASE LINE
2300 CEILING CREASE LINE
2300 CEILING CREASE LINE
1300 CEILING CREASE LINE
400 min

BEDROOM 2

BEDROOM 3

MASTER BEDROOM

EN-SUITE

CPD

BATHROOM.

GALLERY.

VOID

BED 4

CPD

DRESSING.

EN-SUITE.

F I R S T   F L O O R

Master bedroom	5.0 x 4.9m + dressing room & en-suite
Bedroom 2	4.9 x 3.6m + en-suite
Bedroom 3	5.0 x 2.9m
Bedroom 4	4.0 x 2.7m
Play area + bathroom	12.2 x 4.5m

DUNDEE

The copyright belongs to Designer Homes

451 sq. m.
including a garage of 36 sq. m.

Overall dimensions 25.20 x 21.60m

FRONT ELEVATION

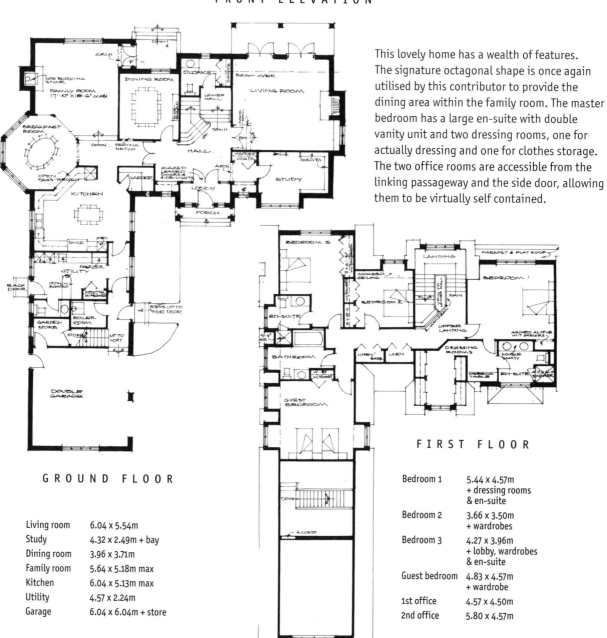

This lovely home has a wealth of features. The signature octagonal shape is once again utilised by this contributor to provide the dining area within the family room. The master bedroom has a large en-suite with double vanity unit and two dressing rooms, one for actually dressing and one for clothes storage. The two office rooms are accessible from the linking passageway and the side door, allowing them to be virtually self contained.

GROUND FLOOR

FIRST FLOOR

Living room	6.04 x 5.54m
Study	4.32 x 2.49m + bay
Dining room	3.96 x 3.71m
Family room	5.64 x 5.18m max
Kitchen	6.04 x 5.13m max
Utility	4.57 x 2.24m
Garage	6.04 x 6.04m + store

Bedroom 1	5.44 x 4.57m + dressing rooms & en-suite
Bedroom 2	3.66 x 3.50m + wardrobes
Bedroom 3	4.27 x 3.96m + lobby, wardrobes & en-suite
Guest bedroom	4.83 x 4.57m + wardrobe
1st office	4.57 x 4.50m
2nd office	5.80 x 4.57m

SOHAM

The copyright belongs to T. J. Crump OAKRIGHTS Ltd.

481 sq. m.
including a garage of 53 sq. m.

Overall dimensions 25.52 x 19.58m

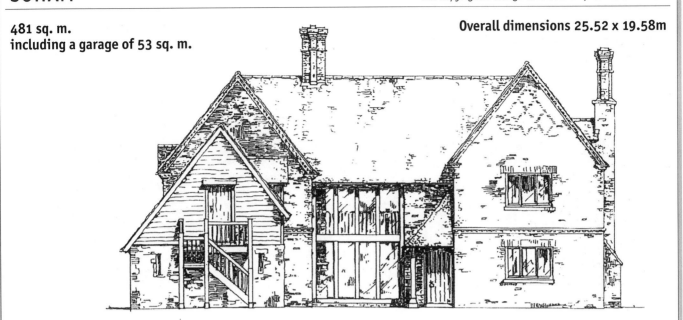

FRONT ELEVATION

One way of achieving size without having an over-high roof line is to break the accommodation down into smaller sections and then link them together as has been done here. The playroom has a separate entrance and this would lend itself to use as a home office. The kitchen and eating areas are open planned but most other rooms are self contained.

Sitting room	7.09 x 5.69m
Dining hall	6.32 x 4.09m
Kitchen	7.29 x 5.42m
Breakfast room	4.37 x 4.03m
Utility	4.27 x 2.79m
Garage	8.97 x 5.92m
Bedroom 1	6.93 x 5.69m + bathroom
Bedroom 2	5.49 x 5.38m + en-suite
Bedroom 3	4.47 x 3.86m + en-suite
Bedroom 4	5.82 x 4.75m
Playroom	4.75 x 3.35m

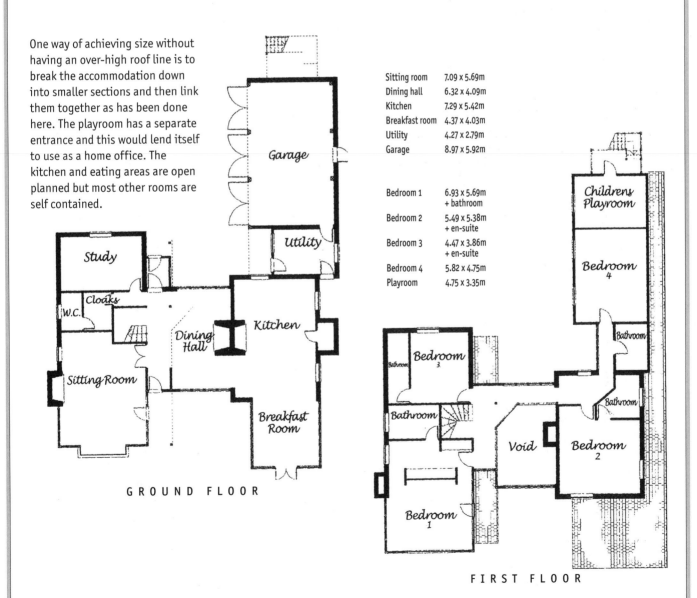

GROUND FLOOR

FIRST FLOOR

397

WARWICK

The copyright belongs to Designer Homes

460 sq. m. including a garage block of 46 sq. m.

Overall dimensions 37.00 x 23.70m

FRONT ELEVATION

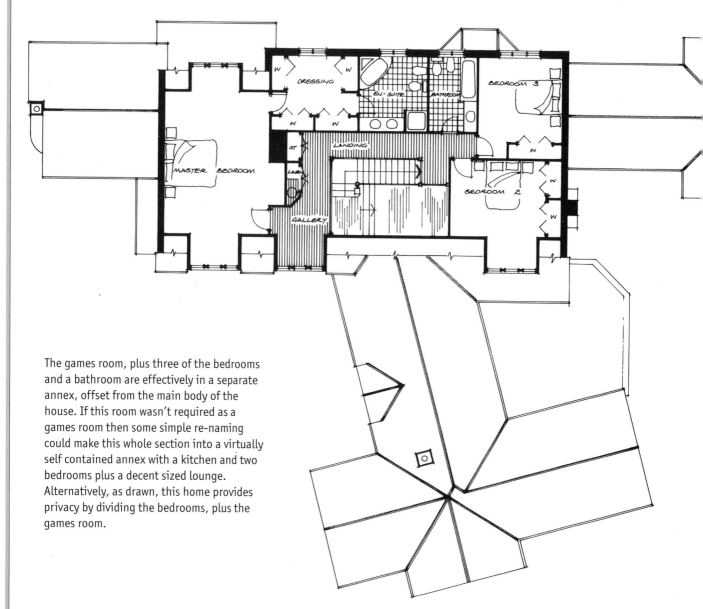

The games room, plus three of the bedrooms and a bathroom are effectively in a separate annex, offset from the main body of the house. If this room wasn't required as a games room then some simple re-naming could make this whole section into a virtually self contained annex with a kitchen and two bedrooms plus a decent sized lounge. Alternatively, as drawn, this home provides privacy by dividing the bedrooms, plus the games room.

FIRST FLOOR

Living room   4.95 x 4.27m
Drawing room   7.16 x 4.57m
Library   4.80 x 4.72m
Dining room   4.72 x 4.04m
Kitchen/
breakfast room   6.25 x 4.27m
Utility   4.27 x 2.40m
Garage   6.00 x 5.90m
Fuel store   3.00 x 1.70m
Games room   5.33 x 3.66m
Bedroom 4   4.19 x 2.90m + wardrobe
Bedroom 5   3.50 x 3.43m + wardrobe
Bedroom 6   3.50 x 3.35m

Master bedroom   5.94 x 4.57m + dressing room & en-suite
Bedroom 2   4.11 x 3.20m + wardrobes
Bedroom 3   3.58 x 3.58m + wardrobe

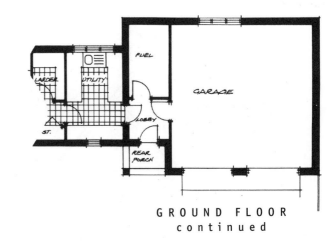

G R O U N D   F L O O R
c o n t i n u e d

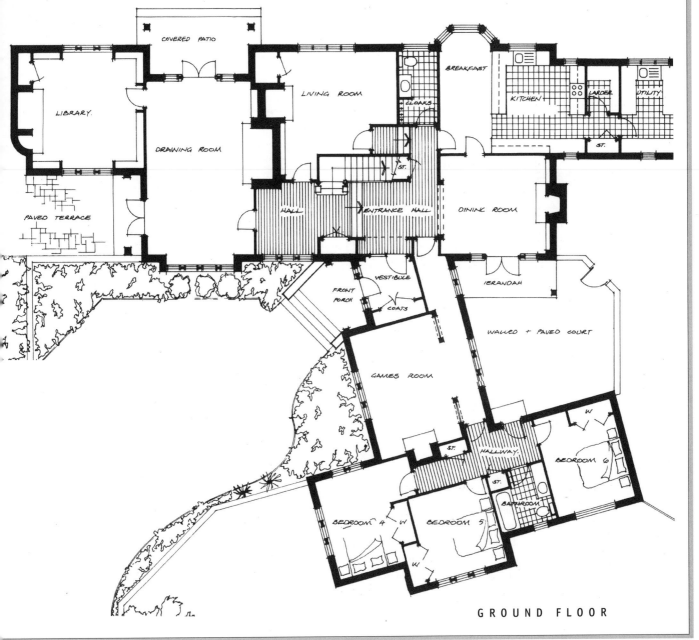

G R O U N D   F L O O R

MUIRFIELD

The copyright belongs to Designer Homes

**464 sq. m.
including a garage
of 44 sq. m.**

Overall dimensions 28.40 x 24.60m

FRONT ELEVATION

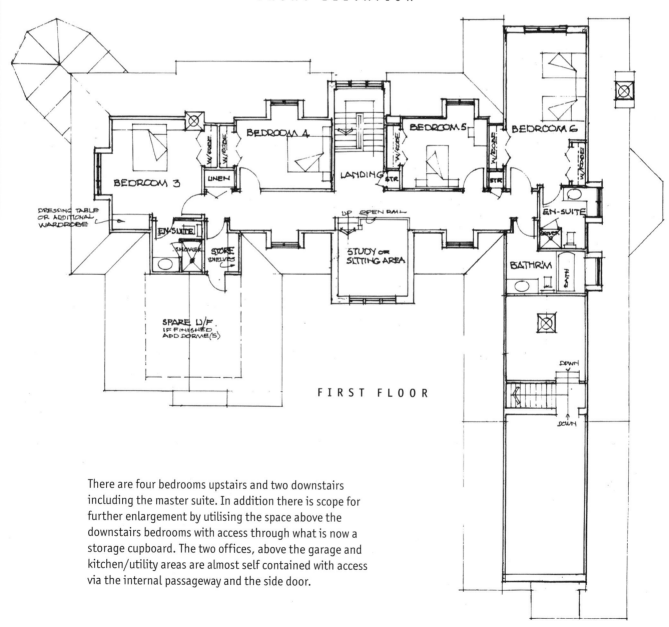

FIRST FLOOR

There are four bedrooms upstairs and two downstairs
including the master suite. In addition there is scope for
further enlargement by utilising the space above the
downstairs bedrooms with access through what is now a
storage cupboard. The two offices, above the garage and
kitchen/utility areas are almost self contained with access
via the internal passageway and the side door.

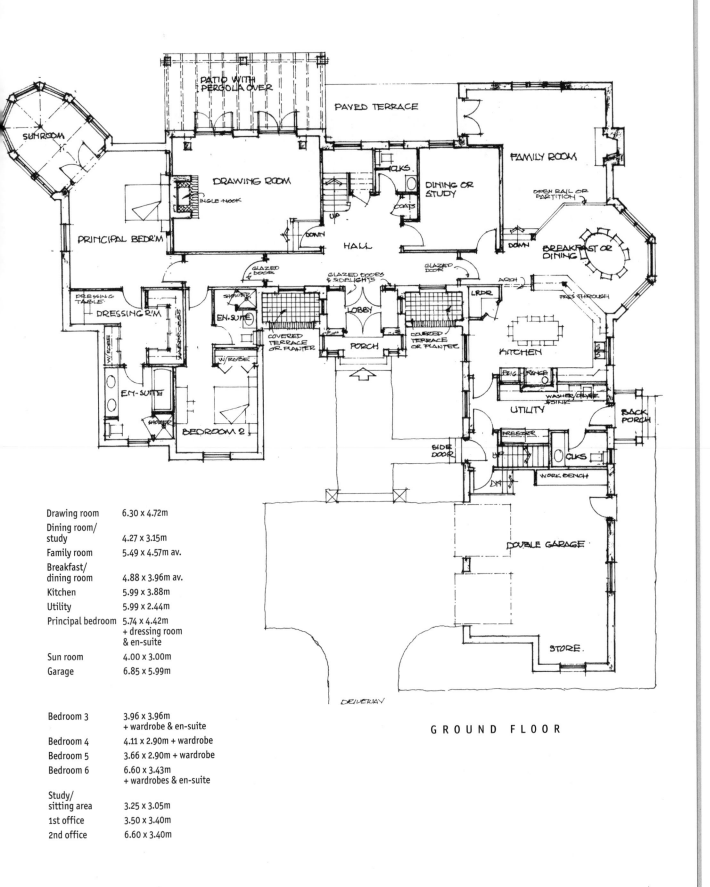

Drawing room	6.30 x 4.72m
Dining room/ study	4.27 x 3.15m
Family room	5.49 x 4.57m av.
Breakfast/ dining room	4.88 x 3.96m av.
Kitchen	5.99 x 3.88m
Utility	5.99 x 2.44m
Principal bedroom	5.74 x 4.42m + dressing room & en-suite
Sun room	4.00 x 3.00m
Garage	6.85 x 5.99m
Bedroom 3	3.96 x 3.96m + wardrobe & en-suite
Bedroom 4	4.11 x 2.90m + wardrobe
Bedroom 5	3.66 x 2.90m + wardrobe
Bedroom 6	6.60 x 3.43m + wardrobes & en-suite
Study/ sitting area	3.25 x 3.05m
1st office	3.50 x 3.40m
2nd office	6.60 x 3.40m

GROUND FLOOR

GLYNEDALE

The copyright belongs to T. J. Crump OAKRIGHTS Ltd.

509 sq. m.
including a garage of 27 sq. m.

Overall dimensions 21.7 x 25.3m

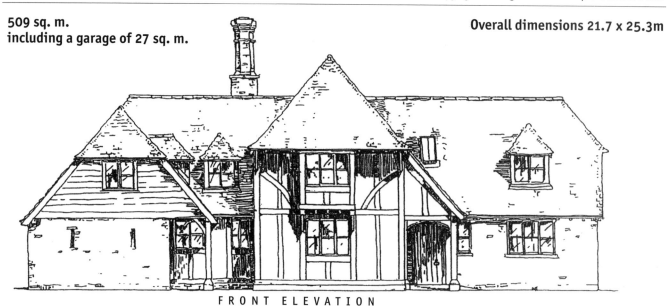

FRONT ELEVATION

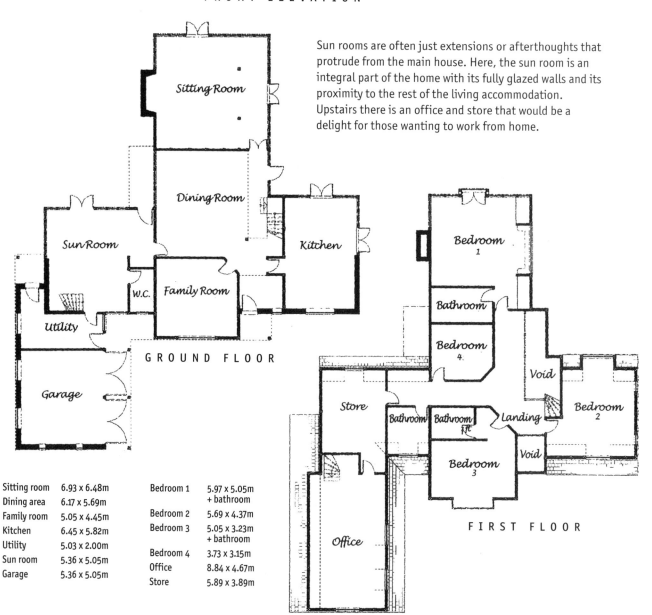

Sun rooms are often just extensions or afterthoughts that protrude from the main house. Here, the sun room is an integral part of the home with its fully glazed walls and its proximity to the rest of the living accommodation. Upstairs there is an office and store that would be a delight for those wanting to work from home.

GROUND FLOOR

FIRST FLOOR

Sitting room	6.93 x 6.48m		Bedroom 1	5.97 x 5.05m + bathroom
Dining area	6.17 x 5.69m		Bedroom 2	5.69 x 4.37m
Family room	5.05 x 4.45m		Bedroom 3	5.05 x 3.23m + bathroom
Kitchen	6.45 x 5.82m			
Utility	5.03 x 2.00m		Bedroom 4	3.73 x 3.15m
Sun room	5.36 x 5.05m		Office	8.84 x 4.67m
Garage	5.36 x 5.05m		Store	5.89 x 3.89m

D238

The copyright belongs to Design & Materials Ltd.

514 sq. m. including a garage of 60 sq. m.

Overall dimensions 26.70 x 20.27m

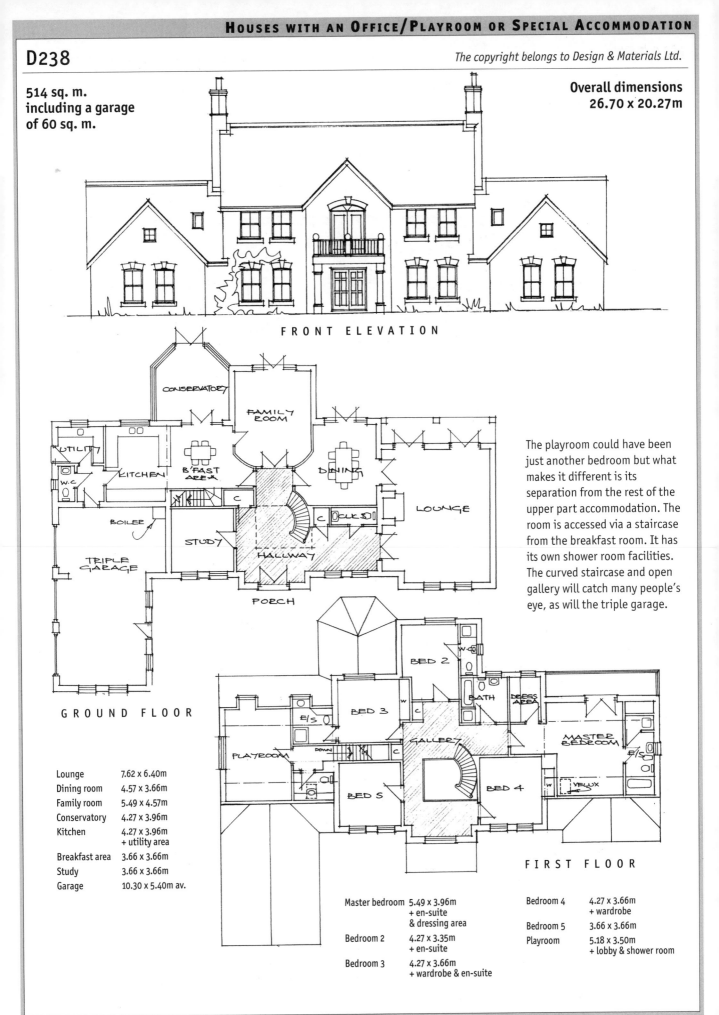

FRONT ELEVATION

GROUND FLOOR

FIRST FLOOR

The playroom could have been just another bedroom but what makes it different is its separation from the rest of the upper part accommodation. The room is accessed via a staircase from the breakfast room. It has its own shower room facilities. The curved staircase and open gallery will catch many people's eye, as will the triple garage.

Lounge	7.62 x 6.40m
Dining room	4.57 x 3.66m
Family room	5.49 x 4.57m
Conservatory	4.27 x 3.96m
Kitchen	4.27 x 3.96m + utility area
Breakfast area	3.66 x 3.66m
Study	3.66 x 3.66m
Garage	10.30 x 5.40m av.

Master bedroom	5.49 x 3.96m + en-suite & dressing area
Bedroom 2	4.27 x 3.35m + en-suite
Bedroom 3	4.27 x 3.66m + wardrobe & en-suite

Bedroom 4	4.27 x 3.66m + wardrobe
Bedroom 5	3.66 x 3.66m
Playroom	5.18 x 3.50m + lobby & shower room

H205

The copyright belongs to Design & Materials Ltd.

555 sq. m.
including a garage of 44 sq. m.

Overall dimensions 31.81 x 21.65m

FRONT ELEVATION

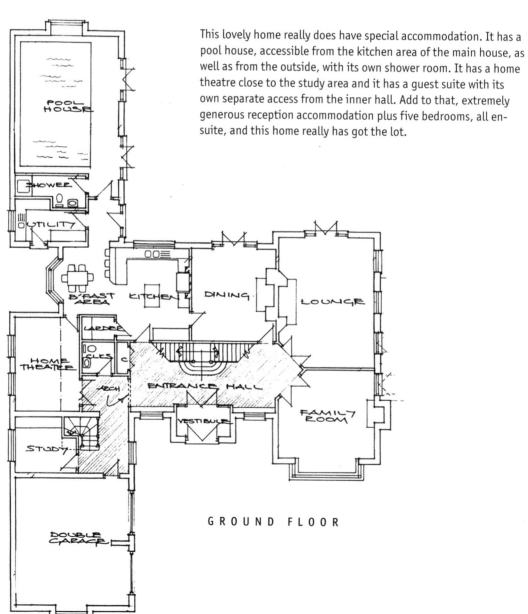

This lovely home really does have special accommodation. It has a pool house, accessible from the kitchen area of the main house, as well as from the outside, with its own shower room. It has a home theatre close to the study area and it has a guest suite with its own separate access from the inner hall. Add to that, extremely generous reception accommodation plus five bedrooms, all en-suite, and this home really has got the lot.

GROUND FLOOR

R E A R   E L E V A T I O N

Lounge	7.32 x 5.49m		Master bedroom	5.85 x 5.49m + dressing area & en-suite
Family room	5.49 x 4.88m		Bedroom 2	5.18 x 4.57m + en-suite
Dining room	5.18 x 4.88m			
Kitchen/ breakfast room	7.15 x 5.18m + utility area		Bedroom 3	5.09 x 3.80m + en-suite
Study	3.50 x 3.05m		Bedroom 4	4.88 x 3.74m + en-suite
Home theatre	5.18 x 3.66m		Bedroom 5	3.80 x 3.50m + en-suite
Pool house	7.62 x 5.90m			
Garage	6.94 x 6.40m		Guest suite	5.30 x 3.60m including en-suite + wardrobe

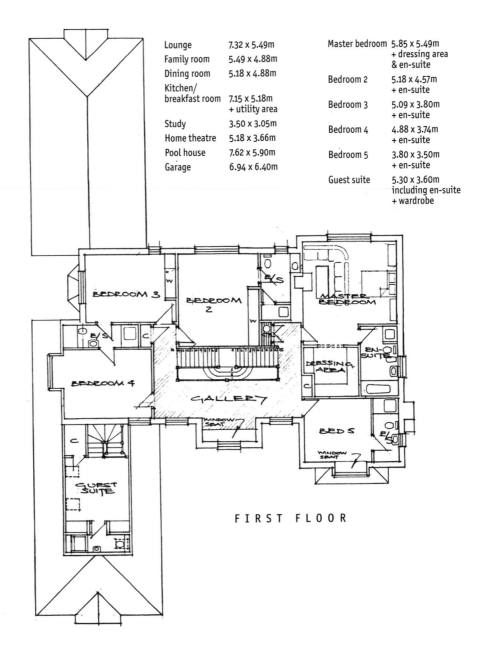

F I R S T   F L O O R

D158

The copyright belongs to Design & Materials Ltd.

654 sq. m.

Overall dimensions 32.62 x 18.76m

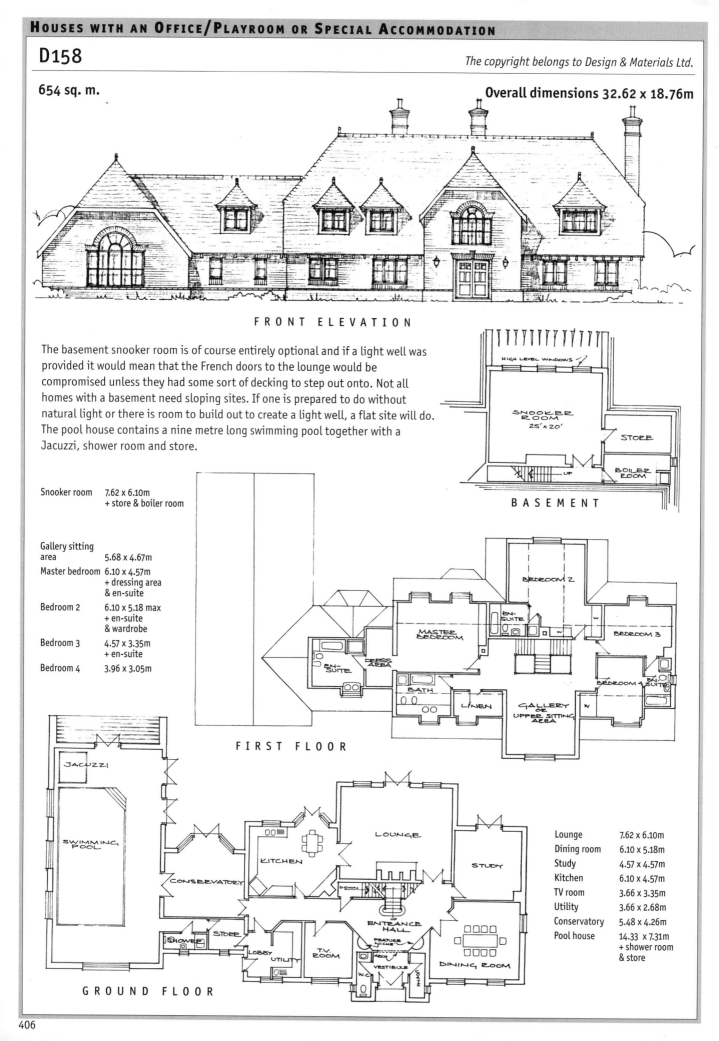

FRONT ELEVATION

The basement snooker room is of course entirely optional and if a light well was provided it would mean that the French doors to the lounge would be compromised unless they had some sort of decking to step out onto. Not all homes with a basement need sloping sites. If one is prepared to do without natural light or there is room to build out to create a light well, a flat site will do. The pool house contains a nine metre long swimming pool together with a Jacuzzi, shower room and store.

BASEMENT

Snooker room	7.62 x 6.10m + store & boiler room
Gallery sitting area	5.68 x 4.67m
Master bedroom	6.10 x 4.57m + dressing area & en-suite
Bedroom 2	6.10 x 5.18 max + en-suite & wardrobe
Bedroom 3	4.57 x 3.35m + en-suite
Bedroom 4	3.96 x 3.05m

FIRST FLOOR

Lounge	7.62 x 6.10m
Dining room	6.10 x 5.18m
Study	4.57 x 4.57m
Kitchen	6.10 x 4.57m
TV room	3.66 x 3.35m
Utility	3.66 x 2.68m
Conservatory	5.48 x 4.26m
Pool house	14.33 x 7.31m + shower room & store

GROUND FLOOR

OUTBUILDINGS

I have railed against boring little boxes as garages and urged that these outbuildings and others have as much design thought and innovation put into them as the rest of the home. Trace the roots of the garage back to the coach house or cart barn and you get to visually exciting structures that can enhance any property.

Permitted Development Rights, discussed in great detail in Building Your Own Home mean that up to half of the garden in most areas can be utilised as outbuildings. This can mean pool houses, cinemas, games rooms, boat houses and of course garages. It can also mean that in many cases it is perfectly feasible to build extra sleeping or living accommodation as an outhouse so long as it is part and parcel of the enjoyment and proper use of the home.

Contributors in this section:
Associated Self Build Architects
Design & Materials Ltd.
Potton Ltd.
Scottish Architects Network

SOUTHILL

8.2 x 8.09m

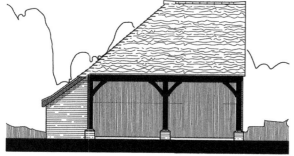

FRONT ELEVATION

SIDE VIEW

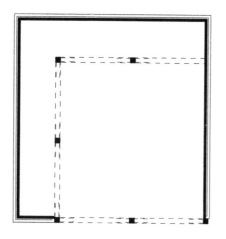

An open fronted double carport with internal storage

WESTON

6.5 x 6.35m

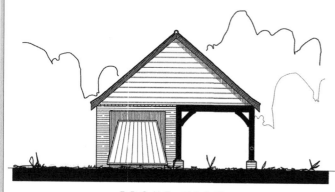

FRONT VIEW

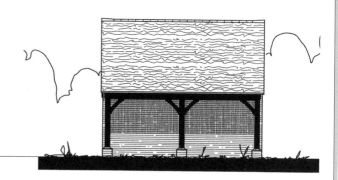

SIDE VIEW

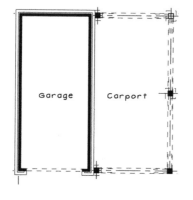

A single garage with additional carport

BASSINGBOURNE

10.4 x 6.5m

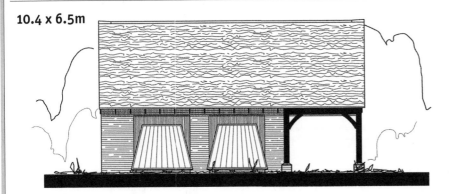

A double garage with additional carport plus storage over

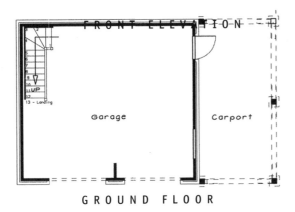

FRONT ELEVATION

Garage   Carport

GROUND FLOOR

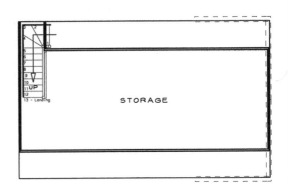

STORAGE

FIRST FLOOR

SHUTTLEWORTH

7.5 x 6.5m

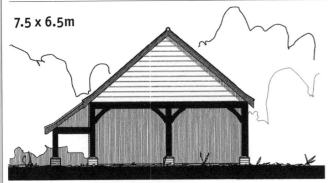

FRONT VIEW

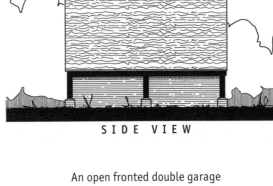

SIDE VIEW

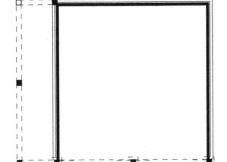

An open fronted double garage with external lean-to storage

THE BOATHOUSE

The copyright belongs to a ScAN architectural practice – Gillespie & Scott

25 sq. m.   **9.2 x 4.1m**

Designed for a seaside
situation, providing superb
daytime accommodation
with facilities.

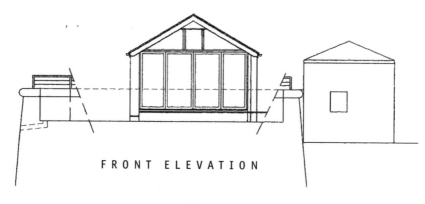

FRONT ELEVATION

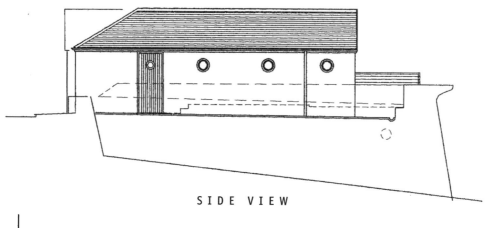

SIDE VIEW

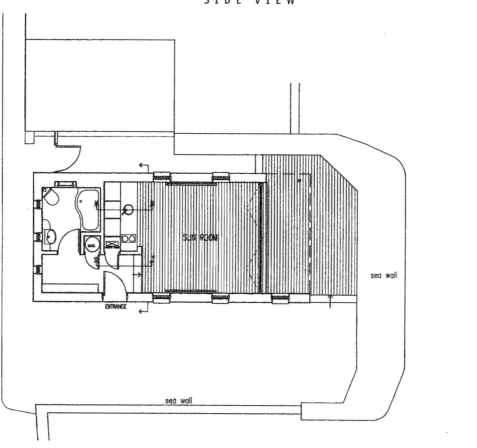

T227

158 sq. m.

Overall dimensions 14.83 x 9.56m

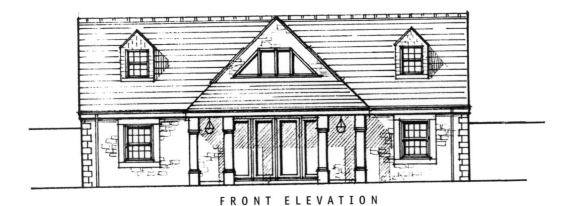

F R O N T   E L E V A T I O N

If you're going to the expense of building a pool house and gymnasium it does perhaps make sense to go that extra bit and include guest and sleeping accommodation in the roof. This outbuilding is the size of many of the smaller houses in this book but the house it serves might well be correspondingly smaller. Alternatively, some small re-arrangements and re-naming could well turn this into staff accommodation.

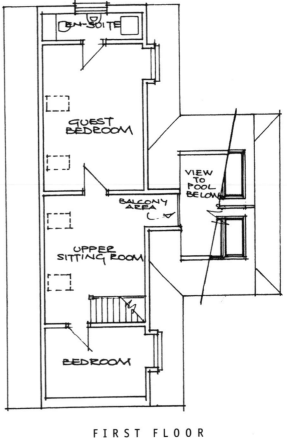

F I R S T   F L O O R

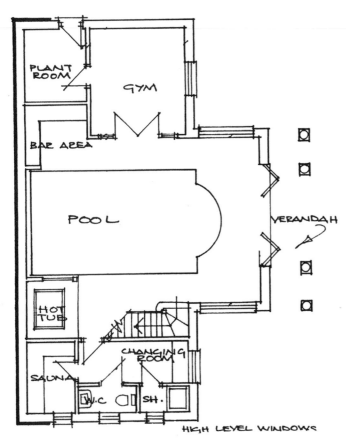

G R O U N D   F L O O R

Pool room	8.94 x 7.33m max including bar area & hot tub.	Guest bedroom	5.42 x 3.87m + en-suite
Changing room	4.22 x 1.64m + WC & shower room	Bedroom	3.87 x 2.57m
Sauna	2.60 x 1.83m	Upper sitting room	4.78 x 3.87m
Gym	3.96 x 3.66m		
Plant room	2.67 x 2.34m		

411

NOTES

COMPANIES WHOSE DESIGNS ARE FEATURED IN THIS BOOK

Associated Self Build Architects (ASBA)
Champions Hall
Drake Street
Rochdale
Lancs
OL16 1PB
Telephone 0800 387310
asba@asba-architects.org

The Border Design Centre
Harelaw Moor
Greenlaw
Berwickshire
TD10 6XT
Telephone/fax 01578 740218
borderdesign@constructionplus.net

T.J.Crump OAKWRIGHTS Ltd
The Lakes
Swainshill
Hereford
HR4 7PU
Telephone 01432 353353
Fax 01432 357733
enquiries@oakwrights.co.uk

Custom Homes Ltd
South Suffolk Business Centre
Alexandra Road
Sudbury
Suffolk
CO10 2ZX
Telephone 01293 822898
Fax 01787 377622
info@customhomes.co.uk

Designer Homes
Pooh Cottage
Minto
Hawick
TD9 8SB
Telephone/fax 01450 870127

Design & Materials Ltd
Lawn Road
Carlton in Lindrick
Worksop
North Notts
S81 9LB
Telephone 01909 730333
Fax 01909 730201
designandmaterials@lineone.net

Potton Ltd
Wyboston Lakes
Great North Road
Wyboston
Bedfordshire
MK44 3BA
Telephone 01480 401401
Fax 01480 401444
sales@potton.co.uk

The Self Build House Company Ltd
Courtfield
Cranston Road
East Grinstead
West Sussex
RH19 3YU
Telephone 01342 312513
Fax 01342 312613
sales@sbhc.co.uk

Scandia-Hus Ltd
Courtfield
Cranston Road
East Grinstead
West Sussex
RH19 3YU
Telephone 01342 327977
Fax 01342 315139
sales@scandia-hus.co.uk

Scottish Architects Network (ScAN)
10 Lynedoch Crescent
Glasgow
G3 6EQ
Telephone 0800 731 3405
Fax 0141 331 2751
architectu@aol.com

The Swedish House Company Ltd
Seabridge House
8 St.John's Road
Tunbridge Wells
Kent
TN4 9NP
Telephone 08707 700760
Fax 08707 700759
sales@swedishhouses.com

FURTHER INFORMATION

Books

BUILDING YOUR OWN HOME 17th edition by David Snell & Murray Armor (Ebury Press)
For twenty-five years this has been the self-builder's favourite source of information. A companion to this book and by the same authors, constantly referred to between these covers, the serious self-builder should read it in conjunction with this book of plans – available with many other self-build books from **Ryton Books Ltd. Telephone 01909 591652**

THE HOME PLANS BOOK by David Snell & Murray Armor (Ebury Press)

THE HOUSEBUILDER'S BIBLE by Mark Brinkley (Ovolo Publishing)

PRACTICAL HOUSEBUILDING by Bob Matthews (Blackberry Books)

ALL ABOUT SELF BUILDING by Bob Matthews (Blackberry Books)

HOW TO FIND A BUILDING PLOT by Speer & Dade (Stonepound Books)

HOW TO GET PLANNING PERMISSION by Speer & Dade (Stonepound Books)

HOW TO FINANCE BUILDING & CONVERTING YOUR OWN HOME by Speer & Dade (Stonepound Books)

Most of the above available from Ryton Books Tel: 01909 591652

Magazines

HOMEBUILDING & RENOVATING Tel: 01527 834400 www.homebuilding.co.uk

BUILD IT   Tel: 020 7772 8307 www.self-build.co.uk

SELF BUILD & DESIGN Tel: 01283 742950

Plotfinding agencies

Buildstore/plotsearch Tel: 0870 870 9994 www.buildstore.co.uk/plotsearch

Plotfinder.net Tel: 0906 557 5400 www.plotfinder.net

Landbank Services Tel: 0118 962 6022 www.landbank.co.uk

English Partnerships Tel: 01908 692692 www.englishpartnerships.co.uk

Exhibitions

THE HOMEBUILDING & RENOVATING SHOW

Run in conjunction with Homebuilding & Renovating magazine. Every spring at the NEC and at various times of the year in Peterborogh, Glasgow, London, Bath and Harrogate. Tel: 01527 834 400

Self build insurances

DMS Services Ltd. Tel: 01909 591652

Buildcare Tel: 0870 872 0908

Capital Cover (Eire only) Tel: 00353 1491 0210

Self build warranties

NHBC – 'Solo' & 'Buildmark' Tel: 01494 434477

Zurich 'Custombuild' & 'Newbuild' Tel: 01252 522000

Buildcare Tel: 0870 872 0908

Project Builder Tel: 020 7716 5050

NHBC (Eire only) Tel: 00353 1496 6268

Architectural, design & engineering associations

The Royal Institute of British Architects (RIBA) Tel: 020 7580 5533

The Royal Incorporation of Architects in Scotland (RIAS) Tel: 0131 229 7205

The Royal Society of Architects in Wales Tel: 02920 874753

The Royal Society of Ulster Architects Tel: 02890 323760

The Royal Institute of Architects in Ireland (RIAI) Tel: 00353 1676 1703

Associated Self Build Architects (ASBA) Tel: 0800 387310

Scottish Architects Network (ScAN) Tel: 0800 731 3405

The Architect's Registration Board (ARB) Tel: 020 7580 5861

The Royal Town Planning Institute Tel: 020 7636 9107

The British Institute of Architectural Technologists (BIAT) Tel: 020 7278 2206

The Institute of Civil Engineers Tel: 020 7222 7722

Government agencies and establishments

The Building Research Establishment Tel: 01923 664000

National Radiological Protection Board Tel: 01235 831 600

HM Land Registry Tel: 020 7917 8888

Floodline Tel: 0845 988 1188

Planning Inspectorates and Appeal Boards

England – The planning Inspectorate Tel: 0117 372 8754

Wales – The Planning Inspectorate Tel: 02920 825007

Scotland – The Scottish Executive Inquiry Reporters Unit Tel: 0131 244 5649

Ulster – The Planning Appeals Commission Tel: 02890 244710

Eire – An Bord Pleanala Tel: 00353 1872 8001

Special interest groups

UK Timber Frame Association (UKTFA) Tel: 01259 272140

The Traditional Housing Bureau Tel: 01344 725757

The Disabled Living Foundation Tel: 020 7289 6111

The Society for the Protection of Ancient Buildings (SPAB) Tel: 020 7377 1644

English Heritage Tel: 020 7973 3000

Historic Scotland Tel: 0131 668 8600

Cadw Tel: 02920 500200

The Council for British Archaeology Tel: 01904 671417

The Council for the Protection of Rural England (CPRE) Tel: 020 7253 0300

The Ancient Monuments Society Tel: 020 7236 3934

The Georgian Group Tel: 020 7387 1720

The Victorian Society Tel: 020 7994 1019

SELFBUILDERS INSURANCES
PROPOSAL

Name of proposer: Mr/Mrs/Ms .... Phone number: ....

Full postal address: ....

.... Post Code: ....

Address of property to be insured: ....

....

Name, address and any reference number of any interested party, e.g. Building Society: ....

....

YOUR PROPOSAL

1. Have you made any other proposal for insurance in respect of the risk proposed? **YES/NO**
   If "yes" give details at 10 below.

2. Has any company or underwriter declined your proposal? *If "yes" give details at 10 below.* **YES/NO**

3. Have you been convicted of (or charged but not yet tried with) arson or any offence involving dishonesty of any kind (e.g. fraud, theft, handling stolen goods etc.) *If "yes" give details at 10 below.* **YES/NO**

YOUR PROGRAMME

4(a). Commencing date of insurance ..../.........../...........

4(b). Date work commenced if a start has been made on the site? ..../.........../...........

4(c). Have there been any incidents on the site which could have given rise to a claim? **YES/NO**
   If "yes" give details at 10 below.

4(d). Target completion date ..../.........../...........
   Standard policy is for 15 months.

THE BUILDING

5(a). Is the building a completely new structure? **YES/NO**
   If "no" refer to DMS Services on 01909 591652 or provide details at 10 below.

5(b). State the value of the new building at builders reinstatement cost. (The minimum premium is for the value up to £80,000) **£**

5(c). Will the new dwelling have brick or masonry walls with or without a timber frame under a tile or slate roof? **YES/NO**
   If "no" refer to DMS Services on 01909 591652 or provide details at 10 below.

5(d). Will the building qualify for a warranty, either N.H.B.C., Zurich Custombuild, surveyors or architects progress certificates **YES/NO**
   If "no" refer to DMS Services on 01909 591652 or provide details at 10 below.

THE SITE

6. Is the site and any existing building on it subject to any special hazard such as flooding, subsidence or other ground conditions **YES/NO**
   If "yes" give details at 10 below.

7. Do the Planning Consent or Building Regulation Approvals indicate any special requirements or special precautions to be taken in the construction of the building? *If "yes" give details at 10 below.* **YES/NO**

SECURITY

8. Does the proposer intend to live within 25 metres of the new work during the construction period? **YES/NO**
   If "yes" a discount can be claimed on the proposal form opposite

9. Will security arrangements on site be to good standard practice on building sites in the local area? **YES/NO**
   (A limit of £20,000 will apply to unfixed electrical, plumbing, heating, kitchen and bathroom fitments which must be contained in a locked building, hut or steel container whenever left unattended)

SPECIAL CIRCUMSTANCES

10. State the circumstances of any unusual circumstances or other facts which might influence the decision of the insurer when considering this proposal.
   If insufficient space please continue on a separate sheet.

I/we declare that all the work to which this proposal relates will be carried out in accordance with the Building Regulations, and that arrangements for the approval or certification of the works under the regulations will be made before any works are carried out.

I/we declare that to the best of my/our knowledge and belief all the statements and particulars made with regard to this proposal are true and I/we agree that this proposal shall be the basis of the contract of insurance between me/us and AXA Insurance. I/we consent to the seeking of information from other insurers to check the answers I/we have provided, and I/we authorise the giving of information for such purposes.

Signature _____   Date _____

SELFBUILDERS INSURANCES
ASSESSING YOUR INSURANCE REQUIREMENTS

STANDARD COVER

| LIABILITIES | Limit of Liability |

A. Employers Liability – *no excess*   £10,000,000

B. Public Liability   £2,000,000
in respect of the site, the natural features on it
including trees and the work proposed – *excess
of £250 for property damage*

CONTRACT WORKS

C. Contract Works insurance to the value declared
in respect of the works and materials for use in
the works, with a standard excess of £500

OPTIONAL COVER

PLANT

D. Plant and tools owned by the proposer, cover on
the site only with a standard excess of £500

E. Employees tools or plant, cover effective on the
site only with a standard excess of £50. (Maximum
2 employees)

F. Plant and tools hired in by the proposer and NOT
covered by Hiresafe or other hirers scheme, cover
for the whole term of the policy with the standard
excess of £500

G. Plant and tools hired in by the proposer and NOT
covered by Hiresafe or other hirers scheme, short
term cover for a 14 day period. (Phone 01909
591652 to arrange)

CARAVAN

H. Caravan on the site, used
as a site hut or temporary
dwelling, excess £250

INCREASED PUBLIC LIABILITY LIMITS

J. Increase Public Liability cover for a 14 day period
if required by an authority to facilitate a drain
connection or similar purpose

K. Public Liability to £1,000,000 and Fire Cover to an
agreed value on existing buildings, walls and other
structures on the site which are not part of the
construction project.

**The above cover extends for the duration of the
building work or 15 months whichever is the sooner.
It applies to mainland UK, C. Isles, IoM, and
Shetlands.**

Public Liability and Employers Liability
premiums account for £100 in the premiums
below:

INCLUSIVE PREMIUMS

Rebuild Cost Up to £	Premium £	Rebuild Cost Up to £	Premium £
80,000 *(min)*	399	90,000	436
100,000	474	110,000	511
120,000	548	130,000	586
140,000	623	150,000	660

*Premiums for larger sums on application
Premiums INCLUDE Insurance Premium Tax*

*The **minimum**
total premium
for Section D, E
& F is £250. It
is recommended
that proposers
requiring this
cover telephone
01909 591652
to discuss their
requirements*

*Premiums will be quoted after
consultation*

*£52.50 per £1,000 value of caravan. (Does not
include cover for personal possessions)*

REVISED LIMIT OF INDEMNITY
    £2,500,000   fixed premium £26
    £5,000,000   fixed premium £46
Premiums will be quoted after consultation

*If living within 25 metres of the new building a
discount is applicable. Refer to 01909 591652
for amount.*

*If excesses on Sections C, D & F are to be
increased to £1000 a discount is applicable.
Refer to 01909 591652 for amount.*

PREMIUM PAYABLE
(Premiums above are inclusive of Insurance Premium
Tax at 5%)

PAYMENT – Please tick as appropriate
❑ Cheque for payment enclosed
❑ Payment to be made by credit card

Card No. ☐☐☐☐ ☐☐☐☐ ☐☐☐☐ ☐☐☐☐   expiry ☐☐☐☐